The Institutional Topology of International Regime Complexes

T0391830

Transformations in Governance

Transformations in Governance is a major academic book series from Oxford University Press. It is designed to accommodate the impressive growth of research in comparative politics, international relations, public policy, federalism, and environmental and urban studies concerned with the dispersion of authority from central states to supranational institutions, subnational governments, and public–private networks. It brings together work that advances our understanding of the organization, causes, and consequences of multilevel and complex governance. The series is selective, containing annually a small number of books of exceptionally high quality by leading and emerging scholars.

The series is edited by Liesbet Hooghe and Gary Marks of the University of North Carolina, Chapel Hill, and Walter Mattli of the University of Oxford.

RECENTLY PUBLISHED IN THE SERIES

A Postfunctionalist Theory of Governance (5 Volumes)
Liesbet Hooghe and Gary Marks et al.

Territory and Ideology in Latin America: Policy Conflicts between National and Subnational Governments
Kent Eaton

Rules without Rights: Land, Labor, and Private Authority in the Global Economy
Tim Bartley

Voluntary Disruptions: International Soft Law, Finance, and Power
Abraham L. Newman and Elliot Posner

Managing Money and Discord in the UN: Budgeting and Bureaucracy
Ronny Patz and Klaus H. Goetz

A Theory of International Organization
Liesbet Hooghe, Tobias Lenz, and Gary Marks

The Rise of International Parliaments: Strategic Legitimation in International Organizations
Frank Schimmelfennig, Thomas Winzen, Tobias Lenz, Jofre Rocabert, Loriana Crasnic, Cristina Gherasimov, Jana Lipps, and Densua Mumford

The Political Commissioner: A European Ethnography
Frédéric Mérand

Interorganizational Diffusion in International Relations: Regional Institutions and the Role of the European Union
Tobias Lenz

International Organization as Technocratic Utopia
Jens Steffek

Ideational Legacies and the Politics of Migration in European Minority Regions
Christina Isabel Zuber

For a full list of titles published in the series, see pp. 286–7

The Institutional Topology of International Regime Complexes

Mapping Interinstitutional Structures in Global Governance

Benjamin Daßler

OXFORD
UNIVERSITY PRESS

OXFORD
UNIVERSITY PRESS

Great Clarendon Street, Oxford, OX2 6DP,
United Kingdom

Oxford University Press is a department of the University of Oxford.
It furthers the University's objective of excellence in research, scholarship,
and education by publishing worldwide. Oxford is a registered trade mark of
Oxford University Press in the UK and in certain other countries

Published in the United States of America by Oxford University Press
198 Madison Avenue, New York, NY 10016, United States of America

British Library Cataloguing in Publication Data
Data available

Library of Congress Control Number: 2023935106

ISBN 978–0–19–888192–6

DOI: 10.1093/oso/9780198881926.001.0001

Printed and bound in the UK by
Clays Ltd, Elcograf S.p.A.

Preface

I have always been fascinated by the amount and complexity of today's international cooperation. When I was an undergraduate student visiting my first courses in International Relations and learning about the complex architecture of Global Governance, its underlying institutions, and their historical evolution, the topic immediately captured my imagination. Growing up in a deeply integrated Europe and all the associated individual privileges like a peaceful childhood, freedom of movement, and the vast opportunities for intensive intercultural exchange, I quickly realized that many of these values are the result of the relentless struggle of policymakers all around the globe who share the belief that international cooperation can provide mutual benefits.

Not least the unleashing of the devastating full-scale Russian war against Ukraine has reinforced my awareness of the value of these privileges, which cannot be enjoyed by people in large parts of our world and, at the same time, their fragility. Today, the global community faces a complex web of fundamental challenges ranging from economic inequality and climate change to political polarization and rising geopolitical tensions. In this context, the functioning of multilateralism in all its different shapes and nuances has never been more crucial for peace and the reduction of global inequalities. By bringing together states under the umbrella of international institutions to work towards common goals, multilateralism is key for addressing the profound geopolitical challenges we face today. However, the process of creating multilateral institutions has proven to be far from simple, and today, in many issue areas, international institutions face existential threats. They are being threatened from within, as established powers like the United States or the United Kingdom, once the leading architects of the Liberal International Order (LIO) and its underlying institutions, openly turn away from some of its principles. They are also threatened from the outside. As the Russian invasion of Ukraine shows, basic principles of this order, like compliance with international humanitarian law, are being openly disregarded.

The solidifying realization over the years of the privileges associated with belonging to this Liberal International Order has spurred my interest in the actual architecture of this order, which seems to be increasingly threatened now. Why is multilateral cooperation oftentimes so differently pursued, and why does it vary in its success across time and (policy) space? I wanted to better understand the "big picture" of global multilateralism, which today is characterized by overlapping and complex international regimes that vary significantly in their actual shape, degree of integration, and amount and diversity of institutions. There are profound differences across different policy areas of global governance. Making sense of the current challenges to global governance requires a deep understanding of the very nature and architecture of regimes underlying the global political landscape.

In this book, I seek to provide a comparative perspective on regime complexes across policy areas and time. I analyze how and why regime complexes, their underlying multilateral institutions, and the institutionalization processes initiated by states differ profoundly across different policy fields. Thereby, this book attempts to provide a comprehensive overview of the challenges facing multilateralism in these five issue areas and offer a better understanding of what needs to be done to overcome them. Whether you are a student or scholar of international relations, a policymaker, or simply someone interested in the current and past developments in global governance, I hope this book offers a refreshing and accessible perspective on the complexities and diverse institutional landscapes of multilateral cooperation.

I am deeply indebted to many persons who have helped me along the way. First, I would like to thank my long-term mentor, Bernhard Zangl. Bernhard, thank you for giving me the opportunity and supporting me in developing this and many other projects. Thank you for helping me develop academically over the last few years. I am also truly thankful to Berthold Rittberger, whose advice and precious comments on the project were always stimulating. I developed the theoretical and empirical approach taken in this book while working on my dissertation at the Geschwister-Scholl-Institute for Political Science at the Ludwig-Maximilians-University Munich. I could not be happier to have been able to work on this project in such a great institution, but most importantly, in such a pleasant and congenial circle of colleagues for the last few years.

I am grateful for the challenging but always extremely stimulating comments by Rainer Hülsse. I could not have wished for a more pleasant and congenial office colleague over the last few years. I am deeply indebted to Felix Biermann and Lisa Kriegmair for their scientifically excellent comments and advice while working on the project but especially for their friendship and support beyond the work on this book. I am also profoundly grateful to my colleagues Tim Heinkelmann-Wild, Rapahela Hobbach, Andreas Kruck, and Sebastian Schindler. Their collegial nature, suggestions, and ideas on the project have inspired and advanced me in many ways, for which I would like to thank them. I would like to also thank my (former) colleagues Christian Kreuder-Sonnen, Hilde van Meegdenburg, Moritz Weiß, Eva Ziegler, Laura Seelkopf, Yves Steinebach, Nina Guérin, Vytas Jankauskas, and Ronny Patz for the regular exchange, the excellent working atmosphere, and the inspiring and constructive comments in the international relations colloquium of the Geschwister-Scholl Institute, but also beyond.

Furthermore, I am incredibly grateful to the many other colleagues who have engaged with my work and commented on papers and chapters, including the two kind and constructive anonymous reviewers at Oxford University Press. I want to thank OUP, particularly Dominic Byatt and the editorial team of the Transformations in Governance series Liesbet Hooghe, Gary Marks, and Walter Mattli for their support during the process. Over the years, I also have benefited greatly from many intellectually inspiring discussions with impressive scholars from the field of International Relations at numerous conferences and workshops. I would like to particularly thank Eyal Benvenisti, Karen Alter, Stephanie Hofmann, Benjamin Faude, Thomas Malang, Diana Panke, Klaus Dingwerth, Phillip Genschel, Michael Zürn, and Alex Thompson. I am also deeply indebted to Nadia El Ghali, who supported me greatly as a research assistant with the manuscript. I would also like to thank Stephen Curtis for editing the manuscript.

I also want to thank my friends, who have ensured that I have always been able to balance and distract myself from this work over the last few years. I am especially grateful to Jonas, Fabian, Jürgen, Bettina, and Matthias, for their constant support and all the joy. Thank you, Sabrina, for being by my side and giving me strength and confidence.

Lastly and most sincerely, I thank my family, Silvia, Joachim, and Francisca. Their unconditional love and support have been crucial in many ways. I cannot thank them enough. I dedicate this book to them.

Contents

List of Figures

List of Tables

List of Abbreviations

ADB	Asian Development Bank
AFDB	African Development Bank
AIIB	Asian Infrastructure Investment Bank
AMF	Arab Monetary Fund
ARIPO	African Regional Intellectual Property Organization
ATAF	African Tax Administrations Forum
BADEA	Arab Bank for Economic Development in Africa
BEPS	Base Erosion and Profit Shifting
BoP	Balance of Payments
BRICS	Brazil, Russia, India, China, and South Africa
CAF	Corporación Andina de Fomento (Development Bank of Latin America)
CATA	Commonwealth Association of Tax Administrators
CBD	Convention on Biological Diversity
CDB	Caribbean Development Bank
CEB	Council of Europe Development Bank
CIAT	Inter-American Center of Tax Administrations
CMI	Chiang Mai Initiative
CRA	BRICS Contingency Reserve Arrangement
CREDAF	Exchange and Research Centre for Leaders of Tax Administrations
CSDP	Common Security and Defense Policy
EAPO	Eurasian Patent Organization
EBRD	European Bank for Reconstruction and Development
ECT	Energy Charter Treaty
EDB	Eurasian Development Bank
EIB	Investment Bank
ENI	Italian National Hydrocarbons Authority (ital. "Ente Nazionale Idrocarburi")
EPO	European Patent Organization
ESM	European Stability Mechanism
EU	European Union
EU COM	European Commission
FAO	Food and Agriculture Organization
G20	Group of Twenty
G7	Group of Seven
IBSA	Indian, Brazilian, and South African Dialogue Forum
IDB	Inter-American Development Bank
IEA	International Energy Agency
IEF	International Energy Forum (IEF)
IMF	International Monetary Fund

IO	International Organization
IOTA	Intra-European Organisation of Tax Administrations
IP	Intellectual Property
IPR	Intellectual Property Rights
IRENA	International Renewable Energy Agency
IsDB	Islamic Development Bank
ISDS	Investor-State Dispute Settlement
LARF	Latin American Reserve Fund
MDB	Multilateral Development Bank
NATO	North Atlantic Treaty Organization
NDB	New Development Bank
OAPEC	Organization of Arab Petroleum Exporting Countries
OAPI	African Intellectual Property Organization
OECD	Organization for Economic Co-operation and Development
OPEC	Organization of the Petroleum Exporting Countries
OPECFID	Organization of the Petroleum Exporting Countries Fund for International Development
PEEREA	Energy Charter Protocol on Energy Efficiency and Related Environmental Aspects
QCA	Qualitative Comparative Analysis
RCT	Regime Complexity Theory
TRIPS	Agreement on Trade-Related Aspects of Intellectual Property Rights
UAE	United Arab Emirates
UN	United Nations
UNDG	United Nations Development Group
UNTC	United Nations Tax Committee
UPOV	International Union for the Protection of New Varieties of Plants
US	United States
USD	United States Dollar
WB	World Bank
WHO	World Health Organization
WIPO	World Intellectual Property Organization
WTO	World Trade Organization

PART I
INTRODUCTION

1

Institutional Centralization/ Decentralization in International Regime Complexes

On October 24, 2014, a ceremony took place in Beijing during which 21 Asian countries signed a memorandum of understanding on establishing the Asian Infrastructure Investment Bank (AIIB). The event was the culmination of intense two-year diplomatic efforts by the Chinese government under President Xi Jinping, who had taken office in 2013. Since then, the Chinese government has been pursuing a foreign policy agenda aimed at creating the so-called "One Belt One Road," an initiative that seeks to expand China's economic influence across the whole of the Eurasian continent and beyond. The AIIB was considered a central institutional element of this "Eurasian Moment" in Chinese foreign policy. However, the AIIB was set up in a policy field that was already densely populated by multilateral development institutions, many of them sharing central development policy objectives and mandates with the AIIB. Unsurprisingly, the United States, the most powerful principal of the World Bank, still by far the largest Multilateral Development Bank (MDB) in terms of membership and financial resources, reacted less than favorably to the establishment of the AIIB and made no secret of the fact that it regarded it as an unwelcome competitor. When one of the US's closest geopolitical allies, the United Kingdom, declared that it intended to join the AIIB, the White House even saw itself forced to react with a "rare public breach in the special relationship" between the two countries (Watt et al. 2015).

When, in January 2009, the International Renewable Energy Agency (IRENA) was founded by a group of 75 states in Bonn, Germany, this formal act marked the end of a yearlong endeavor on the part of a German-led coalition that was deeply dissatisfied with the lack of urgency in multilateral action against the climate crisis within the preexisting International Energy Agency (IEA). Although the IEA had worked on climate and energy transition issues for quite some time, many of its members were apparently not

The Institutional Topology of International Regime Complexes. Benjamin Daßler, Oxford University Press.
© Benjamin Daßler (2023). DOI: 10.1093/oso/9780198881926.003.0001

convinced about its ability to satisfy their demands for more efficient multilateral action on the topic and joined the newly created IRENA. As of late 2022, IRENA has become a truly global international energy institution with 168 members. Again, although it joined IRENA later, the United States was not in favor of the organization's establishment as it considered it an unnecessary duplicate and competitor to the IEA. The IEA itself reacted to this increased interinstitutional competition by bureaucratic reforms aimed at strengthening its renewable energy competencies and an uptick in renewable energy policy activities (van de Graaf 2013a; Heubaum and Biermann 2015).

Even though rarely expressed explicitly by supranational bureaucracies themselves, this implicit sense of competition among multilateral institutions and their supporting states is not limited to the policy field of development aid and energy governance. The way states coordinate and govern political issues on the international level has changed profoundly over recent decades. In many issue areas, new intergovernmental arrangements have been created whose functions overlap with or complement those of preexisting international institutions. States have created new supranational organizations like the AIIB in the development field or IRENA in energy governance and have signed numerous new intergovernmental treaties like the Paris Agreement on Climate Change or the Iran Nuclear Deal to tackle a wide range of political issues. Today there are thousands of international organizations actively engaged in interstate politics and hundreds of thousands of intergovernmental treaties (Hathaway and Shapiro 2017: xviii).

This development has not only led to a dramatic increase in the density of governance systems, which, in many issue areas, has produced what scholars refer to as "regime complexes" (Alter and Meunier 2009; Keohane and Victor 2011; Orsini et al. 2013; Urpelainen and van de Graaf 2015). This increasingly fragmented governance architecture (Biermann et al. 2009; Oberthur and Stokke 2011; Zelli and Van Asselt 2013; Kim 2020) has also fundamentally affected the relationship between states and international institutions: States have increasingly begun either to shift their activities away from what were hitherto regarded as "core institutions" towards other intergovernmental arrangements or to create completely new international institutions leading to a situation that Morse and Keohane (2014) describe as "contested multilateralism." One of the most important characteristics of these evolving institutional complexes has long been described as "the absence of hierarchy among institutions and rules ...—[a] feature that drives the critical dynamics and strategic interactions that characterize politics within a regime complex" (Alter and Raustiala 2018: 332).

However, the proliferation of new intergovernmental institutions in many policy fields has also been accompanied by the evolution of diverse forms of interaction among multilateral institutions themselves: Today, international institutions coordinate or imitate policies, defer and refer to each other, or even conflict over jurisdictions (Barnett and Finnemore 2004; Biermann 2008; Alter and Meunier 2009; Park 2014; Abbott et al. 2015; Harsch 2015; Lipson 2017; Pratt 2018; Gehring and Faude 2014; Clark 2021). Scholars working on the complexity of global environmental governance were amongst the first to provide important insights into the quality, dynamics, and consequences of such institutional interactions (Bäckstrand 2006; Biermann et al. 2010; Johnson and Urpelainen 2012; Zelli 2011; Oberthur and Stokke 2011; Orsini 2013; Andrade and de Oliveira 2015; van Asselt and Zelli 2014; Green 2014; Biermann and Kim 2020). As this literature points out, the issue area of environmental governance is characterized by a regime complex which is fragmented, decentralized, and densely populated by many different transnational institutions without central coordination (Abbott 2012). Other issue areas are equally marked by the emergence of overlapping institutions that have cultivated diverse forms of interaction and interinstitutional cooperation. Within the international trade regime, for instance, the World Trade Organization (WTO) currently maintains formal relationships with 31 other multilateral institutions while, on the other hand, more than 60 other institutions retain observer status within the WTO (Orsini et al. 2013: 28). In many cases, other intergovernmental organizations like the European Union (EU) defer to the WTO in order to solve trade disputes with states or other supranational organizations. Still, in some cases, supranational organizations like the EU that possess overlapping mandates are reluctant to defer to the WTO or to respond adequately to trade litigations pursued within the context of the WTO (Yildirim 2018). So the actual degree of centralization within regime complexes appears to vary widely across issue areas of global governance.

Some of these issue areas appear to be marked by strong degrees of hierarchization and centralization, despite the emergence of more and more regional institutional arrangements. The area of financial stability and balance of payments assistance is a key example. Here, the lion's share of everyday policy processes is shaped by a single institution, the International Monetary Fund (IMF). Alternative and more regional institutions like the Chiang Mai Initiative (CMI), the Latin American Reserve Fund (LARF), or the only recently established European Stability Mechanism (ESM) which were created, inter alia, to mirror some of the IMF's key policy objectives, have so far predominantly operated in its shadow while linking their institutional rules closely to those of the IMF. Even the financial stability institution created by the so-called BRICS group of states (consisting of Brazil, Russia, India, China, and South Africa), the BRICS Contingent Reserve Arrangement (CRA), tied parts of its lending programs directly to those of the IMF. These institutional linkages appear especially remarkable given the clearly articulated revisionist ambitions of the BRICS when it comes to the dominant position of the IMF in the international financial system where they consider themselves to be significantly underrepresented (Cooper 2016). Many scholars have therefore concluded that, despite the emergence of alternative financial stability institutions, the IMF has so far remained the most central and influential international institution when it comes to the fight against international financial crises (Climie 2018; Schwarzer 2015; Clark 2022).

In other policy fields like development aid, the interinstitutional structure appears to be different. Here the World Bank (WB) coordinates its development projects with an increasing number of other multilateral development funds and institutions and finds itself increasingly confronted with competition for projects by these alternative institutions (Humphrey 2014). In the case of the WB, the emergence of alternative development donors has even made the organization offer credits less restrictively to remain competitive (Hernandez 2017), and to initiate other mechanism to cope with the new realities on the ground (Güven 2017). Despite these efforts by the WB to consolidate its central position within the development aid complex, many states have reinforced their development aid policies outside of the WB's institutional environment and have joined alternative institutions like the Asian Infrastructure Investment Bank. Thus, it appears that the interinstitutional structure of the development aid complex is much more decentralized and contested, with various institutional actors competing for a central position to shape everyday policymaking in the issue area.

As I will argue throughout the present book, understanding these differences in institutional topologies across various policy fields of global governance is essential because they have broader implications for international relations that go beyond the often small-scale and issue-area-specific policymaking in individual regime complexes. The preexisting institutional landscape in a policy field sets the stage on which interstate politics is made. Given the current fundamental disruptions, crises, and conflicts caused by political shocks like the COVID-19 pandemic, the Ukraine war, or the most recent global financial crisis, varying institutional topologies constrain or enable states to address policy issues on the global level. They determine the institutional opportunities that states have at their disposal, thereby limiting or increasing the prospects of effective multilateral responses to these disruptions. They also affect how states can navigate under the condition of power shifts and increasing geopolitical tensions between the West and the East. The ways in which these shifts transform multilateral cooperation differ markedly across regime complexes with varying institutional topologies. As this book will argue, within specific institutions, the degree of conflict and the speed of institutional adoption can be affected by whether these complexes are ordered in accordance with a centralistic or strongly decentralized design. Under conditions characterized by power shifts and an increasing propensity for interstate conflicts, variation in institutional opportunity structures, which are reflected in the underlying topology of a given regime complex, are becoming ever more relevant. Although institutional topologies are, of course, only one, structural factor among many that shape the overall outcomes of the current fundamental and transformative processes in international politics, I hold that they do make a difference to how states are able to address international issues across varying issue areas of global governance. It is precisely this variation in the degree of centralization obtaining in institutionalized forms of cooperation within different regime complexes of global governance that this book intends to shed light on.

The Empirical Contribution: Mapping Institutional Topologies in Global Governance

How can the varying topologies underlying international regime complexes be mapped and explained? By exploring this question, the book addresses important gaps in the burgeoning literature on regime complexity, but also adds important nuances to the current debate on the future trajectories of the so-called liberal international order (LIO). While the regime complexity (RC) literature has delivered many insights into the consequences of institutional complexity for specific policy fields, as well as relations among states and institutions (Raustiala and Victor 2004; Alter and Meunier 2009; Hofmann 2009; Drezner 2009; Keohane and Victor 2011; Orsini et al. 2013; Morse and Keohane 2014; Hooghe et al. 2019; Urpelainen and van de Graaf 2015) or even among institutions and nonstate actors (Green 2022), it has so far fallen short of a coherent and theoretically grounded conceptualization of the interinstitutional structures underlying different policy fields of global governance. Although the literature recognizes that these structures are far from homogenous (Biermann 2008; Alter and Meunier 2009; Gehring and Faude 2014; Harsch 2015; Pratt 2018; Clark 2021; Green 2022), in the existing literature on regime complexes there is a striking lack of comparative analyses across policy fields.

Moreover, the RC literature has so far remained relatively limited regarding its analytical perspective on the phenomenon of institutional complexity. It has predominantly analyzed the structures of institutional complexes from a "within policy field perspective" using a variety of different concepts and methods. Surprisingly, there are hardly any structured comparisons across different policy fields using coherent conceptualizations and measurements of institutional topologies. I argue that this is, again, due to the dominant research focus of the RC literature: As these early studies (Biermann et al. 2009; Hofmann 2011; Gehring and Faude 2013; 2014; Riles 2014) have been predominantly interested in the *consequences* but not the *causes* of complexity, there was no urgent need for a comparative perspective. Their investigations were mainly driven "by an apparent lack of consensus in the academic literature on the consequences of fragmentation" (Biermann et al. 2009: 14) for specific institutions. Therefore, their analyses have predominantly remained on the level of individual institutions (e.g., Graham 2014; Hanrieder 2015) or specific dyads of institutions (e.g., van de Graaf 2013a; Heubaum and Biermann 2015; Henning 2017) but have hardly shifted their focus to the overall structure of institutional complexes. For instance, by tracing the evolution of the EU's Common Security and Defense Policy (CSDP), Stéphanie Hofmann (2011) argues that institutional overlap has direct consequences for the strategic choices states have at their disposal. Conceiving of institutional complexity as an independent, explanatory variable, she engages in exploring the impact of complexity on the CSDP's underlying specific institutions. Taking an international law perspective, Annelise Riles (2014) argues that there are also legal consequences for individual states arising from institutional complexity as they can make use of the growing number of institutional inconsistencies to avoid costly rules. Consequently, according to Asif Efrat and Abraham Newman (2016), states tend to support institutions with the lowest regulatory approach, thereby encouraging a dangerous race to the bottom, which ultimately weakens international law. Thus, what the majority of regime complexity literature has in common is the perception of interinstitutional structures as an explanatory factor that allows us to understand why individual states engage in strategies such as forum shopping (Murphy and Kellow 2013), regime shifting (Helfer 2009), regime integration and separation (Johnson and Urpelainen 2012), or the creation of competitive institutions (Morse and Keohane 2014).

The book proposes a conceptualization of institutional topologies in international regime complexes that allows variation to be mapped across virtually every policy field of global governance. It argues that institutional topologies can be compared across these different policy fields if we think of them as social networks. This relational structure among institutions established to govern the same policy field is defined as the institutional topology of a regime complex. While some complexes are marked by high degrees of centralization, others exhibit decentralized structures. To measure this topology of institutional complexes, the book proposes to think of them as social networks structured by the interaction of their constitutive actors, institutions, and states. Taking a social network perspective allows for the "fine-grained conceptualization and measurement of structures" (Hafner-Burton et al. 2009: 561) and thus enables an abstract picture of a complex's underlying institutional activities to be drawn that can be compared across policy fields, even if they differ greatly regarding the characteristics of the underlying institutions or states involved.

Its ability to descriptively analyze the degree of centralization of institutional cooperation across a potentially large set of completely different policy fields makes the network perspective complementary to other quantitative methods of analyzing regime complexity systematically (Gholiagha et al. 2020; Kreuder-Sonnen and Zürn 2020; Haftel and Lenz 2021). These sophisticated approaches allow for a fine-grained quantification of different qualities of interinstitutional structures, for instance, the degree of policy and membership overlap (Haftel and Lenz 2021) or dyadic conflicts among a complex's constitutive institutions (Gholiagha et al. 2020; Kreuder-Sonnen and Zürn 2020). While these approaches zoom in on the micro level of dyadic institutional overlap and conflict, thereby providing important insights into the quality of regime complexity, the network approach provides a structural perspective focusing on the degree of centralization of institutional cooperation within different policy fields.

Drawing on a rich set of original quantitative and qualitative data this book provides an in-depth comparative analysis of the institutional topologies underlying five highly relevant issue areas. Exploiting an original dataset comprising over 73,800 pages of official IO documents and additional material from a total of 48 international institutions, the book maps institutional topologies by means of social network analysis complemented by in-depth qualitative process analyses. It thereby offers novel empirical insights for the study of regime complexity through comprehensive comparative studies drawing on both kinds of analysis and on quantitative and qualitative data that shed new light on institutional trajectories in five highly dynamic policy fields of global governance. Following the logic of a most-similar-system design, it compares the competitive structures and topologies underlying the institutional complexes of (1) financial stability and development aid, (2) tax avoidance and intellectual property protection, as well as (3) the policy field of energy governance over time.

This most-similar-system design allows me to analyze whether the variation in one specific market characteristic covaries with the institutional topologies underlying the compared policy areas, which will allow the book's theoretical framework to be evaluated. Throughout its three empirical chapters, the book contrasts issue areas that are strikingly similar with respect to a whole array of characteristics but nonetheless differ in one specific market characteristic. This case selection thereby isolates the effect of each market characteristic of a policy field on its regime complex's underlying topology. These comparative network analyses are further complemented by detailed process-tracing exercises of critical institutionalization processes within each of the five regime complexes. The qualitative case studies show that, despite the many similarities of each pair of policy fields under investigation, individual differences regarding market characteristics are associated with different institutionalization processes, these processes having been characterized by centripetal or centrifugal tendencies that have led to significantly varying institutional topologies over time.

The Argument and Theoretical Contribution: Varying Institutional Opportunity Structures and the Topology of Regime Complexes

The book's main argument is structural. It holds that (de)centralization dynamics in regime complexes and the resulting variation in the institutional topologies underlying them are crucially shaped by the "market characteristics" of their policy area. Different issues of global governance and their underlying cooperation problems are associated with different institutional opportunity structures, which produce varying incentives for states to engage in the creation or support of alternative institutions. These differences in issue area characteristics as a result create varying endogenous institutionalization dynamics which, over time, reinforce the centrifugal or centripetal dynamics in the complex's underlying topology. Within issue areas exhibiting high propensities to institutional competition due to the presence of pro-competitive market characteristics, centrifugal dynamics reinforce the evolution of decentralized institutional topologies. Conversely, within issue areas that are marked by anticompetitive characteristics, the resulting institutional opportunity structures create centripetal effects which tend to cement these regime complex's underlying centralistic topologies.

Taking Phillip Lipscy's (2015; 2017) theory of policy area competition and institutional change as a starting point, the book refines and complements his concept of institutional competition by conceptually disentangling these market characteristics and theoretically linking them to *interinstitutional* dynamics that produce either centripetal or centrifugal effects on a regime complex's underlying topology. Drawing on theories regarding the economic good characteristics of institutional cooperation (Cornes and Sandler 1996; Kaul et al. 1999; 2003; Mattli 1999; Kölliker 2001; Daßler 2022), the book complements Lipscy's concept of policy area competition by conceptualizing the (non)excludability of institutional benefits as an additional important determinant of policy area competition and thus of the evolution of (de)centralized institutional topologies. More precisely, it claims that institutional competition is not only a consequence of network effects and barriers to entry (Lipscy 2015; 2017) but is also shaped by the excludability or otherwise of institutional benefits.

The book argues that the varying propensity for competition within policy areas, which depends on their specific configuration of market characteristics, can operate in two distinct ways, crucially shaping the topology of regime complexes: First, highly competitive market structures produce centrifugal effects on the topology of institutional complexes, as states face strong incentives to pursue institutionalized forms of cooperation via small-scale and decentralized institutions which, in turn, favors the development of more contested and fragmented interinstitutional structures. Second, policy areas characterized by low degrees of competition produce centripetal effects on the topology of their institutional complexes, as cooperation tends to be pursued in a more universalistic and large-scale fashion, which consequently favors the development of comparatively uncontested, centralistic, and hierarchical structures among institutions. By synthesizing existing arguments on institutional competition with public good theories (Snidal 1979; Mattli 1999; Kölliker 2001; Fischbacher and Gachter 2010) and by putting the different market characteristics of policy fields into context, the book proposes and subsequently empirically tests a comprehensive theory of how policy area characteristics and their associated institutional opportunity structures affect the evolution of the different institutional topologies underlying individual regime complexes.

This argument and its inherently structural analytical focus address important gaps in the RC literature. A large chunk of this literature has engaged in unraveling the different consequences of the alleged ever-increasing complexity of global governance. While various scholars nowadays refer to this evolving literature as the "Regime Complexity Theory" (RCT), a large part of it has so far remained rather descriptive. Early studies that explored the phenomenon of regime complexity aimed to describe and conceptualize this new empirical phenomenon and to unravel its consequences for interstate politics (Biermann et al. 2009; Drezner 2009; Hofmann 2009; Urpelainen and van de Graaf 2015) or for particular international organizations or regions (Betts 2013; Brosig 2011; 2015; 2017). As such, this early literature focused on *the consequences* of the evolution of complex institutional structures for different kinds of international actors rather than on *their causes.*

The literature has, furthermore, remained quite divided regarding its evaluation of these consequences. This is especially the case when it comes to the (de)centralized relations among international institutions with overlapping mandates and functions. A rather optimistic camp expects that, when a growing number of institutions govern the same issue area, this leads to improved interinstitutional cooperation and division of labor among them (Gehring and Faude 2014; Pratt 2018). It is thus seen as an effective and realistic response to globalization which helps to increase the benefits of cooperation and the flexibility of states (Kellow 2012; Burke-White 2003). According to Judith Kelley (2009), the increasing proliferation of overlapping institutions can help to strengthen the legitimacy of interstate cooperation. Referring to the election monitoring complex, she argues that consensus and coordination among different monitoring institutions can bolster their legitimacy and thereby increase the domestic influence of these supranational actors. According to these optimistic accounts, the increasing proliferation of institutions should lead to cooperative, rather decentralized structures for institutional complexes, where reciprocal and equal relations among multiple institutions can exist. This is visible in the many instances where international institutions occupying the same policy field coordinate their policies while at the same time specializing and specifying their individual policy profile. Following this functional logic, states should benefit from membership in multiple and even overlapping institutions, as the evolving coordinative structure among them will enhance the efficiency of their policy-specific regulations. This optimistic strand in RCT implicitly expects the growing complexity of institutional structures to tend to relax interinstitutional hierarchies, thereby producing more fragmented, decentralized topologies which are marked by cooperative interinstitutional coordination and deference.

On the other hand, there is a more pessimistic camp that argues that the increasing number of institutions sharing similar jurisdictions leads to regulatory and legal uncertainty, higher transaction costs, and growing inequality among states since it helps especially powerful states to increase their influence and control institutional outcomes (Henning 2019; Zelli and van Asselt 2013; Benvenisti and Downs 2007; Urpelainen and van de Graaf 2015; Biermann et al. 2009; Pratt 2018; Clark 2021). Those who take this view expect the growing proliferation of competing international institutions to reinforce interinstitutional conflict, privileging those institutions that have powerful member states. These theories therefore implicitly expect that topologies among international institutions governing the same issue area should reflect the distribution of power among states insofar as they are willing and able to create institutions to pursue their specific interests (Henning 2017). Following a logic of contested multilateralism (Morse and Keohane 2014), from the perspective of these theories, powerful states exploit the increasing complexity of international regimes to pursue their individual policy goals while impeding their political competitors from pursuing their interests.

While both scenarios for developments among international institutions—cooperation and deference (e.g., Biermann 2008; Gehring and Faude 2014; Pratt 2018) as well as conflict and competition (e.g., Raustiala and Victor 2004; Davis 2009; Helfer 2009)—have been studied intensively, they have so far fallen short of explaining why their implicit expectations diverge regarding the general dynamics that lead to varying institutional topologies across different issue areas. Although it provides important insights into the consequences of the ever-increasing complexity of global governance, the RC literature has hardly perceived this structure as a dependent variable in need of explanation. Consequently, it has so far failed to supply concepts and theories located at a structural level that would allow them to empirically assess and explain the variance of these structures across issue areas.

The present book takes one step back to address the gap resulting from this focus on institutional structures as an explanatory factor: We have limited knowledge of the structural causes that have led to interinstitutional structures evolving so differently across policy areas of global governance. Institutional complexity, this book will argue, is not a constant but a variable; it ranges from fragmentation and fierce interinstitutional competition at one extreme to strictly hierarchical topologies among institutions with overlapping mandates at the other. And we need to know more about this variance. Following the call by Henning and Pratt (2020: 2) to "strengthen the foundation for comparative analysis of regime complexes," it offers the first systematic comparison of institutional topologies underlying various policy fields providing both an empirically grounded, network-based conceptualization and mapping of these structures and a theoretical explanation for their variation across global governance issue areas.

In this way, the book contributes to a better understanding of both the empirical manifestation of interinstitutional structures across various policy fields of global governance and the structural determinants of institutional competition in regime complexes that pave the way for the manifestation of (de)centralized institutional topologies. By enhancing our understanding of the causes of varying institutional structures, the book also seeks to challenge the existing implicit notion that specific interinstitutional structures are associated per se with either negative or positive consequences for institutionalized forms of interstate cooperation. Much more, it argues that it is necessary to explore the policy-area-specific causes of variation in interinstitutional topologies in order to understand its consequences for international politics: While hierarchization and centralization might be associated with efficient and effective institutional outcomes in some issue areas, other policy problems can be more efficiently addressed when there are multiple, overlapping, and competing institutional fora in which states (re)negotiate the issue-specific rules of the game.

These arguments, as developed in this book, carry important theoretical implications beyond regime complexity. Today's IR scholarship is understandably concerned with the tectonic geopolitical shifts that are taking place in the context of an increasingly conflictual international system marked by power shifts among states and fundamental ideological cleavages within their societies. Many scholars see the LIO and its underlying institutions as being existentially threatened by a domestic nationalist and populist backlash and the associated shrinkage of support in liberal democracies or by the rising influence of autocratic states like China or Saudi Arabia in global governance. As the Russian invasion of Ukraine, which ruthlessly breaches international law, has so terribly demonstrated, concerns about the fragility of the LIO and its underlying international institutions are legitimate. These changes in the conflictual nature of the international system are generally undermining efforts at institutionalization across many issue areas. But it is the book's central argument that the speed and degree of disruption caused by this geopolitical transformation are shaped by issue-area-specific institutional opportunity structures and the endogenous centripetal or centrifugal effects they create. Therefore, it is crucial to understand the endogenous effects that policy area characteristics exert on the evolution of different institutional topologies. And our understanding of this crucial policy-area-specific variance is precisely what this present book seeks to improve.

Structure of the Book

Part II of this book, comprising Chapters 2 and 3, develops the conceptual and theoretical framework and introduces the book's research design. Part III, comprising Chapters 4–7, empirically evaluates that framework. Part IV puts the book's argument and empirical findings into context and concludes with an outlook and agenda for further research.

In Chapters 2 and 3, I present the central theoretical concepts and arguments of this book: Chapter 2 introduces the relational concept of institutional topologies that allow for a comparative perspective on the (de)centralization of international regime complexes. Drawing on literature on authority and recognition in global governance, the chapter argues that institutional topologies are reflected in the interaction among the constitutive elements of regime complexes, states, and institutions. Chapter 3 introduces this book's theory of institutional topologies in regime complexes: The degree to which interinstitutional structures in regime complexes are exposed to centrifugal or centripetal trajectories crucially depends on the configuration of the characteristics of their underlying policy problem. Drawing on, but also refining and complementing, Lipscy's (2015; 2017) theory of policy area competition and institutional change, the book introduces the three market characteristics of policy fields that determine the degree of the book's main independent variable, the propensity for competition within policy areas: (i) The excludability or otherwise of benefits associated with institutionalized forms of cooperation within a certain policy field, (ii) the presence or absence of network effects associated with cooperation on a respective policy, and (iii) barriers to entry as material or political hindrances for states in setting up international institutions within a particular issue area. In this chapter, I propose to think of these market characteristics as indicator variables of a policy field's (latent) propensity for competition. The excludability of institutional benefits is associated with higher tendencies to competition; their nonexcludability comes with lower ones. The absence of network effects increases a policy field's underlying propensity for institutional competition, the presence of strong network effects inhibits it. Finally, high barriers to entry are associated with lower dispositions to institutional competition; low barriers encourage it.

The overall configuration of these market characteristics creates varying institutional opportunity structures under which states navigate their issue-specific cooperation. Whether institutionalized forms of cooperation among states follow centralized or decentralized and fragmented patterns is strongly affected by an issue area's underlying propensity for competition.

Depending on the configuration of market characteristics, this high (or low) propensity for institutional competition significantly shapes the incentives or disincentives for states to engage in competitive regime creation or institutional contestation. These varying opportunity structures create endogenous effects on individual regime complexes: Over time, high propensities for competition have centrifugal effects on institutional topologies. Procompetitive market characteristics, such as the provision of excludable institutional benefits, the absence of network effects, and low barriers to entry, facilitate and thereby reinforce the creation of alternative institutions. Moreover, they come with incentives for states to create exclusive institutional structures and relax hierarchies among competing institutions. Over time, these centrifugal effects on institutional competition lead to the evolution of decentralized institutional topologies in regime complexes. Conversely, low propensities for competition over time have centripetal effects on a regime complex's underlying topology. The presence in policy fields of anticompetitive market characteristics like the provision of nonexcludable institutional goods, the presence of strong network effects, and high barriers to setting up competing institutions, hamper interinstitutional competition and bind interstate cooperation to central and inclusive institutions. Over time, these centripetal effects of low propensities for institutional competition lead to the evolution of decentralized institutional topologies in regime complexes.

Part III, the empirical section of this book, begins by introducing the book's operationalization of institutional topology, its comparative research design, and empirical strategy in Chapter 4. By synthesizing the literature on institutional authority with network theory, I claim that institutional topologies can be compared across different regime complexes if we perceive them as social networks. The relative centrality of particular institutions is thus reflected in their network position vis-à-vis all other institutions as well as the states engaging in institutionalized forms of cooperation within the same complex. Taking a network perspective on institutional complexes further allows fine-grained structures to be compared not only within but also across different policy areas. As I will set out in greater detail throughout Chapter 4, a network analysis of institutional complexes allows one to go beyond an assessment of dyadic relations and hierarchies among different sets of institutions, the main preoccupation of most of the existing literature on international regime complexes. As an inherently relational concept, network analysis allows an individual institution's authority to be evaluated vis-à-vis the authority of all the other institutions in a complex in order to map the topology underlying the institutional complex in question accurately. The conceptualization of institutional topologies covers two dimensions: (1) the distribution of recognition among international institutions and (2) the recognition of institutions by states.

Chapters 5–7 provide a detailed structural comparison of a total of five different regime complexes and their institutional topologies as well as their competitive structure in order to probe the book's main theoretical claims. Over 73,800 pages of official institutional documents and additional material are analyzed in these chapters to assess the institutional topologies underlying five different policy fields of global governance: development aid, financial stability, intellectual property protection, tax avoidance, and energy governance. Moreover, drawing on qualitative data, each chapter traces specific institutionalization processes within each of the policy fields. These process-tracing analyses pinpoint the causal mechanisms linking the policy fields' respective market characteristics with their institutional topology.

Chapter 5 examines the impact of the excludability or otherwise of institutional goods in the policy field of tax avoidance and intellectual property on the policy areas' underlying institutional topologies. It starts by laying out important similarities between both policy issues before fleshing out their main difference: the two policy fields differ strongly regarding the type of good associated with institutionalized forms of cooperation. While in the issue area of tax avoidance, states cooperate to provide goods from which noncooperators cannot be excluded, in the intellectual property field, they cooperate to provide institutional goods that are excludable. The chapter demonstrates how this major difference among both issues translates into profoundly varying propensities for institutional competition. While the Organisation for Economic Co-operation and Development (OECD) is rarely challenged in the issue area of tax avoidance due to its provision of public goods, the World Trade Organization (WTO) and the World Intellectual Property Organization (WIPO) in the policy area of intellectual property are subject to regime shifting and institutional contestation strategies by states seeking to mitigate the negative effects of their exclusion from key trade networks. Network analysis corroborates the theory's expectation that the issue area's low propensity for competition has spurred the evolution of centralized institutional topologies in the regime complex of tax avoidance and decentralized interinstitutional structures in the issue area of intellectual property.

In Chapter 6 the book compares the institutional topologies underlying the policy fields of financial stability and development aid. It starts with a detailed analysis of these issue areas' similarities before pointing out their profound differences as regards the network effects associated with cooperation. Institutional cooperation on international financial stability benefits strongly from large membership and inclusive collaboration, but these network effects are less pronounced in the policy field of development aid. The chapter shows that states depend on the IMF's universal and large-scale design in the policy field of financial stability. At the same time, the creation and maintenance of institutional alternatives has proven to be politically difficult, costly, and therefore continually unsuccessful, which has ultimately resulted in the dominant and central position of the IMF and hence a strongly centralized institutional topology. By contrast, the World Bank does not benefit from such network effects in the policy field of development aid. The chapter shows how pursuing institutionalized forms of development cooperation outside the universal and large-scale institution of the World Bank in more specialized and regional formats is comparatively attractive and suitable. The qualitative process-analytical part of the chapter demonstrates how this highly competitive environment has led to the creation of several alternative multilateral development institutions in direct competition with the World Bank. Corroborating the book's underlying argument, in comparison to the institutional complex of financial stability, institutional topologies in the policy field of development aid appear strongly decentralized.

Chapter 7 applies a different research logic to study the effect of barriers to entry on topologies within institutional complexes. In contrast to the previous two chapters, this one does not engage in a static comparison of two policy fields but in a longitudinal analysis of one policy field's institutional topology, energy governance. I demonstrate how barriers to entry to institutionalized forms of cooperation in the issue area have been successively reduced over the last decades while many other characteristics, like network effects and the type of good provided by institutions have not changed over the same period. While before and throughout the early 1990s, institutionalized forms of cooperation on the issue of energy governance were an exclusive option for a small group of powerful states, the chapter demonstrates that, over time, shrinking political, material, and technological hurdles have significantly increased the policy field's propensity for institutional competition. The liberalization of the energy market following the end of the Cold War, the potential to exploit new forms of energy in many regions, and the exponential rise in the availability of renewable energy technologies incentivized several new state actors to engage in institutionalized forms of cooperation in the issue area. As the longitudinal analysis of the institutional networks underlying the energy governance complex reveals, it has indeed become more decentralized and contested over time, particularly at the expense of the International Energy Agency (IEA), which was for many decades the clear-cut institutional center of global energy governance.

Part IV of this book provides concluding reflections on the generalizability of the argument and its relationship with two prominent alternatives and considers potential avenues for further research. Chapter 8 evaluates the book's main finding in light of two prominent alternative explanations: neorealism and neofunctionalism. It argues that, while these alternative accounts add important insights to the study of specific institutionalization processes within specific institutional complexes, they have a hard time explaining the variance in institutional topologies observed across issue areas. By laying out how these alternative explanatory factors interact with policy area characteristics, I underline the relevance of considering the market characteristics of policy fields to explain variation in interinstitutional structures across issue areas. In its concluding Chapter 9, the book ends by reflecting on the implications for the literature on regime complexes, future research agendas on institutional complexity, and the importance of policymakers reflecting upon issue-specific differences with regard to the feasibility and attractiveness of interstate cooperation.

PART II
THEORETICAL FRAMEWORK

2

Rallying Together or Drifting Apart? Toward a Comparative Perspective on Institutional Topologies Underlying International Regime Complexes

This part of the book presents the theoretical framework that guides the analyses in the three subsequent empirical chapters. In the following section, I develop the book's conceptualization of the (de)centralized institutional topologies underlying international regime complexes, i.e., its explanandum. Subsequently, in the second part of this framework, building on Lipscy's (2015; 2017) theory of policy area competition and intra-institutional change, I develop a structural explanation for the significant variation in these topologies across different issue areas of global governance.

Prevailing arguments in the existing literature on regime complexity emphasize the importance of state power and interests or the functional advantages and disadvantages of specific institutional designs in the politics of regime complexity. My theory, by contrast, suggests that it is necessary to consider the profound differences in institutional opportunity structures associated with different policy issues as well. These differences in market characteristics create significantly different incentives for states to engage in institutionalized cooperation on that issue in whatever form, irrespective of their individual interests and power capabilities or the perceived benefits of specific institutional design features. While power-based and functional arguments are undoubtedly essential elements of an encompassing explanation for the politics of international regime complexes, I argue that their effects on the long-term evolution of policy-specific institutional topologies are contingent on the underlying market characteristics of the issue area in question.[1] To fully grasp the long-term trends in the evolution of centralized/decentralized institutional topologies, I suggest that it is necessary to understand how different policy issue characteristics translate into the varying propensities for institutional competition that create the endogenous

The Institutional Topology of International Regime Complexes. Benjamin Daßler, Oxford University Press.
© Benjamin Daßler (2023). DOI: 10.1093/oso/9780198881926.003.0002

centripetal or centrifugal trajectories under which states navigate their multi-lateral activities in regime complexes. Before making this argument in greater detail, the following section clarifies what the book conceives of as institutional topologies, its regime-complex-specific variable of interest, and how they manifest themselves empirically. Drawing on institutionalist literature, it develops a conceptualization of institutional topologies that allows the centralization/decentralization of interinstitutional structures to be compared across time and policy space.

Following the broad perception of Koremenos et al. (2001: 762), I conceive of international institutions as "explicit arrangements negotiated among international actors, that prescribe, proscribe, and/or authorize behavior." This broad definition explicitly encompasses a diverse set of differently designed institutions, ranging from rather informal arrangements like the Group of 20 (G20) and the African Tax Administration Forum (ATAF) via intergovernmental treaties like the Convention on Biological Diversity (CBD) or the Energy Charter Treaty (ECT) to international organizations like the International Monetary Fund (IMF) and the World Bank (WB). While these institutions differ considerably in their individual design characteristics, they all have in common that to a greater or lesser extent they sometimes directly constrain the behavior of international actors. They set norms, standards, and rules that guide international political action (Duffield 2007).

I therefore agree with literatures stressing the relevance of institutional design to, e.g., the effective functioning of institutional arrangements (Rosendorff and Milner 2001; Coglianese 2000; Bernauer 1995b) or the room for strategic maneuver that institutions provide for states seeking their individual policy goals (Koremenos et al. 2001; Johnston 2001). I nevertheless argue that these institutional design characteristics are less important when it comes to an individual institution's centrality in a particular regime complex. As I will lay out in this theory chapter in greater detail, some policy issues favor the central position of more flexibly and informally designed institutions, others may encourage states to create more formally designed institutional arrangements with explicit enforcement mechanisms. Thus, irrespective of their individual degree of institutionalization, institutions can occupy central positions within their regime complexes. In many issue areas, central international institutions are highly institutionalized. In the realm of human rights, for instance, the United Nations (UN) exhibits a high degree of formalization and institutionalization and, despite criticism or even outright contestation by some of its members, it is among the most frequently used international institutions when it comes to human rights issues (see, e.g., Alston and Mégret 2020). In other issue areas, however, informal and poorly institutionalized institutions are important central fora for multilateral cooperation. In the issue area of tax avoidance, for instance, the Group of 20, the informal club of the twenty most powerful industrial economies in the world, greatly impacts on the norms and standards in the field of international tax policy. It is therefore important to note that, while institutional design certainly matters for effective policymaking by international institutions, institutionalization and a high degree of formalization are not prerequisites for occupying central and authoritative positions within regime complexes.

Institutional complexes emerge whenever states set up more than one institutional arrangement to coordinate and regulate the same policy issue. Virtually every issue area is governed by "an array of partially overlapping and nonhierarchical institutions" (Raustiala and Victor 2004: 279), characterized by poorly delineated mandates and potentially competing among themselves for authority (Alter and Meunier 2009; Alter and Raustiala 2018). Regime complexes emerge either as an unintended consequence of functional differentiation (Zürn and Faude 2013), institutional mandate expansion (Humrich 2013), or issue linkages and package deals (Muzaka 2011). Moreover, regime complexes can result from deliberate state action, such as engaging in contested multilateralism (Colgan et al. 2012; Morse and Keohane 2014; Urpelainen and van de Graaf 2015). Coalitions of dissatisfied states find the pathway to institutional adaptation blocked and decide to engage in regime shifting or competitive regime creation (Morse and Keohane 2014: 389).

In a given issue area populated by overlapping institutions, states can decide which institution they should refer a cooperation problem to (Drezner 2009; Jupille et al. 2013), which rules to comply with (Benvenisti and Downs 2007; Raustiala and Victor 2004), and which institution to transfer their financial and political capital to (Hofmann 2009). This implies that institutions, as agents of their member states, can be expected to act in accordance with their principals' demands (Hawkins et al. 2006). Institutional complexes are therefore necessarily marked by an overlap of political mandates among their constitutive institutions. Following Raustiala and Victor's (2004: 279) definition, I conceive of institutional complexes as "array[s] of partially overlapping and nonhierarchical institutions governing a particular issue-area."

Within these complexes, states can select from a set of institutional alternatives oftentimes differing in their design characteristics and functional scope. Because of these state choices, relational structures emerge among established institutions and their newly created contenders (Biermann et al. 2009;

Gehring and Faude 2014; Henning 2017; Haftel and Lenz 2021; Kreuder-Sonnen and Zürn 2020; Pratt 2018; Lenz 2021). As Lenz (2021) convincingly demonstrates in his book on interorganizational diffusion, these ties are also consequential, as far as regional institutions are concerned, since central and influential regional institutions like the EU have the potential to significantly influence institution-building processes in other regions of the world. Within some regime complexes, quasi-hierarchical structures emerge that are characterized by a few inclusive and more encompassing institutions at the center of the regime complex. Here, states cultivate synergistic and cooperative relations among institutions. Other complexes are more fragmented. In these settings, established institutions and their contenders compete on eye level and states pursue forum-shopping and regime-shifting strategies to make use of contradictory rules, competing mandates and foundational policies.

It is therefore important to note that the absence of a formally agreed hierarchy among the international institutions set up to govern the same policy issue does *not* imply the absence of relational structures between these institutions. On the contrary, the coexistence of institutional arrangements addressing the very same policy problems may encourage the formation of relational structures among these institutional actors that do encompass some form of social hierarchy which may be highly contested resulting in decentralized forms of institutional cooperation, but could equally well be harmonious and universal, resulting in centralized forms of cooperation with a clear-cut institutional center. I define these varying interinstitutional structures as the topologies of regime complexes.

While some institutional complexes are strongly centralized, others exhibit decentralized topologies. An institution's relative position within its complex is, I argue, a function of its recognition by other institutions and states (Avant et al. 2010; Sending 2017; Lake 2009, 2011; Zürn et al. 2012). Central positions within institutional complexes allow actors to exercise authority by directly or indirectly constraining others (Heupel and Zürn 2017: 4; Bogdandy et al. 2010: 11; Zürn et al. 2012: 70; Hooghe and Marks 2015). Only if international institutions are recognized by states and other institutions claiming to govern the same policy issue, can they constrain, initiate, or encourage political actions by states on the issue in question. An international institution's centrality in a particular complex thus hinges on its success in "claim[ing] the right to perform regulatory functions like the formulation of rules and rule monitoring or enforcement" (Zürn et al. 2012: 70) within its policy area. This conceptualization of authority as a recognized claim to govern is closely linked to assumptions formulated by the more general literature on recognition processes and their relevance for international politics

(Honneth 1995; Wendt 2003; Greenhill 2008; Kavalski 2013). In line with these theories, I argue that recognition matters for international politics and especially for international institutions as supranational actors. Recognition matters "because it represents the process through which actors come to exist as actors within the international system and take on a particular identity within that system" (Greenhill 2008: 344).

Thus, for international institutions, recognition by other actors such as states or other supranational institutions—even if they are institutional or political competitors—represents a significant prerequisite to exercising authority. If they are recognized by states and other institutions claiming to govern the same policy issue, they can constrain, initiate, or encourage political actions by states on the issue in question. An international institution's authority thus rests on its success in "claim[ing] the right to perform regulatory functions like the formulation of rules and rule monitoring or enforcement" (Zürn et al. 2012: 70) vis-à-vis other important actors in their policy areas. What follows from this perception of authority as the degree of recognition of an institution's claim to govern is that there are potentially varying distributions of authority among institutions governing the same issue area. This distribution of recognition among international institutions reflects a complex's underlying topology, and the topologies underlying particular institutional complexes can actually be assessed and mapped if we take a relational perspective. Assessing the degree of recognition received by a specific institution in direct relation to the degree of recognition received by all other institutions of the complex allows one to take a structural perspective that goes beyond one focusing on single institutions or dyads of competing institutions. This perspective has so far been taken mainly by scholars interested in the phenomena of institutional complexity. I argue that each institution exhibits a distinct relational position within its complex, thus allowing us to evaluate a regime complex's institutional topology accurately. How can varying institutional topologies across issue areas of global governance be explained? What conditions reinforce centralizing/decentralizing tendencies in regime complexes? In the following Chapter 3, I develop an argument highlighting the importance of issue area characteristics that hamper or promote interinstitutional competition in regime complexes.

Note

1. Chapter 8 of this book lays out this argument in greater detail. More specifically, it shows how the effect of state power and institutional design features on institutional topologies

underlying regime complexes are *moderated* by the market characteristics of issue areas. Referring to the empirical cases analyzed in the empirical chapters, Chapter 8 claims that the effect of state power and interest, as well as the functional benefit of specific institutional design characteristics on the long-term centripetal or centrifugal trajectories within regime complexes, can be either reinforced or attenuated by varying market characteristics in different issue areas.

3
Theorizing Institutional Topologies in International Regime Complexes

Drawing on a rational-institutionalist framework, this book argues that varying market structures within policy fields provide diverging incentives for states to engage in institutionalized forms of cooperation. This, in turn, spurs the formation of varying institutional topologies, ranging from decentralized and more fragmented structures to strongly centralized, more hierarchical ones. States—understood as bounded, rational, and uniform actors—seek to cooperate on issues where they expect the outcome of cooperation to be beneficial and represent a mutually preferable equilibrium (Oye 1985; Abbott and Snidal 1998; Koremenos et al. 2001). While scholars have stressed that external conditions like the situational dependency structure or type of collaboration problem have an impact on whether states seek to coordinate via international institutions and how they design them (Martin 1992), they have so far not paid much attention to how policy-specific characteristics actually affect relationships and hierarchies among overlapping and/or competing institutions thereby crucially shaping the institutional topology of regime complexes. By drawing on a combination of economic and institutionalist theories, I seek to fill this gap.

Taking Lipscy's (2015; 2017) seminal theory on policy area competition and intra-institutional change as a starting point, this book's main proposition is that states seeking to achieve cooperative outcomes on global policy issues are affected and constrained by the political problem structure they engage in, just as firms are constrained by the characteristics of their respective industrial markets. These constraints significantly impact the way states pursue institutionalized forms of cooperation on a specific issue, thereby significantly shaping the way institutional complexes are structured and hierarchically ordered. Economic theories have long pointed to the relevance of structural differences across industries, shaping not only the degree of concentration within markets, but also the type and design of organization as well as the hierarchies emerging from these varying conditions (George et al. 2005: 259 ff.; Bryson and Rusten 2010). Within certain industries, market

The Institutional Topology of International Regime Complexes. Benjamin Daßler, Oxford University Press.
© Benjamin Daßler (2023). DOI: 10.1093/oso/9780198881926.003.0003

characteristics like barriers to entry, economies of scale, network effects, or the provision of nonexcludable public goods incentivize the formation of oligopolies or even monopolies, where only a small number of organizations control a large proportion of market share (see, e.g., Auster 1977; Katz and Shapiro 1994; Markovich 2008).

While it is important to stress that industrial organizations differ greatly from international institutions in many respects (Lipscy 2017: 25), the way states, as members of international institutions, are affected and constrained by the characteristics of their respective environments when it comes to decisions about the design and scope of institutionalized forms of cooperation is quite similar: Within certain areas of global governance, like, for example, the mitigation of global climate change, incentives to cooperate via universal and large-scale institutions are high, as the positive effects of reduced carbon emissions rise significantly with the number of participating states. Thus, states are incentivized to pursue institutional forms of cooperation via rather large-scale and universal institutions. Smaller-scale and exclusive institutions, by contrast, are unattractive options. Consequently, there is very little inclination to compete institutionally in these policy areas. On the other hand, there are policy areas where states do have incentives to pursue cooperation through comparatively small-scale and exclusive institutions. One example is the issue area of development aid, where the coordination of redistributive measures might even be hampered if larger numbers of states took part owing to greater heterogeneity of interest. Within these issue areas, small-scale, independent, and exclusive institutional outside options are much more attractive. In these policy fields, therefore, there exists a strong propensity for institutional competition.

By introducing the concept of policy area competition to the study of international institutions, Lipscy (2015; 2017) was the first to theorize the external institutional environment's effects on intra-institutional change processes in international institutions. Lipscy's theory highlights the link between preexisting outside options and their attractiveness for states and an institution's propensity for intra-institutional reform. His theory convincingly explains how the probability of success for revisionist states seeking to change preexisting institutional privileges and the rules within specific institutions is contingent on the availability and attractiveness of outside options in the broader institutional environment of a policy field. The theory developed in the following section of this book adopts Lipscy's notion of the relevance of policy area competition to explain the politics in international regime complexes. However, it also differs from his argument in four significant ways. First, and most importantly, the theory differs regarding its explanandum. While Lipscy's theory seeks to explain the prospects for change and reform within individual institutions, this book's theory explains how the market characteristics of policy issues shape the evolution of interinstitutional structures underlying the entire regime complex. Thus, what in Lipscy's theory is an important independent variable on his theorized causal pathway is the primary dependent variable in this book's theory: the centralization/decentralization of a regime complex's institutional topology. In a nutshell, Lipscy's theory convincingly explains how the availability and attractiveness of institutional outside options, reflected in the centralized/decentralized topology of the entire regime complexes, shapes intra-institutional reform and change. This book's theory, developed below, explains, by contrast, how opportunity structures associated with the specific policy issue at hand shape the evolution of these (de)centralized interinstitutional structures in the first place. A second important difference is the conceptualization and operationalization of regime complexity, i.e., the availability of institutional outside options in Lipscy's theory and the (de)centralization of the complex's interinstitutional structure in the theory put forward in this book. While in Lipscy's theory complexity is operationalized as the sheer number of competing institutions available to states in a specific regime complex (Lipscy 2017: 31–4), this book takes a relational perspective. Conceptualizing institutional topologies as the interinstitutional structures underlying the entire regime complex allows us not only to capture the "density" of individual regime complexes in quantitative terms, but to map the hierarchical (de)centralization among its constitutive elements. Third, while borrowing Lipscy's concepts of network effects and barriers to entry as essential characteristics of policy areas that determine the propensity for institutional competition in individual issue areas, this book's theory adds a third important characteristic impacting competition in regime complexes, the excludability or nonexcludability of institutional benefits, to this two-dimensional concept of policy area competition. Drawing on economic and political science theories respecting the provision of public goods, I argue that policy-area competition is shaped not only by network effects and barriers to entry, but also by the degree to which institutional cooperation is beneficial to those states that refrain from participating. While network effects and barriers to entry impact the costs of creating alternative institutions, the (non)excludability of institutional benefits creates incentives or disincentives for the strengthening of alternative arrangements due to the existing institution's positive externalities. Thus, depending on this variable's value, it either reinforces or hampers institutional competition, independently of the pro- or anticompetitive effect of network effects and barriers to entry. Combining these three market characteristics, as well as linking their specific configurations to the evolution of different topologies in regime complexes allows interinstitutional structures to be mapped and analyzed across issue areas and time. Fourth, and finally, this book's theory expands on Lipscy's (2015; 2017) argument by claiming that constellations of policy area characteristics favoring institutional competition, i.e., the absence of network effects and low barriers to entry, not only render intra-institutional reform more likely, but also create centrifugal effects that affect the entire regime complex by incentivizing states to create or strengthen institutional competitors, even if they have been accommodated by intra-institutional reforms. This is because even though such reforms are likely to occur under the condition of policy area competition, the literature has shown that, due to the general stickiness of international institutions, these reforms are often far from perfect, providing strong incentives for underprivileged states to strengthen alternative institutions, in particular in cases where there is a high propensity for institutional competition (see, e.g., Rixen et al. 2016; Zangl et al. 2016; Pratt 2021).

I argue that there are two important ways in which competition within policy fields shapes the structure of institutional complexes: First, competitive market structures tend to create *centrifugal effects on the topology underlying institutional complexes*, as they facilitate and reinforce the creation of alternative institutions, incentivize exclusive institutional structures, and relax hierarchies among institutions within the complex. Second, policy areas marked by strongly anticompetitive market characteristics tend to produce *centripetal effects on the topology underlying institutional complexes*, as they hamper the creation of alternative institution while incentivizing inclusive cooperation via large-scale institutions, thereby favoring more central institutional topologies. Before discussing these two effects in greater detail in the next section, let me introduce three "market characteristics" of policy areas indicating the degree of institutional competition within different policy fields: the excludability or nonexcludability of benefits associated with institutionalized forms of cooperation, network effects, and the barriers to entry to institutionalized forms of cooperation. These three market characteristics can be understood as indicators allowing to approach the degree of my latent, independent variable, which is a policy field's underlying propensity for competition. Figure 3.1 summarizes and illustrates the overall argument of my theory.

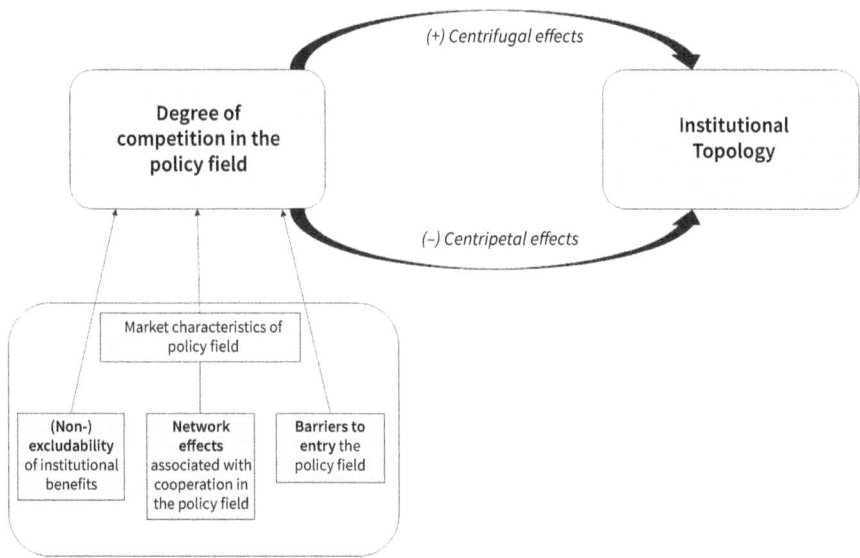

Figure 3.1 Market Characteristics of Policy Fields, Competition and the Topology of Regime Complexes

The Excludability/Nonexcludability of Institutional Benefits and Institutional Topologies in Regime Complexes

Economists and political scientists have produced a burgeoning literature on how the type of good provided by economic or state actors affects incentives for private as well as political actors to engage in its supply (Clarke 1971; Ostrom 1990; Cornes and Sandler 1996; Kaul et al. 1999; Kaul et al. 2003). This literature differentiates whether a good is rivalrous/nonrivalrous, and excludable/nonexcludable. The first, internal dimension addresses potential distributional conflicts over a particular good among institutional members on the basis of whether its supply is finite or infinite. Rivalrous goods, if consumed by one individual, are no longer available for consumption by others. Classical examples of rivalrous goods in the economic market include food, clothing, and other physical products. In international politics rivalrous goods are oftentimes associated with conflicts over resources among states. Natural resources such as oil, natural gas, and minerals are prime examples of goods for which states compete at the international level because they are limited in supply and can only be used by one country at a time. As became painfully apparent, especially for the European Union, in the course of the

Russian war of aggression against Ukraine that was unleashed in early 2022 and was immediately followed by import restrictions on some of Russia's natural resources, such rivalrous goods can lead to severe conflicts over access to them. Nonrivalrous goods are goods that can be consumed by multiple individuals at the same time, and do not diminish in availability as a result. Classical examples of nonrivalrous goods in the economic sphere include public goods such as clean air, knowledge, or cultural knowledge or certain artifacts. In international politics, nonrivalrous goods are likewise resources that can be used by multiple states or private actors at the same time without diminishing the supply. In theory, they include information, such as scientific research and data, and cultural work including art, music, and literature. However, especially in transnational politics, nonrivalrous goods, despite their potentially infinite supply, are often associated with serious conflict among states over their proper use and protection. This is particularly relevant when it comes to the protection of intellectual property, where nonrivalrous goods can be politically and legally transformed into rivalrous, but more importantly, excludable goods to limit their consumption and earn profits.

The (non)excludability characteristic is the second dimension of economic goods and, as I will argue in what follows, one with significant consequences for the likelihood of competition in regime complexes. The excludability dimension of an economic good or resource is its ability to be restricted to specific individuals or groups. In the economic literature, this dimension is used to classify goods as either private, which means they can be excluded from use by others, or public, which means that consumers cannot be excluded from using them. Examples of private goods provided by states through international cooperation are the reciprocal security guarantees given by states in military alliances. These goods, the security guarantees, are essentially private because other states outside the alliance are excluded from their consumption. Typical examples of purely public goods provided through multilateral cooperation include, e.g., the protection of the global environment against climate change and biodiversity loss mitigation measures. These goods provided by cooperating states are public goods because noncooperating states cannot be excluded from the benefits associated with them. The benefits of protecting the global environment, such as clean air and water, are enjoyed by all countries, irrespective of their individual contributions. Nevertheless, many goods provided through international cooperation can be described as "impure public goods," meaning that they only fit one of the two criteria for public goods, nonexcludability and nonrivalry in consumption. Goods that are mostly nonexcludable but remain rivalrous in consumption are referred to by the literature as common pool resources (Steins and Edwards 1999: 242); goods that are nonrivalrous in consumption but are excludable are referred to as "club goods" (Kaul et al. 1999: 5). Table 3.1 below classifies these different types of good provided by international institutions according to their main characteristics as introduced above and provides empirical examples.

I argue that, within international regime complexes, it is the external dimension of an institutional good provided through multilateral cooperation, the possibility of excluding others states from the benefits associated with cooperation, that strongly affects a policy field's propensity for institutional competition. The attractiveness of outside options depends on whether there are positive externalities for nonparticipating states, or, on the contrary, benefits can be enjoyed exclusively by institutional members. In the latter case, incentives to join existing institutions or create new ones are high. Take, for instance, the establishment of a military alliance which grants exclusive, reciprocal security guarantees to its member states. For nonparticipating states, there are no benefits associated with the production of that good, i.e., the exclusive security guarantees. Quite the opposite. The very existence of this exclusive military alliance creates incentives for nonmembers to engage in counter-institutionalization by creating their own military alliance so that they can also enjoy security guarantees. If cooperation on specific issues is associated with providing nonexcludable goods, incentives to shift to or create other institutions to compete with existing ones are low. Even if states do not participate in a given institution, they cannot be excluded from the goods associated with the cooperation of the institutional members. Multilateral cooperation on the issue of global health is associated with nonexcludable benefits. The eradication of a particular disease through multilateral initiatives brings about benefits for all states irrespective of their contribution to

Table 3.1 Types of Good Provided by International Institutions; Empirical Examples

	Rivalrous	Nonrivalrous
Excludable institutional goods	*Private goods* (Example: intergovernmental commodity-pricing cartels)	*Club goods* (Examples: military alliances)
Nonexcludable institutional goods	*Common-pool resources* (Examples: international institutions regulating the use of biological resources)	*Purely public goods* (Examples: institutions aimed at mitigating climate change)

Note: Author's own illustration. For more nuanced and detailed differentiations of various types of good see, e.g., Kaul et. al 2003, Barrett 2007; Sandler 2004: 82; Cornes and Sandler 1996.

the specific initiative. The very existence of such initiatives—like the WHO's Global Polio Eradication Initiative, founded in 1988 and widely considered a multilateral success story as the number of polio cases has since decreased dramatically—reduces incentives for states to set up alternative institutions as they cannot be excluded from the good, the (quasi-)eradication of polio, irrespective of their participation. When it comes to the propensity for institutional competition in specific issue areas, therefore, it matters whether institutional cooperation is associated with benefits resembling a club good (Mattli 1999: 59–64), which member states enjoy exclusively, or benefits resembling a public good, where nonparticipating states enjoy the benefits stemming from cooperation equally, irrespective of their participation in the institution in question (Snidal 1979: 539–44). Consequently, institutionalization processes in issue areas differ with respect to their underlying (de)centralization dynamics. Regime complexes in which states cooperate to provide nonexcludable goods are shaped by centripetal effects that prompt the evolution of centralized topologies. Conversely, in complexes where multilateral institutions are set up to produce excludable goods that can only be enjoyed by their members, centrifugal effects accelerate and reinforce the evolution of decentralized institutional topologies. The following paragraphs spell out these two different dynamics in greater detail.

Issue areas with nonexcludable institutional benefits (public good provision): If policy issues require that institutions are set up to provide public goods, institutional competition can be expected to remain comparatively low, favoring the evolution of centralized institutional topologies. The main reason is the free rider problem (Runge 1984: 156; Carraro and Siniscalco 1998: 2; Fischbacher and Gachter 2010). Once institutions that produce public goods are established, incentives to create alternative institutions decrease sharply. Nonparticipating states benefit from the public good provided by others without having to bear any costs themselves. Moreover, in issue areas where institutions provide public goods, nonmembers face positive externalities through the cooperation of others. Still, in many issue areas of global governance, institutions are set up to provide global public goods. One reason is that especially powerful states have a substantial interest in their provision: As pointed out by realist scholars, by supplying global public goods, great powers can stabilize the institutional order thereby fortifying their central position and reassuring themselves against potential revisionist behavior by emerging powers (Gowa 1989; Nye 2002; Gilpin 2016). The preexistence of a public good institution creates disincentives for outsider states to engage in the creation of institutional alternatives (Hofmann 2011). For instance, if a group of states decides to set up an environmental agreement in which they obligate themselves to reduce their carbon dioxide emissions, the positive effects on global climate are not restricted to member states, but are equally beneficial to those states that refrain from cooperation. Thus, within issue areas where the provision of nonexcludable goods is central to institutional cooperation, states that refrain from cooperation enjoy positive externalities arising from the cooperation of others (Kölliker 2001: 130; Mattli 1999: 59-64). Here, positive external effects for outsiders are significantly higher than the internal costs of participation (Kölliker 2001). This, in turn, significantly reduces the attractiveness of outside options. Even more, the nonexcludability of cooperative benefits creates strong incentives for members of existing public good institutions to opt for a strategy of "buying nonmembers in," thereby unintentionally further weakening institutional competition and reinforcing centripetal tendencies within a regime complex. As institutional members are interested in the distribution of costs and the expansion of the institutions' underlying rules and norms, they have to offer nonparticipants benefits in exchange for their participation, co-opting them by, for example, "trading institutional privileges for institutional support" (Kruck and Zangl 2019: 321). Such privileges can entail the provision of soft and nonbinding arrangements which allow nonmembers access to institutional resources without requiring the legally binding commitments associated with sovereignty costs (Abbott and Snidal 2000). Consequently, the attractiveness of institutional outside options is low in issue areas where institutions provide nonexcludable goods. States have no incentives to engage in competitive regime creation or forum shopping, so institutional competition remains weak which, in turn, has centripetal rather than centrifugal effects on the institutional complex's underlying topology.

Issue areas with excludable institutional benefits (club good provision): If policy issues allow states to set up institutions that provide club goods from which nonparticipants can effectively be excluded, institutional competition can be expected to be comparatively high, favoring the evolution of decentralized institutional topologies. Here, free riding on the provision of nonexcludable goods by others is impossible. Moreover, as compared to issue areas where public goods are central to institutional cooperation, there are no positive externalities for nonmembers. Positive internal effects for members are significantly higher than positive external effects for outsiders (Kölliker 2001: 134–8). Even more, institutional clubs are oftentimes associated with negative externalities for nonmembers. For instance, if a group of states decides to establish a military alliance with reciprocal security guarantees, the good provided by the institution in question can only be enjoyed by member states (Bernauer 1995a; Buchanan 1965: 2; Cornes and Sandler

1996: 34; Sandler and Tschirhart 1997: 337). Incentives for states to either join existing institutions or to create their own in order to enjoy similar benefits are, consequently, high (Brummer 2007: 536). However, joining existing institutional clubs is not always possible, as membership depends on the club's conditions for acceptance and the member states' willingness to accommodate outsiders. While in some cases states may have good reasons to "privatize" the output of their institutionalized cooperation by selectively offering excludable goods to nonmembers thereby incentivizing them to join and participate in financing the institution in question (Frey 1984: 215), in other cases states may have a strong political and strategical interest in preventing certain states from gaining access to the excludable good provided by their institution. If admission to existing clubs cannot be realized, incentives for counter-institutionalization rise significantly, as the good in question cannot otherwise be enjoyed. The preexistence of such an institutional club also comes with negative effects for nonparticipants. The establishment of exclusive security institutions can lead to increasing uncertainty among nonmembers who view the exclusive institution as a potential threat, provoking them to engage in counter-institutionalization. For nonparticipants to enjoy the benefits provided by security institutions, it is necessary for them to either join existing arrangements or to create their own institutional club. This, I argue, creates centrifugal effects in a regime complex's underlying topology. In issue areas where the threat of exclusion from essential institutional benefits is real, states oftentimes find themselves forced to enter institutional arrangements, if accession is possible after all, whose rules are not in line with their interests to avoid the negative effects of being excluded from the good provided by the institutional club. For instance, a decision to abstain from a certain free-trade arrangement comes with prohibitively high costs for states as they may find themselves excluded from essential markets, so they eventually agree upon rules harmful to their economic development to avoid the negative effects of exclusion (see in particular Gruber 2001; Murphy 2009; Slapin 2009). Thus, and in contrast to issue areas where institutions provide public goods, excludability allows cooperators to force the unwilling into institutionalized forms of cooperation rather than having to co-opt them. Here, the preexistence of institutions providing excludable goods alters the preferences of states (Hofmann 2011). For states forced to join to avoid the negative consequences of exclusion, as well as for states capable of pursuing independent institutional alternatives, there are strong incentives to create or strengthen institutional alternatives to mitigate the negative effects of the existing club's disadvantageous rules. Engaging in strategies like competitive regime creation, regime shifting (Helfer 2004, 2009) or forum shopping

(Busch 2007) becomes rational. Consequently, in issue areas marked by the institutional provision of excludable goods, centrifugal effects shape the evolution of regime complexes' underlying institutional topologies.

Synthesizing the above considerations allows us to hypothesize that:

Hypothesis 1: All else being equal, in policy areas where institutionalized cooperation is associated with the provision of excludable goods, the propensity for interinstitutional competition is higher, and institutional topologies are more decentralized.

Hypothesis 2: All else being equal, in policy areas where institutionalized cooperation is associated with the provision of nonexcludable goods, the propensity for interinstitutional competition is low and institutional topologies are more centralized.

Network Effects and the Topology of Regime Complexes

This section introduces the second market characteristic of policy fields that impacts on the evolution of centralized or decentralized institutional topologies underlying regime complexes. Like the excludability or nonexcludability of institutional benefits, network effects associated with cooperation on a respective policy issue shape a policy field's underlying propensity for competition (Lipscy 2015: 343; Lipscy 2017: 28). Lipscy (2015; 2017) derives his institutionalist concept of network effects from the economic literature on market structure and competition. The concept refers, in its basic understanding, to a phenomenon in which an increase in the number of consumers improves the value of a particular good or service (Katz and Shapiro 1985; 1994: 94). For users, the utility derived from consuming the good increases with each additional agent that joins the group of customers. A classic example for an economic market with strong network effects is modern communications technology industry: The utility that a consumer derives from using, e.g., a certain web-based messenger service, clearly depends on the number of other people that have decided to opt for that specific messenger. In this way, the attractiveness of alternative messengers decreases dramatically in line with the number of consumers opting for the same service, which, in turn, makes it hard or even impossible for alternative suppliers to enter the market. Another prime example of a good associated with strong network effects are social media platforms such as Facebook, Instagram, or Twitter. Their value increases as more people join and use them, as this allows users to connect with a larger network of friends, family, and acquaintances and creates a positive feedback loop, where more users lead to more value, which in turn attracts more users. As a result, the platform becomes more valuable the more people use it, which makes it more likely that even more people will use it. This powerful network effect makes it particularly difficult for competitors to position themselves as attractive alternatives. Consequently, the market for social media platforms has produced comparatively strongly centralized structures, with a small number of large firms dominating the business with almost no competition (Baran et al. 2015).

Network effects further produce indirect binding effects on customers: For example, a customer purchasing a particular electronic hardware product will be concerned about the number of other agents purchasing similar hardware because the amount and variety of software that is supplied for use with a given hardware product will be a function of the number of hardware units that have been sold (Katz and Shapiro 1985: 424; Gandal 2002). Streaming platforms, such as Netflix and Spotify, are another prime example of goods with strong network effects for customers. The value of these platforms increases as more content creators and users join. This creates a positive feedback loop where more content leads to more value, which in turn attracts more content creators and users. For customers, the more users and content creators on the platform, the more diverse and extensive the content library becomes. This makes it more likely that customers will find content they want to watch or listen to, which makes the platform more valuable to them. This creates a powerful network effect that can be difficult for competitors to overcome. Thus, if network effects are present within a particular industrial market, firms with large established clienteles are more attractive to new customers than firms with fewer customers, independent of the quality or price of the products on offer (Cabral et al. 1999: 200 f.). If there are strong network effects present within a respective industrial market, competition among firms is significantly hampered and large shares of the market tend to be controlled by only a small number of large enterprises.

Following Lipscy (2017), I argue that the idea of network effects as a determinant of competition within markets can be transferred to the realm of interstate cooperation on global policy issues. In the context of international institutions, such effects emerge when the utility of a particular institution increases with the total number of participating states (Lipscy 2015: 343; Lipscy 2017: 28–31). Thus, network effects in a policy field are present when cooperative outcomes benefit greatly from there being relatively more participating states. Conversely, if the number of member states does not influence the attractiveness of institutions within the respective policy field, network effects can be considered low or absent. Whether network effects are present or not varies strongly across policy areas: While, e.g., military alliances or development institutions do not necessarily profit from having more participating states, international institutions that regulate standardization issues benefit greatly from having greater numbers of participants: the potential transaction costs associated with their regulatory activities decrease significantly the more states adopt their' standards (Lipscy 2017: 28; Braunstein and White 1985). Another issue area where there are significant network effects present is international trade. When states create trade institutions, they gain access to new markets and resources, which can increase economic growth and prosperity. The relative potential for an increase in growth, however, depends on the size of the international trade institution in question. The greater the number of participating states, the more trade and cooperation can be realized, which, in turn, makes it more likely that other countries will try to join the trade institution. Within issue areas where network effects are present, universal and inclusive cooperation is feasible and attractive as the utility of including additional states is high for members of the institution. At the same time, the marginal utility of joining an existing institution increases for outsiders the more states join it, thus decreasing incentives to foster cooperation by means of small-scale institutional alternatives (Lipscy 2017: 28). On the other hand, within issue areas where there are no network effects associated with institutionalized cooperation, it is more attractive for states to cooperate via small-scale and exclusive institutions, as there will be no utility from including additional members but increasing transaction and coordination costs.

In some policy areas where there are no network effects, cooperative outcomes may even be worsened by higher numbers of participants. This is especially the case in issue areas where policies are associated with positive societal resonance, which hinges on the visibility of an individual state's willingness to act. Take as an example intergovernmental efforts to respond to humanitarian crises. Though the cooperative outcome might be improved in overall terms by there being large numbers of donors, the visibility of an individual state's helpfulness will be lower the greater the number of states and supranational actors that are involved. Furthermore, political considerations about the specific targets of aid can be more easily implemented if the number of participating states is low. More, and potentially divergent, political motivations and thus interests can significantly detract from the individual utility of states. Consequently, in these issue areas higher numbers of participating states provide strong incentives for states to pursue smaller-scale forms of institutionalized cooperation and reduce the attractiveness of larger and more universalistic institutions. This, in turn, fuels competition, as it incentivizes states to engage in the creation of more small-scale and exclusive institutional outside options.

The presence of network effects, on the other hand, tends to curb competition among institutions in a particular policy area since they tend to bind states into universalistic cooperative arrangements (Lipscy 2017: 28). Just as customers are bound to particular suppliers in industrial markets with strong network effects, states tend to become bound into large, universalist institutions when it comes to cooperation in policy areas with strong network effects. Within such areas, pursuing outside options is unattractive and associated with comparatively high costs. Additionally, member states have strong incentives to prevent dissatisfied states from exiting when network effects are present because the utility of cooperation on policy issues is dependent on the number of participating states, so that status quo states are strongly incentivized to accommodate dissatisfied fellow members within the existing institution in order to avoid their exit. Counter-institutionalization becomes less likely, as the accommodation of dissatisfied states by institutional members is a feasible strategy to avoid the losses in utility associated with institutionalized cooperation if the number of members is reduced.

Strong network effects tend, as a result, to absorb competition by strengthening existing inclusive and centralized structures. They further reduce the attractiveness of outside options by making them costly and difficult to pursue. As the utility of institutionalized cooperation is dependent on the overall number of participating states, it is necessary to form a sufficiently large coalition of states willing to join the alternative institution. International institutions associated with strong network effects are thus much more prone to what Pierson (2000) refers to as the "institutional status-quo bias": As cooperative outcomes are much more effective in the context of large universalist institutions, they tend to be more stable and more attractive than hypothetical small-scale alternatives.

Two interlinked theoretical expectations regarding the presence of network effects and the evolution of centralized or decentralized institutional topologies in regime complexes can be derived from these considerations:

> Hypothesis 3: If there are network effects associated with institutionalized forms of cooperation, the propensity for competition in the policy field is low, hence institutional topologies tend to be centralized.
>
> Hypothesis 4: If there are no network effects associated with institutionalized forms of cooperation, the propensity for competition in the policy field is higher, hence institutional topologies tend to be decentralized.

Barriers to Entry and the Institutional Topology of Institutional Complexes

This section introduces the third and final market characteristic of policy fields that impacts on the evolution of centralized/decentralized institutional topologies underlying regime complexes: barriers to entry as material hindrances to creating international institutions in the first place. These barriers include all the material and immaterial costs states must bear when they seek to set up institutional arrangements to cooperate on a specific policy issue. Just as firms seeking to enter a new industrial market are constrained by the specific costs and hindrances associated with producing and distributing products within this market, states are constrained by the material and immaterial costs associated with institutionalized cooperation on a particular policy issue. These hindrances and costs vary considerably across issue areas and can therefore be either a catalyst for interinstitutional competition or, if they are high, an obstacle for states preventing interinstitutional competition. Following Lipscy's conceptualization (2015: 343; 2017: 28–30), I will refer to the hindrances and costs associated with institutionalized cooperation in a particular policy field as barriers to entry.

The term barriers to entry is used extensively by economic and legal scholars basically to describe the market structure among competing firms and, more specifically, how the concentration, i.e., the number of significant firms in an industrial field, hinders or allows other organizations to increase their returns on capital within a specific market (see, e.g., Caves and Porter 1977; Conner 1991; Cetorelli and Straham 2006). Typical examples of barriers to entry into economic markets include high capital, marketing, or distribution costs that make it difficult for new firms to start producing and selling their goods. Economies of scale can be another significant barrier insofar as they make it more difficult for new and smaller competitor firms to compete on price with established contenders. A prime example of a market with significantly high barriers to entry is the airline industry, where the high cost of purchasing or leasing aircraft, obtaining landing slots and routes, and marketing and advertising services, make it difficult for new firms to enter the market. Examples of the immaterial barriers that hamper competition in economic markets are, for instance, government regulations that require firms to acquire expensive licenses and permits or patents, trademarks, and copyrights which can prevent new firms from producing and selling similar products as established firms. Barriers to entry vary greatly among markets. While in the airline industry, capital and distributional costs are significant, in the software app industry, these costs are lower. In general terms, while high barriers to entry tend to reduce competition and increase the concentration and centralization of the market, the absence of significant barriers to entry tends to increase competition as it allows more competitors to enter the market.

Lipscy (2015; 2017) transfers this idea to the realm of international institutions by conceptualizing institutional barriers to entry more broadly as *hindrances to alternative forms of cooperation (for states) within a specific policy field*. Barriers to entry thus determine how costly it is for states to build alternative institutional arrangements within a specific policy area. The very direct material costs states face when deciding to create new institutions include the necessary funding for initial meetings and conferences, staff salaries, office space and equipment, and travel expenses for member states. These costs vary significantly depending on an institution's purpose and policy-specific mandate. The higher the initial costs of institution building within a particular policy field, e.g., because of the specialized and scarce expertise or bureaucratic formalization required, the lower the expected competition among institutions within the given area (Lipscy 2017: 29–30). Setting up alternative institutions to existing ones is less feasible if the costs of institution-building are high.

As in the case of the market characteristics of (non)excludability and network effects, barriers to entering regime complexes vary greatly across issue areas of global governance. While, for instance, the costs of setting up fora for consultation and dialogue like the G7, the G20, the BRICS International Forum, the Asia Cooperation Dialogue, or the IBSA Dialogue Forum are relatively low, the costs of establishing an international security institution are much higher: States not only need to create military and civil platforms which allow shared use, they also need to share sensitive information and military knowledge. Setting up an international military institution like NATO is thus associated with very high financial as well as immaterial costs for states interested in institutionalized cooperation. In other policy fields of global governance these costs are comparatively low. In the issue area of trade, the creation of international institutions is associated with much lower costs. The costs that states face if they decide to set up a new multilateral trade agreement will primarily be related to negotiations and administrative expenses. The overall resources that need to be devoted to keeping an international trade organization running are therefore significantly lower than those that states need to invest in international security organizations. All in all, some institutions are more difficult to set up than others: it varies across issue areas and according to the specific underlying policy problems that have to be addressed by the prospective institution.

Besides material or immaterial setting-up costs, another policy area characteristic that can serve as a significant barrier to entry to an institutional complex for states is what which Lipscy (2017) refers to as the "exclusivity of cooperation." While there are some issue areas, in which states can unproblematically pursue cooperation on the same policy via several alternative institutions without jeopardizing their positions within existing institutions, other issue areas make simultaneous cooperation much more costly or even impossible (Lipscy 2017: 29). States can, for instance, pursue development aid policies via different unrelated institutions simultaneously without damaging their respective cooperative outcomes, but it may be much more problematic for states to be members of multiple security organizations or monetary unions. Thus, "at the high end of exclusivity, it is generally impractical to pursue membership in more than one monetary union at a time due to the transaction costs associated with multiple currencies and monetary policy regimes" (Lipscy 2017: 29). Exclusivity of cooperation within respective policy fields tends per se to reduce the availability of outside options irrespective of the material and immaterial costs of their creation, as fewer configurations of institutions are possible. Furthermore, exclusivity binds states to existing institutions, as it raises the cost and risk associated with exit by limiting the ability of states to opt for institutional alternatives.

Within policy areas where barriers to entry are low, the creation of outside options is attractive, and it is feasible for states to pursue cooperation even on a small scale or via multiple institutions (Kastner et al. 2016: 147 f.). In this way, barriers to entry also determine how cooperative outcomes can be achieved and to what extent it is attractive for states to pursue unilateral action. In political environments where the costs of entering the international stage and pursuing cooperation are low, each state's outside option is the best alternative negotiated agreement compared to its existing institutional arrangements. As its best alternative is most feasible in policy areas where barriers to entry are low, the value of any one particular institutional compromise diminishes, which thus incentivizes states to either pursue unilateral action or cooperate via alternative institutions (Voeten 2001; Fisher et al. 2011; Kastner et al. 2016). Policy areas that exhibit no or only very weak barriers to entry thus spur interinstitutional competition as they significantly boost the attractiveness of outside options available to states seeking to cooperate on the respective policy issue.

It is important to note, however, that barriers to entry are not a static concept—quite the opposite, in fact: Barriers to entry into a policy field are inherently prone to change. If, for instance, technological progress eliminates certain hindrances to cooperation within a particular policy field, institutionalized cooperation becomes feasible for more states. Thus, barriers to entry into the institutional complex are reduced as more states become potential cooperators on the issue. Think of the regulation of energy production and trade as an example. For a long time, the supply of energy largely relied on oil and gas sources that only a small number of states were able to exploit. As rapid technological progress in the field of (renewable) energy production allowed more and more states to produce significant amounts of energy, they were also increasingly able to engage in institutionalized cooperation on energy policies. The rapid growth of solar and wind power has allowed countries with abundant sunshine and strong winds, such as Spain and Germany, to become significant players in the global renewable energy market. This has led to the development of new industries and jobs in these countries, as well as increased economic growth and competitiveness. China is another example. Owing to the rapid technological development of its industry, it has become a major producer of solar panels and wind turbines and has also invested heavily in hydroelectric power and biofuels. As a result, it has become both one of the world's largest producers of renewable energy and a major exporter of renewable energy technology. Thus, in the regime complex of energy governance, over time outside options to the existing institutions have become more feasible for nonmember states over time, which, in turn, has significantly enhanced interinstitutional competition in the field of energy governance.

Based on these considerations two more interlinked theoretical expectations concerning the degree of competition within different policy fields of global governance can be formulated:

Hypothesis 5: The higher the respective barriers to entry to an institutional complex, the lower its propensity for interinstitutional competition and hence the more centralized its institutional topologies.

Hypothesis 6: The lower the respective barriers to entry to an institutional complex, the higher its propensity for interinstitutional competition and hence the more decentralized its institutional topologies.

The specific market characteristics underlying various policy fields confront states with very different incentives and constraints regarding how to pursue institutionalized cooperation effectively in different issue areas. How do these structural constraints and incentives translate into varying institutional topologies? More precisely, why do we observe strongly centralized topologies in some policy fields while others are marked by decentralization and fragmentation?

The final section of this chapter theorizes two ways in which the propensity for competition exerts a long-term effect on the evolution of institutional topologies in regime complexes. First, when the market structure of policy fields is highly competitive, which means that there are no, or only weak, network effects associated with cooperating on the respective issue, institutionalization is associated with relatively low costs or institutions produce goods that are excludable, then this market structure tends to produce centrifugal effects on the institutional topology of the respective institutional complex prompting decentralization and fragmentation of the institutional complex. Second, and contrariwise, noncompetitive policy areas, characterized by strong network effects associated with cooperation on the respective issue, high costs of institutionalization, and the provision of nonexcludable public goods by its institutions, tend to reinforce centripetal effects on the institutional topology of institutional complexes, enabling integrative cooperation and centralistic topologies among institutions.

Centrifugal and Centripetal Effects in Regime Complexes

The previous section developed the argument that different issue areas of global governance can differ significantly in terms of their market characteristics and, thus, of their propensity for competition. The specific market structure of policy fields, determined by the configuration of the three market characteristics introduced in the previous section, shapes how institutionalized cooperation between states is pursued and, thus, the structure of the institutional complex in question. This section elaborates on the underlying mechanisms by showing how 'competitive and noncompetitive configurations of market characteristics play out.

In the previous section the three characteristics were treated as variables that independently exert effects on the topologies of the regime complex. However, it is clear that the strength of their effect (whether centripetal or centrifugal) on the evolution of centralized/decentralized topologies also depends on the value of the other market characteristics present in the issue area in question. The specific expression of a particular market characteristic can mitigate or reinforce the effect of another on a policy field's overall propensity for competition.

On the one hand, therefore, the simultaneous presence of pro-competitive characteristics can reinforce their individual centrifugal effect on institutional topologies. For example, network effects strongly reinforce the mitigating effect on competition of existing material barriers to cooperation. As network effects confer functional advantages on existing large-scale integrative institutions, they also act as a significant barrier to entry for states seeking to create institutional competitors. Thus, in policy areas with strong network effects and high barriers to entry, the propensity for institutional competition is low, and institutionalization processes are likely to follow centripetal trajectories. This combination of anticompetitive policy characteristics may also undermine the procompetitive effect of excludability that may still be present in a given policy area. A similarly reinforcing effect exists between nonexcludability and network effects. Policy areas where institutionalized cooperation aims at providing nonexcludable goods are often also characterized by network effects. In the case of cooperation on climate change, for example, states cannot be excluded from the benefits of cooperation, even if they do not bear the costs of creating them. At the same time, the benefits of effectively mitigating global warming through multilateral initiatives increase with the number of participating states. Thus, there is both an incentive to free ride on the efforts of institutional members and a disincentive to pursue alternative forms of institutional cooperation. For states interested in effective climate change mitigation, on the other hand, the incentives to join existing large-scale institutions that provide the nonexcludable good are much stronger than those to create institutional alternatives.

On the other hand, the simultaneous presence of pro- and anticompetitive characteristics can act in opposite directions thus canceling out their respective centripetal and centrifugal effects. Take, for instance, the simultaneous presence of strong network effects, which curbs institutional competition in a regime complex, and excludable institutional goods, which reinforces the propensity for competition. The former makes it particularly attractive for states to join preexisting large-scale institutions and abstain from creating new alternatives from scratch. The latter, on the other hand, forces states to engage in institutionalized forms of cooperation as free riding is not possible. In particular, if joining preexisting clubs is not possible, states might still be willing to engage in institution building despite the comparatively high costs of entering regime complexes with strong network effects and preexisting large-scale institutions. In these cases, the absence or presence of barriers to entry is decisive. If these barriers are (too) high for states not willing or able to join preexisting institutions, institutional topologies are likely to develop following status quo–biased, centralized patterns. If the hurdles to the establishment of new multilateral institutions are low, states might, on the contrary, be incentivized to engage in competitive institution building despite their *ex ante* competitive disadvantage stemming from network effects in the field. Take the example of institutionalized cooperation in the field of security and defense. Military alliances such as NATO or the former Warsaw Pact are alliances between countries that agree to provide military aid to one another in the event of an attack. The creation of these alliances is subject to strong network effects present because the value of being a member of the alliance increases as more countries join. First, the more countries that are part of an alliance, the greater the potential for collective defense. The presence of many countries in an alliance increases its deterrent effect, as potential aggressors are less likely to attack a country that is part of a large and powerful alliance. Second, more members mean more resources and capabilities. Military alliances allow countries to pool their resources and capabilities, such as military equipment and personnel, to better defend against threats. The more members an alliance has, the more resources and capabilities it will have at its disposal. At the same time, these institutions provide purely excludable goods, security guarantees, that can only be enjoyed by members. Nonparticipating states can, therefore, only enjoy institutional benefits if they either decide to join a preexisting institution or create their own defensive alliance. However, in the case of military cooperation, barriers to entry are significantly high. Military alliances are complex and highly specialized institutions that require a significant investment of resources and expertise to establish and maintain. Forming a military alliance requires the establishment of a joint command structure, which requires significant coordination and cooperation between participating states. This can be a difficult and time-consuming process, especially if the participating states have different military cultures and organizational structures. Moreover, military alliances require a significant investment in military hardware and infrastructure. This includes the acquisition of advanced weapons systems, the construction of military bases, and the development of joint communications and intelligence-gathering capabilities. This can be a costly endeavor, and many states do not have the resources to invest in joint infrastructure of this kind. Besides these high material hurdles, creating new multilateral defense institutions requires a high degree of trust and cooperation between participating states. This can be difficult to establish, especially if there are historical or political tensions between the states. Additionally, the sharing of sensitive military information and decision making can also be challenging, especially if there are different levels of commitment among participating states. Thus, in the case of institutional cooperation on security and defense issues, the pro-competitive effect of excludable good provision is canceled out by the high initial costs of institution building, as well as the presence of strong network effects.

As these considerations demonstrate, it is crucial to consider the specific configuration of market characteristics in order to be able to capture the overall propensity for institutional competition in regime complexes. It is the combination of all three market characteristics which determines the long-term centripetal or centrifugal trajectories of institutional topologies underlying regime complexes. How do these centripetal and centrifugal effects converge into centralized or decentralized topologies? The paragraphs that follow lay out the causal mechanisms that link a policy area's propensity for competition with the evolution of different institutional topologies.

Policy areas that are marked by highly competitive structures tend to promote the creation of many relatively unrelated institutions, forming somewhat fragmented and decentralized institutional complexes. In these complexes, institutional authority tends to be more contested among several institutions, as pursuing institutional outside options is feasible and attractive for states dissatisfied with existing institutional arrangements. Strong propensities to competition within policy fields thus exert centrifugal effects on institutional topologies. This effect occurs because, in these policy areas, there are many more attractive forms of cooperating on the policy issue in question than the large-scale, universalistic form under one specific institutional arrangement. Outside options are often unfeasible and unattractive, by contrast, in policy fields where competition is low and exit is often associated with comparatively high costs. Noncompetitive political environments thus exert centripetal effects on the structure of institutional complexes as they drive states towards centralized and rather universalistic cooperation via large-scale institutions and make counter-institutionalization and small-scale cooperation less likely.

Scholars have long pointed out that outside options are crucial to understanding differences in bargaining outcomes in the context of international institutions (see, e.g., Voeten 2001; Slapin 2009; Urpelainen 2012; Lipscy 2017: 25 ff.). Some policy areas, e.g., financial stability, are marked by comparatively strong but rather one-sided dependencies among states seeking to achieve cooperative outcomes. As far as market characteristics are concerned, such policy fields are marked by high barriers to entry—which significantly restrain the number of states capable of setting up and maintaining effective institutional cooperation in the first place. Institutionalized cooperation is thus directed toward powerful states, who can use their structural advantages to assure institutional privileges and exclusive benefits (Baccini et al. 2011; Drezner 2009). This, in turn, reduces the attractiveness of pursuing outside options for powerful states as they benefit from burden and cost sharing within the institution while shaping and controlling its outcomes.

In policy areas marked by low degrees of competition, centripetal tendencies are also reinforced by the comparatively high costs of remaining outside established institutional arrangements: Some states would be better off if a particular institution set up in an uncompetitive environment by powerful states did not exist. However, given that it does, they may feel it necessary for them to join (Gruber 2001: 709–10). In other words, policy fields marked by particularly low propensities for interinstitutional competition among states tend to produce institutions where the costs for laggard states of not participating are too high, even though these states might have preferred the original status quo of no international organization at all (Slapin 2009: 190; Gruber 2001). In these circumstances, even the strategy of sticking to their usual' modus operandi in the international arena, namely unilateral action, becomes unattractive as the mere existence of a powerful institution within uncompetitive policy fields may dramatically alter the costs associated with nonparticipation (Gruber 2001: 710). Consequently, uncompetitive environments reinforce centralization as they bind states to powerful, large-scale institutions.

Furthermore, within policy areas marked by a low propensity for competition, there may also be high reputational costs associated with not participating in an existing institution: For instance, powerful states or even private actors like international companies may blame and eventually shun a country for not joining an international organization that they deem to be "good," while joining a highly regarded international organization may confer some benefit on states, regardless of how these states feel about the organization's policy, which they would not have received if they had not joined the organization (Slapin 2009: 190). Within policy areas marked by low degrees of competition, states are thus much more bound to the institutional status— quo. Incentives for large-scale cooperation are also strong, as network effects encourage powerful states to include additional members in existing institutions instead of pursuing cooperation on a uni-, bi-, or minilateral basis. Thus, within uncompetitive political environments where outside options are unattractive, it is possible for universal institutions to remain stable for a long time despite potentially significant shifts in relative power (Lipscy 2017: 46).

This, in turn, cements their dominant position in the institutional complex thereby reinforcing centralized institutional topologies.

Furthermore, if network effects are present within uncompetitive policy environments, exit or shifting to other institutional fora are not attractive options either. Pursuing policy goals alone is associated with high costs not only for the "exiters" but also for the states that remain as the institution's utility is dependent on the number of its participants and therefore suffers if that number is reduced. Thus, within policy areas where institutionalized cooperation is associated with strong network effects, "letting states go" is not a preferable option for institutional members, which incentivizes them to accommodate potential leavers in order to preserve the institutional status quo (Slapin 2009: 192). Strong network effects can in this way impede counter-institutionalization and bind states to existing universal institutions.

The provision of nonexcludable goods by institutionalized forms of cooperation in policy fields can further reinforce such centripetal effects. In these issue areas, interinstitutional competition is low because nonparticipating states have strong incentives to free ride on the positive effects that stem from others' cooperation but from which they cannot be excluded. At the same time, competitive institution building in policy fields where institutionalized cooperation has been established to produce public goods is comparatively costly. States must invest in the provision of goods without being able to control their consumption. Therefore, engaging in the provision of public goods is associated with competitive self-restraint vis-à-vis other states. Policy areas exhibiting uncompetitive market structures tend to produce solidary, centripetal effects that spur interstate cooperation via inclusive, dominant, and large-scale institutional arrangements. Due to the high costs of exit and counter-institutionalization, the number of institutions in the respective policy fields can be expected to remain limited, and cooperative outcomes tend to reflect the interests of their respective "power centers." The structure of institutional complexes within such uncompetitive policy environments can thus be expected to be shaped by path dependency favoring the evolution of strongly centralized institutional topologies.

Within policy areas where barriers to entry are low, network effects are weak, and institutional cooperation is associated with the provision of excludable goods, outside options to existing forms of institutionalized cooperation are, by contrast, much more attractive, which, in turn, exerts centrifugal effects on the structure of the institutional complex involved. Within such competitive political environments, exit and counter-institutionalization are associated with much lower costs and hence are much more feasible for states both within and outside existing institutions. If outside options are attractive due to low barriers to entry and weak network effects, dissatisfied states are more likely to engage in counter-institutionalization. It is not unusual for states to renounce their membership in an international organization entirely. However, a more common response is the reallocation of diplomatic and financial resources to bilateral initiatives or other multilateral fora (Lipscy 2017: 42f.). Additionally, the absence of network effects within highly competitive policy areas allows states to exit institutions without significantly reducing the benefits of cooperation for the remaining states. Status quo states within these institutions are thus expected to be much less opposed to changes in institutional membership than they might be in policy areas where institutionalized cooperation is associated with strong network effects. At the same time, in competitive policy settings where institutions are set up to produce excludable goods, states lack the opportunity to free ride on the benefits derived from the cooperation of others. To gain cooperative benefits, states must either join existing institutions or create alternative institutional "clubs." The excludability of institutional benefits consequently incentivizes states to contest existing institutional topologies.

Highly competitive policy environments, in this way, provide a structural setting of institutional renegotiation, marked by attractive outside options and comparatively low costs to exit. Furthermore, pursuing institutionalized cooperation on a small scale is an attractive alternative to membership in universal arrangements, as the outcome of cooperation is not dependent on the number of participants. Challenges to the status quo of institutions set up in highly competitive policy areas appear much more frequently than they do in policy fields marked by low degrees of competition. Therefore, the structure of institutional complexes is expected to be more unstable and prone to change in favor of decentralized institutional topologies. The number of institutions set up by states is likely higher within policy areas where the degree of competition is low. Additionally, the hierarchy among these institutions should be relatively shallow. Figure 3.2 illustrates and sums up the argument about the effect of market characteristics on the institutional topologies of regime complexes by comparing two ideal-types of policy area (competitive and uncompetitive) and their long-term effect on the evolution of institutional topologies.

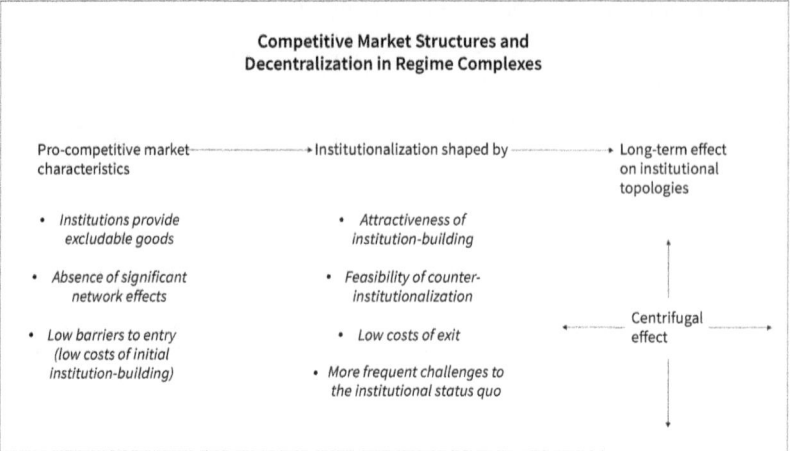

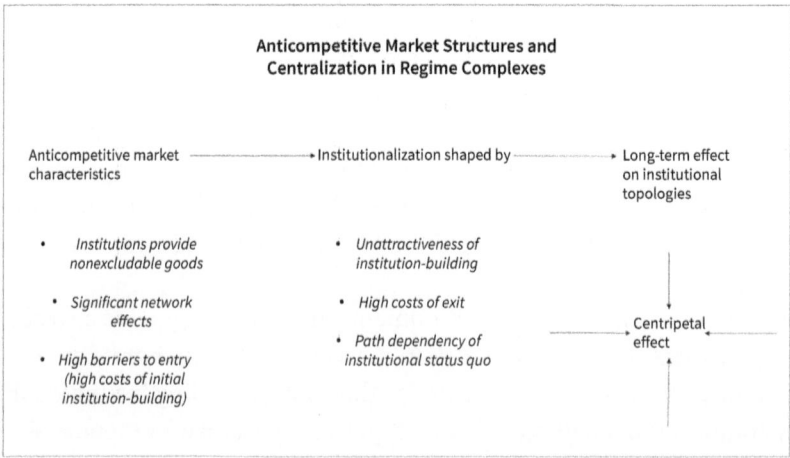

Figure 3.2 Centrifugal and Centripetal Effects of Market Characteristics on the Structure of Institutional Complexes

Conclusion

By drawing on, but also complementing, recent institutionalist literature on institutional change—more specifically on Lipscy's (2015; 2017) theory of policy area competition and intra-institutional renegotiation— Chapters 2 and 3 developed a theory of (de)centralized institutional topologies in international regime complexes. Combining literature on institutional authority and recognition with network theory, Chapter 2 introduces the concept of institutional topologies taking a relational perspective. Existing literature on regime complexity has so far primarily focused on specific issue areas and their underlying regime complexes, shying away from cross-policy-area systematization. I argue that the (de)centralization tendencies in regime complexes underlying different issue areas of global governance can be captured by systematically comparing the network positions of international institutions vis-à-vis all other institutional actors sharing similar policy mandates. The overall structure that results can then be systematically compared across issue areas of global governance, which allows the "comparison shortage" in the literature on international regime complexes to be overcome.

Following this network-based conceptualization of institutional topologies, this chapter develops the argument that differences in institutional trajectories across various issue areas of global governance are systematic and driven by centripetal and centrifugal dynamics stemming from variation in the policy issues' market characteristics excludability or nonexcludability, network effects, and barriers to entry. Rather than explaining institutional trajectories as being simply based on state interests, or the advantages or disadvantages of institutional design, I argue that the competitive environment within which states renegotiate international institutions significantly shapes the long-term evolution of institutional topologies. This chapter thus proposes that a shift in explanatory focus toward the issue-area level of analysis allows us to assess the endogenous dynamics in regime complexes that follow systematic patterns generalizable across all policy fields of global governance.

PART III
EMPIRICAL ANALYSIS

4

Preparing the Ground

Operationalization, Research Design, and Empirical Strategy

Part II developed the main theoretical argument of this book: that institutional topologies underlying international regime complexes are crucially shaped by the market characteristics of their policy issue. This policy-area-specific competition shapes the evolution of institutional topologies through two contrary long-term effects—centripetal and centrifugal—which depend on an issue area's specific configuration of the three market characteristics of (non-) excludability, network effects, and barriers to entry. In this second part of the book, I provide a comprehensive examination of this argument across five policy fields of global governance: tax avoidance, intellectual property protection, financial stability, development aid, and energy governance. Using original data from these five different regime complexes and their constitutive international institutions, this empirical part of the book maps and compares their underlying institutional topologies. Drawing on qualitative process evidence, each of the empirical chapters presents extensive case studies tracing the theorized competition mechanisms and corresponding centripetal or centrifugal effects in each of the five issue areas. Exploiting a most-similar-system case design, each of the empirical chapters demonstrates the effect of a specific market characteristic on the evolution of the policy field's regime complex and its topology by comparing two issue areas that show remarkable similarity in two of their market characteristics but differ fundamentally in the third. The empirical analysis offers robust evidence for the book's central claim about the effect of market characteristics on the evolution of different institutional topologies in regime complexes. Differences in the issue areas' propensity for competition correlate with significant differences in their regime complexes' underlying topologies. The qualitative examination of the institutionalization process further highlights the importance of the theorized mechanisms that unfold the centripetal or centrifugal dynamics in the five regime complexes under investigation. While

The Institutional Topology of International Regime Complexes. Benjamin Daßler, Oxford University Press.
© Benjamin Daßler (2023). DOI: 10.1093/oso/9780198881926.003.0004

pro-competitive constellations of market characteristics incentivize states to pursue cooperation via many unrelated and competing institutions, the presence of anticompetitive characteristics significantly hampers interinstitutional competition by incentivizing states to centralize their cooperation via large, inclusive, and comparatively uncontested institutions.

In this chapter, I lay out the book's general empirical strategy by introducing its conceptualization of institutional topologies, justifying the case selection, and elaborating on the observable implications that follow from the hypotheses developed in the previous theory chapter. The first section develops a conceptualization of institutional topologies underlying regime complexes. Drawing on concepts from institutionalism and social network analysis, it proposes to capture the centralization/decentralization of institutional topologies from an interinstitutional, hence relational, perspective. To map the topologies underlying international regime complexes, I propose to think of them as social networks structured by the interaction of their constitutive actors, institutions, and states.

Operationalizing Institutional Topologies

Taking a social network perspective allows for the "fine-grained conceptualization and measurement of structures" (Hafner-Burton et al. 2009: 561) and thus enables an abstract picture to be drawn of a complex's underlying cooperative activities, which can be compared across policy fields, even if they differ greatly regarding the characteristics of their underlying institutions or the number and natures of the states involved. IR scholars have increasingly opted for a network perspective to study an array of international political phenomena ranging from interstate conflicts over international law to transnational advocacy (Morin et al. 2017; Greenhill and Lupu 2017; Carpenter et al. 2014; Lupu and Voeten 2012; Dorussen and Ward 2008). Its ability to descriptively analyze the degree of centralization in institutional cooperation across a potentially large set of completely different policy fields makes the network perspective complementary to other quantitative methods of systematically analyzing regime complexity (Haftel and Lenz 2021; Kreuder-Sonnen and Zürn 2020; Gholiagha et al. 2020). These sophisticated approaches allow for a fine-grained quantification of different qualities of interinstitutional structures, e.g., the degree of policy and membership overlap (Haftel and Lenz 2021) or dyadic conflicts among a complex's constitutive institutions (Kreuder-Sonnen and Zürn 2020; Gholiagha et al. 2020). While both approaches zoom in on the micro level of dyadic institutional overlap and conflict, thereby providing important insights into the quality of complexity, the network perspective provides a structural perspective focusing on the degree of centralization of institutional cooperation within different policy fields. While this focus on the structural characteristics of regime complexes risks omitting information on the individual actor level, it represents a powerful lens through which social relations among international actors and hence, the "topology" underlying international politics can be assessed.

The network approach allows one to assess quantitatively and, most importantly, to visually and numerically compare these often complicated interinstitutional structures across institutional complexes. From a network perspective, an institution's authority stems from its centrality within the networks underlying its regime complex. The more central an institution, the higher its degree of authority. Following the conceptualization of authority as a recognized claim to govern, these central network positions result from high degrees of recognition by other institutions and states engaging in the institutional complex in question.

I propose to map acts of recognition among (1) all the international institutions of a particular policy field and (2) the institutions and states actively engaged in that issue area of global governance.

Depending on the intensity and quantity of ties with other actors in their complex, institutions occupy more or less central positions within their network. Conditioned by the constellation of individual network positions among their entities, the overall topology of regime complexes may vary significantly across issue areas of global governance. While some institutional complexes may exhibit strongly centralized network structures, others may have decentralized structures. The topology of regime complexes thus represents a gradual variable with maximal centralization as one extreme value and strong decentralization and fragmentation as the other.

It is important to note that these "extreme cases" depicted in Figure 4.1— completely centralized topologies on the one hand, and the highest possible degree of decentralization on the other, i.e., a situation where all the institutions governing a specific issue area obtain an equally central position within their network—are unlikely to be observed. While the former would imply a perfect interinstitutional hierarchy, the latter implies perfect decentralization and a total absence of hierarchy.

In reality, institutional topologies are much more complex. Even in relatively centralized complexes, fewer central institutions enjoy at least some degree of recognition that prevents the formation of a perfectly star-shaped network. Moreover, even in institutional complexes marked by high degrees

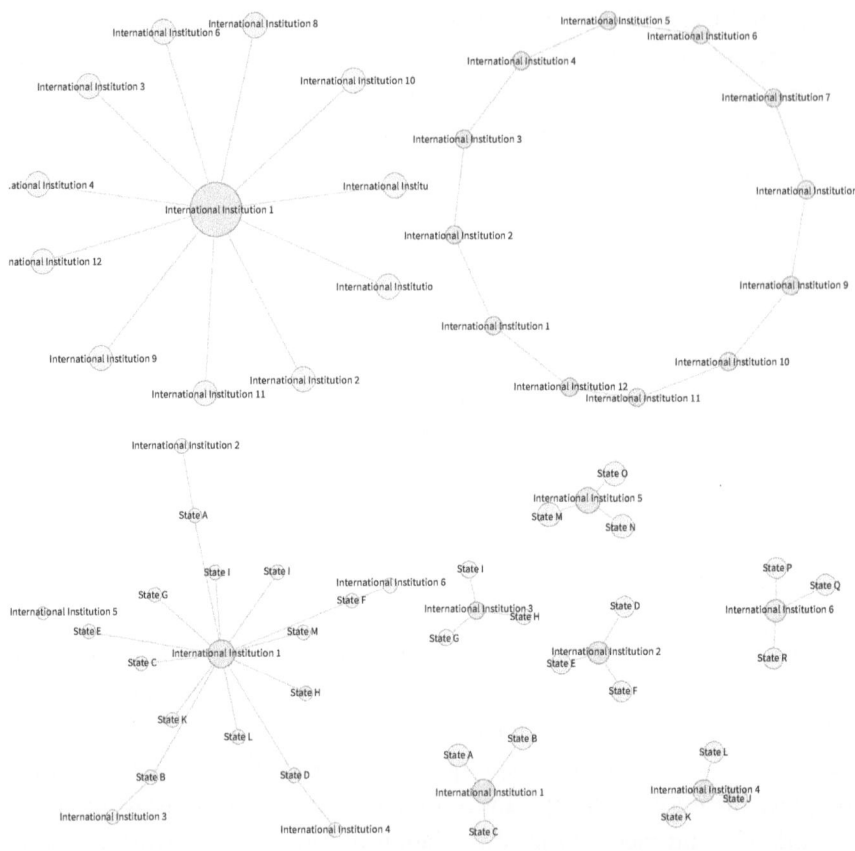

Figure 4.1 Extreme Types of (De-) Centralized Institutional Topologies

of decentralization, marginal differences in the centrality scores obtained by individual institutions are highly likely to be observed. Topologies are much more likely to lie somewhere in between these extreme values. How can we capture and compare these potentially fine-grained differences in topologies among institutional complexes? I argue that the network approach offers a suitable and useful toolkit for measuring and mapping these differences across institutional complexes, so I propose to measure the two dimensions of institutional authority networks in the following way:

(1) To map the institutional topologies, I analyze references made by all the relevant institutions of a complex. Following Pratt (2018), I claim that the underlying structure of the complexes is constituted by instances of interinstitutional policy coordination and reference (Pratt 2018: 562–3). These references may occur in institutional resolutions,

annual reports, or other official documents published by a respective international institution. If such documents contain an explicit reference to another institution governing the same issue area, this constitutes an interinstitutional relation and thus an edge between two nodes in their respective reference network. The ties among institutions within these reference networks are directed and weighted, which implies that they do not necessarily have to be reciprocal and that they may differ in their quantity and, hence, in their intensity. To this end, during my research for this book I collected more than 73,800 pages of official institution documents from forty-nine international institutions in five policy fields, allowing me to accurately map the networks of references underlying the policy-specific institutional complexes.

(2) To measure the second dimension of institutional topologies, i.e., institution—state relationships, I map the formal membership and/or participation of the most relevant states in terms of cooperative engagement in a particular policy field.[1] I claim that, besides recognition by competing or complementary institutions, formal membership by important states in institutionalized cooperation within a policy field represents another important indicator of an institution's centrality within its complex (Hurd 1999; Haftel and Hofmann 2019; Greenhill and Lupu 2017). In contrast to the interinstitutional reference networks, the membership networks are neither directed nor weighted. Membership networks are symmetrical and unweighted, which means that ties either do exist or do not. Every time a state formally participates in a particular institution this represents an undirected and unweighted tie between that state and that institution. As I will lay out below, this has important implications for the calculation of the centrality measures underlying either the directed and weighted references, or the undirected and unweighted membership networks.

The network approach provides a variety of measurements that describe the relative position of individual nodes in a network. These individual "centralities" allow the relative positions of institutions within the reference and membership networks underlying their respective institutional complexes to be compared. Taken together, these individual network positions of all the institutions that make up a complex form its distinct topology. Mapping authority networks among international institutions thus allows one to analyze both the relative positions of individual institutions vis-à-vis all other institutions in the complex as well as the complex's overall topology.

The first and most basic concept that allows the centrality of individual institutions to be assessed from a network perspective are the so-called "in-degree centralities." The degree centrality of a node indicates the number of ties it has with all the other nodes in the network. In directed networks, such as interinstitutional reference networks, it is important to differentiate between the in- and out-degrees of a particular node. The in-degree of a node captures all incoming references from the rest of the network; the out-degree represents the number of actors this node refers to. While the in-degree centrality of an institution within its directed reference network can be used to measure the "popularity" of a particular node within its network (Scott 2017: 80; Ward et al. 2011: 250; Hämmerli et al. 2006), the out-degree represents its active participation in that network (Scott 2017:80; Jansen 2006: 132). Thus, both in-degree and out-degree centrality can be interpreted as indicators of a node's centrality or importance in a network. However, they provide different insights into the node's role. A node with high in-degree centrality may be seen as a leader or influencer; a node with high out-degree centrality may be seen, on the other hand as a connector or active participant. To approach the centrality of every individual institution in a complex, capturing the in-degree centralities of all the institutions that form part of the reference network is therefore an important first step. The more often an institution is referred to by all the other institutions in the reference network, the higher its degree of recognition and, hence, its interinstitutional authority. In the case of undirected networks such as institutional membership networks it is unnecessary to differentiate between individual in- and out-degrees as these networks are symmetrical in the sense that ties are reciprocal per se. As a result, the degree centrality of a node within an undirected network simply reflects the overall number of connections it has with all the other nodes in the network.

The second important centrality concept that allows one to approach a network-based measurement of the centrality of institutions is their individual "betweenness centrality" within their respective reference and membership networks. The betweenness centrality of a node captures the extent to which it lies between other nodes in its network (Scott 2017:99; Ward et al. 2011: 250). Technically, the betweenness centrality of a particular node captures the number of shortest paths that pass through it (Brandes 2001: 2; Freeman 1977: 35). Nodes with a high betweenness centrality possess important "brokerage" positions as they connect otherwise rather isolated parts of a network. They are therefore able to use their network position to influence the flow and transmission of information and to initiate interactions among unconnected nodes in the network (Scott 2017: 99–100; Rusinowska et al.

2011: 5; Jansen 2006: 135). Moreover, high betweenness centralities often also imply "that other nodes are dependent for access to information" on the node in question (Ward et al. 2011: 250). Institutions with high betweenness centralities can be considered as having high degrees of communicative control and structural autonomy within their respective interinstitutional networks. These institutions, furthermore, have higher social and epistemic capital than those with lower betweenness centralities (Barnett et al. 2014: 11): They are often able to influence political debates in different parts of the network thereby constraining or furthering political agendas.

The same applies to the state membership networks underlying institutional complexes. Institutions with a high betweenness centrality in these networks connect otherwise rather isolated groups of states, thereby acquiring important brokerage positions between these groups. These institutions are particularly useful for states, as they provide information and the possibility of communicating across a larger set of actors in their network. Being recognized as a linking element enabling the exchange of information and communications implies institutional authority. A high degree of betweenness centrality means that the institution is well connected and able to facilitate communication and cooperation between different states. This is important because it enables the institution to address and resolve issues effectively within the regime complex in addition to acting as a catalyst for cooperation and coordination among states, a role that is essential for maintaining stability and addressing global challenges. Taken together with their individual in-degree centrality, the betweenness centrality of institutions is another important indicator of their relative position within their complex.

Another useful toolkit offered by the network perspective for ascertaining the overall topology of regime complexes are the centralization scores of entire interinstitutional and membership networks. The centralization of a particular network can be calculated using the individual centrality scores of all the nodes within it. In degree-based network centralization records whether any of the institutions in the network is involved to a particularly high degree in the direct relations between the other actors in the network (Jansen 2006: 139). High in-degree centralization scores for institutional networks indicate that there is one single institution, or a very small number of institutions, that has been obtaining a disproportionately large share of all the references or state memberships in its network. To calculate the in-degree centralization of a particular interinstitutional reference network, the sum of the deviations between the in-degree centrality of the most central institution and all the others is calculated and then divided by the maximum possible deviation in that network. High in-degree centralizations thus indicate that references are predominantly directed to a single institution or a small number, while the remaining institutions are much less frequently referred to. Low in-degree centralizations, on the other hand, indicate that references are relatively equally distributed across all institutions in the network.

Besides centralization based on the distribution of incoming ties among all institutions, in reference networks it can also be helpful to assess variation in reference intensity among institutions. As reference networks are directed and weighted, the intensity of incoming references may differ significantly among individual institutions. This diversity or homogeneity of reference intensities can be measured by calculating the coefficient of variation of individual in-degree weights (see, e.g., Sartori and Schiavo 2015: 118; Serdült 2002: 137). The coefficient of variation is defined as the ratio between the standard deviation and the mean. Larger coefficients of variation indicate greater deviation between the individual institutions of a network with respect to the intensity of their incoming references; small coefficients, by contrast, suggest greater homogeneity. While the latter suggests more decentralized topologies, the former hints at more centralized ones.

The same calculations can be applied to the second centrality measure based on the betweenness of individual institutions within their respective network. Betweenness centralization can be interpreted as the degree of monopolization of resources, and information flows by actors occupying significantly central positions in the network (Jansen 2006: 141; Lu et al. 2010: 34). High betweenness centralization scores indicate that one or a small number of institutions controls information flows among the rest of the otherwise relatively unconnected institutions in the network. Analogous to the calculation of a network's in-degree centralization, in calculating the betweenness-based centralization of a particular interinstitutional reference network, the sum of the deviations between the betweenness centrality of the most central institution (in terms of betweenness) and all the others is calculated and then divided by the maximum possible deviation in the network. More significant betweenness centralization scores indicate a monopolization of information flows in the network, as there is only one or a minimal number of institutions with high scores. By contrast, less significant scores indicate that no institution has obtained a unique brokerage position linking otherwise separated parts of their network.

Taken as a whole, the network approach provides a whole array of measures that help to overcome significant gaps and shortcomings in large parts of the existing literature on regime complexity: It not only allows one to approach the often very abstract understanding and conceptualization of institutional authority in an empirically more suitable fashion. It also enables comparison between interinstitutional topologies across various issue areas of global governance. By taking a network approach, this book introduces a more relational understanding of institutional authority than existing, often more abstract approaches.

Case Selection, Research Strategy, and Observable Implications

In the following section of this chapter, I outline the research logic underlying the ensuing three empirical chapters. As reflected in the hypotheses formulated in the theory chapter, I treat all three market characteristics as binary variables. Cooperation on a specific policy issue is either associated with network effects or it is not. Cooperating on a particular issue either allows nonparticipants to be excluded from institutional benefits or it does not. And barriers to engaging in institution-building in a specific policy area are either present or not present. I argue that the combination of these market characteristics determines the competitive structure of issue areas.

Moreover, I conceive the propensity for institutional competition of policy fields as a latent variable that cannot be observed or measured directly (Treier and Jackman 2008; Goertz 2006). As such, I conceptualize the propensity for competition of a policy field as an additive index ranging from 0—which means that the policy area exhibits no pro-competitive market characteristics at all—to 3, which means that all three market characteristics are pro-competitive. In my conceptualization there are, as a result, eight possible combinations of market characteristics and four different degrees of institutional competition within regime complexes (see Table 4.1). This additive conceptualization of the propensity for competition based on my binary indicator variables allows me to test my hypotheses about the effect of individual market characteristics on institutional topologies following the logic of most-similar-systems design. I will now lay out this logic in greater detail. To be sure, network effects, and barriers to entry can be thought of as continuous rather than binary variables. The conceptual simplification of treating the indicators as binary ones, however, comes with significant advantages, especially when systematically testing this book's main argument across the subsequent empirical chapters. Conceptualizing the propensity for competition as an additive index allows one to deliberately select policy fields that are similar with respect to two market characteristics (and other potentially confounding variables) and vary only with respect to one. Thereby, I compare regime complexes following the logic of most-similar-systems design (see,

Table 4.1 Market Characteristics and the Propensity for Competition in Policy Fields

	Nonexcludable benefits of institutionalized cooperation		Excludable benefits of institutionalized cooperation	
	Network effects +	Network effects −	Network effects +	Network effects −
Barriers to entry +	*Weakest propensity for competition (0)*	*Rather weak propensity for competition (1)*	*Rather weak propensity for competition (1)*	*Rather strong propensity for competition (2)*
Barriers to entry −	*Rather weak propensity for competition (1)*	*Rather strong propensity for competition (2)*	*Rather strong propensity for competition (2)*	*Strongest propensity for competition (3)*

Note: Author's own illustration. Numbers in brackets indicate the presence of pro-competitive market characteristics.

e.g., Levy 2008: 10; Teune and Przeworski 1970: 32–4; Anckar 2008). Most-similar-systems designs are especially well suited to deductively testing derived theories when there is little knowledge of the value of the dependent variable (see also Anckar 2008: 394–5). It allows one to compare cases that are similar in as many aspects as possible but differ regarding one characteristic, i.e., the independent variable of interest. Keeping all other market characteristics and other relevant confounding variables constant allows the effect of one specific market characteristic, the independent variable of interest, on institutional topologies, my dependent variable of interest, to be evaluated.

This most-similar-systems design allows one to analyze whether the variation in one specific market characteristic covaries with institutional topologies underlying the compared policy areas. This, in turn, provides an opportunity to test each of the theory section's hypotheses separately on the market characteristics of policy fields and the institutional topologies of their respective regime complexes. Accordingly, the three empirical chapters that follow contrast issue areas which, as demonstrated throughout each of those chapters, are strikingly similar with respect to a whole array of characteristics but still differ regarding one specific market characteristic. This case selection allows us to isolate the effect of each market characteristic of a policy field on its regime complex's underlying topology.

Moreover, this logic not only allows the covariation between individual market characteristics and institutional topologies to be tested, but it also makes it possible for me to qualitatively assess whether the observable implications of my proposed competition mechanism are at work within

the five regime complexes I am assessing. While the absence of an anticompetitive characteristic in one of the compared policy fields should result in
more profound and fierce competition among states when it comes to institutionalization processes within that field, in the other field, where the anticompetitive characteristic is present, there should be much less institutional
competition among states and more inclusive and centralistic patterns of
cooperation. Thus, this research design allows me to use qualitative process-
level observations to check whether there is evidence for the theorized causal
mechanism linking market characteristics and institutional topologies.

The empirical analyses throughout Chapters 5–7 accordingly all follow the
same logical structure (see Table 4.2). Each chapter starts with a detailed comparison of the policy fields I am analyzing. Most importantly, the chapters
explain why the investigated policy fields are similar in many respects but
also show how they differ regarding the market characteristics of interest.
The chapters successively map this book's dependent variable of interest,
i.e., interinstitutional topologies underlying the respective individual regime
complexes. Employing a comparative analysis of the networks underlying
both institutional complexes allows the fine-grained interinstitutional structures that emerge in the issue areas to be contrasted. Each empirical chapter
concludes with case studies of institutionalization processes within both policy fields, thus providing additional detailed qualitative evidence for the
book's theoretical claims.

How can specific market characteristics and their respective effects on
competition be observed empirically? Based on the theoretical considerations and derived hypotheses developed in Chapter 3 of this book, there
are concrete observable implications of the presence and absence of each
of the three individual market characteristics. These observable implications will guide the empirical case comparisons of the ensuing chapters
(see Table 4.3).

The excludability or nonexcludability of benefits: The provision of nonexcludable goods by international institutions in issue areas comes with states
profiting from existing cooperation by others. While refraining from criticiz-
ing existing forms of institutionalized cooperation, noncooperators should
generally be unwilling to engage in the production of the public good via
alternative institutions, as they are able to enjoy the positive effects of the
cooperation by other states without having to bear any costs themselves. More
specifically, as the cooperation of others is associated with positive effects
for the noncooperators, in issue areas where cooperation provides public
goods, noncooperators ought frequently to express their satisfaction with the
institutional status quo. On the other hand, the states that bear the costs of

Table 4.2 Case Selection Logic Underlying the Three Empirical Chapters

The (Non-) Excludability of Institutional Benefits and Institutional Topologies (Chapter 5)	Network Effects	
	Nonexcludable benefits of institutionalized cooperation	Excludable benefits of institutionalized cooperation
Barriers to entry +	*Case*: Tax Avoidance *Expected Propensity for Competition:* Low *Expected Topology:* Centralized	*Case*: Intellectual Property *Expected Propensity for Competition*: High *Expected Topology:* Decentralized

Network Effects and Institutional Topologies (Chapter 6)	Nonexcludable Benefits of Institutionalized Cooperation	
	Network effects +	Network effects –
Barriers to entry +	*Case*: Financial Stability *Expected Propensity for Competition*: Low *Expected Topology:* Centralized	*Case*: Development Aid *Expected Propensity for Competition*: High *Expected Topology:* Decentralized

Barriers to Entry and Institutional Topologies (Chapter 7)	Network Effects	
	Barriers to entry +	Barriers to entry –
Excludable benefits of institutionalized cooperation	*Case*: Energy Governance ("Fossil Age") *Expected Propensity for Competition*: Low *Expected Topology:* Centralized	*Case*: Energy Governance (Today) *Expected Propensity for Competition*: High *Expected Topology:* Decentralized

public good provision should be proactively trying to persuade noncooperators to join in order to stop them from free riding and to carry their fair share of the burden. Thus, in policy areas where institutions provide nonexcludable goods, efforts by institutional members to accommodate the demands of institutional outsiders are commonly observable. However, these negotiations tend to be difficult as nonparticipators need to be offered concrete privileges in order to move away from the status quo of noncooperation. Existing international institutions in these areas will therefore typically aim to be as inclusive and universal as possible. The provision of excludable goods by international institutions, on the other hand, should be associated with states eager to generate the benefits of cooperation themselves, as free riding is not possible. The status quo for noncooperators may even be associated with negative effects, which results in their being generally interested in creating new institutions. In these issue areas, institutional conflict is likely to occur frequently and in the case of nonreform of existing institutions, states should be eager to create their own, competing institutions.

Network effects: The presence of network effects in a particular issue area of global governance comes with a generally strong demand for cooperation among states. States have an incentive to coordinate and cooperate with one another to maximize the benefits of collective action. States that cooperate via multilateral institutions in issue areas with strong network effects should be particularly open to the accession of nonmembers, or even proactively seek to accommodate their demands. Institutions with large memberships should, furthermore, exhibit functional advantages in issue areas with strong network effects. They will be able to provide the intended good more effectively with cooperation and address the issue-specific challenges and problems much more effectively than small-scale regional institutions. Counter-institutionalization processes should therefore be particularly difficult to initiate for states, as the critical number of states required to provide institutional benefits is high and states that are already cooperating via existing institutions face no incentives to join additional formats. In issue areas without significant network effects, the opposite should be observable. As the functional benefits of cooperation are independent of the size of institutions, the creation of even regionally limited, small-scale alternative institutions is feasible. Thus, in these issue areas large-scale inclusive institutions should exhibit no functional superiority vis-à-vis regional small-scale alternatives. Moreover, states face incentives to pursue cooperation on these issues via several institutions simultaneously and may therefore be more likely to innovate, functionally differentiate new institutions from their pre-existing competitors, and pick and choose among a more diverse set of institutions to address issue-specific challenges.

Barriers to entry: The presence of barriers to entry in issue areas of global governance are generally seen when a limited circle of states is capable of initiating institutionalization processes. Attempts at institutionalization should thereby be marked by large amounts of dedicated material and immaterial resources and states struggling to provide these resources in the first place. Moreover, the requirements for effective cooperation are high and are recognized as such by states. Institutionalization processes in issue areas marked by high barriers to entry are therefore likely to be marked by struggles over proper rulemaking and the formulation of obligations and sanctions.

Table 4.3 Observable Implications

	Nonexcludability	Excludability	Network Effects Present	Network Effects Absent	Barriers to Entry Present	Barriers to Entry Absent
Observable Implications	*Nonmembers of existing institutions benefit from existing cooperation* *Institutional members proactively encourage nonmembers' participation* *Rather soft than hard law to increase incentives for free-riding states to join*	*Nonmembers are excluded from institutional benefits* *Incentives to join existing clubs to avoid negative externalities* *Incentives to engage in the creation or support of institutional alternatives*	*States perceive large-scale institutions as functionally superior to regional alternatives* *Institutions tend to be designed inclusive and (quasi-)universal* *States dissatisfied with existing large-scale institutions struggle to establish functioning alternatives*	*Functionality and specialization of regional and more small-scale institutions* *Regionally limited scope and membership of institutions* *Dissatisfaction with existing institutions can easily be translated into competitive institution-building*	*Limited circle of states capable of initiating institutionalization processes* *Institution-building requires large material and immaterial resources* *Enforcement costs make institutionalization particularly difficult*	*More states willing and able to create institutions* *Institution-building requires only limited resources* *Coalitions of like-minded states can smoothly negotiate on the rules of the game*

The absence of barriers to entry, contrariwise should generally come with a wider circle of states willing and able to initiate institutionalization processes. Attempts at institutionalization should be marked by smooth and uncomplicated negotiations, and states should be capable of setting up institutions, irrespective of the material and immaterial resources they have available. Moreover, the requirements for effective institutionalized cooperation should be low. Institutionalization processes in issue areas marked by low barriers to entry are therefore likely to exhibit smooth decision-making processes concerning the rules of cooperation and potential enforcement mechanisms.

Conclusion

This chapter presents the network-based operationalization of institutional topologies that will guide the ensuing three empirical chapters of this book. Moreover, it elaborates on the most-similar-systems case selection logic that motivates the composition of those chapters. It has also made the case that, if we consider the recognition of international institutions by their relevant policy-specific competitors and member states engaged in the respective domain as important indicators of their individual position in the regime complex's everyday policymaking, the resulting institutional reference and membership networks allow a fine-grained mapping of the complex's overall topology. Drawing on diverse descriptive network measures allows the degree of centralization that characterizes individual regime complexes' institutional topologies to be structurally compared. The chapter has further elaborated on the empirical strategy of the next three chapters. Each of the ensuing chapters provides a structural comparison of two issue areas that are similar with respect to two of their underlying market characteristics but differ with respect to a third. This most-similar-systems design allows the effect of a single market characteristic to be isolated while controlling for the two other market characteristics. Finally, the chapter has developed and presented its theory's observable implications. More specifically, it has spelled out how the presence or absence of particular market characteristics translates into significant constraints or incentives for states to engage in the creation or strengthening of alternative institutions. These empirical manifestations, which depend on the specific constellation of market characteristics in the issue areas in question, will guide the individual case studies of institutionalization processes in the following three empirical chapters.

Note

1. I conceive of a state's formal membership of an institution as being constituted by its legal participatory status and/or its regular and institutionalized contributions to an institution's regular activities, e.g., by contributing financial resources to its budget.

5

Excludability/Nonexcludability and Institutional Topologies in the Regime Complexes of Tax Avoidance and Intellectual Property

This empirical chapter provides a structural comparison of the regime complexes of tax avoidance and intellectual property. It compares their underlying institutional topologies and analyzes how the similarities and differences in their market structures have affected the evolution of varying institutional topologies. This book's theoretical argument, developed in Chapter 2, holds that the structures among institutions set up in the same policy field are crucially shaped by the market characteristics of policy fields: Barriers to entry, network effects, and the type of good provided by international institutions set the competitive environment in which states engage in (re)negotiating their institutionalized forms of cooperation. While issue areas marked by higher propensities for competition produce centrifugal effects on the structure of institutional complexes resulting in more fragmented interinstitutional topologies, policy fields characterized by low propensities for competition tend to produce centripetal effects that lead to centralization and hierarchization among the respective institutions. This chapter tests the first set of hypotheses on the effect of the type of good provided by institutions on the evolution of interinstitutional structures in regime complexes. The hypotheses hold, first, that issue areas where states create institutions to provide nonexcludable goods exhibit centripetal institutional trajectories: The preexistence of institutions aimed at the provision of public goods incentivizes states to either refrain from cooperation and opt for a strategy of free riding or to join existing large-scale institutions thereby reinforcing centralized patterns of institutionalization. Conversely, the theory holds that issue areas where institutional goods are essentially excludable, and membership can be restricted exhibit centrifugal trajectories. States face strong incentives to strengthen or create alternative arrangements to counter the potentially

The Institutional Topology of International Regime Complexes. Benjamin Daßler, Oxford University Press.
© Benjamin Daßler (2023). DOI: 10.1093/oso/9780198881926.003.0005

negative externalities of the cooperation of others and to enjoy the benefits of cooperation from which other clubs of states can effectively exclude them.

While the market characteristics network effects and barriers to entry capture the costs and benefits of establishing institutionalized forms of cooperation, the type of good characteristic, by contrast, has to do with the outer scope of institutional benefits. Whether and how nonparticipating states can be excluded from the benefits of institutionalized cooperation hinges on the type of good provided by the institutions in a particular policy field. By drawing on theories that stress the relevance of economic goods characteristic of the proliferation of institutionalized cooperation among states, in Chapter 2 I have argued that the type of good provided by the institutions in a particular policy field strongly influences its underlying propensity for competition.

Policy fields in which institutions are set up to provide public goods from whose consumption nonparticipating states cannot be excluded effectively exhibit low degrees of interinstitutional competition. On the other hand, in policy fields where institutionalized cooperation is associated with the provision of club goods, institutional members can effectively exclude nonparticipants from benefits. In policy fields where states cannot be excluded from cooperative benefits, incentives for the creation of competitive or complementary institutions are low, since there is the possibility of free riding: nonparticipating states do not have to bear any of the costs associated with the establishment of institutionalized cooperation but can still benefit from the cooperation of others. Thus, states will not invest too heavily in the proliferation of alternative institutions outside of existing ones. Take, for instance, the issue area of climate change mitigation: Once a group of states sets up an institution aimed at delivering policies to mitigate carbon emissions, incentives for states to create alternative institutions decrease sharply as they enjoy the positive effects, i.e., the' reduction of carbon emissions by participating states and the associated reduction in global climate-related risks, without having to bear any of the costs themselves. In turn, I argue, this produces centripetal effects on the topologies underlying institutional complexes: Existing institutions are strengthened rather than seriously contested, and states tend to refrain from incurring the costs of establishing credible alternatives. Policy fields in which institutionalized cooperation produces nonexcludable outcomes can thus be expected to exhibit more centralistic, enduring structures with relatively uncontested institutions at their centers.

On the other hand, I argue that policy fields exhibit higher propensities for competition if institutional members can effectively exclude nonparticipating states from institutional benefits. In such issue areas, where they lack the opportunity to free ride on the positive externalities of existing institutions, states are forced to seek cooperative benefits by either joining existing institutions or by setting up alternative ones. Furthermore, there are incentives to foster cooperation via multiple institutions simultaneously as the option to remain outside a particular institution can be associated with negative consequences. Thus, I argue that policy fields in which noncooperators can effectively be excluded from the benefits stemming from multilateral institutions are marked by higher degrees of interinstitutional competition and thus exposed to centrifugal effects when it comes to the evolution of their underlying institutional topologies. To test these assumptions regarding the type of good provided by international institutions and its effect on the structure of institutional complexes, this chapter systematically compares the institutional topologies underlying the regime complexes of tax avoidance and intellectual property.

Similarities between the Policy Fields of Tax Avoidance and Intellectual Property

The issue areas of tax avoidance and intellectual property share important characteristics regarding the benefits and obstacles associated with interstate cooperation. In fact, they are remarkably similar when it comes to the functional need for cooperation among states.

Within the policy field of tax avoidance, states cooperate to harmonize their taxation policies in order to mitigate incentives for tax evasion, which can lead, in turn, to harmful tax competition among states (Dagan 2004; Eden and Kudrle 2005: 104; Rixen 2011; Hakelberg 2015; Ndikumana 2015). Cooperation among states on the issue of tax avoidance can help ensure that taxes are collected properly, a crucial endeavor for states, as the associated revenues help to fund essential public services such as healthcare, education, and infrastructure. Moreover, institutionalized forms of cooperation among states in this issue area ensure that tax laws and regulations are consistent across different jurisdictions. States can thereby mitigate the incentives for companies and individuals to engage in transnational tax avoidance strategies by exploiting differences in laws and regulations. Finally, international institutions in the field of tax avoidance allow states to detect and combat illegal activities such as money laundering and illicit financial flows that are often closely tied to tax-avoiding strategies.

Intergovernmental cooperation on intellectual property rights (IPRs), on the other hand, seeks to establish rules among states that regulate the protection of immaterial goods (Maskus 1998; Raustiala 2006; Sell 2017). As IPR protection provides legal mechanisms that enable creators and inventors to protect their rights to their creations, cooperation among states is the only proper solution that ensures these rights are respected and protected beyond national borders. IPR protection is an important aspect of international trade as it allows for the transfer of technology and the exchange of creative works. By means of institutionalized cooperation, states can ensure that IPR laws are compatible and trade can take place smoothly.

In both fields, states bargain about institutional rules addressing the (re)distribution of economic profits. In the field of tax avoidance, they negotiate about tax rates and jurisdictions and appropriate standards of national rule setting. In the issue area of IPRs, they bargain about the adequate degree of compensation to be paid to private entities for the use of their immaterial goods by foreign third parties, and appropriate standards of national IP protection. These similarities in the underlying cooperation problems should, from a rational-institutionalist perspective (Koremenos et al. 2001; Abbott and Snidal 1998; Keohane and Victor 2011; Jupille et al. 2013), translate into comparable institutional configurations in both fields. We should observe that the institutional topology underlying both issue areas provides equally central positions to institutions offering the most "fitting" design in terms of utility maximization for states. At least, there should be no profound differences in how institutionalized forms of cooperation are pursued in both policy fields.

Moreover, variation in institutional competition, and thus in topologies, cannot be explained by the interests of powerful states alone, as suggested by neorealist arguments (Benvenisti and Downs 2007; Drezner 2009; Ikenberry and Lim 2017). These interests are strikingly similar in both cases. In both issue areas, economically powerful states strive to make binding rules to counter the redistribution of income. In the case of tax avoidance, they seek to avoid the shifting of private capital to tax havens, which are predominantly situated within economically small states. In the case of intellectual property, they seek to tackle the issue of the unpaid use of technologies, knowledge, or brands belonging to their domestic firms by counterfeiting industries abroad that are predominantly located in economically weaker, less developed states. States like the US, Germany, or Japan, which are powerful in both policy areas, have traditionally been strong proponents of stricter and more binding rules in line with their economic interests and have forcefully articulated these ambitions within the context of international institutions such as the

OECD and the WTO (Sell 2010a; Kaminski 2013; Muzaka 2011). By contrast, in both fields, economically weaker states have argued for more flexible regulations. For them, attracting capital through low tax rates as well as revenues through the cheap production and retail of unlicensed products is key to their economic development (Drahos 2002; Netanel 2009; Deere 2009). However, as I will show in the next section, in both issue areas these similarly asymmetric power structures and interest constellations among developed and developing nations have not translated into equally centralized patterns of institutional cooperation catering to the interests of the powerful states. Power structures among negotiating states alone cannot account for varying institutional topologies across both issue areas.

In contrast to the policy field of development aid, for example, where there is no fundamental disagreement about the overarching goals of interstate cooperation, namely, the stimulation of economic growth and the reduction of poverty, in the policy fields of tax avoidance and intellectual property, fundamentally different and conflictive perceptions do exist as to what the overarching goals of institutionalized cooperation should be between economically strong and developed countries and economically weak and developing countries. In both issue areas, economically powerful states have strong interests in establishing binding institutional mechanisms to counter both tax evasion and avoidance through the shifting of profits or income to low-tax-rate jurisdictions (so-called "tax havens") and the unpaid use of the intellectual property of their technology-based industries by counterfeiters (located predominantly in economically developing countries). Conversely, economically weak and developing countries seek the advantages provided by the nonregulation of tax policies and IPRs: They aim to increase their welfare by attracting capital through low tax rates and the cheap production and retail of unlicensed products. While high intellectual property standards are therefore associated with costs for developing economies, developed states are crucially interested in their institutionalization.

Broadly speaking then, intergovernmental cooperation on the issue of intellectual property protection seeks to establish rules among states to regulate the protection of patents, copyrights, and trademarks. These rules negotiated among states give private entities, most importantly firms, "temporary exclusive rights to make, use, sell and withhold goods and services" (Sell 2017: 309). International institutions in the field of intellectual property protection take various forms, ranging from fully-fledged international organizations like the Word Intellectual Property Organization (WIPO) to multilateral treaties like the Convention on Biological Diversity (CBD). Still, what they have in common is that they all engage in the formulation and, at least to some extent, the monitoring of compliance with IPRs (see, e.g., Helfer 2009; Muzaka 2011). I thus conceive of international institutions as being part of the intellectual property complex if they obtain a mandate from their member states to formulate intellectual property norms or guiding principles and support the monitoring and implementation of IPRs within member states.

In the policy field of tax avoidance, on the other hand, states seek cooperation to harmonize their taxation policies to mitigate incentives, especially for multinational firms, to take advantage of lower corporate tax rates abroad, which can lead to harmful tax competition among states (see, e.g., Eden and Kudrle 2005: 104; Rixen 2008a; 2011; Hakelberg 2015; Ndikumana 2015). It is thus important to note that I conceive of the policy area of tax avoidance as consisting of intergovernmental cooperation aimed at preventing the shift of corporate profit to low-tax countries by both legal and illegal means. While the former is the more obvious reason for intergovernmental cooperation as it can be addressed directly by harmonizing tax policies among states, institutionalized cooperation on the issue of illegal forms of tax avoidance, which, for the sake of differentiation, is often referred to in the literature as tax evasion (see. e.g., Hakelberg 2016: 511; Wildasin 2002: 179), is also of great interest to states, e.g., in order to allow the transnational prosecution of tax crimes (see, e.g., Kerzner and Chodikoff 2016; Gravelle 2015).

Various forms of multilateral international institutions, ranging from international organizations such as the OECD or the European Union (EU) through regional institutions like the Intra-European Organization of Tax Administrators (IOTA) to relatively informal consultation and dialogue fora like the G20 engage in the policy field for the purposes of strengthening their member states' ability to collect tax revenues by limiting the possibilities for tax avoidance. The political economy of taxation is very complex, including many different potential instruments like personal income tax (PIT), value-added tax (VAT), general sales tax (GST), and corporate income tax (CIT). Therefore, for the sake of simplicity, I will focus exclusively on institutions with a mandate to support and foster cooperation on CIT. I justify this definitory simplification of the policy field of tax avoidance on the grounds of the particular importance and universality of CIT: Not only is it a truly global tax policy, as, with a few rare exceptions, almost every country in the world has formulated a separate CIT policy, but it is also a crucial revenue raiser for poor states, where multinational firms constitute a reliable source of tax revenue (Genschel and Seelkopf 2016: 325–6). For the empirical analysis in this chapter, I thus conceive of an international institution as being part of the tax avoidance complex if it (also) formulates guidelines, recommendations, or rules for participating states that address the issue of tax avoidance by increasing its member states' abilities to collect corporate income tax revenues.

The issue areas of tax avoidance and intellectual property share more than just essential characteristics regarding power and interest heterogeneities among potentially cooperating states. Notably, both policy areas exhibit striking similarities regarding barriers to entry and network effects. To begin with, material and immaterial hurdles to setting up institutionalized forms of cooperation in both areas are relatively moderate. States do not need vast material or immaterial resources to initiate cooperation on IPRs. Due to their intangible nature, there are no significant material hurdles impeding states from engaging in institutionalized cooperation on IPRs (Muzaka 2011: 763; Emmert 1990: 1318). Even though they often lack technology-based industries, also developing countries foster cooperation on IPRs, e.g., to protect traditional and indigenous knowledge or biological and genetic resources (Finger and Schuler 2004; Dutfield 2010: 4–5). Unlike, e.g., in the issue area of financial stability where states require vast financial resources to set up institutions capable of solving balance of payments issues affecting their members, in the issue area of IPRs, states can engage in cooperation irrespective of their financial resources. Even economically weak countries can set up intellectual property institutions to protect traditional and indigenous knowledge or biological or genetic resources (Daßler et al. 2019).

Furthermore, virtually every state today runs national or subnational patent offices where the bureaucratic and legal expertise necessary to engage in intergovernmental cooperation on intellectual property issues exists (WIPO 2019a). The same holds for tax avoidance: Just like in the field of IPRs, states do not need vast capacities to cooperate on the issue of tax avoidance at the international level. Modern corporate income tax policies and the associated bureaucratic and legal expertise, with a few rare exceptions, have spread across the globe and been introduced in low-income countries too over the last few decades (Seelkopf et al. 2016). Moreover, the regular and frequent bilateral exchange of information among governments regarding their taxation policies is well established in most countries, so that governments are usually aware of other states' taxation policies, further decreasing the costs of cooperation on tax avoidance issues (Dehejia and Genschel 1999: 404).

However, in both issue areas, there are similar challenges regarding enforcement. To effectively implement the measures against tax avoidance proposed by international institutions, members must make substantial resources available that are exclusively devoted to tax enforcement (Slemrod and Wilson 2009: 1262; Troiano 2017). This implies a need for international legal expertise beyond existing national capacities that allows the enforcement of institutional provisions. The same holds for the policy field of intellectual property protection. To counter the inflow of unlicensed goods, states need specifically trained customs authorities that can identify and confiscate them efficiently. Especially for states lacking these well-equipped and trained customs authorities, the major problem will be their "failure to get [their] ... laws and international obligations adequately and effectively enforced" (Massey 2006: 232). The case of the Chinese government's long-lasting struggle to contain the problem of "piracy" in order to fulfill their institutional obligations illustrates this. For China, high enforcement costs over a long period of time have been a significant obstacle to deepening institutional cooperation on intellectual property, which they needed to gain access to Western markets (Massey 2006). Thus, both issue areas are remarkably similar regarding barriers to initiating institutionalized forms of cooperation.

Both policy fields are further similar regarding network effects associated with institutional cooperation. In both cases, the "marginal utility of joining an activity" (Lipscy 2017: 28) does not increase but decreases with the total number of participating states. For tax havens that generate a large proportion of their economic growth by attracting foreign capital through low tax rates, the marginal utility of joining a tax avoidance institution decreases as the numbers of institutional members grow. For them, "being a tax haven in a world where every other state is also a tax haven is not very profitable, but being the sole tax haven in an otherwise tax-haven free world is potentially very profitable" (Genschel and Plümper 1997: 637). The more states decide to join a tax institution, the lower the incentives for the remaining nonparticipating states. Indeed, the complete abolition of harmful tax competition is only thinkable given the existence of a genuinely universal institution (Rixen 2011: 204; Dehejiha and Genschel 1999). The same holds for the issue area of intellectual property protection. With increasing numbers of cooperators, abstaining becomes more valuable for states interested in deregulating intellectual property. The demand for the unlicensed products sold by their counterfeiting industries increases as more states abolish their own "piracy firms". This, in turn, may incentivize states with important counterfeiting industries to abstain from cooperation as more and more other states decide to commit themselves to institutionalized rules protecting IPRs. The role of Brazil and India in the dispute surrounding the production and export of generic drugs through compulsory licenses is an excellent example of such an effect. The establishment of the large-scale Trade-Related

Aspects of Intellectual Property Rights (TRIPS) agreement in 1995 prompted many economically weak countries to look for alternatives to the expensive and now patent-protected pharmaceuticals that they desperately needed to tackle the spreading HIV/AIDS epidemic. Both India and Brazil promoted the generic drugs produced under compulsory licenses by their domestic pharmaceutical industry, which led to a significant decrease in prices for HIV/AIDS drugs in economically weak countries while strengthening their pharmaceutical industries that specialized in the production of generic drugs (Coriat 2008: 9; Dauvergne and Farias 2012: 910–11; Grace 2004). Thus, in both issue areas, states interested in deregulation rather than institution-alization benefit from higher numbers of states joining the institutions in question.

In contrast to, e.g., the policy field of financial stability,[1] where there are strong network effects curbing institutional competition by creating incentives for all states to participate in one universal institution (Lipscy 2017: 68–70), in the issue areas of tax avoidance and intellectual property, these effects are absent. To counter the absence of strong network effects in both policy fields, the advocates of solid rules have firmly pushed for large-scale and universalistic forms of cooperation: In the policy field of IPRs, developed countries in particular with their powerful technology-based industries have advocated strongly for institutional arrangements that allow them to "globalize their preferred conception of [IPR] control" (Sell 2003: 19). In the policy field of tax avoidance, the OECD already issued a report back in 1998 recognizing that "there are limitations on unilateral or bilateral responses to a problem that is inherently multilateral and ... [the OECD needs to identify] ways in which governments can best establish a common framework within which countries could operate individually and collectively to limit the problems presented by countries and fiscally sovereign territories engaging in harmful tax practices" (OECD 1998: 8).

Thus, in contrast to, e.g., the policy field of financial stability, neither of the policy fields currently under analysis exhibits strong and uniform network effects associated with institutionalized forms of cooperation. While both are quite comparable when it comes to network effects associated with institutionalized cooperation, the barriers and hindrances to engaging in cooperation and the fundamental policy issues and conflicts involved, I argue they still differ in one important aspect: While states cannot be excluded from the benefits derived from institutional cooperation on the issue of tax avoidance, institutional benefits associated with cooperation on IPRs are highly excludable and, hence, restricted to member states.

Why the Policy Fields of Tax Avoidance and Intellectual Property are Still Different: The Excludability/ Nonexcludability of Institutional Benefits

Despite these many similarities, the following section shows how the two policy fields differ significantly in their underlying propensity to institutional competition. In the field of tax avoidance, institutional benefits are nonexcludable. Here, nonparticipating states benefit strongly from the cooperative efforts of others. As Dehejia and Genschel (1999) show, economically weak states have much less interest in institutional cooperation than economically strong ones; since they differ considerably in the size of their tax bases, smaller states' potential tax revenue losses from reducing rates are relatively low.

By contrast, the positive effect of attracting foreign capital into their tax base is comparatively high. When it comes to the harmonization of taxes, therefore, "cooperation would leave the small state with less tax revenue than under tax competition (absent side payments)" (Dehejia and Genschel 1999: 411). Once a group of states engages in institutionalized cooperation to tackle tax avoidance, virtually all nonparticipating states benefit from the cooperating states' efforts to harmonize their tax rates. Outsiders are not excluded but face positive externalities from the competitive self-restraint exercised by members as they now face less competition for foreign capital (Kammas and Philippopoulos 2009; Shaviro 2001). As corporations interested in shifting their capital to a jurisdiction with low tax rates are left with a smaller range of potential tax havens, the race to the bottom may eventually even slow down. Therefore, once a group of states institutionalizes their cooperation on tax avoidance, other states have no incentive to join or create alternative arrangements. Furthermore, participating states have incentives to "buy nonmembers in" (Kruck and Zangl 2019) in order to expand the scope of their rules. This, in turn, reduces interinstitutional competition in the field.

The "public good issue" caused by the nonexcludability from institutional benefits of nonparticipating states is further reinforced by what scholars refer to as spillover effects associated with tax harmonization: As many economist scholars argue, in the absence of cooperation, tax revenues and tax rates become too low to finance an efficient amount of public goods (see, e.g., Zodrow and Miszkowsi 1986; Keen and Merchand 1997: 33; Bjorvatn and Schjelderup 2002: 111). More specifically, Bjorvatn and Schjelderup (2002) have argued that there are spillover effects from the provision of public goods by a particular country that offer other states the opportunity to free ride.

Assume states invest parts of their tax revenues in public goods like, e.g., measures aimed at reducing carbon emissions or sponsoring research and development, which both have positive spillover effects across jurisdictions. These states face the problem of free riding by other states in the sense that the latter enjoy the benefits of the provision of good without having to incur any costs, such as imposing higher taxes to finance these goods themselves (Bjorvatn and Schjelderup 2002: 111).

These spillover effects affect a policy field's propensity for interinstitutional competition. States that decide to cooperate on the issue of tax avoidance by harmonizing their tax rates can use their higher tax revenues to increase the provision of these public goods, which, in turn, reinforces incentives for nonparticipating states to defect and abstain from alternative venues of cooperation. They will then refrain from increasing their taxes as they can free ride on the strengthened provision of public goods by cooperators creating spillover effects in their respective jurisdictions. The incentive for nonparticipating states to commit themselves to stricter tax rates immediately decreases once a group of states harmonizes their tax rates to increase the supply of international public goods. Without their having to take any action themselves, they become even more attractive jurisdictions for transnational capital thanks to the competitive self-restraint of the cooperators.

In the field of IPRs, contrariwise, institutional benefits are excludable. If states decide to abstain from an IPR institution, they are excluded from the privileges exclusively enjoyed by members of the "IPR club." These privileges entail access to club members' domestic markets or the possibility of protecting their own patents. The very nature of cooperation on intellectual property standards results in the creation of institutional clubs. Outsiders cannot enjoy the conveniences associated with intellectual property club membership. Quite the opposite: The creation of intellectual property clubs creates negative externalities for states with a preference for intellectual property deregulation. They are worse off than they were before the institution was established (Slapin 2009). After institutions have been set up to establish IPRs, there are fewer potential markets for their (unlicensed) products, and they face higher prices for licensed products from club member jurisdictions. The creation of IPR institutions even forces states interested in deregulation to pay for licenses that allow the use of desperately needed foreign goods (Dosi and Stieglitz 2014: 2). Many studies have shown that countries that abstain from IPR institutions receive less foreign direct investment and fewer joint ventures, especially in research and development facilities (Mansfield 1995), which significantly hampers their economic growth (Gould and Gruben 1996).

Furthermore, firms from countries with high intellectual property protection standards often refuse to license their products to companies from states that only reluctantly enforce IPRs, fearing that contracts will not be enforceable (see, e.g., Sherwood 1990). Countries that decide not to cooperate on the issue of internationally binding IPRs are likely targets of economic pressure by states interested in enforcing these rules. For instance, throughout the Uruguay Round, which resulted in the foundation of the World Trade Organization (WTO), including the TRIPS agreement in 1995, the US put intense pressure on countries reluctant to agree to strict intellectual property standards. The US government directly threatened Mexico with access restrictions to the US market for their agriculture businesses. During the subsequent negotiations, in 1987, when Mexico refused to make substantial changes to its intellectual property system, the US cut its so-called "Generalized System of Preferences" (GSP) benefits by USD 500 million (Drahos 2002: 776). Due to the excludability of the institutional benefits associated with intellectual property protection, Mexico had no choice but to fulfill the institutional obligations demanded of it.

Another example illustrating the threat of exclusion associated with intellectual property cooperation is China's norm-compliant behavior following its economic liberalization reforms that started in the early 1980s. When China decided to liberalize its economy following the "Cultural Revolution" in 1979, one of the main political projects its government was to implement was the so-called "Open Door Policy," which aimed to modernize the domestic economy (Zhang 1997: 70). A substantial part of this policy was a reform of the underdeveloped Chinese intellectual property system, which was conceived to be a necessary condition for attracting investment, especially from the US. Only membership in this international intellectual property club was perceived as allowing them access to associated institutional benefits. Indeed, when the US and China concluded a bilateral trade agreement in 1979, China acknowledged the importance of intellectual property standards and its willingness to establish an enforceable and reliable intellectual property system (Zhang 1997: 71). Still, the US side indicated that "in the absence of adequate protection, the representatives would not be permitted to sign the agreements" (Yang 2003: 136). The fact that China was not yet a member of WIPO at that time was a significant hurdle to the implementation of the treaty. Finally, in 1980, in order to be able to implement the trade deal with the US and to follow through on its "Open Door Policy", China decided to join the WIPO (Zhang 1997: 72). Thus, in the case of China's attempt to modernize its economy after the Cultural Revolution, membership of existing institutional clubs governing intellectual property and the associated access to institutional benefits like increased foreign direct investment were perceived to be necessary in order to enable it to pursue its efforts at economic liberalization: China was not able to attract foreign investment through bilateral trade agreements, as members of existing intellectual property institutions refused to intensify trade relations unless China committing itself to the institutional rules of the intellectual property club. Despite their initial reluctance and resistance to stronger IPRs, in order to pursue its economic liberalization policy, China was thus forced to join an existing institutional arrangement, namely the WIPO.

Consequently, for noncooperators, the disadvantages of exclusion from the benefits of intellectual property cooperation outweigh the costs of IPR commitments. Once intellectual property institutions have been established, unilateralism is no longer a rational option, even for states with profound interests in noncooperation. On the contrary, outsiders face strong incentives either to join institutions, thereby trying to mitigate rules from within, or to create or strengthen alternative clubs promoting less strict IPR protection standards to mitigate the harmful effects of noncooperation. It becomes a rational strategy to shift cooperation to those institutional clubs providing exceptions and less strict intellectual property rules. These tendencies rooted in the excludability of institutional benefits reinforce institutional competition in the policy field of IPRs. Here, compared to the policy field of tax avoidance, excludability creates strong incentives for states to engage in a (re)negotiation of institutions. Strategies like competitive regime creation or regime shifting and forum shopping are rational and exert centrifugal effects on the regime complex's underlying topology.

Table 5.1 summarizes the main differences and highlights the crucial similarities between the policy issues of tax avoidance and intellectual property protection. While both policy fields are comparable when it comes to barriers to entry and the network effects associated with institutionalized cooperation, they differ markedly with respect to the excludability of nonparticipating states from institutional benefits: In the field of tax avoidance, nonparticipating states cannot be excluded from the positive effects associated with institutionalized cooperation by other states, but in the policy field of intellectual property protection, institutional outsiders can effectively be excluded from enjoying these benefits. According to my theory, these differences promote the development of diverging topologies within the policy fields' underlying institutional complexes.

Table 5.1 Market Characteristics of the Policy Fields of Tax Avoidance and Intellectual Property Protection and Effects on their Topologies

Market Characteristic / Issue Area	Barriers to Entry	Network Effects	(Non-) Excludability of Institutional Benefits	Degree of Competition and Effects on Topology
Tax Avoidance	*Moderate:* Initiating institutionalized cooperation with the aim of regulating and monitoring tax compliance does not require vast material resources as bureaucratic and technocratic expertise exists on the national level and as intergovernmental exchange and information flows among states on a bilateral basis are already well established. There are high enforcement costs associated with the implementation of institutional obligations.	*Rather Weak:* "Tax havens" benefit from more participating states as competition for capital is gradually reduced with growing numbers of participating states and the utility of joining decreases.	*Nonexcludability of Institutional Benefits:* Cooperation on the issue of tax avoidance creates incentives for nonparticipants to free ride on reduced tax competition while abstaining from institutionalizing tax harmonization themselves. Positive spillover effects of increased public good provision by countries harmonizing their tax rates on nonparticipating states further reduce incentives to engage in alternative institution building.	*Mitigated Competition:* To ensure the effective functioning of institutionalized cooperation on the issue of tax avoidance, cooperators need to buy nonparticipants in by, e.g., offering informal institutional privileges to noncooperators; No incentives to engage in alternative regime creation or forum-shifting strategies. **Centripetal effects on the topology of the institutional complex**
Intellectual Property Protection	*Moderate:* Setting up institutionalized cooperation does not require vast material resources due to the intangible nature of IPRs and the fact that the bureaucratic and technocratic expertise required for cooperation on IPRs already exists on a national level in the form of National Patent Offices. Comparatively high enforcement costs	*Rather Weak:* "Pirates" benefit from large-scale cooperation on IPRs as their counterfeiting industry gains relevance, which is why their utility from joining decreases with a larger number of participants.	*Excludability of Institutional Benefits:* Noncooperation on intellectual property protection leads to the exclusion from institutional benefits, e.g., in the form of market access restrictions on domestic firms. States are therefore incentivized to join institutions even if strict intellectual property rules are against their interest.	*Reinforced Competition:* To mitigate the negative consequences of membership of the intellectual property "club" states are forced to engage in counter-institutionalization and regime-shifting strategies. **Centrifugal effects on the topology of the institutional complex**

Mapping Institutional Topologies: A Comparative Network Analysis of the Institutional Complexes of Tax Avoidance and Intellectual Property

To assess the topologies underlying the tax avoidance and intellectual property complexes, I propose to think of them as social networks. Within these networks, each institution's relative centrality shapes the overall topology of the complex. Areas dominated by one central institution with others located on the network's fringes exhibit strongly centralized interinstitutional structures. Issue areas whose underlying institutional networks have no clear-cut center, by contrast, exhibit more decentralized structures.

In all three empirical chapters of this book, institutional networks are measured along two important dimensions. The first dimension captures references among all relevant institutions within the complex. In line with Pratt (2018), I argue that structures within interinstitutional networks are constituted by instances of policy coordination and deference among institutions (Pratt 2018: 562–3). These acts of recognition occur in official IO documents. When they explicitly reference another IO governing the same issue area, it constitutes an IO relation and an edge between two nodes in the respective institutional complex's network. The more an institution is referred to by all the other institutions in a particular policy field, the more central its position within the institutional complex's reference network. I complement this dimension of analysis with another that captures formal participation in institutions by states that are actively engaging in the policy field. The institutional topology underlying regime complexes can be considered fragmented in policy fields where states pursue cooperation via many unrelated institutions and where references to these institutions are distributed equally. Conversely, institutional structures are centralized if states pursue cooperation on a policy issue predominantly by means of large-scale, universalistic institutions and where references among institutions are directed at only one or a very small number of institutions. I selected the sample of states based on quantitative criteria indicating the degree to which a particular state had a substantial interest in cooperation on the issue in question.

To identify the relevant institutions set up in each of the two policy fields, as a first step, I consulted several existing studies of the two issue areas and their underlying institutions.[2] For the policy field of intellectual property protection, I also consulted an official publication by the African Regional Intellectual Property Organization (ARIPO). The document contains a list of, amongst other things, international institutions set up by states to cooperate on the issue of intellectual property protection (ARIPO 2019). For the policy field of tax avoidance, the OECD published a similar document about a "platform for collaboration on tax." The document explicitly lists other multilateral tax organizations with whom it seeks to "establish an effective institutional setting ... and to produce concrete outputs" (OECD 2016: 6) on the policy issue of tax avoidance. Both documents were consulted to complement the list of the most relevant multilateral institutions engaging in the policy field. Based on the above considerations and selection criteria, I created the following set of institutions, summarized in Table 5.2, to analyze the network structures underlying the intellectual property and the tax avoidance complexes.

Table 5.2 International Institutions in the Policy Fields of Intellectual Property Protection and Tax Avoidance

Intellectual Property Protection	Institution	Year of Creation
	World Intellectual Property Organization (WIPO)	1967
	Convention on Biological Diversity (CBD)	1992
	African Regional Intellectual Property Organization (ARIPO)	1976
	Eurasian Patent Organization (EAPO)	1995
	European Patent Organization (EPO)	1977
	Food and Agriculture Organization (FAO)	1945
	World Trade Organization/TRIPS Council (TRIPS)	1995
	International Union for the Protection of New Varieties of Plants (UPOV)	1961
	World Health Organization (WHO)	1948
	African Intellectual Property Organization (OAPI)	1962
Tax Avoidance	Group of 20 (G20)	1999
	African Tax Administration Forum (ATAF)	2009
	Commonwealth Association of Tax Administrators (CATA)	1978
	Inter-American Center of Tax Administrations (CIAT)	1967
	Organisation for Economic Co-operation and Development (OECD)	1948
	European Commission (EU COM)	1967
	Intra-European Organization of Tax Administrations (IOTA)	1997
	UN Tax Committee (UNTC)	1980
	Exchange and Research Centre for Leaders of Tax Administrations (CREDAF)	1982

For this sample of institutions, I collected official institutional documents to map the reference networks underlying both policy fields. These documents include, among other things, official annual reports by the respective institutions containing reviews of institutional activities, reports on organizational events like conferences or annual meetings, financial statements, statistical reports, or reflections on political strategies. Each time a specific institution is directly mentioned within a document that I analyzed, this constitutes a referential tie between the institution mentioned and the institution from which the document was collected. Speaking in network terms, each reference linking two institutions from the same subfield constitutes an edge between these two network nodes. The resulting network graphs thus represent the intensity and direction of reciprocal references among all relevant institutions of the institutional complex during the observation period.

To map these interinstitutional reference networks, I analyzed documents over a period of more than five years. Thus, all the documents collected for the institutions in the issue areas of tax avoidance and intellectual property protection originate from 2013–18. I subsequently created sets of documents comprising all the data gathered for a particular institution. Afterwards, I quantitatively analyzed these sets of documents to capture the number and direction of references among the institutions in question. I then performed several weighting procedures to enhance reference intensity comparability. The number of references within a particular set of institutional documents were weighted according to their relative size, i.e., the total number of document pages collected for a respective institution over the period of observation. The resulting reference networks are directed, meaning that they show both incoming and outgoing references to and from the institutions involved.

The sociomatrices underlying the institutional complexes' membership networks were collected in an undirected fashion, however. In these networks, states and institutions have no weighted or directed connections. Following a binary system, the sociomatrices contain cells for each state–institution pair in which "1" indicates membership and "0" indicates non-membership of a respective institution. Based on this coding, I constructed sociomatrices indicating the membership to the sample of institutions of the previously selected relevant states engaging in the respective policy area during 2013–18.[3]

In the reference network graphs, the relative size of each node is based on its respective in-degree centrality. The in-degree centrality of each institution indicates the total of all incoming references from other institutions in the complex. The color shade of a node, on the other hand, uniquely indicates its particular betweenness centrality, i.e., the relative number of shortest paths between all pairs of institutions that pass through it. The "thickness" of ties among institutions further indicates the intensity of a particular IO relation: The more a particular pair of institutions refer to one another, the more pronounced their tie in the network graph will be. In the membership network graphs, which are undirected, the size of each node simply indicates its degree centrality, i.e., the overall number of connections that node has with all the other nodes in the network. States pursuing institutionalized cooperation via many institutions simultaneously are shown as larger nodes in the graph than states which cooperate via a small number of institutions only. At the same time, the size of each institution's node indicates the number of relevant states obtaining formal membership of it. Figures 5.1 and 5.2 compare the reference and the membership networks in the policy fields of tax avoidance and intellectual property protection.

Figures 5.1 and 5.2 indicate that interinstitutional structures differ across both policy fields. The IPR issue area, with its more competitive institutional environment, exhibits a more fragmented topology in both the reference and the membership network compared with the tax avoidance complex. Here, the OECD occupies the most central position in both networks. In the IPR issue area, however, the central positions occupied by the WIPO and the WTO/TRIPS are more contested, e.g., by the CBD or by regional institutions like EPO or ARIPO. In the IPR network, institutions with broad and rather unspecific mandates like the CBD and the WHO take comparatively central positions. When comparing the differences in centrality scores among institutions across both complexes, the difference in in-degree and betweenness centrality from all other institution is greater in the case of the OECD than in that of the WIPO (see Figures 5.3 and 5.4). In contrast to the institutional complex of tax avoidance, in the IPR complex, institutional activity appears not to be clustered around a well-defined center but to be spread across several centrally positioned institutions.

Divergent structures are reflected not only in the individual positions of institutions, but in both reference networks' underlying normalized in-degree and betweenness centralizations. While the reference network underlying the tax avoidance complex exhibits a high degree of in-degree and betweenness centralization, the IPR equivalent exhibits lower degrees of both weighted in-degree and normalized betweenness centralization.

Figure 5.4 further indicates that the institutional complex of tax avoidance exhibits a clear-cut institutional center as regards the betweenness centrality of its institutions. The OECD is by far the most central institution in terms of betweenness, which means that it occupies the position within the reference

Reference Network Tax Avoidance

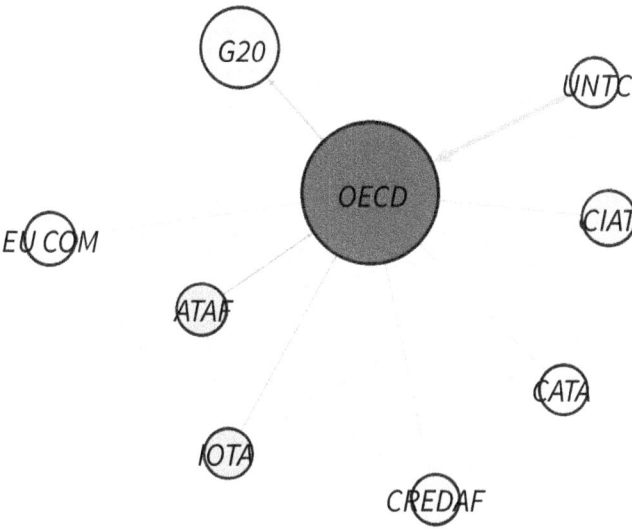

Reference Network Intellectual Property

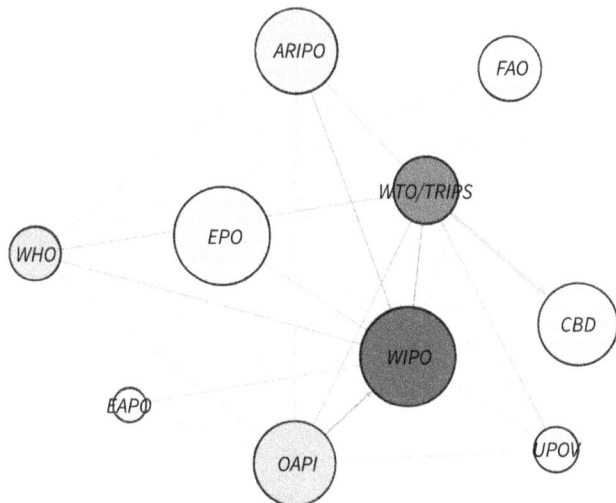

Figure 5.1 Reference Networks of the Institutional Complexes of Tax Avoidance and Intellectual Property (2013–18)

Note: Graphs were created with the network visualization tool Gephi (v. 0.9.2). The color shade of the node indicates an institution's betweenness centrality.

Membership Network Tax Avoidance

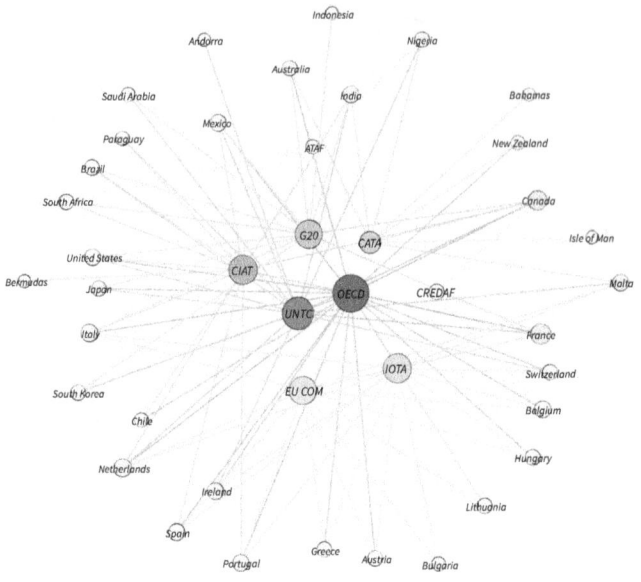

Membership Network Intellectual Property

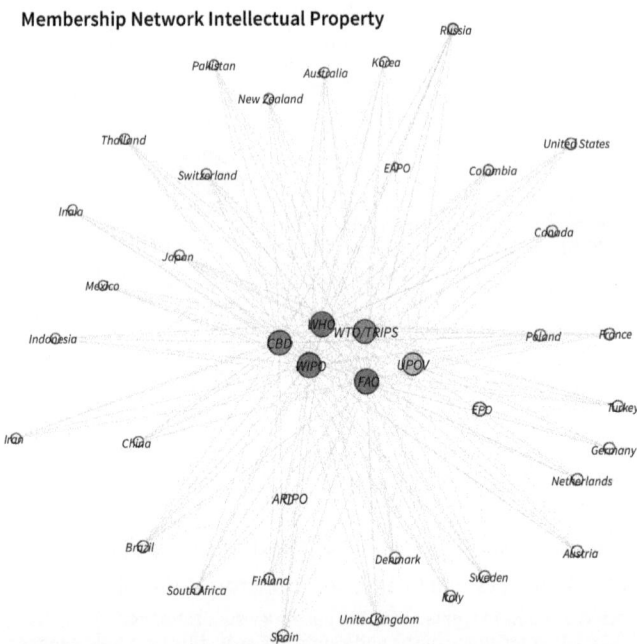

Figure 5.2 Membership Networks of the Institutional Complexes of Tax Avoidance and Intellectual Property (2018)

Note: Graphs were created with the network visualization tool Gephi (v. 0.9.2).

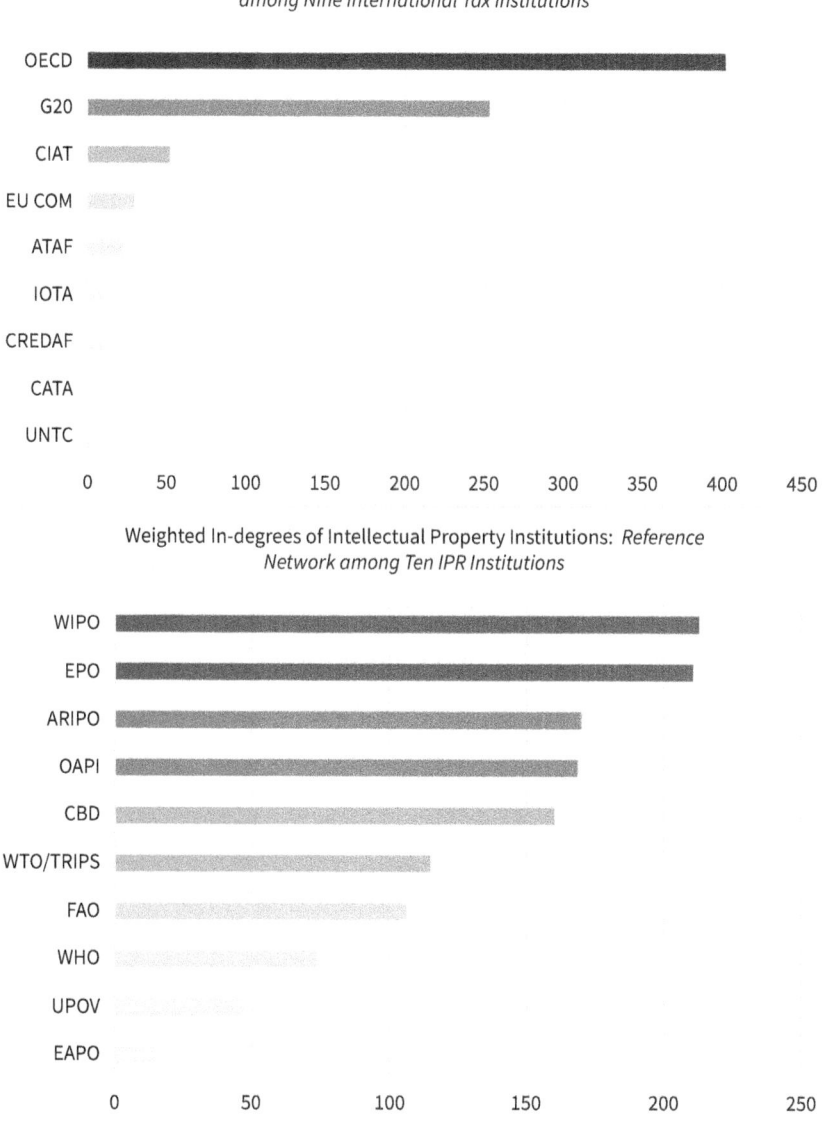

Figure 5.3 Weighted Indegrees of Tax Avoidance and Intellectual Property Institutions

network that intersects with the highest number of shortest paths between all other institutions. The normalized betweenness centrality of the second and third most central institutions in the network, IOTA and ATAF, is less than 50 percent that of the OECD. Within the institutional complex of intellectual

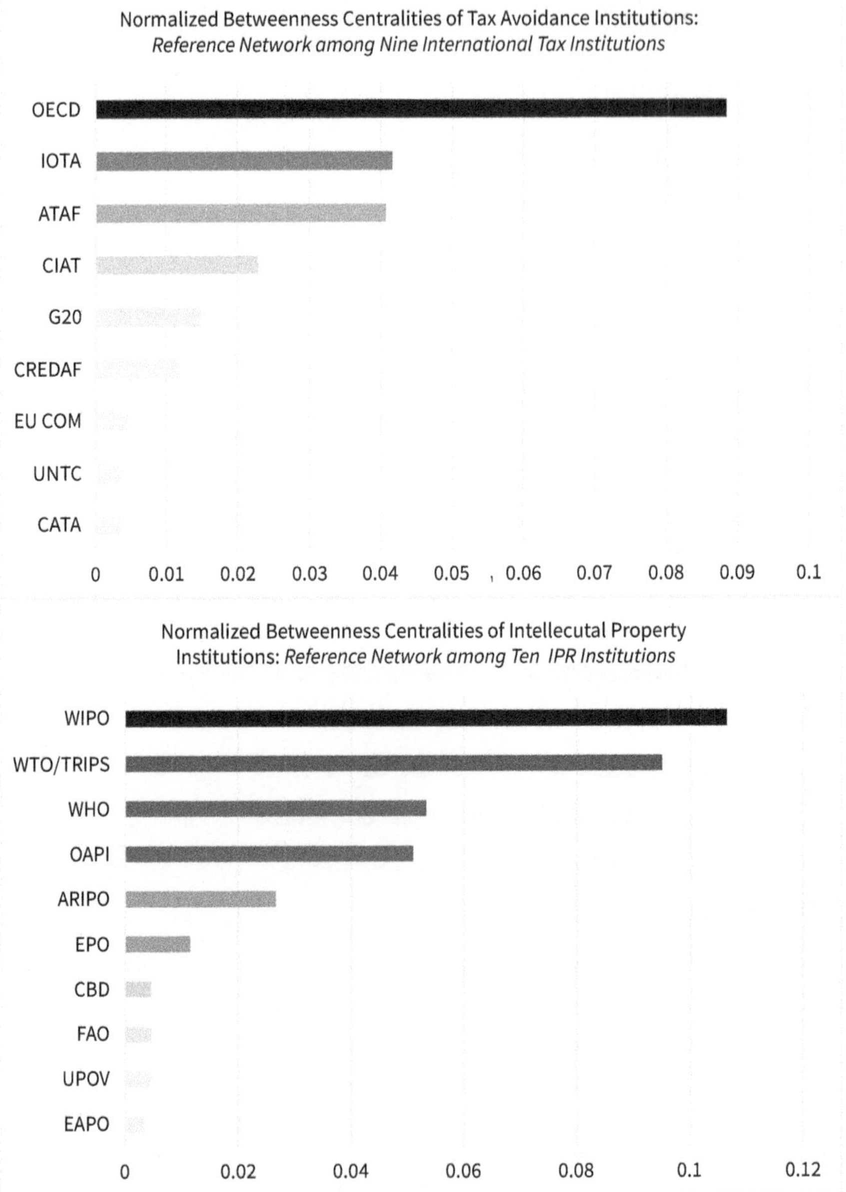

Normalized Betweenness Centralities of Tax Avoidance Institutions:
Reference Network among Nine International Tax Institutions

Figure 5.4 Normalized Betweenness Centralities of Tax Avoidance and Intellectual Property Institutions

property, WIPO occupies the most central position in terms of betweenness. It is closely followed by the WTO/TRIPS with only slightly smaller normalized betweenness centrality. The WHO and OAPI exhibit a normalized betweenness centrality that is approximately 50 percent that of the WIPO. The differences regarding individual normalized betweenness scores among institutions of both institutional complexes further indicate that the reference network underlying the institutional complex of intellectual property is more fragmented. While the OECD occupies an important brokerage position among institutions that are otherwise scarcely connected, the WIPO, by contrast, has a similar brokerage position to the WTO/TRIPS. In sum, the network analysis suggests that the two institutional complexes differ considerably with respect to their underlying institutional topology. While the institutional complex of tax avoidance exhibits more centralistic structures, with the OECD occupying a dominant position in both the underlying reference and the membership network, the intellectual property complex appears more decentralized and contested with several institutions, amongst them regional IPR arrangements like EPO or ARIPO as well as more broadly mandated institutions in terms of policy scope like the WHO or CBD, competing for equally central positions.

Going beyond this mere covariation analysis of market characteristics and institutional topologies, the next section presents two case studies of institutionalization processes in both complexes. The section shows that in the policy field of tax avoidance, the nonexcludability of institutional benefits created centripetal effects on the complex's underlying structures strengthening the OECD's position in particular. In the policy field of IPRs, by contrast, higher propensities for interinstitutional competition due to the excludability of institutional benefits created centrifugal effects on the complex's underlying structures, resulting in more decentralized patterns of institutional cooperation through the WTO, the WHO, the CBD, and other fora.

Excludability and Centrifugal Effects in the Regime Complex of Intellectual Property Protection

The network analyses I conducted in the previous part of this chapter indicate that, unlike the institutional complex of tax avoidance, the institutional complex of intellectual property rights (IPRs) has no clear-cut authoritative center in terms of institutionalized cooperation among states engaging in the field. Both in terms of interinstitutional references and membership by relevant states in the field, the IPR complex appears to exhibit a much more decentralized topology. In the following section of this empirical chapter, I claim that the evolution of these diverging topologies was favored by the policy fields' fundamental differences regarding the excludability/nonexcludability of institutional benefits. While institutionalized cooperation within the policy field of tax avoidance is associated with nonexcludable institutional benefits, which incentivize nonmembers to abstain from cooperation, institutionalized cooperation within the policy field of IPRs is associated with excludable institutional goods from which nonparticipants can effectively be cut off. This is because cooperation on intellectual property issues is predominantly undertaken with a view to providing club goods to IPR cooperators: States that decide not to cooperate on the issue are excluded from important trade networks or directly sanctioned economically. They are thus unable to obtain benefits that only members of the "IPR club" can enjoy. Noncooperation is thus associated with economically harmful effects. As a result, even states that are not interested in the global regulation and enforcement of IPRs have incentives to formally join IPR institutions in order to avoid the exclusion from institutional benefits associated with noncooperation. At the same time, once they have joined the institution in order to enjoy its exclusive benefits, these states have strong incentives to counter the negative effects of stricter IPR norms on their economies by fostering cooperation via alternative or even competitive institutions to establish alternative, laxer IPR norms. This mechanism, I argue, gives strong encouragement to interinstitutional competition thereby producing centrifugal effects on the underlying institutional complex and its interinstitutional hierarchies.

In this section of the book, I provide qualitative empirical evidence for these centrifugal effects within the IPR complex. More precisely, I trace the institutionalization processes that led to the establishment of the TRIPS agreement in 1995 and its subsequent contestation by developing and emerging states. During the Uruguay Round that led to the establishment of TRIPS, developing and emerging countries were exposed to strongly negative economic consequences resulting from their initial nonparticipation. These negative externalities forced them to finally back down and join TRIPS. As I will show, their main motive was to prevent themselves from being excluded from important trade clubs, a fate directly associated with noncooperation and experienced by states that tried to stay outside existing IPR institutions. Over the years that followed, many developing countries fostered cooperation on IPRs via alternative institutions like the Convention on Biological Diversity (CBD) or the World Health Organization (WHO) in order to mitigate the strongly negative effects of TRIPS on their economies, as indicated, e.g., by their increasing inability to provide public health services to their people during the HIV/AIDS crisis.

As I will show, these attempts were successful especially as two large-scale institutions, the WHO and CBD, were gradually granted the authority to formulate IPR-related norms that would partially mitigate the negative effects of TRIPS on developing and emerging states. Thus, in the institutional complex of IPR, the ability of institutional cooperators to effectively exclude noncooperators from institutional benefits forced developing and emerging states to join institutions that provided rules and norms that were essentially not in their interest. As they were still forced to join the institution in order to avoid being excluded from important benefits exclusively enjoyed by members of the "IPR club," incentives increased to foster cooperation via other institutions where they could establish alternative IPR norms to mitigate the negative effects of TRIPS. This, in turn, fueled interinstitutional competition within the IPR complex resulting in the dispersion of institutional authority and the gradual development of decentralized institutional topologies.

Before the start of the Uruguay negotiation process, the international regulation of IPRs was of no great concern to many governments. IPR issues were mainly dealt with—though to a very limited extent and rather noncommittally—under the umbrella of the WIPO, which administered the so-called Berne Convention, dating back to 1886, and the Paris Convention, dating back to 1883 (Guzman 2002: 948–9). While in the early 1980s, industrialized economies like the United States successfully fought off attempts by developing countries to weaken the patent-related obligations of the treaties underlying the WIPO, the hard and long-lasting negotiations made them conclude that raising intellectual property standards further within the WIPO framework was not a realistic goal (Helfer 2004: 20). Throughout the years that followed, especially the rapidly growing technology-based industries in many developed countries began to push for stricter and more binding international IPRs. With a continuously growing trade surplus in intellectual-property-reliant goods, which contrasted sharply with an overall trade deficit, US business advocacy networks pushed their government for internationally expanded and more strictly enforced IPRs (Sell and Prakash 2004: 157). These advocacy networks stressed that businesses were exposed to the negative effects of the existing institutional arrangements within the WIPO framework as these regulations would not be able to prevent the unlicensed use of intellectual property in developing countries. According to C. L. Clemente, then vice-president counsel of Pfizer, this form of "piracy" was getting out of hand: "Why is it that another government can base a policy of helping the consumers in their country to steal foreign owned technology?" (quoted in Weissman 1996: 1088).

Another problem for technology-based industries in developed countries with regard to the existing IPR institutions was that cooperation within these frameworks was far from universal. Not only did several important newly industrializing countries like India, Singapore, or Taiwan not participate in the agreements,[4] many states only selectively ratified the provisions of the Berne and Paris Conventions, thereby making "it difficult to determine the exact obligations between two member states" (Emmert 1990: 1337). For these developing countries, institutionalized cooperation aimed at the establishment of internationally enforceable IPRs was considered costly and associated with strongly negative consequences: For them, patent protection was seen as "an obstacle to technology transfer, which they need for development and enhancing their capacity to undertake research leading to patentable inventions of their own" (Adede 2003: 30). For a long time, developing and newly industrializing countries thus anticipated the high costs of institutionalized cooperation on IPRs and shied away from legally binding commitments.

Throughout the unfolding negotiations on the intake of stricter IPR rules to the General Agreement on Tariffs and Trade (GATT) framework in the context of the Uruguay Round (1986–94), a broad coalition of industrialized states led by the US worked at emphasizing and increasing the costs for noncooperators by explicitly framing institutionalized IPR cooperation as a prerequisite for further trade facilitations from which noncooperators would be excluded. They also successfully framed internationally binding IPRs as a normatively desirable goal and a mandatory prerequisite for fair and balanced trading agreements. Noncooperators were thereby at least indirectly accused of producing "broader negative effects on U.S. competitiveness, its trade balance, and American jobs" (Sell and Prakash 2004: 158). Consequently, only those states that committed themselves to IPR agreements should be allowed to profit from trade facilitations and enhanced access to the important sales markets in developed states: Agreeing to the institutionalization of strong IPRs was thus directly linked to an enhanced potential for economic growth (Adede 2003: 31–2). Only states that agreed to strong IPR rules within the GATT negotiations were to profit from trade privileges offered by club members; states that remained outside the proposed IPR framework would be excluded from privileged trade relationships and, even worse, were to experience the strongly negative consequences of nonparticipation.

Those states especially that were initially strongly reluctant to accommodate the demands of the industrialized states for stricter IPRs were increasingly pressured with threats of trade sanctions if they continued to resist enhanced IPR protection within the GATT framework. In 1988, the US Trade Representative (USTR) put several emerging economies such as India and Taiwan, which were not part of the Paris Conventions and were blocking the intake of IPRs to GATT negotiations, on its "Special 301 watch list" threatening to impose trade sanctions if these countries did not revise their patent laws accordingly (Weissman 1996: 1078). The only remaining way for many of the affected developing countries to mitigate these negative effects of nonparticipation was to join the proposed club of IPR cooperators as "compliance with TRIPS … [could effectively] shelter the foreign party [from US sanctions]" (Finger and Nogues 2002: 336).

Not only did these threats of sanctions by the US expose the negative consequences of nonparticipation, developing countries further saw themselves increasingly confronted with the concrete risk of a complete breakdown of the Uruguay Negotiation Round if they blocked the inclusion of IPRs into the trade talks any longer. Especially for developing and emerging economies, this was perceived as an unacceptable negative consequence of remaining outside the proposed IPR institution as they perceived it to be of the highest importance to "remain in the multilateral system rather than be caught in the middle of an impending trade war that might result in due to the failure of GATT … [which] calls for a '"fair"' and possibly a uniform standard of patent protection laws" (Patnaik 1992: 37). For them, solving IPR disputes multilaterally appeared to be a better solution than unilateral bargaining with powerful industrialized states, which is why membership of the IPR club was considered a promising way of getting a "multilateral mechanism for dispute settlement that would avoid unilateral actions by developed countries" (Correa 2000: 11). To protect themselves from unilateral action by powerful states, they considered it a lesser evil to join the proposed IPR institution. Albeit anxious about the costs of an enhanced IPR commitment, they considered it to be less costly than sticking to a strategy of refraining from cooperation that was associated with the risk of being excluded from the club of respected and privileged trading nations.

Confronted with the severely negative consequences associated with noncooperation and recognizing that they had simply "[run] out of alternatives and options … [because] if they did not negotiate multilaterally they would each have to face the United States alone" (Drahos 2002: 774), developing and emerging countries finally gave up their resistance and agreed to put IPRs on the Uruguay Negotiation Round's agenda. The negotiations that ensued were marked by only very minor and modest concessions from the developed countries to developing economies and TRIPS negotiations were essentially already completed by the end of 1991 (Singh 2006: 70). Developing and emerging countries thus conceived of their decision to agree upon stricter IPR rules within the WTO framework as a necessary evil to avoid the threat of exclusion from important trade clubs and being at the mercy of unilateral actions by the US from which they perceived they would only be protected within the institutional framework providing IPRs.

When the agreement finally became effective in 1995, many developing and emerging countries had already begun to express their discontent with its provisions and, as many of them had been pushed into the agreement by the prohibitively negative consequences of noncooperation, they started to intensify their cooperative efforts to mitigate the negative impacts of TRIPS obligations on their economies by drawing up alternative, especially more flexible IPR rules outside of the WTO/TRIPS environment. One of the most profound problems for developing countries was that the obligations codified in the agreement prevented patients in developing countries—especially HIV/AIDS patients—from accessing vital drugs (Kalantzis-Cope 2016: 6; Daßler et al. 2019: 595–6). So, from the mid-1990s onwards, a coalition of emerging countries under the leadership of Brazil and South Africa forcefully pushed for an institutionalized solution to this essential public health issue within the framework of the World Health Organization (WHO) (Viana 2002: 311; Helfer 2004: 42). They argued that the negative consequences of TRIPS on the ability of states to address domestic public health issues needed to be addressed within and by the WHO.

As a result, the WHO did indeed gradually intensify and expand its institutional activities with regard to IPRs. In its so-called "revised drug strategy" it decided to undertake the "monitoring and analysis of the impact of trade agreements on essential drugs in partnership with four WHO collaborating centers ... [and to] monitor all relevant issues under discussion at WTO that may have implications for the health sector" (WHO 2001: 4). Moreover, in 2003, on the initiative of the public health coalition of developing and emerging countries, the WHO decided to formally institutionalize the monitoring of negative consequences of IPRs for public health provisions by WHO members by establishing a whole new body with the exclusive task of examining the effect of IPRs on the development of new drugs and also allowing proposals to be formulated to review TRIPS in the future (WHO 2003; Helfer 2004: 44). Thus, in order to mitigate the negative effects of TRIPS, which they had been forced to join due to their exposure to the strongly negative externalities associated with noncooperation on the issue of IPRs, developing and emerging countries gradually undermined the TRIPS agreement by shifting policy-related authority towards an alternative institution, the WHO.

Another issue for many emerging and developing countries regarding the undesirable adverse effects of the TRIPS agreement concerned the "patentability" of biological resources. Especially those developing nations with rich and diverse biological resources at their disposal argued that the TRIPS agreement would allow industrialized states to unrestrictedly grant patents on genetic resources thereby aggravating their efforts to protect those resources as well as their own commercial use of them within their very own borders (Helfer 2004: 28–9; Dutfield 2010). As formulated by then President Ali Hassan Mulinyi of Tanzania:

> [m]ost of us in developing countries find it difficult to accept the notion that bio-diversity should [flow freely to industrial countries] while the flow of biological products from industrial countries is patented, expensive and considered private property of the firms that produce them. This asymmetry reflects the inequality of opportunity and is unjust. (Mulinyi, quoted in Jacoby and Weiss 1997: 89)

To mitigate these risks of an exploitation of their biological resources by industrialized states enabled by TRIPS provisions, a coalition of developing and emerging countries under the leadership of China and India subsequently called for institutionalized solutions to this problem outside of the WTO/TRIPS framework. For them, the Convention on Biological Resources (CBD) which was established in 1992, provided a possibility to pursue IPR norms that contrasted with those of the TRIPS agreement, presenting an institutional alternative capable of mitigating the adverse effects of TRIPS on the use of their biological resources. India especially, a country with very rich biological diversity and knowledge of the traditional use of such resources, acted to further strengthen the provisions of the CBD, which, it considered, "give better protection to the rights of developing countries [than TRIPS]" (Kruger 2001: 172). Indeed, in contrast to TRIPS, the CBD formulated concrete rights for biodiversity-rich states to "control genetic resources within their borders and to determine conditions of access to them. Access may be granted only upon mutually agreed terms and subject to the prior informed consent of the state providing the resources" (Helfer 2004: 31). Together with China and several NGOs with a focus on the protection of biodiversity, India subsequently pushed for the institutionalization and reinforcement of these norms contrary to those of TRIPS by formulating rules and guidelines for affected members to the CBD. These attempts were ultimately successful when, in 2001, the CBD's Convention of Parties (COP) decided to establish a working group of experts to address the relationship between IPRs as formulated by TRIPS and the regulation of access to and benefits from the use of genetic and biological resources (Helfer 2004: 33).

This working group's conclusions and proposals were finally also formally implemented within the so-called "Bonn Guidelines on Access to Genetic Resources and Fair and Equitable Sharing of the Benefits Arising out of their Utilization," which were adopted by the CBD's Sixth COP in 2002. The guidelines reflect the CBD member states' ambition to counter the negative consequences of TRIPS on developing countries' ability to use and protect biological resources within their domestic context by stressing the need to:

> provide capacity-building to guarantee the effective negotiation and implementation of access and benefit-sharing arrangements, especially to developing countries ... [and to] contribute to the development by Parties of mechanisms and access and benefit-sharing regimes that recognize the protection of traditional knowledge, innovations and practices of indigenous and local communities ... [by means of i.a.] [m]easures to encourage the disclosure of the country of origin of the genetic resources and of the origin of traditional knowledge, innovations and practices of indigenous and local communities in applications for intellectual property rights. (CBD 2002)

Reflecting the interests of developing and emerging countries, the institutional provisions of the Bonn Guidelines significantly strengthened the rights of "biological-resource-exporting" states vis-à-vis biotechnology industries from biological-resource-importing countries seeking to patent and commercialize such resources.

In the endeavor of the economically rising states Brazil and India, which both possessed large and diverse quantities of biological resources, the role of the CBD in global IPR governance was further expanded in the years that followed the implementation of the Bonn Guidelines. Under their leadership, a coalition of "Like-Minded Megadiverse Countries (LMMC)" successively pushed for more and even stronger benefit-sharing mechanisms under the CBD (Buck and Hamilton 2011: 48). With the support of several non-governmental environmental groups, which significantly raised the public's attention to the issue of an unregulated exploitation of biological resources by industrialized states' so-called "life industry" and against the fierce resistance of many developed states such as Japan, the US and also the EU, the LMMC were able to reach an agreement on the so-called Nagoya Protocol in 2010 (Wallbott et al. 2014: 36). The protocol further enhanced the CBD's authority in IPR governance: In contrast to TRIPS, it lays down concrete rules regarding access to genetic resources as well as benefit sharing (Kamau et al. 2010). Among other things, it gives provider countries (of biological resources) legal permission to restrict free access to their genetic resources and to require users (of biological resources) to share the benefits, while also committing providers to establishing comprehensible rules that give users legal certainty about the conditions of access and benefit sharing (Kamau et al. 2010; Daßler et al. 2019: 605). At least partially, this institutional "Access and Benefit Sharing" (ABS) mechanism thus allowed developing and emerging economies to mitigate the negative effects of TRIPS on their ability to regulate the use of their biological and genetic resources. As institutionalized cooperation on IPRs was essentially pursued in the form of an exclusive club with privileges only for states that cooperated, developing and emerging states had to agree to TRIPS to avoid the harmful and severely negative economic consequences associated with being excluded from that club. This, in turn, gave significant impetus to interinstitutional competition within the complex of IPR governance as it dramatically raised incentives especially for developing countries to engage in counter-institutionalization.

As the episodes leading to the strengthening and intensification of the WHO's as well as the CBD's involvement in global IPR governance have shown, developing countries were indeed partially successful in their attempts to shift IPR authority to alternative institutions outside the WTO framework. They successfully established new IPR rules and expanded the existing ones underlying the CBD through the implementation of the Bonn Guidelines and the institutionalization of the Nagoya Protocol, thereby creating norms that aimed at countering the negative effects of TRIPS in respect of the unregulated patentability of biological and genetic resources within their domestic realms. And they brought about the establishment of a new institutional body within the WHO explicitly aimed at monitoring the negative consequences of TRIPS on the provision of public health in developing countries and formulating reform proposals to mitigate these negative effects.

The very nature of global IPR governance, which is premised on the provision of club rather than public goods with exclusive benefits for participating states but seriously negative consequences for noncooperating states created a comparatively competitive environment with regard to institutionalized cooperation: The threat of being excluded from important institutional benefits had pushed developing and emerging states into institutionalized cooperation in providing rules that were essentially bad for them. To mitigate these negative effects, in the years following the establishment of the TRIPS agreement they strove to find opportunities to transfer the issue of IPR governance to alternative institutions, which would offer them the opportunity to create alternative IPR norms to allow for a partial mitigation of the negative consequences of TRIPS.

Thus, after joining TRIPS to avoid being denied the trade club membership they desperately needed and unilateral sanctions by powerful IPR proponents, it became highly attractive for these states to engage in counter-institutionalization outside the focal IPR institutions, TRIPS and WIPO, in order to promote and strengthen the authority of an alternative IPR institution, which significantly intensified interinstitutional competition within the complex. This, in turn, exerted centrifugal effects on the underlying institutional complex as it gradually undermined the authority of the so far focal institutions, the WIPO and TRIPS, while redistributing authority towards alternative institutional arrangements like the CBD, the WHO, and the FAO, which provided them with the ability to institutionalize alternative and, especially, more flexible and less strict IPR norms and rules.

Considering the conflicting rather than compatible IPR norms underlying the various institutions engaged in the policy field, it appears highly likely that interinstitutional competition will intensify in the foreseeable future. As they are increasingly confronted with the institutionalization of competing arrangements promoting more flexible IPR norms, the proponents of strict and binding IPR rules have begun to foster alternative venues for cooperation: To counter the exceptions and flexibilities provided by, e.g., the CBD and the WHO, developed countries have themselves begun to shift IPR cooperation back to WIPO and, more forcefully, to highly exclusive forms of cooperation, for instance via bi- and minilateral trade agreements in which they formulate even stricter IPRs than those enshrined in TRIPS (see, e.g.,Sell 2010b; Helfer 2009).

Tax Avoidance and the Nonexcludability of Institutional Benefits: Trading Institutional Weakness for Centrality

In the issue area of tax avoidance, the nonexcludability of institutional benefits played a crucial role in the OECD member states' struggle to establish and expand more binding and encompassing institutions. Although the OECD had deepened its cooperation on the issue including more internal rules among member states, non-OECD members like Panama, the Cook Islands, or Macau continuously declined any participation in their initiatives but acted as "renegade states" (Eden and Kudrle 2005). Rather than feeling any incentives to join the OECD's institutional projects or to create alternative institutions by themselves, for a long time they benefitted from the OECD's regulatory efforts without having to bear any costs. Most importantly, they profited substantially from transnational firms' tax evasion practices in response to higher tax rates in OECD jurisdictions (Kudrle 2008). In response to higher rates in many OECD states, there were huge capital shifts in particular to small tax havens (Slemrod and Wilson 2009). Due to this "competitive self-restraint" by the OECD members, among nonmembers, there were no incentives to strengthen alternative tax avoidance institutions either, which, in turn, strongly mitigated institutional competition in the field. Moreover, institutional competition was further hampered by the fact that the OECD actively engaged in efforts to create a more encompassing tax regime by "buying nonmembers in," thereby weakening alternative institutional arrangements that had emerged over time, like the UN Tax Committee regional institutions such as the Intra-European Organization of Tax Administrations (IOTA).

Since the early 1990s at the latest, however, the OECD has been intensifying its efforts to tackle this growing issue of noncooperation by tax havens (see Rixen 2008b; Lesage and van de Graaf 2015: 84–5). In 1998 it introduced concrete measures to intensify international cooperation beyond its members by creating the international "Forum on Harmful Tax Practices" (OECD 1998: 52–5). Most importantly, the Forum explicitly aimed at including noncooperators as it intended "that nonmember countries ... [should be] associated with the recommendations to the extent possible ... [and] to ensure that the application of the guidelines by member countries will not simply result in the displacement of investment to harmful preferential regimes in nonmember countries" (Weiner and Ault 1998: 607). These considerations clearly indicate that the OECD was aware of the free-riding problem associated with institutionalized cooperation on tax avoidance. Simultaneously, the cautiously formulated ambitions also indicate that the organization was aware that the incentives for nonmembers to cooperate were prohibitively low. The OECD consequently needed to design its institutional arrangement in a way that made it more attractive for nonmembers to cooperate instead of simply abstaining from the institution's tax avoidance initiatives while still benefitting from their effects: They had to trade institutional weakness for nonmembers' participation.

For a long time, economically less powerful states favored the so-called UN Tax Model, including more source-based taxation, which corresponded with their economic interests more than the OECD tax model favoring residence-based taxation, which corresponded more with capital-exporting interests (Baistrocchi 2013: 17). Furthermore, among non-OECD countries, pursuing cooperation on tax matters via the United Nation's Tax Committee was perceived to be more legitimate, due to the UN's universal membership and the fact that it provides an equal voice to economically weaker countries (Lesage and van de Graaf 2015: 86). It was only in the light of severe tax scandals involving banks in Switzerland and Lichtenstein and the aggravating financial crisis throughout the years 2008–9 that a group of 17 OECD members led by France and Germany called upon reinforcing efforts for multilateral cooperation within and beyond the OECD framework (Lesage 2010: 2–3). Not only were many countries interested in securing their tax revenues in view of the escalating sovereign debt crisis, the issue of Tax Avoidance was also directly linked to the outbreak of the crisis as "[t]ax havens were depicted at least as permissive causes of the crisis" (Lesage 2010: 2). With the explicit endorsement of the more diverse G20 (Group of 20 Heads of State 2009), in 2009 the OECD reinforced its efforts to establish institutionalized cooperation on tax matters beyond its own limited group of members. By reorganizing its "Global Forum on Transparency and Exchange of Information for Tax Purposes" into a nonbinding institutional arrangement that was "open to all states and [had] a clearly defined purpose" (Kudrle 2014: 205), the OECD aimed to coopt reluctant nonmembers that had so-far ridden free on their tax-rate-increasing policies.

To incentivize reluctant nonmembers to participate in the proliferation of its public good, the OECD offered them benefits in exchange for institutional participation. They offered significant material and immaterial support to nonmember states, e.g., through the "OECD-SAT Multilateral Tax Centre," the first of its kind set up outside the OECD world in which "OECD tax specialists … train local taxation civil servants" (Clifton and Diaz-Fuentes 2014: 262). Through this center, the OECD aimed inter alia at supporting "a consistent implementation of BEPS outcomes [i.e., the OECD project aiming to tackle Base Erosion and Profit Shifting (BEPS)] for the benefit of developing countries with almost ten events per year" (OECD 2018: 37). Thus, the OECD aimed to guide nonmembers towards implementing their epistemic standards and norms, thereby reducing incentives for these states to cooperate on tax matters outside of the OECD environment. China in particular clearly recognized the benefits associated with intensified cooperation under the proposed OECD frameworks. In 2017, China joined the Multilateral Convention to Implement Tax Treaty Related Measures to Prevent BEPS (MLI), which, according to the OECD, marked a milestone in the areas of tax transparency and compliance indicating China's efforts to become a leading actor in the definition and implementation of international tax policies (OECD 2017: 37). Tax collaboration with the OECD allowed China and many other emerging countries to "benefit from the OECD standards on tax governance and modernize ... [their] own anti-tax evasion system" (Zhu 2016: 4). Thus, by acknowledging the nonexcludability of institutional benefits associated with its institutional efforts against tax avoidance, the OECD was seeking to ensure the participation of nonmembers in its tax avoidance projects by offering them exclusive privileges. The organization aimed at guiding them towards the implementation of OECD standards while at the same time reducing incentives for these states to engage in the development of conflicting standards by initiating cooperation on tax matters outside of the OECD environment. Thus, the OECD pursued a strategy of trading privileges for institutional support and centrality.

Moreover, the OECD put strong emphasis on the fact that its cooperative arrangements with nonmembers were soft-law instruments (OECD 2015: 5). This lack of an adequate enforcement mechanism allowed states to join the OECD's arrangements without having to fear any sovereignty costs (Grinberg 2016: 166). Especially towards China, the OECD relaxed its demands so as not to endanger its participation in its projects. In 2009, when the OECD Tax Centre reinforced its efforts against tax avoidance by publishing a list of "noncooperative" tax havens including Hong Kong and Macau, China put its cooperation with the OECD on tax matters on hold. China's annoyance was so great that they eventually insisted on excluding the OECD from the G20 summit in London in March 2009 (Clifton and Diaz-Fuentes 2014: 73–4). The OECD hastily removed both Hong Kong and Macau from its tax haven list to ensure China's future participation in the organization's tax initiatives. This concession was finally crowned by success. In 2013 China signed the OECD's "Multilateral Convention on Mutual Administrative Assistance in Tax Matters," which provides an inclusive framework enabling participating countries to swiftly implement the automatic exchange of tax information (OECD 2013). The convention was widely considered a great success and was strongly endorsed by the G8 and the G20 respectively. As claimed by the OECD itself, the Convention "is the most comprehensive multilateral instrument available for all forms of tax co-operation to tackle tax evasion and avoidance" (OECD 2019d) and, as of October 2019, has 130 jurisdictions formally participating (OECD 2019d).

The OECD also intensified its accommodation towards nonmembers through its Base Erosion and Profit Shifting (BEPS) project which "provides 15 Actions that equip governments with the domestic and international instruments needed to tackle tax avoidance" (OECD 2019b). While, for its member states, the OECD considers the implementation of the minimum standards of this package as obligatory, several nonmember states, though actively involved in the development of these standards, were merely "invited" to implement them by becoming "BEPS Associates" (Christians 2016: 1603). Embodied in its "BEPS package" the OECD "provides 15 Actions that equip governments with the domestic and international instruments needed to tackle tax avoidance" (OECD 2019e). This indicates the OECD's awareness of the free riding problem that would have arisen if members had implemented the initiative alone. The organization aimed at courting noncooperators by involving them in the deliberation process thereby increasing the likelihood that they would actually implement the BEPS standards, while at the same time "maintaining the position that the organization is not imposing any rules on sovereign states" (Christians 2016: 1608). Because of increasing tax rates and further policy instruments then implemented by OECD members, nonmembers would have become an even more attractive destination for corporate capital.

The uncertain legal status of the institutional arrangements offered to nonmembers by the OECD further allowed them to be "opportunistic about their decision to cooperate or remain autonomous in specific tax policy matters" (Christians 2016: 1616). Simultaneously, the inclusion of institutional outsiders in the agenda-setting and policy-formulation stage of the project allowed nonmembers to shape the conditions under which BEPS cooperation took place, thereby reducing their incentives to strengthen institutional alternatives. China, for instance, used its hosting of the G20 summit in 2016 to present and underscore its ideas on relevant measures against BEPS, which were eventually added to the final policy package (Avi-Yonah and Xu 2018: 4–5). Indeed, "China's influence on BEPS outcomes is presumably evidenced by the inclusion of location savings and specific market advantages in the Action 8 Deliverable (2014) [… which] recognizes that features of the geographic market in which business operations occur, i.e., location savings and other local market advantages or disadvantages can affect comparability and arm's length prices" (Li 2016: 20). Thus, the BEPS project initiated by the OECD clearly reflected Chinese interests, underscoring the determination of the organization to make China one of the key partners in developing the BEPS agenda. These efforts were ultimately successful as China has gradually become "one of [the] most active countries in endorsing its obligations under the BEPS project" (Avi-Yonah and Xu 2018: 23). Also regarding the overall number of participants, BEPS can clearly be considered a success for the OECD. By late 2019, even tax havens like Macau, Monaco, Luxembourg, Anguilla, Bermuda, Liberia, Hong Kong, and the Cook Islands had joined the initiative (OECD 2019f). The participation of these states in the project seems especially remarkable as they had been extremely uncooperative with regard to international tax issues for such a long time and had even been characterized as renegade states in the international tax system, as their "tax practices [were] salient to the regime and [their] behavior [did] not comply with the regime's descriptive norms and practices" (Eden and Kudrle 2005: 106).

The G20 strongly supported the OECD's leading role in the context of BEPS from 2013 at the latest when the leaders stated in their final declaration that they "fully endorse[d] the ambitious and comprehensive Action Plan—originated in the OECD—aimed at addressing base erosion and profit shifting with mechanisms to enrich the Plan as appropriate ... welcome[d] the establishment of the G20/OECD BEPS project and ... encourage[d] all interested countries to participate" (G20 2013). By catering to the interests of important nonmember states and thereby further reducing the attractiveness of other institutional options, the OECD was able to fortify its position within the institutional complex of tax avoidance: Due to the nonexcludability of benefits stemming from the OECD's cooperative efforts to reduce harmful tax competition, nonmembers were able to free ride on the competitive advantages associated with OECD members' formal commitments. The OECD thus had to accommodate the interests of nonmembers to ensure their participation. It was ultimately successful, but only at the cost of trading institutional privileges and weakness for institutional support as many nonmembers joined its soft institutional arrangements like the Global Forum or BEPS.

In fact, it appears that it was precisely because of its strong emphasis on its self-image as a "purveyor of soft law" (Christians 2016: 1614) that the OECD was able to fortify and even expand its central role within the institutional complex of tax avoidance. In a policy field in which nonparticipants cannot per se be excluded from institutional benefits, in order to be successful, institutions providing public goods need to offer forms of cooperation that are more attractive than noncooperation. Offering soft and nonbinding institutional arrangements to nonmember states combined with substantial capacity-building support can be, as the case of the OECD's tax avoidance initiatives demonstrates, one solution to this problem. On the other hand, the OECD was forced to trade institutional support for institutional weakness: The predominantly soft and nonbinding instruments come with serious enforcement problems. While the OECD offered access to information-sharing mechanisms and substantial material support to persuade nonmembers to cooperate, the substantial institutional concession agreed with nonmembers can be considered rather limiting. The nonbinding character of the OECD's institutional arrangements means that "legal uncertainty concerns" (Eberhartinger and Petutschnig 2015: 23) among practitioners responsible for surveilling and implementing the OECD guidelines and recommendations are very likely to arise. Regarding the policy field's propensity for interinstitutional competition, one likely effect is certainly that it becomes even less attractive for states to foster forms of institutionalized cooperation outside the OECD framework. By catering to the interests of important nonmember states and thereby further hampering institutional competition, the OECD was able to fortify its central position within the institutional complex of tax avoidance. Due to the nonexcludability of benefits associated with cooperation on the issue, it had to accommodate the interests of nonmembers to ensure their participation. It was ultimately successful, but only at the cost of trading institutional privileges and weakness for institutional support as many nonmembers joined its soft institutional arrangements like the Global Forum or BEPS.

It appears very likely that the OECD will not only remain the uncontested center of cooperation for states engaging in the issue area of tax avoidance, but that it will further expand and fortify its position as an "informal World Tax Organization" (Cockfield 2005) which uses "nonbinding but persuasive methods to curate the international tax order as we recognize it today" (Christians 2016: 1614). Within the policy field of tax avoidance, due to its low propensity to interinstitutional competition, incentives for states to create and sustain credible alternative forms of institutionalized cooperation independent from, or even contrary to, the OECD regime are very low. Any attempts to counter the OECD's centrality within the tax avoidance regime complex will be further impeded if the organization continues to be successful in establishing accommodative, inclusive, and soft institutional arrangements like BEPS or the Global Forum in line with nonmembers' interests. If these arrangements maintain their soft and nonbinding character, nonmembers will continue to avoid the costs of joining newly created more binding and effective institutions while selectively committing themselves to, or opportunistically defecting from, the OECD's soft rules. Consequently, the low propensity for competition in the field works against the goals of the proponents of more effective and legally binding institutional instruments aimed at the reduction of harmful tax avoidance. Table 5.3 summarizes the findings of the previous two empirical sections.

Conclusion

This chapter has provided a comparative analysis of the institutional topologies underlying the international regime complexes of tax avoidance and intellectual property protection. It began by laying out the key similarities

Table 5.3 The Excludability/Nonexcludability of Institutional Benefits in the Policy Fields of Tax Avoidance and Intellectual Property Rights—Empirical Observations

Structural Characteristics	Policy Field	Tax Avoidance	Intellectual Property Rights
Empirical evidence for the (non-) excludability of institutional benefits and mechanisms of institutional (non-) competition		*Nonexcludability:* Nonmembers profit from institutionalized cooperation by the OECD by free riding on the members' commitment to refrain from undertaxation while at the same time receiving support with their own tax-related capacity building aimed at increasing tax revenues. *Nonexcludability:* To ensure participation by nonmembers, the OECD provides access to information exchange mechanisms without insisting on any formal commitments by nonmembers. The OECD's predominantly soft instruments offered to nonmembers allow for selective cooperation without inflicting any sovereignty costs on nonmembers. ***Pressure on institutional members to accommodate nonmembers to avoid free riding; (dis)incentives to engage in the creation or support of alternative institutions.***	*Excludability:* Nonmembers of the WIPO treaties and states that refuse to institutionalize cooperation on IPRs during the Uruguay Round were denied access to essential trade markets. Nonmembers of the IPR club received less foreign investment and were excluded from trade privileges offered to IPR cooperators. *Excludability:* Only TRIPS members were shielded from unilateral sanctions like the US "301 watch list." Multilateral dispute resolution mechanisms to solve trade conflicts were denied to nonparticipants ("Shielding function" of TRIPS). ***Pressure on nonmembers to join IPR institutions to avoid exclusion; incentives to engage in the creation or support of institutional alternatives.***
Institutional Competition within the Complex		Attractiveness of soft and nonbinding OECD arrangements further reduces incentives for nonmembers to strengthen alternative institutions or to create new alternative arrangements. ***Limited institutional competition.***	Developing and emerging states were forced to join TRIPS undertaking obligations against their interests. To counter these negative effects, developing and emerging states increasingly engaged in regime shifting and counter-institutionalization. ***Extensive institutional competition.***
Institutional Topology		Centralization	Decentralization

between the cooperation issues states face in both areas. In both policy fields, institutions are set up to regulate the (re)distribution of economic revenue. Both issues are further characterized by strong interest divergences between economically powerful, industrialized states on the one side, and economically less developed states on the other. In both issue areas, the material and political hurdles to setting up international institutions to address the underlying policy challenges are only moderate, although, again in both fields, there are enforcement mechanism that complicate the design necessary to establish functioning institutions. Both issue areas also share an absence of significant network effects. In both fields, in fact, the incentives for states that have an interest in the (non)regulation of the issue to participate diminish as the number of cooperating states increases. The potential economic gains associated with being the sole tax haven in the system (in the case of tax avoidance), or the only jurisdiction that provides legal scope for counterfeiting or copying industries (in the case of intellectual property protection), tend to increase rather than decrease the more potential competitor jurisdictions decide to join institutions that regulate tax avoidance or IPRs.

However, the chapter also demonstrated that both issues differ significantly regarding the (non-) excludability of institutional benefits derived from the cooperation of others. In the case of tax avoidance, states can free ride on the cooperative efforts of others. In the issue area of IPRs the contrary is the case. Noncooperation is associated with significant costs that force states to join, even if cooperation on IPRs is against their interests. Due to the absence of major barriers to entry and network effects, however, there are strong incentives to engage in counter-institutionalization and the strengthening of alternative, less stringent IPR institutions. The resulting dynamics, it has been argued, result in long-term centripetal effects on institutional topologies in the case of tax avoidance, and long-term centrifugal effects in the case of intellectual property. The ensuing comparative network analysis of interinstitutional structures underlying both regime complex corroborates these theoretical expectations. While the networks underlying the issue area of tax avoidance are strongly centralized, with the OECD as the clear-cut institutional center, the networks underlying the issue area of IPRs are significantly more fragmented. Here, both WTO/TRIPS and WIPO face several alternative international institutions with comparably central positions. The qualitative analysis of institutionalization processes within the issue area of IPR demonstrates that this more decentralized structure was strongly influenced by the costs of excludability. Even though it was against their interests, many developing countries were forced to join TRIPS to avoid exclusion from trade networks. At the same time, they were incentivized to strengthen alternative IPR institutions where they pushed for the institutionalization of IPR exceptions and more flexible rules. The case study of institutionalization processes in the issue area of tax avoidance demonstrates the opposite institutional dynamics. Here, the nonexcludability of institutional benefits forced those states interested in the regulation of taxation to accommodate non-cooperators. They faced no costs as a result of abstention but rather the opposite, economic incentives to refrain from joining the OECD's initiative. Consequently, in the field of tax avoidance, strong centripetal dynamics strengthened the OECD as the most central and comparatively uncontested institution in the complex, but this centrality came at the cost of institutional weakness, as cooperators had to buy nonmembers in and provide them with flexibility and other institutional privileges.

Notes

1. See also pp. 123–24 of this book explaining the high network effects in the policy field of financial stability. With increasing numbers of cooperating states, the utility derived from financial stability institutions increases strongly, thereby creating incentives for states to foster cooperation universally rather than regionally.
2. A description of the case selection logic and the operationalization, additional robustness checks, as well as a list of the documents gathered for each institution, can be found in Appendix A.
3. For the policy field of tax avoidance, I consulted the OCED dataset on Statutory Corporate Income Tax Rates to identify 17 states with the relatively lowest CIT rates and 19 states with the relatively highest CIT rates, as reported for the year 2018 (OECD 2019c). For the policy field of intellectual property protection, I consulted the WIPO dataset on total patent applications (direct and PCT national phase entries) to identify 33 states with the highest total number of patent applications, as reported for the year 2017 (WIPO 2019b); I further checked these figures against the latest ranking provided by the WIPO ranking of total IP filing activity by country for the year 2017 (WIPO 2018: 8–9). Note that, if a certain state terminated its membership of an institution within the period of observation (2013–18), the IO–state relationship was coded "0" in terms of membership. This ensures that the membership networks reflect the most recent patterns of institutionalized state cooperation, i.e., membership status in the analyzed institution by the end of the year 2018.
4. At the beginning of the Uruguay Round in 1986, these countries were not signatory parties to the Berne Union (see Emmert 1990: 1340).

6

The Benefits and Disadvantages of Large-Scale Cooperation

Network Effects and the Topologies of the Regime Complexes of Financial Stability and Development Aid

This chapter explores the institutional topologies of the regime complexes of financial stability and development aid. While these prominent issues in international political economy share many characteristics, they exhibit decisive differences with respect to universal and large-scale cooperation incentives. In this chapter, I will argue that those differences lie in what economists refer to as network effects: increasing marginal utilities derived from cooperation with growing numbers of participants. Within regime complexes, network effects are present if larger numbers of cooperating states improve cooperative outcomes. I contend that network effects associated with cooperation on a particular political issue can create strong centripetal effects in regime complexes. They reduce the attractiveness of outside options, binding states to large-scale, universalistic institutions instead. In policy fields where cooperation among states is not associated with network effects, on the other hand, centrifugal forces tend to push institutionalization processes toward more pronounced institutional competition. All else being equal, if there are no network effects present, pursuing cooperation in the respective field via small-scale institutions or bilateral arrangements is an attractive alternative to large-scale and universal forms. States are thus incentivized to engage in counter-institutionalization or to cooperate via several arrangements simultaneously, favoring the evolution of decentralized institutional topologies in the issue area of global governance. In his book *Renegotiating the World Order: Institutional Change in International Relations* Lipscy (2017) demonstrates how the degree of interinstitutional competition in terms of barriers to entry and network effects within the policy fields of development aid and financial stability strongly influenced the way institutional privileges within the two "Bretton Woods" institutions, the World Bank (WB) and the International Monetary Fund (IMF), were renegotiated. While the

The Institutional Topology of International Regime Complexes. Benjamin Daßler, Oxford University Press.
© Benjamin Daßler (2023). DOI: 10.1093/oso/9780198881926.003.0006

IMF proved to be relatively rigid and inflexible regarding the redistribution of voting shares among member states in response to shifting economic power, the WB reacted much more flexibly and adaptively (Lispcy 2017: 63–90). In this chapter, I go beyond micro-level analysis of individual and institutional change and turn to the overall macro level. I analyze how the differences in network effects associated with institutional cooperation affect the overall topology of both regime complexes, noting that, in accordance with the theory's premise, the substantial differences in network effects associated with institutionalized cooperation should result in strongly diverging institutional topologies in them.

This chapter proceeds as follows. In line with the layout of the previous empirical section, I start with a definition of both policy areas. After that, I justify the case selection and the comparative research design underlying the chapter. First, I argue that these two policy fields are well suited for comparison, because of their similarities in respect not only of the economic and redistributive character of their underlying policy problems and conflicts but also of the market characteristics, barriers to entry and the excludability of benefits associated with cooperation on the issues. Second, I show that, despite these similarities, the policy fields differ significantly when it comes to the network effects associated with cooperation on the underlying policy issues: By drawing on, but also refining, Lipscy's (2017) conceptualization of network effects within the policy fields in question, I elaborate on these differences in greater detail.

Subsequently, I turn to my dependent variable of interest, the institutional topologies underlying both issue areas. I analyze and compare their underlying interinstitutional structures employing comparative network analyses. I conclude the chapter by complementing the structural assessments of both regime complexes with in-depth case studies of institutionalization processes in both policy fields. Drawing on qualitative evidence, I show that in the issue area of financial stability, there have been several attempts to establish regional alternative institutions to the IMF over the last few decades. However, states' awareness of substantial network effects has continuously mitigated interinstitutional competition, ultimately reinforcing the IMF's central position within the institutional complex. In the policy field of development aid, in strong contrast, due to the absence of network effects, states have strong incentives to create regional, specialized, and independent institutional alternatives to the WB. This chapter will highlight how these incentives led to more frequent and substantial challenges to the WB's central position in the development aid regime complex.

Similarities between the Policy Fields of Financial Stability and Development Aid

The issue areas of financial stability and development aid are particularly well suited to being used to compare the impact of network effects on the structure of their respective institutional complexes. This is because both policy fields are remarkably similar as regards their underlying fundamental problem with cooperation, and especially regarding the market characteristics of barriers to entry and the type of good provided by their institutions. At the same time, they differ significantly regarding the network effects associated with institutionalized cooperation on the two policy issues. This book's theory suggests that the degree of competition within an issue area, constraining or enabling institutionalized forms of cooperation among states, decisively shapes the institutional complex's underlying topology. Like the previous one, this chapter follows the logic of a most-similar-system design. I argue that the similarities between both policy fields regarding their fundamental economic problem with cooperation and especially regarding their market characteristics allow the influence of network effects on the topology of the two institutional complexes to be isolated.

In both issue areas, states tackle the consequences of disparate developments in national economies perceived as harmful to global economic growth. Intergovernmental cooperation within the policy field of development aid is pursued to provide development funding and assistance to economically less developed countries to reduce poverty, e.g., by financing projects which aim to improve the local economic or educational infrastructure, thereby stimulating growth within these economies (see, e.g., Lipscy 2015: 345; Groves and Hinton 2013; Hook and Rumsey 2016). Economically less developed countries from the Global South in particular rely heavily on foreign aid and investment to support their economies and improve the well-being of their citizens. Institutionalized forms of cooperation leverage collective resources and expertise to address common development challenges more effectively. Multilateral institutionalized cooperation within the policy field of development aid primarily takes the form of multilateral development banks (MDBs). These institutions are predominantly financed by their respective member states and, in the context of their everyday policy making, provide financial and technical support to their members (see, e.g., Faure et al. 2015: 10–14). MDBs typically pool financial and bureaucratic resources thereby increasing the amount of funding available for development projects. Moreover, they provide a source of financing for states with weak credit ratings and limited access to international capital markets. For the empirical analysis within this chapter, I thus conceive of an international institution as part of the policy area of development aid if its main policy objective is the provision of development funding and assistance to reduce poverty by stimulating economic growth in target countries.

In the policy field of financial stability, states also engage in multilateral cooperation to address macroeconomic issues: They foster cooperation via multilateral institutions to prevent or cope with financial crises and related balance of payments difficulties of their member states (Crockett 1997; Agosin 2001: 32; Weiss 2009: 4–5; Lipscy 2015: 345; Moschella 2010). More precisely, financial stability institutions are set up by their member countries to provide conditional loans to financially struggling members, thereby reducing the risk that locally limited financial crises spread to other member countries (Clark and Huang 2001: 6; Trachtman 2010: 721). These institutions are therefore designed as lenders of last resort, helping to prevent the spillover of financial shocks and associated potential widespread harm to the global economy. They are also created to provide policy advice and technical assistance to member countries, helping them implement economic policies that promote stability and growth. In general, institutionalized forms of cooperation on the issue of financial stability helps to promote a more stable and resilient global economy, which benefits all countries. For the empirical analysis in this chapter, I conceive of international institutions as part of the policy area of financial stability if the preservation of the financial stability of member countries belongs among their primary policy goals—goals they pursue by providing conditional loans to struggling member countries.

Both policy fields thus share the overarching goal of interstate cooperation to stabilize and promote economic prosperity on a global level. Moreover, in both issue areas achieving this general policy objective is perceived to be in the economic interests of both developing and industrialized states (see, e.g., Brown 2000; Widmaier 2003). Moreover, the policy areas of financial stability and development aid exhibit relatively high entry barriers. To establish institutionalized forms of cooperation, states in both areas need to have significant fiscal and political power at their disposal. To create institutions that manage accumulated financial reserves in order to provide conditional loans to members in the context of financial crises, states need huge financial capabilities (Desai and Vreeland 2011: 116; Lipscy 2017: 70). Countries that struggle with high sovereign debt and limited economic growth are dependent on foreign capital to create safeguards against cases of financial instability. Due to this lack of fiscal capabilities, the number of states with the potential to initiate and sustain international financial stability institutions is limited. The same holds for the policy field of development aid, where the initiation and maintenance of adequate multilateral development funds and institutions require large amounts of money, which, for many economically weak states, represents an insurmountable barrier to setting up MDBs without the support of powerful economies.

Within the policy field of financial stability, then, these comparatively high barriers to fostering institutionalized cooperation can be illustrated empirically by the protracted efforts of many Asian states to create an independent financial stability institution in response to the Asian Financial Crisis of the late 1990s. After several initiatives such as Japan's proposed Asian Monetary Fund (AMF) could not be implemented due to lack of political and financial support from China and the United States (Ciorciari 2011: 928), it was not until 2009 that the Chiang Mai Initiative (CMI) was established. Initially, the institution was created simply for bilateral swaps among the participating Asian countries; it was explicitly not designed as a fully-fledged monetary fund. Only when the emerging power China, together with Japan and South Korea, increased their political and financial contributions to the initiative did the CMI's institutionalization progress further. This progress led to the establishment of the ASEAN+3 Macroeconomic and Research Office (AMRO) in 2011, which serves as a surveillance facility for CMI members (see, e,g, Chabchitrchaidol et al. 2018; Haihong 2017; Grabel 2019: 56–7) and the doubling of the CMI's size from US$120 to 240 billion in 2012 (Loewen 2018: 110). Without these immense financial and political commitments by the three "currency reserve giants," South Korea, Japan, and China, the establishment of the CMI could not have been realized (Loewen and Hilpert 2010: 2–3). However, despite these strong efforts, the CMI remains strongly dependent on the IMF and cultivated close institutional ties with its legacy contender (Loewen 2014). The case of the CMI multilateralization thus illustrates the high barriers to states engaging in the establishment of institutionalized financial stability arrangements.

In the policy field of development aid, barriers to the initiation of institutionalized forms of cooperation exist not only in the form of the financial capacities required to cooperate on development projects. It is also crucial for states to have the technical and bureaucratic expertise provided by, for instance, domestic development NGOs or aid agencies to pursue development cooperation effectively (see, e.g., Dietrich 2016; Lundsgaarde 2012; Milner 2006). Besides these structural hindrances for states willing to engage in institutionalized development cooperation, there is another, more political barrier to engaging in multilateral development financing: the need for diplomatic leverage within the aid-recipient countries. In order to coordinate and pursue development aid projects effectively, states need political backing and a willingness to accept financial help on the part of the recipient state. Only where trust and institutionalized relations are established among donors and recipients can bi- or multilateral aid be pursued effectively (see, e.g., Parks et al. 2016; Minasyan 2016). For states that do not have this diplomatic leverage, establishing multilateral development aid institutions with the goal of financing projects in third countries is hardly possible. Since many states are without either the financial capabilities or the diplomatic leverage to institutionalize development cooperation, they frequently lack the "Go It Alone" power (Gruber 2001) to pursue cooperation via institutions outside existing institutional arrangements.

Institutions in the policy fields of financial stability and development aid are also similar as far as the type of good provided by their underlying institutions is concerned. In both issue areas, institutionalized cooperation aims at providing nonexcludable public goods, which means that the benefits of cooperation are not limited to institutional members but can also be enjoyed by institutional outsiders. The benefits of preserving financial stability during financial shocks are not limited to members of a particular institution (Kawai 2017: 312; Trachtman 2010: 721–2; Houben et al. 2004; Nieto and Schienasi 2007). States that are not part of an institutionalized financial stability arrangement still gain if conditional loans to a struggling state prevent contagion and spillover (Claessens and Forbes 2004; Trachtman 2010: 721). For nonparticipating states, an existing arrangement thus provides the opportunity to free ride, at least to some extent, on other states' provision of financial stability. The danger of adverse spillover effects in cross-border financial crises is reduced without nonparticipating states having to bear any costs. The same holds for multilateral development institutions where nonparticipating states still benefit from poverty alleviation, which stimulates overall economic growth and reduces the negative consequences of structural poverty for the rest of the world. This "free-riding" problem within the issue area of development aid, many scholars argue, has a negative effect on the overall willingness of especially small states to contribute financially, as they can free ride on the donations of others (Pincus 1965; Olson and Zeckhauser 1966; Mosley 1985; Chong and Gradstein 2008).

Why the Policy Fields of Financial Stability and Development Aid are Still Different: Varying Network Effects

As has been stated, the issue areas of development aid and financial stability exhibit significant similarities. In both, states tackle economic problems arising from an increasingly globalized world economy. In both, economically strong states pursue institutionalized forms of cooperation to contribute to economically weaker states' financial stabilization and economic development in order to sustain or improve economic growth. Both fields are also comparable in terms of the type of good provided by their underlying institutions and the barriers that restrict entry to their respective institution complexes. But they differ significantly regarding their respective propensity for interinstitutional competition. Building on Lipscy (2017), I argue that this is due to significant differences between the policy fields regarding the network effects associated with intergovernmental cooperation. As I will show in the subsequent sections of this chapter, the institutional complex of financial stability exhibits strong positive network effects for states seeking institutional cooperation, which means that the utility of institutionalized cooperation increases strongly the more states join an institution for that purpose. On the other hand, the issue area of development aid exhibits quite the opposite: institutionalized cooperation in this field is not associated with network effects. In this issue area, the utility stemming from cooperating on that issue decreases with the number of states that join in, which creates incentives for states to foster cooperation outside existing institutional arrangements.

The most important reason for the absence of network effects in the field of development aid is the political credit and leverage that states seek when cooperating on the issue (Lipscy 2017: 69). The higher the number of states participating in an arrangement that seeks to provide development assistance to target countries, the less visible and assignable is an individual country's contribution and hence, its political credit and leverage in the form of, e.g., political goodwill and changes in the policy stance of the recipient country or an enhanced position on its markets (Martens 2005: 652). This, in turn, spurs interinstitutional competition among states as pursuing institutional options outside large-scale, multilateral institutions becomes much more attractive.

Furthermore, with more participating states, the number of political interests that need to be considered when institutions pursue development projects increases, making it more challenging to decide on the recipients and targets of aid. This may significantly reduce the efficiency of aid allocation by an institution incentivizing states to pursue development goals via alternative, more regionally focused institutions. For states, it appears highly rational to pursue cooperation in development aid via many unrelated MDBs simultaneously, as there are no high costs simply additional benefits associated with "switching between institutions." Pursuing specific globally oriented development projects through the institutional framework of the World Bank does not restrict a member state's ability to pursue other, potentially more specialized and regionally focused projects via other MDBs.

On the other hand, cooperating on the issue of financial stability is associated with strong network effects: An institution's ability to prevent financial contagion and spillovers crucially hinges on the number of states participating (Lipscy 2017: 68–70). This is because the efficiency of a financial stability institution's policies in times of financial crisis strongly depends on its functional range. Quasi-universal institutions can quickly take measures in different countries affected by financial turmoil, thereby reducing the risk of contagion and spillover for so far unharmed member states. Institutions with only regional or small-scale membership, on the other hand, cannot effectively prevent contagion as their measures are limited to fewer states.

Moreover, as Lipscy (2017) convincingly argues, large-scale institutions set up in the issue area of financial stability provide political cover and the opportunity to shift blame for unpopular measures during financial crises (Lipscy 2017: 68–9). Regional or rather small-scale institutions cannot, in terms of membership, provide this kind of political cover, as responsibilities and thus attributed blame can be directed more clearly at the respective member states' governments. A good example is Germany's politics of blame diffusion during the European Sovereign Debt crisis in the late 2000s. As Schwarzer (2015) convincingly demonstrates, Germany's push for IMF involvement in the solution of the European Sovereign Debt crisis was strongly driven by considerations that "part of the responsibility for unpopular decisions to … implement tough conditionality" (Schwarzer 2015: 612) could be displaced onto this "external actor." Involving a large-scale and universal actor such as the IMF makes it easier to push through the tough and unpopular policy decisions necessary to tackle financial crises. Thus, the more universal and inclusive an institution set up to bail out struggling member countries, the more likely that member states' governments will be shielded from public blame for harsh austerity measures, whereas regionally limited, small-scale financial stability arrangements cannot provide this kind of political cover. Here, responsibilities can be attributed more directly to member states, especially the economically powerful member states that contribute large shares of potential bailout packages.

Taken together, while institutions in the issue area of financial stability benefit substantially from higher numbers of participating states, those in the field of development aid do not necessarily gain from higher numbers of participants, which tend rather to reduce an individual state's benefits from cooperation. Table 6.1 sums up these considerations regarding market characteristics in the fields of development aid and financial stability and further explicates the theory's expectations with respect to the underlying institutional topology of the institutional complexes: Within the institutional complex of financial stability, there should be a clear institutional center of authority; within that of development aid, however, authority can be expected to be distributed more evenly among several institutions.

As summarized in Table 6.1, the issue areas of development aid and financial stability are similar with regard to their broader goals of economic cooperation and, more importantly, their market characteristics, barriers to entry and the type of good provided by their institutions. However, they differ significantly regarding the network effects associated with institutionalized cooperation. While large numbers of institutional members substantially increase the utility of cooperation for states when it comes to safeguarding financial stability, large numbers of participating states in the field of development aid can even reduce the utility of cooperation for states. Network effects curb institutional competition as states seek cooperation via large-scale and rather universalistic institutions. Thus, network effects create centripetal effects as they bind states to existing, universalistic institutions and hamper the creation of alternative institutional arrangements. Therefore, my theory expects centralized interinstitutional topologies in the field of financial stability.

On the other hand, my theory expects the absence of network effects to reinforce institutional competition as states are not bound to large-scale and inclusive institutions but are incentivized to pursue cooperation via relatively small-scale and independent ones. If there are no network effects presents, policy fields thus tend to exhibit centrifugal effects as they increase the attractiveness of institutional alternatives outside of existing, potentially large-scale institutions. I thus expect the topology underlying the development aid complex to be more decentralized and fragmented.

I will empirically test this argument in two steps. In the first, and throughout the next part of this chapter, I compare the network structures among institutions within the regime complexes of financial stability and development aid to analyze the topologies underlying both institutional complexes. In the second step, I will analyze institutionalization processes within both institutional complexes to provide qualitative causal evidence for my theory. More precisely, the following section analyzes how the presence and absence of network effects have affected states' institutionalization efforts in both issue areas, thus exerting strong centripetal effects in the policy field of financial stability and centrifugal effects in the institutional complex of development aid. Strong network effects associated with cooperation on financial stability made it challenging to create credible and politically independent

Table 6.1 Market Characteristics of the Policy Fields of Development Aid and Financial Stability and the Expected Structure of their Institutional Complexes

Market characteristic / Issue Area	Barriers to Entry	Type of Good	Network Effects	Mechanisms of Competition and Expected Topology of the Institutional Complex
Development Aid	*Rather high:* - Institutions need large financial resources - Institutions need technical and bureaucratic expertise - Institutions need member states with diplomatic leverage to pursue development projects in third countries	*Nonexcludable:* + positive effects of cooperation for nonparticipating states: reduction of global poverty; stimulation of global economic growth	*No Network Effects:* - More participating states increase heterogeneity of interest impeding specialized and regionally focused development projects - Large numbers of participating states decrease individual states' ability to claim credit and gain political leverage in recipient states - Visibility of individual responsibilities taken on by states decreases as more states participate (*but is actually wanted!*)	*Less Centralized* States are not bound to universalistic forms of cooperation; outside options are attractive; *Centrifugal effects due to the absence of network effects*
Financial Stability	*Rather high:* - Institutions need large financial resources - Institutions need technical and bureaucratic expertise - Institutions need member states with high creditworthiness	*Nonexcludable:* + positive effects of cooperation for nonparticipating states: conditional loans to struggling countries prevent the spread of financial shocks	*Strong Network Effects:* + Large number of participating states increases the institution's ability to absorb financial shocks + Large number of participating states increases the institution's ability to provide political cover necessary to push through conditionalities and avoid moral hazard + Visibility of individual responsibilities taken by states decreases the more states participate (*and is also not wanted!*)	*More Centralized* States are tied to large-scale and inclusive forms of cooperation; outside options are oftentimes unattractive; *Centripetal effects due to the presence of strong network effects*

alternatives to the IMF. Conversely, the absence of network effects in the issue area of development aid spurred interinstitutional competition among states. Over time, the resulting more competitive environment led to various credible and independent institutional alternatives to the World Bank, such as the Asian Infrastructure Investment Bank (AIIB) and the New Development Bank (NDB).

Mapping Topologies: A Comparative Network Analysis of the Institutional Complexes of Financial Stability and Development Aid

In order to assess the topologies among multilateral institutions engaged in the policy fields of financial stability and development aid, like in the previous chapter, I propose to think of both complexes as social networks. Within these networks, the relative position of each institution not only determines its position in the underlying hierarchy of the regime complex but also determines the complex's overall structure. Areas dominated by one or a small number of central and inclusive institutions with other institutions operating in their shadows exhibit strongly centralized interinstitutional network structures. By contrast, issue areas where cooperation is pursued via many different and unrelated institutions exhibit much more decentralized interinstitutional network structures and hierarchies. In a nutshell, whether an institutional complex within a specific policy field is characterized by a high degree of fragmentation or a strongly centralized institutional topology is reflected in the network structure of institutions created by states to cooperate on a policy issue.

To further complement this measurement of institutional topologies, as in the previous empirical chapter, I also analyze the most relevant states' formal membership of the respective institutions in terms of their cooperative engagement in the policy field. To map these membership networks, I selected a sample of the states most active in intergovernmental policy coordination on the issue governing each policy field. The selection was based on quantitative criteria indicating the degree to which a particular state had a substantial interest in coordinating policy on the issue in question.[1]

Mapping the membership structure of the respective complex further allows me to control whether the reference network structure observed among the institutions in question also holds for states' membership within the field. This does not imply that institutions with a comparatively central position in their respective reference network are automatically expected to obtain a central position in the membership network of the institutional complex. Still, if the reference structures and the membership networks differ significantly, this will be an interesting empirical variance that will need explanation. Thus, mapping both the reference network among institutions and the underlying state membership network allows for a more robust measurement of topologies across different institutional complexes.

To analyze whether we observe variation regarding these structures within the issue areas of development aid and financial stability, I first identified the relevant institution within each of the two policy fields. To this end, I consulted several existing studies of the two issue areas and their underlying institutions. In the case of the development aid complex, I also consulted the OECD's Multilateral Development Finance database, which includes an extensive list of multilateral donor agencies (OECD 2019b). Furthermore, I used official statements by the institutions about alternative institutional arrangements to complement the sample of MDBs. The World Bank, for instance, provides a list of institutions that provide financial support to developing countries, including MBDs and other multilateral financial institutions on its website (World Bank 2018a). For the policy field of financial stability, the IMF has published a report about its engagement with other multilateral financial institutions where it lists those that were established to avert financial instability or due to dissatisfaction with the Fund's conditionality and concerns about its governance (see IMF 2013; Lipscy 2017: 75).

Based on these criteria, the following set of institutions was identified. Table 6.2 lists the selected institutions together with their respective year of creation.[2]

For this sample of development aid and financial stability institutions, I collected official institutional documents to map the reference networks underlying both regime complexes. These documents include, for example, official annual reports, reviews of institutional activities, reports on organizational events but also financial statements, statistical reports, and reflections on political strategies. Each time a particular institution is directly mentioned within an analyzed document, this constitutes a link between the institution mentioned and the institution from which the document was collected. The resulting network graphs thus represent the intensity and direction of reciprocal references among the international institutions involved during the period under observation.

As in the previous chapter, to minimize the effect of random events on the frequency of interinstitutional references, I collected documents covering several years. All documents collected for the institutions of the financial stability and development aid policy fields originate from 2013–18. Each

Table 6.2 International Institutions in the Policy Fields of Development Aid and Financial Stability

Development Aid	Institution	Year of Creation
	World Bank (WB)	1944
	Asian Development Bank (ADB)	1966
	African Development Bank (AFDB)	1963
	Asian Infrastructure Investment Bank (AIIB)	2016
	Arab Bank for Economic Development in Africa (BADEA)	1974
	Caribbean Development Bank (CDB)	1969
	Council of Europe Development Bank (CEB)	1956
	Development Bank of Latin America (CAF)	1968
	Eurasian Development Bank (EDB)	2006
	European Bank for Reconstruction and Development (EBRD)	1991
	European Investment Bank (EIB)	1958
	Inter-American Development Bank (IADB)	1959
	Islamic Development Bank (IsDB)	1975
	New Development Bank (NDB)	2014
	OPEC Fund for International Development (OPECFID)	1976
	United Nations Development Group (UNDG)	1997
Financial Stability	International Monetary Fund (IMF)	1944
	Arab Monetary Fund (AMF)	1976
	BRICS Contingent Reserve Arrangement (CRA)	2015
	Chiang-Mai-Initiative (CMI)	2010
	EU Balance of Payment Assistance Facility/ European Stability Mechanism (EU BoP/ESM)	2002
	Latin American Reserve Fund (LARF)	1976

set of institutional documents, comprising all the data gathered for each institution, was subsequently quantitatively analyzed to capture the number and direction of references among the respective organizations. To improve the comparability of the reference data collected from each institution, I again performed several weighting procedures. For every set of documents collected for the period of observation, I weighted the number of outgoing references by the relative number of document pages collected for the respective institution. The resulting reference networks are directed, meaning that they show both incoming and outgoing references of the respective institutions.

The membership networks for the two policy fields, on the other hand, are undirected as they are solely based on the membership status of states in the respective IOs within a particular institutional complex.[3] The ties between states and institutions were thus coded in a binary way, where "1" indicates membership and "0" indicates nonmembership of a particular institution. Based on this coding, sociomatrices were constructed indicating the membership of the previously selected states engaged in the respective policy area during the period of observation 2013–18.[4] While these network graphs indicate the institutions states through which states engaged in the policy field formally pursue institutionalized cooperation, they do not reflect the intensity or quality of the IO–state relation. However, as mentioned earlier in this section, this is not what the membership networks are intended to capture. Much more, they are supposed to "control" whether the hierarchical structures among IOs captured by means of the reference networks are also reflected in the patterns of institutionalized state cooperation within the institutional complex. Thus, analyzing the relative position of each institution within both the interinstitutional authority and the membership network allows for a more robust measurement of the underlying topology of each institutional complex.

In the reference network graphs, the relative size of each node is based on its in-degree centrality.[5] The color shade of each node, on the other hand, indicates its betweenness centrality, i.e., the relative number of shortest paths between all pairs of institutions that pass through it. The "thickness" of ties among institutions further indicates the intensity of specific interinstitutional references. In the membership network graphs, which are undirected, the size of each node simply indicates its degree centrality, i.e., the overall number of connections it has with all the other nodes in the network. Figures 6.1 and 6.2 compare the reference and membership networks in the development aid and financial stability policy field.

The network graphs intuitively indicate that the development aid institutional complex is more decentralized than the financial stability complex. While the financial stability complex does possess a clear institutional center in both networks, the IMF, references are more dispersed across institutions in the networks underlying the development aid complex. As far as centrality is concerned, the World Bank has a similar network position to the Asian Development Bank (ADB), the European Investment Bank (EIB), the Inter-American Development Bank (IADB), and the African Development Bank (AFDB). They all intensively refer to and are referred to by almost all the other institutional members of the network. By contrast, references among financial stability institutions are predominantly directed toward the IMF, with all other institutions only very seldom referring to one another. Furthermore, while states coordinate their institutionalized cooperation on the issue

Reference Network Development Aid

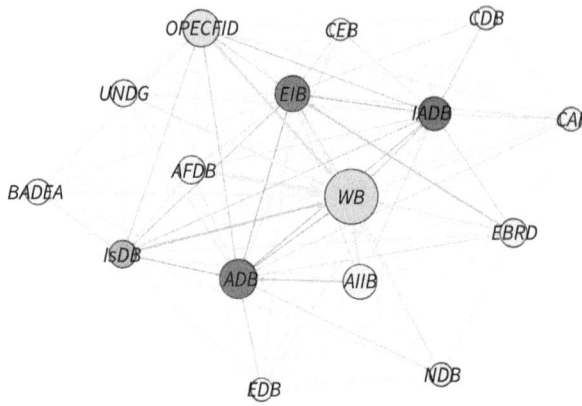

Reference Network Financial Stability

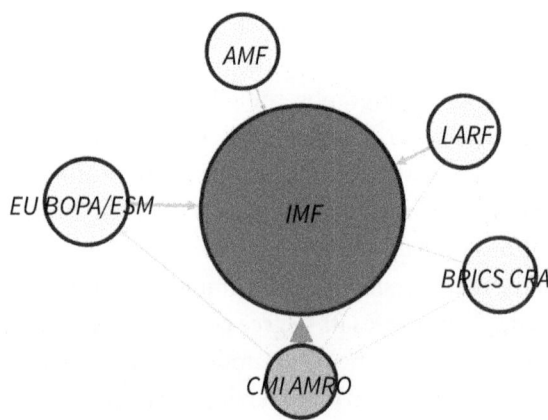

Figure 6.1 Reference Networks of the Institutional Complexes of Development Aid and Financial Stability (2013–2018)

Note: Graphs were created with the network visualization tool Gephi (v. 0.9.2). The size of the nodes indicates the institution's in-degree centrality, i.e., the number of institutions referring to it. The color of the node indicates the institution's betweenness centrality.

of development aid via numerous different MDBs, the most relevant states in the field of financial stability have all acquired membership of the IMF while only very selectively participating in alternative institutional arrangements.

Furthermore, institutions in the two policy fields in question here, financial stability and development aid, differ significantly as regards their relative positions within their respective reference network. One important measure

Membership Network Development Aid

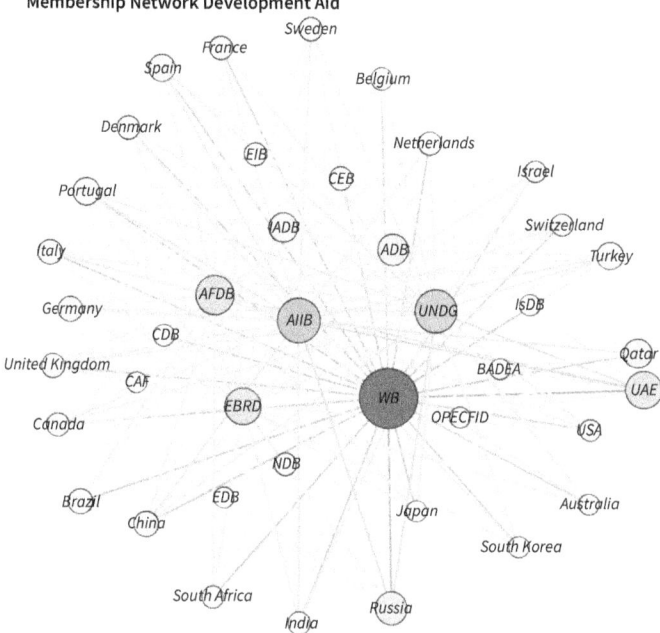

Membership Network Financial Stability

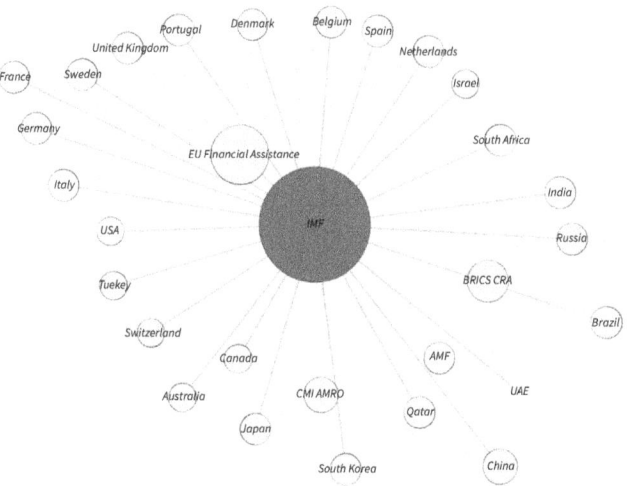

Figure 6.2 Membership Networks of the Institutional Complexes of Development Aid and Financial Stability (2018)

Note: Graphs were created with the network visualization tool Gephi (v. 0.9.2).

that can be used to capture these differences systematically is in-degree centrality. High in-degree centrality is associated with a more central position within a reference network: The greater the number of other institutions referring to a particular institution in the complex, the higher its authority within the network. Low in-degree centrality, on the other hand, indicates a less central position in the network. While the concept of in-degree centrality allows us to capture the position of institutions within their underlying reference network in terms of the absolute number of incoming ties from all other institutions in the network, the centrality of an institution within its reference network can also be measured in terms of betweenness. To recap, institutions obtaining high betweenness centralities acquire "broker positions" among the other institutions in their network. They connect otherwise rather isolated parts of the overall network and are therefore able to use their network position to influence the flow and transmission of information and initiate interactions among unconnected nodes. They consequently obtain high degrees of communicative control and structural autonomy within their network. Figure 6.3 compares the normalized in-degree centralities, Figure 6.4 the normalized betweenness centralities of the reference networks underlying the development aid and financial stability complexes.

Figures 6.3 and 6.4 illustrate that the distributions of incoming referential ties differ significantly between the two institutional complexes. Within the development aid complex, there are three MDBs—the EIB, the ADB, and the WB—which are referred to by more than 90 percent of all institutions of the complex, thus all obtaining an equally central position within the underlying reference network. Furthermore, in the same complex there are five MDBs—the AFDB, the IADB, the IsDB, the UNDG, and the EBRD—which are referred to by two-thirds or more of all other institutions, thus obtaining only slightly less central positions in the reference network than the previous three. The AIIB is still referred to by more than 50 percent of all other MDIs. Two MDBs, the OPECFID and the NDB, are referred to by 40 percent of all other MDBs. Only two MDBs, the BADEA and the CEB, are referred to by less than a fourth of all other MDBs within the development aid complex. In terms of incoming referential ties by other MDBs, there is thus no single central institution in the complex's underlying reference network.

In the institutional complex of financial stability, by contrast, the IMF is the only institution within its reference network which is referred to by all other institutions. Except for the AMF and the EU BoP/ESM, which are referred to by 60 percent of all other institutions, the remaining financial stability institutions, the Chiang Mai Initiative (CMI), the Group of Brazil, Russia, India, China, and South Africa Contingent Reserve Arrangement (BRICS CRA),

Normalized In-degree Centralities of Development Aid Institutions: *Reference Network among 16 MDIs*

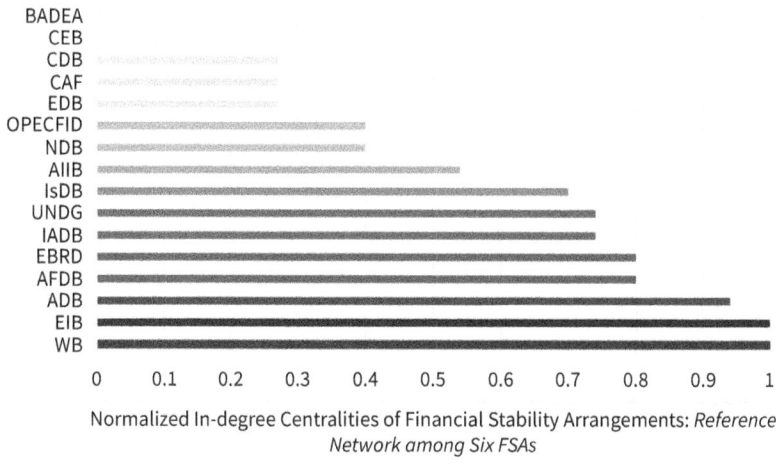

Normalized In-degree Centralities of Financial Stability Arrangements: *Reference Network among Six FSAs*

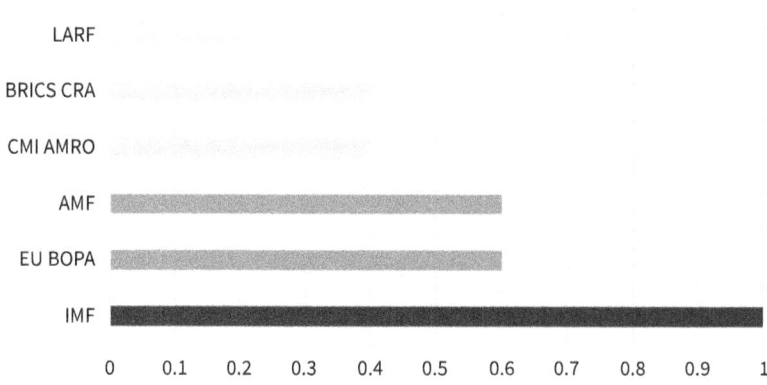

Figure 6.3 Normalized In-Degree Centralities by Institutions: Development Aid Complex and Financial Stability Complex Reference Networks

and the Latin American Reserve Fund (LARF), are referred to by only 40 percent or less. In terms of incoming referential ties from other financial stability institutions, the IMF thus clearly holds the single most central position within the complex's underlying reference network.

Figure 6.4 further shows great differences regarding the betweenness centrality of institutions in both complexes. Within the financial stability complex, the IMF, with a normalized score of 0.6, is the most central institution in terms of betweenness. In the development aid complex, by contrast, the ADB and the IADB are the most central institutions in terms of betweenness within

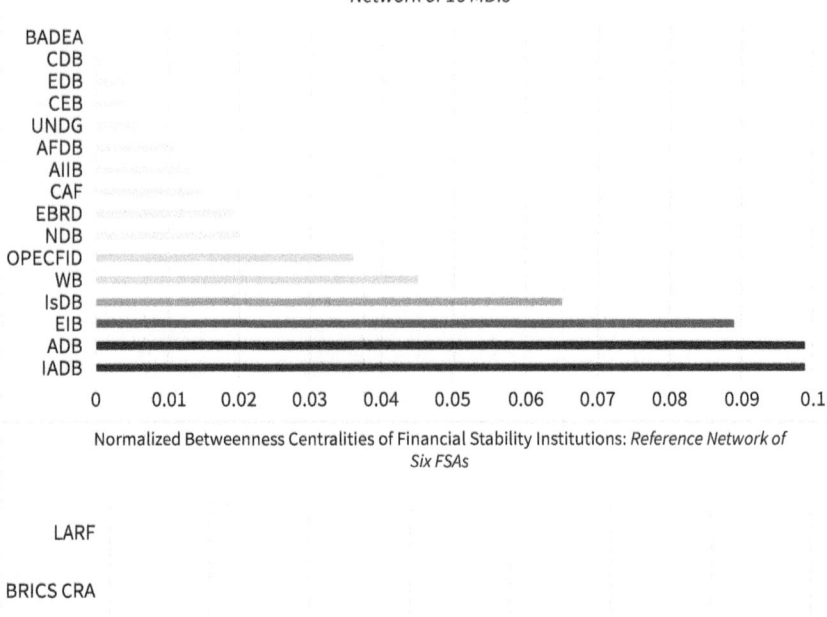

Figure 6.4 Normalized Betweenness Centralities by Institutions: Development Aid Complex and Financial Stability Complex Reference Networks

the underlying reference network. Within the reference network of the financial stability complex, the IMF is followed by the CMI. All the other financial stability institutions are much more minor in terms of their betweenness centrality: The ADB and the IADB are followed by the EIB, exhibiting a only slightly lower betweenness centrality. While the difference between the first and second highest normalized betweenness scores in the reference network of development aid is comparatively small, in the financial stability complex, this difference is substantively larger. Furthermore, in the development aid network of 15 MDBs, only the BADEA is not located on any shortest path between a pair of other MDBs. By contrast, in the network underlying the financial stability complex, four out of six FSAs are not located on any short-est path. Compared to its "Bretton Woods twin," the IMF, the WB possesses a less central position within the institutional reference network of its policy field as regards betweenness centrality. This further indicates that the IMF maintains an important brokerage position among otherwise scarcely con-nected institutions, while the World Bank, on the other hand, appears to lacks such a brokerage position.

In sum, the analysis of the institutional networks underlying the insti-tutional complexes of development aid and financial stability suggests that they differ significantly. While the network underlying the financial stabil-ity complex has a clear and dominant institution at its center, the IMF, the network underlying the development aid complex suggests a much more decentralized institutional topology.

What mechanisms and associated processes have shaped the evolution of these centralized or decentralized institutional topologies underlying the regime complexes of financial stability and development aid? In the next section of this empirical chapter, I will go beyond this initial covariance analysis. By drawing on in-depth case studies of institutionalization pro-cesses in both fields, the chapter will demonstrate that the observed structural variation across both policy fields results from substantial variation in net-work effects. Strong network effects associated with cooperation on the issue of financial stability have driven states toward universalistic centralized cooperation via the IMF while making the creation and sustainment of alter-native institutions complicated. The absence of network effects in the field of development aid has, on the other hand, incentivized states to foster cooper-ation via several smaller-scale institutional arrangements, thereby relaxing institutional hierarchies and spurring decentralization in the institutional complex.

Reinforcing Centralization: Network Effects and Centripetal Tendencies within the Institutional Complex of Financial Stability

The quantitative network analysis in the previous section of this chapter revealed that, despite the establishment of a series of alternative interna-tional financial stability institutions like the LARF, the BRICS CRA, the EU BoP/ESM, or the CMI during the last few decades, the IMF still maintains the most central position within the institutional complex of financial sta-bility. In the following section, I provide qualitative evidence pointing to the relevance of network effects associated with cooperation on the policy issue of financial stability. I demonstrate that the presence of strong network effects significantly constrains states in their efforts to establish institutional alternatives to the IMF. More precisely, this chapter provides qualitative evidence for network effects in the issue area of financial stability. It does so by empirically fleshing out three mechanisms through which the IMF's universality and broad membership led to its involvement in the management of recent financial crises while simultaneously impeding the creation of emancipated and independent regional alternative institutions.

Unlike small-scale and regionally limited institutional alternatives, the IMF has been perceived as being able to effectively counter contagion risks in the context of financial turmoil due to its global reach and universal membership. Moreover, thanks to its universal membership, the Fund has been considered capable of tying its loans to strict conditions, thereby reducing the risk of moral hazard by recipient states. Finally, involving the universal IMF has been a valuable means for governments to effectively shield themselves from attributions of public responsibility. Their involvement in unpopular and harmful austerity measures has been less visible than it would have been had those measures been imposed by more regional institutions alone. Thus, network effects bind states to the IMF while rendering more regionally focused institutional options much less attractive and feasible, even if dissatisfied states have a strong interest in pursuing these alternatives outside the IMF environment. Network effects exert a strong centripetal influence on the topologies underlying the institutional complex of financial stability in favor of its largest and most inclusive institution, the IMF.

Throughout this chapter, I will qualitatively analyze how the efforts of states to create and expand alternative institutional arrangements to the IMF in response to financial crises and increasing dissatisfaction with IMF policies were severely curbed by their worries about, and anticipation of, alternative institutions' inability to prevent financial contagion due to their limited scope in terms of membership. Thus, although several institutional alternatives to the IMF were initiated and created, their member states cautiously designed them to remain in close political and functional linkage to the IMF and its programs, thereby fortifying the Fund's central position within the institutional complex.

States seek institutionalized cooperation on the policy issue of financial stability to reduce the risk of international financial turmoil and, in the event of a financial crisis, to provide cumulative assistance to struggling states in order to avoid the crisis spreading (Trachtman 2010: 3–4; Gomel 2017; Constancio 2012). Most financial crisis events during recent decades were marked by strong spillover effects between the financial markets of countries even if they were not subject to the initial shock that caused the crisis (see, e.g., Baig and Goldfajin 1999; Samarakoon 2011; Luchtenberg and Vu 2015; Lipscy 2017: 69). Institutionalized cooperation seeking to counter financial contagion during financial crises is therefore exposed to strongly positive network externalities. The effectiveness of institutional counter-contagion measures depends on the number of states these measures can reach. Small-scale financial-stability institutions are much less able to shield their members from financial contagion, as their measures cannot be applied to countries outside their jurisdiction. Thus, the higher the number of states participating in a specific institution, the more effectively this institution can mitigate the risk of contagion.

Furthermore, to counter financial imbalances related to sovereign debt and balance of payment issues affecting member states, financial-stability institutions provide loans to their financially struggling member states. Institutionalized cooperation aimed at providing balance of payment assistance is strongly associated with the problem of moral hazard (see, e.g., Vaubel 1983; Dreher and Vaubel 2004; Lee and Shin 2008): The prospect of receiving loans in cases of financial turmoil or sovereign debt crisis "is likely to generate a moral hazard by reducing the incentive [for the borrowing country] to stay solvent" (Vaubel 1983: 294). To mitigate the problem, financial-stability institutions need to provide financial assistance contingent on the implementation of specific policies, which is referred to as conditional financial assistance or simply "conditionality" (Dreher 2009: 233; Vreeland 2006: 2; Lipscy 2017: 68). Institutionalized cooperation which aims to provide loans linked to strict political conditions exhibits strongly positive network effects thanks to the political cover that is needed when a state has to implement such unpleasant conditions. Universal and inclusive institutions can diffuse responsibility for unpopular measures while small-scale and regional institutional arrangements as a result of their limited membership and local political sensitivities are more straightforward targets for blame (Lipscy 2017: 68). In his empirical analysis of Japan's role and influence within the IMF, Lipscy (2017: 91–119) shows that attempts to establish an Asian regional alternative to the IMF in response to the Asian Financial Crisis of 1997–98 were critically hampered by Japan's and China's reluctance to add their own conditionalities to their newly established financial-stability institution, the CMI:

> The regional framework, because of its limited membership and skewed economic power, does not provide sufficient political cover for China and Japan to provide balance of payments lending in an effective and credible manner independent of IMF conditionality [which is why] Japanese policymakers have sought to make CMI and CMIM financing contingent on IMF conditionality, and 80–90 percent of

its bilateral currency swaps are tied to the presence of an IMF program. (Lipscy 2017: 98)

As I will subsequently demonstrate, the IMF's ability to provide political cover and reduce the risk of financial contagion due to its universal membership exerts strong centripetal effects beyond the CMI multilateralization process in Asia. It significantly affects the structure of the broader institutional complex of financial stability. I will trace three specific attempts to build regional institutional arrangements to provide financial stability more independently of the IMF. None of the three attempts resulted in regional independence from the IMF, but instead fortified the Fund's central position within the institutional complex. In Latin America, initiatives to expand and broaden institutionalized cooperation on financial stability beyond the small-scale LARF by establishing the "Bank of the South," with the primary goal of providing balance of payments assistance to every state in the region of South America independently of IMF conditionality, have been unsuccessful. In Europe, despite the establishment of the EU Balance of Payments (BoP) Facility and, later, the European Stability Mechanism (ESM), when it came to implementing bailout programs for struggling member states during the euro crisis, the EU decided against a regional strategy.

Instead, member states opted for the inclusion of the IMF and its conditionality programs while cautiously designing their institutional arrangements so that they were closely related to the IMF. In the case of the BRICS Credit Reserve Arrangement (CRA), despite the initiator states' expressed willingness to transform it into a credible alternative to the IMF, the institution has not yet properly decoupled all its loans from IMF conditionality. On the contrary, the institution still operates on a relatively small-scale basis. The following sections show that, in each of these cases, considerations of the lack of universality and associated network effects played a crucial role in thwarting the expansion of regional alternatives to the IMF. Despite these regionalization attempts, all three processes resulted in the opposite outcome, the fortification of the IMF's central position within the institutional complex of financial stability.

Financial Stability Regionalization Efforts in Latin America

In Latin America several states have long been struggling to create a regional financial-stability institution to gain more independence from the IMF. Up to now, these attempts have failed, however, as states could not design these institutions to be completely independent from the IMF. Back in 1978, a regional financial-stability institution, the so-called "Andean Reserve Fund," was established by the states of Bolivia, Columbia, Venezuela, Ecuador, and Peru. The institution was intended to grant financing to its members in order to solve "balance of payments problems of the member countries ... [and] facilitate their access to financial markets ... thereby ... [contributing] to obtaining additional financing for the execution of industrial development sectoral programs" (Andean Group 1976). In 1991, the Andean Reserve Fund was transformed into a "Latin American Reserve Fund" (LARF) with the explicit aim of expand its scope in terms of membership and inviting other countries from the region to join (Ocampo and Titelman 2009: 251).

The attempts to expand the Fund's membership to the whole region of Latin America have been far from successful with up to now only Costa Rica and Uruguay (in 2000 and 2009 respectively) having formally joined LARF (Garcia 2016: 200). Furthermore, LARF's actual role in promoting financial stability in the region can be seen as somewhat limited. Owing to LARF's limited capital resources of US$2.3 billion and functional constraints like the inability of its member states' central banks to produce convertible currencies on demand, many Latin American states opted for IMF financial assistance instead during the 1990s (Ponsot 2009: 4; Garcia 2016: 200). Thus, calls for a strengthening and expansion of institutionalized cooperation in Latin America outside of the IMF, for instance, through the transformation of the LARF into a fully-fledged "Latin American Monetary Fund," intensified with the beginning of the 2000s (Fondo Latinoamericano de Reservas 2000; Agosin 2001: 32).

The most ambitious attempt to create a credible institutional alternative to the IMF that goes beyond the scope of the LARF was initiated by Venezuela, Brazil, and Argentina, which proposed the establishment of a "Bank of the South" (BOS) in 2007 (Rosales 2013: 28). These initiator countries were subsequently joined by other MERCOSUR countries like Paraguay, Uruguay, Bolivia, and Peru, who shared the goal of gaining more independence from the predominantly very critically evaluated IMF programs by establishing the BOS as an alternative source of financing for its member states when they were experiencing balance of payment issues (Heredia 2007). These objectives were further substantiated in the negotiations that followed. The parties agreed to analyze the possibilities of either strengthening the Latin American Reserve Fund by integrating new partners and creating new instruments or establishing a new "Fund of the South" to insure its members against financial risks by pooling their resources (Quintana 2008: 748; Ortiz 2007: 4).

Venezuelan then-president Hugo Chávez went even further by proposing to link the creation of the new financial-stability institution with the parties' complete withdrawal from the IMF. However, none of the other states involved in creating the BOS was willing to take such a step because they were very aware of the economic benefits associated with their membership in as universal and large-scale an institution as the IMF. It was argued that withdrawing from the IMF could amount to a default on sovereign bonds and raise the costs of further borrowing (*The Economist* 2007). This was because of a critical network effect associated with cooperation on financial stability: None of the designated member states, except for Brazil, enjoyed a high investment grade rating, while the IMF, with its broad and universal membership, is able to use its high rating to allow its members access to lower interest rates on the capital markets (Artana 2010). Put differently, none of the participating states except for Venezuela was willing to waive the positive effects of membership of the IMF on their access to the capital market. Thus, a complete replacement of the IMF as the "lender of last resort" by the BOS was not an option. Eventually, Venezuela too dropped the idea of linking the creation of the BOS to a withdrawal from the IMF (Quintana 2008: 744).

Throughout the further negotiations on the design of the BOS, Brazil especially took a strongly critical stance toward establishing the institution as a fully-fledged financial-stability arrangement and directly referred to another network effect associated with institutionalized forms of financial-stability cooperation: the issue of moral hazard arising from unequal financial contributions and statecraft among members of small-scale institutions. As the potentially largest donor, Brazil argued strongly against the proposed "no conditionality" design of the institution's lending practices which implied that the BOS would not place any restrictions on repayment beyond the established terms of the loans (McElhinny 2007). As the largest provider of capital to the proposed institution, Brazil insisted that the BOS should be designed in a way that it does "not bailout unwise borrowers." (Quintana 2008: 755).

Other parties, however, especially Venezuela and Ecuador, strongly opposed the idea of the BOS providing conditional loans to its members. They argued that the Bank should avoid dictating policies to lenders, especially as all members were intended to have equal voting rights and would therefore be able to block decisions on such conditionalities (Doleac 2015). Put differently, they worried that a strictly regionally designed and small-scale institution would lack an essential function of its universal competitor, the IMF: the political cover stemming from universality needed to push through harsh economic conditionalities on neighboring countries in the region seeking credits from the regional institution in question.

As it became clear that the BOS would not impose conditions on its loans to members due to a lack of the political will and ability to impose them on other members of the regional institution, Brazil also raised doubts about whether the institution's capital, which without conditionalities could not be expanded by assets from the private capital market due to expected high interest rates, would be large enough to gain independence from IMF loans in the event of financial turmoil (Schaller 2007). Furthermore, Brazil worried that the BOS would not be able to effectively counter financial contagion and external financial shocks: Instead of assigning the role of a currency manager to the institution, which would be necessary to enable it to take flexible measures in a situation of financial crisis, "the option chosen was to focus on a much smaller role as a single international lender" (Doleac 2015). In addition, Brazil argued that the institution's proposed capital resources were far from sufficient to safeguard the country in the event of financial turmoil in a way that would reduce its dependence on IMF loans. For example, Brazil's external debt in 2005 was $226 billion, which was thirty times the amount of the new Bank's planned capital deposits (Schaller 2007). As far as Brazil was concerned, the IMF, with its universal membership and much higher capital pool, could not be replaced by a regional institution: The relatively small amount of resources that could be accumulated under a small-scale regional institutional arrangement was thus perceived to be inadequate to replace the IMF's considerable financial resources stemming from its broad membership. This shows that Brazil was perfectly aware of the network effects associated with international cooperation on the issue of financial stability. Brazil was not willing to emancipate itself from the IMF because it was aware of the benefits associated with its universal membership. Owing to the strong network effects associated with cooperation on the issue, a regionally limited financial-stability institution cannot duplicate the crucial functions of its universal competitor, the IMF. When the institution was formally established in December 2007, it was given the sole function of a development bank, thus abandoning the idea of creating a regional alternative to the IMF in its role of a lender of last resort (Hart-Landsberg 2009:13).

To sum up, the attempts to establish an alternative financial-stability institution to the IMF in Latin America that went beyond the scope of the existing LARF and could serve as a fully-fledged Latin American Monetary Fund failed. They failed because the states involved were not able to reproduce the benefits of large-scale cooperation on the issue of financial stability. A regional alternative's lack of the political cover necessary to push through conditionalities on its loans and its associated small reserve-accumulation capabilities strongly limited the expected benefits for the participating states,

especially Brazil. Thus, the centripetal effects produced by the strong network effects associated with cooperation on the issue of financial stability
reinforced the central position of the IMF in the institutional complex by
inhibiting the creation and expansion of a Latin American regional alternative arrangement.

Financial Stability Regionalization Efforts during the European Sovereign Debt Crisis

In Europe, the positive network effects associated with large-scale cooperation on the issue of financial stability also played a crucial role when it
came to the question of how to institutionalize financial-stability cooperation at a regional level and whether to involve the IMF in the deteriorating
European Debt Crisis after 2009. Before the crisis, institutionalized cooperation to preserve financial stability played a minor role in the context of the
European Union (EU). In 2002, the so-called Balance of Payments Assistance Facility (BoP) was established. The institution aimed at "providing
medium-term financial assistance for Member States' balances of payments"
that would encourage member states "to adopt, in good time in a situation
where orderly exchange rate conditions prevail, economic policy measures
likely to prevent the occurrence of an acute balance of payments crisis and to
support its efforts towards convergence" (EU Council 2002). However, the
BoP remained restricted to EU members outside the Euro area as, since the
Treaty of Maastricht, "potential imbalances were no longer seen as a problem
within the integrated currency union" (Schwarzer 2015: 606).

   When the sovereign debt crisis in Greece deteriorated in 2010, calls for a
regional institutionalized solution in the form of a new Euro area lending
facility became louder. Although the Greek government had begun informal talks with the IMF about how to address its severe balance of payment
problems, among the majority of the "leading players of the European establishment," there was unanimity that the Fund should not be involved in this
institutional solution (Blustein 2015: 4–5). In an article published by the
Financial Times in March 2010, Germany's Finance Minister Schäuble proposed to establish a "European monetary fund" which would take on the
role of a lender of last resort, a task that "the IMF has assumed in many
crises and ... produced strong results. [... This] prospect of emergency aid
connected with hard corrective fiscal action would boost the confidence of
financial markets, thus preventing a deepening of the crisis and obviating the
eurozone members' need to call upon the IMF in future" (Schäuble 2010).

Especially the German chancellor, Angela Merkel, and several Northern European countries pulled the break (Howarth and Schild 2021). They feared that a "Europe-only" solution would produce substantial moral hazard by increasing incentives to avoid austerity measures and reducing incentives for debt relief within the Euro area, eventually "leading to a 'transfer union,' in which the taxpayers of big, rich countries would subsidize less prosperous member states" (Blustein 2015: 5). These countries were aware of a critical network effect associated with institutionalized forms of cooperation on the issue of financial stability: While universal and large-scale institutions can effectively discipline member states thanks to their perceived neutrality and legitimacy, regional institutions with clear responsibilities and power structures among members were considered an obstacle to implementing and surveilling conditionalities. More precisely, the proximity of the lending countries' governments to the potential financial aid recipients was considered to be a serious problem with respect to the surveillance and implementation of conditionalities. Bringing in a disciplining actor from outside of the regional context was considered a more attractive option (Schwarzer 2015: 610–11). In contrast to a regional institution, the IMF was considered capable of resisting partial political influence endogenous to the EU community and was therefore perceived to be able to enforce harsher programs (Seitz and Jost 2012: 11).

Consequently, during an EU summit in Brussels in March 2010, Chancellor Merkel forcefully called for IMF involvement: "It's simply a fact that because at present the handling of deficit procedures isn't sufficiently regulated, Europe isn't in the position to solve such a problem on its own" (Merkel 2010, qtd. in Francis 2010). Thus, while a regionally legitimized institution was considered likely to have a hard time pushing through painful austerity reforms against one of its members, the IMF, with its quasi-universal membership, was perceived to be capable of providing more political cover to fulfill this disciplinary task.

The German government, which would have been the most significant contributor to an institutionalized "Europe-only solution," feared that, under an exclusively regional institutional arrangement, it would become an easy target for blame, not only from the publics of the debtor states but even more from their very own domestic audience. "The German public ... would never accept an emergency loan unless it came with severe conditions, enforced by arbiters with recognized neutrality and competence—and the IMF was the only institution that came close to this description" (Blustein 2015: 6). Merkel feared that if it was predominantly "German taxpayer's money" that was used in Greece, a polarized internal political debate in Germany would inevitably flare up (Feldenkirchen et al. 2010). The IMF's potential role as a "scapegoat" (Seitz and Jost 2012: 11; Nelson et al. 2010: 5), due to its neutrality stemming from its universal membership, thus created a strong impetus to take the option of a regional-only solution off the table.

Besides the advantage of providing political cover for the surveillance and enforcement of harsh conditions, there were also economic reasons for a strong IMF involvement in the potential institutional arrangement addressing the balance-of-payments issue of Euro area member states, which were directly linked to its large membership: As a universal international organization, the IMF enjoys preferred creditor status so that its loans have to be paid back before any other creditors involved are reimbursed (Seitz and Jost 2012: 11), which was thought to have a calming effect on financial markets. Furthermore, the IMF was perceived to be more capable of actually sanctioning noncompliance, by, e.g., holding back credit tranches (Schwarzer 2015: 611), than EU member states who would have to fear "cutting off their nose to spite their face" because refusing to pay could eventually lead to the destabilization of their own currency. This credibility advantage enjoyed by the IMF was perceived to be boosting the financial market's confidence in the debtor states' creditworthiness. Compared to regional and fairly small-scale financial institutions, the large and diverse membership of the IMF and its associated strong network effects incentivized states to involve it in addressing the crisis.

Furthermore, IMF involvement was expected to help debtor states regain access to the capital market and provide EU member states with the opportunity to solve "ratification issues" within the domestic context without undermining the credibility of the lending promise given to the struggling debtor. As the IMF was involved, the risk of nonratification that existed in several EU member countries was less relevant to the credibility of the "lending promise" which "should help calm markets thereby reducing the probability of a liquidity crisis" (Schwarzer 2015: 616). Thus, involving the IMF with its preferred creditor status based on its universal membership could also be considered a valuable means of mitigating the risk of financial contagion and the spillover of liquidity problems through increasing the financial market's confidence in the lending commitment of the member states.

In their decision to establish the Troika in March 2010, a body consisting of representatives from the European Commission and Central Bank as well as the IMF, the Euro area's heads of state and government declared that the loans to Greece would "involv[e] substantial International Monetary Fund financing" and that bilateral loans contributed by Euro area member states should only be a "mechanism complementing International Monetary Fund financing [and have] to be considered ultima ratio, meaning in particular that market financing is insufficient" (EU Council 2010). In the subsequent institutionalization processes that eventually led to the establishment of the European Financial Stability Facility (EFSF) and European Financial Stabilization Mechanism (EFSM) in 2010 and the European Stability Mechanism (ESM) in 2011, Euro area member states carefully established close institutional linkages with the IMF. Not only were all the underlying procedures inspired by the design and practice of the IMF, something that the EU member states explicitly emphasized in the institution's underlying treaties (Salines et al. 2012: 675; EU Council 2012). They also explicitly endorsed close cooperation with the Fund (Schwarzer 2015: 611–12). The treaty establishing the ESM, for instance, stated that "[t]he active participation of the IMF will be sought, both at technical and financial level … [and that a] euro area Member State requesting financial assistance from the ESM is expected to address, wherever possible, a similar request to the IMF" (EU Council 2012: 5).

Thus, while establishing the EFSF, EFSM, and ESM can be conceived of as an expansion of institutional cooperation on the issue of financial stability within the context of the EU, it did not compromise or undermine the IMF's relevance in the policy field. Quite the opposite. Strong positive network effects associated with cooperation on the issue of financial stability reinforced IMF involvement during EU member states' efforts to decide on emergency loans for financially struggling members. They also played a crucial role in the design of the newly created institution and the decision to take plans for a regional-only solution like the European Monetary Fund off the table. Likewise, strong institutional and procedural links between the IMF and the newly established EU institutions and the contractual obligation on member states to involve the IMF when seeking their assistance fortified the Fund's central position within the hierarchy of the institutional complex of financial stability.

Financial Stability Regionalization Efforts by the BRICS Group of States

The BRICS group—Brazil, Russia, India, China, and South Africa—made the most recent push to establish an alternative to the IMF. In 2014 it formally installed the New Development Bank (NDB), intended to provide development lending, and the BRICS Contingency Reserve Arrangement (CRA), which seeks to "parallel the IMF's role of providing short-term liquidity to address financial crises" (Helleiner and Wang 2018: 575). In substantive terms, the CRA, with a size of US$100 billion, with China providing the lion's share of financial liquidity (US$48 billion), can be considered a serious attempt to institutionalize an "instrument [that] will contribute to promoting international financial stability, as it will complement the current global network of financial protection," as Brazil's Foreign Ministry said when declaring the CRA's establishment (*China Daily* 2015). Many observers even argued that the establishment of the CRA would mark a turning point for global financial politics and might be a serious challenger to the IMF's dominance, as the institution would have "the potential to break the pattern not only of US–EU global dominance but also of the harmful conditions typically attached to balance of payments support" (Weisbrot 2014).

Still, even though these ambitions were publicly articulated by the BRICS leaders at the summit in Ufa, Russia, where the establishment of the new financial stability arrangement was concluded, the BRICS states cautiously designed it in close linkage to the IMF's institutional procedures and resources. Most importantly, Article 5 of the "Treaty for the Establishment of a BRICS Contingent Reserve Arrangement" states that only 30 percent of the maximum amount accessible to a requesting party "shall be available subject only to the agreement of the Providing Parties" (BRICS 2014). Every time a member applies for more than 30 percent of its maximum emergency funding, it must first apply for a structural adjustment loan and conditionality from the IMF (BRICS 2014; Bond 2016: 613; Würdemann 2018: 586–7).

I argue that this institutional design in close relation to the IMF was again due to the BRICS states' awareness of the positive network effects associated with institutionalized forms of cooperation on the issue of financial stability and the related benefits associated with membership of the universal IMF. A central issue for the BRICS group, which forced it to link the CRA institutionally to structural IMF loans once borrowing exceeded 30 percent was precisely its limitation in terms of membership and the resulting limited loan pool available to its members: Although members' individual contributions to the CRA are comparatively high, the institution's overall financial resources are relatively modest, thus limiting its ability to avoid financial balance of payments issues affecting its members. For instance, in 2002 Brazil received a standby credit arrangement from the IMF in the sum of about US$30 billion, which exceeded the maximum funding available for Brazil from the CRA independent of the IMF—US$5.4 billion—by almost 600 percent (Steil and Walker 2014).

Thus, while the IMF, with its broad and universal membership despite individually smaller financial contributions, is able to provide loans big enough to adequately address severe balance of payments financing problems, the CRA "will not be a game changer in the case of major balance of payments pressure of any of the BRICS countries" (Würdemann 2018: 585). This issue could be addressed by expanding the membership of the CRA, which so far is not the BRICS' intention due to their lack of institutional control and surveillance mechanisms to safeguard the loans they provide. Thus, the CRA does not offer an alternative source of balance of payments loans to IMF conditionality for nonmember states. Together with the requirement of an IMF agreement, once the requested funding exceeds 30 percent of the maximum available for each member, the CRA is even considered by some observers to be "providing a means of empowering and re-legitimizing the IMF" (Bond 2016: 614).

That the BRICS states are aware of the CRA's limited capacities to address external financial shocks adequately is further reflected in their cautious unilateral accumulation of foreign exchange reserves in parallel to the CRA. These unilateral financial safety measures exceed the maximum individual loans available from the CRA. In the case of China, unilaterally accumulated foreign exchange reserves in 2014, when the CRA was formally created, had a value of almost US$4000 billion while their maximum access to CRA loans without IMF involvement amounted to only US$6.2 billion (Steil and Walker 2014). Thus, in the event of financial turmoil in which all five countries were exposed to balance of payments problems simultaneously, the CRA's resources would quickly be exhausted (Bond 2016: 615), forcing the countries to either draw on their unilaterally accumulated foreign exchange reserves or to apply to the IMF for larger external funds. Thus, network effects associated with institutionalized forms of cooperation on the issue of financial stability tied the BRICS to the universal and large-scale IMF.

Another issue directly related to the CRA's limited capacity due to its small membership is its lack of resources to conduct independent surveillance and implement the safeguarding policies necessary to supervise its approved financial loans: As the CRA lacks the institutional instruments that provide the expertise and experience to ensure that debtor states are repaying its loans, it is dependent on external safeguard measures (Würdemann 2018: 587). Furthermore, especially as the group of states participating in the CRA is small, it is hard to resist the temptation to draw on the institution's resources to delay necessary adjustments. Without the surveillance and strict conditions overseen by a universal institution's bodies, it is challenging to make sure that the state applying for funding is not taking advantage of the institution's nonconditionality without addressing the potentially endogenous problem that led to its balance of payments problems in the first place (Kahn 2014). Thus, due to the small scale of the CRA, it could not provide its members with the essential network effects that arise from large-scale cooperation on the issue of financial stability. This, in turn, created a strong impetus for the BRICS states to link the provision of large loans in the context of the CRA to a parallel application for IMF conditional loans, thereby increasing the institution's dependence on the Fund.

To sum up, in all three episodes of regional institutionalization attempts in the policy field of financial stability discussed in the previous section of this chapter, network effects associated with cooperation on the issue impeded the creation of regional balance of payments facilities that were completely independent of the IMF. The Fund's universal membership and associated advantages compared to its regional alternatives, like its ability to credibly impose conditionalities and safeguard their application or its ability to provide substantial loans and advise how to absorb financial shocks and prevent financial contagion effectively, made states initially willing to create serious institutional alternatives shy away from constructing them with complete independence from the IMF.

The opposite is, in fact, the case. States' anticipation of the IMF's advantages stemming from universality made them include explicit institutional linkages and ties with the IMF in their regional institutional arrangements to ensure their functionality. And by creating these strong institutional dependencies, states reinforced and fortified the IMF's central position in the institutional complex of financial stability.

While the strong network effects associated with institutionalized cooperation on the issue of financial stability created strong centripetal effects on the institution complex by reinforcing hierarchies and interinstitutional dependencies, in the next section of this chapter, the opposite is revealed to be the case in the policy field of development aid. Within this policy field, the lack of positive network effects drives states to diversify their cooperative efforts on development aid, creating strongly centrifugal effects on the institutional topology underlying the policy field's institutional complex.

Centrifugal Tendencies in the Institutional Complex of Development Aid

The network analysis conducted earlier in this chapter revealed that, compared to the institutional complex underlying the issue area of financial stability, the institutional complex underlying development aid exhibits much more fragmented topologies. There, authority is dispersed across several institutions, all of which have comparably central positions within its membership and reference networks.

Building on Lipscy's (2017: 69–70) conceptualization of network effects in the context of institutionalized cooperation, in this section of the chapter, I claim that there are two main reasons why—in sharp contrast to intergovernmental cooperation on the issue of financial stability—it is unattractive for states to pursue development aid exclusively via large-scale and universalistic institutions: the reduced political leverage and credit associated with the funding of development projects within large-scale institutions on the one hand, and efficiency losses due to more significant interest heterogeneity among states as compared to smaller-scale regional institutional arrangements on the other. Thus, compared to the issue area of financial stability, increasing numbers of participating states in development institutions are not experiencing greater utilities derived from that specific form of institutionalized cooperation. Rather to the contrary, I hold that the absence of network effects in the policy field of development aid creates strong incentives to create more regionally focused, relatively small-scale development institutions independent from or even competing with existing ones. In the following, I lay out this argument in greater detail.

Engaging in institutionalized cooperation in the form of Multilateral Development Banks (MDBs) can help states to pursue welfare policies beyond their domestic context (Lumsdaine 1993), to provide domestic economic interest groups with an improved position in the aid recipients' market, or "to enhance political alliances with the recipient country government [and] to obtain political goodwill and changes ... in the decisions and policy stance of that government" (Martens 2005: 652). Furthermore, powerful states can use MDBs as a means to influence the allocation of aggregated aid flows to pursue geopolitical or commercial interests (see, e.g., Tuman and Strand 2006; Kilby 2006; Kilby 2013).

To what extent these donor-specific interests can be realized in the context of concrete development projects within MDBs very much hinges on the outcome of bargaining processes, in which both wealthier donor countries and poorer recipient countries "coalesce and vote on policies that guide aid allocation and/or on specific proposals for development projects and programs" (Nielson et al. 2017: 159). With increasing numbers of institutional participants and, thus, potentially conflicting interests, realizing an individual donor state's policy objective is more complicated. Especially within large MDBs like the WB or the ADB, where powerful states dominate the everyday decision-making processes (see, e.g., Dutt 1997; Kilby 2006; Kilby 2011; Dreher et al. 2009; Lim and Vreeland 2013; Clark and Dolan 2021), less powerful members have a hard time pushing for their preferences to be considered. Interest heterogeneity underlying large-scale development aid institutions may reinforce this issue for less powerful members, creating strong incentives for them to pursue their policy goals via outside options.

Furthermore, small-scale institutional arrangements providing development aid can help states to achieve the kind of political credit associated with aid disbursement to within their domestic context as well as in the recipient state's society (Lipscy 2017: 69). Beyond political and economic leverage, "visibly" contributing to poverty alleviation in developing countries can not only signal a strong commitment to the goal of poverty reduction to domestic constituencies, it can also be a tool of "soft power" by, e.g., improving a donor state's reputation in the recipient country (Bry 2017). Within large-scale institutions, a state's contribution to concrete development aid projects is much less visible as projects are funded by aggregating the contribution of all member states. Within small-scale and more regionally focused institutions, contributions can be assigned more easily to individual states, thus allowing them to claim credit for these projects, thereby increasing their influence over future investments.

Thus, adverse effects associated with large-scale cooperation on the issue of development aid can incentivize states to disperse their institutionalized cooperation via many relatively unrelated institutions, thereby reinforcing interinstitutional competition, which creates substantial centrifugal effects on the institutional complex. In the subsequent section of this chapter, I will provide qualitative evidence for these centrifugal effects on states' institutionalization efforts due to negative network externalities by tracing the process that led to the establishment of the AIIB in 2015. I argue that this case is well suited to illustrating how the absence of positive network effects prompts states to foster institutionalized cooperation outside large-scale and universal institutions. First, despite the initially strong resistance of the United States, the AIIB was established in direct competition with the World Bank and the Asian Development Bank by China and many other Asian States with concrete reference to these institutions' lack of consideration of Asian infrastructure needs despite the great demand in the region. Second, due to their lack of influence on development lending in large-scale institutions like the World Bank and the Asian Development Bank and their anticipation of enhanced political leverage over funding projects, many European states like Germany and Italy eventually joined the AIIB. In contrast to their struggle to emancipate their financial stability institutions from the IMF during the European Debt Crisis, in the case of the AIIB, European states did not hesitate to support the counter-institutionalization project within the institutional complex of development aid. They expected to be able to exert direct political influence on infrastructure projects within a more regional and specialized institution like the AIIB.

Successful Institutionalization in the Development Aid Area: The Institutionalization of the AIIB

The following section will trace how the absence of network effects in the policy field of development aid comes with a highly competitive institutional environment with strong incentives, especially for states dissatisfied with existing universal institutions, to create alternative, regionally focused and more specialized ones. In the aftermath of the Global Financial Crisis that unfolded in 2008, China and other emerging economies began to intensify their efforts to gain a greater say within established large-scale MDBs like the Asian Development Bank (ADB) and the World Bank (WB), which, they complained, were dominated for the most part by the United States, Japan, and their European Allies (Danner 2019: 82). Despite efforts to reform the decision-making process and to give emerging economies and developing countries a greater voice within these two institutions (see, e.g., Vestergaard and Wade 2015; Strand and Retzl 2016: 59–61) China in particular continued to express its dissatisfaction with the World Bank and the ADB's policies. From 2013, when the new Chinese government under President Xi Jinping took office, the focus of Chinese development policy was increasingly on promoting and expanding infrastructure projects within the Asia-Pacific region. Within the context of its "One Belt One Road Initiative," China aims to finance development projects with the concrete goal of "trade promotion, infrastructure development, and regional connectivity to boost economic linkages between China and dozens of countries along a land route (the Silk Road Economic Belt) and a sea route (the 21st century Maritime Silk Route)" (Weiss 2017: 2).

Within the large-scale existing institutions, the WB and the ADB, the Chinese calls for infrastructure projects to be given more significant consideration in the institutions' overall funding of development found hardly any hearing. Between 2004 and 2011, a large share of Chinese project proposals to the ADB and World Bank were not supported by the United States and many of its Western Allies (Strand et al. 2016: 57). Within these institutions with broad-based membership, interest heterogeneity was a major problem that prevented China from pursuing its development strategy of infrastructure financing. Furthermore, because of their large and heterogenous lending portfolio, the WB's and the ADB's resources exclusively available for funding infrastructure projects were far below the actual need: A research paper published by the Asian Development Bank Institute estimated that in Asia between 2010 and 2020, there would be an overall "infrastructure investment need of about US$750 billion per year during this 11-year period." (Asian Development Bank Institute 2009: 5). A more recent policy paper published by the WB further suggests that the infrastructural needs of developing countries amount to annual investments of US$819 billion to sustain their economic growth (Ruiz Nunez and Wei 2015). In 2013, while the WB's overall lending commitments amounted to US$31.5 billion (World Bank 2019a), its infrastructure projects were valued at only US$11.7 billion (Weiss 2017: 5). Owing to the heterogenous development policy interests of its 189 member states, the WB currently maintains projects in eleven different sectors, e.g., energy and extractives, education, industry and trade, health and social protection, each of which contains multiple different subsectors of the recipient state's economy (World Bank 2016). To pursue the strategy of targeted infrastructure funding, it thus became an attractive option for states interested in such projects to foster multilateral development cooperation on a smaller and more specialized scale outside of the large-scale and universal WB.

In another large-scale development institution, the ADB, which already existed and could have been used to pursue multilateral infrastructure development projects, China did not succeed in increasing the institution's infrastructure development activities either. Japan and the United States, which together held almost 26 percent of the institution's voting shares, as compared with China's only 5.5 percent, continued to "dominate ADB lending in Asia" (Chow 2016: 1272), which enabled them to reject China's infrastructure development project proposals. The ADB actually finances only less than 2 percent of Asia's infrastructure needs (Callaghan and Hubbard 2016: 135). In more general terms, the interest of many especially Western donor countries in financing major infrastructure projects has decreased substantially since the beginning of the 1980s. This is also reflected in a significant decline in infrastructure financing at MDBs: "Since then, the MDBs have largely embraced a view of economic development, shared by the United States and other developed economies, that places a greater emphasis on developing a robust investment climate (legal, political, economic ministries, for example) in developing countries rather than on funding basic infrastructure" (Weiss 2017: 4). Conflicts of interests have therefore intensified as China has increased its focus on infrastructure development under its "One Belt One Road Initiative". As a result, China was incentivized to pursue development cooperation outside of large-scale and universal MDBs by creating more specialized and small-scale institutions.

When proposing the institutionalization of an MDB with an exclusive focus on infrastructure development projects in Asia, the Chinese government stressed above all that, unlike the WB, the AIIB would not attach political conditionalities to its loans as "politics should not enter into the discussion of whether and under what circumstances a development project is worth pursuing" and a borrower should only be judged "based on pure economic considerations" (Liao 2015). In contrast to the policy field of financial stability, where the utility of institutionalized cooperation among states is strongly dependent on the institution's ability to impose conditions on recipient countries in order to avoid moral hazard and assure the institution's access to the capital market, which in turn is dependent on the number of participating states, in the field of development aid an institution's renunciation of political conditions increases its attractiveness for potential recipient states: As the AIIB was intended "to issue loans with fewer or no conditions, [... the AIIB is] more appealing to many recipient countries [than the WB]" (Chow 2016: 1263).

Thus, the nonattachment of political conditionalities to its loans can allow a newly created MDB to fund development projects in countries not targeted by existing development institutions due to their inability or unwillingness to comply with conditions, which, in turn, fuels competition among institutions within the development aid complex. Put differently, the nonexistence of network effects in the field of development aid makes it much more attractive for states to establish specialized and more regional cooperative arrangements than in the field of financial stability because these institutions' effectiveness is not dependent on large and economically heterogenous membership. On the contrary, pursuing projects explicitly targeted at infrastructure development is more manageable if like-minded donor states work together to promote infrastructure projects without attaching political conditions to the recipient countries.

Due to the lack of network effects associated with institutionalized cooperation on development funding, the establishment of the regional and specialized AIIB was also considered a valuable tool to increase economic leverage in the Asian region, which China had not been able to achieve via large-scale institutions like the World Bank and the ADB. Infrastructure projects funded by the regional AIIB looked promising for the sizeable Chinese construction sector interested in expanding its economic activities abroad (Talley 2015). Furthermore, the newly founded institution was perceived as a helpful venue for reinvesting China's massive foreign reserves in infrastructure projects abroad, thereby reducing the risk of inflation in the domestic economy (Hecan 2016: 162). As compared to the World Bank, within the context of its newly created regional competitor, the AIIB, China had more leverage on concrete infrastructure projects and could therefore channel more financial contributions to specific projects as compared to projects funded by the WB or the ADB, where the Chinese project-specific contributions were much smaller: While China held an initial capital subscription of US$29.8 billion in the AIIB, the total amount of capital it subscribed to the WB's International Bank for Reconstruction and Development (IBRD) was only one-third of this, namely, US$10.7 billion (AIIB 2019: 29; World Bank 2019b).

In the case of the AIIB, the absence of strong network effects, which in the institutional complex of financial stability binds states strongly to the IMF and impedes the creation of independent institutional alternatives, also incentivized many Western states—despite the initially strong resistance of the US—to join the newly created development institution. Only three months after 21 Asian states had signed a memorandum of understanding on establishing the AIIB in October 2014, the member of the British Commonwealth New Zealand officially applied for membership in January 2015. The United States immediately began to forcefully discourage its allies from joining the new institution (Danner 2019: 82). More precisely, the US government tried to convince its allies that "China ... [would] use the bank to set the global economic agenda on its own terms, forgoing ... environmental protections, human rights, anticorruption measures and other governance standards" (Perlez 2015).

Still, even for one of the US's closest ally, the United Kingdom, the newly created regional and highly specialized infrastructure development institution represented a highly attractive alternative venue. The new institutions enabled the UK to pursue specialized infrastructure development projects beyond the World Bank thereby increasing its economic influence in Asia. When the then Chancellor of the Exchequer George Osborne announced that the UK would become a prospective founding member of the AIIB in March 2015, he explicitly stressed the UK government's ambition to use AIIB membership to intensify and deepen its economic ties with Asia:

This government has actively promoted closer political and economic engagement with the Asia-Pacific region and forging links between the UK and Asian economies to give our companies the best opportunity to work and invest in the world's fastest growing markets is a key part of our long-term economic plan. Joining the AIIB at the founding stage will create an unrivalled opportunity for the UK and Asia to invest and grow together. (Osborne 2015)

The statement clearly indicates that the British government expected an economic benefit from enhanced cooperation between British companies and their Asian counterparts in the context of infrastructure projects promoted by the AIIB. Thus, pursuing these interests via an institution specializing in infrastructure development in Asia was perceived to be a more appealing strategy than listening to the advice of the UK's powerful ally, the US, to stay away from the institution. The US reacted with annoyance to the UK's decision to join the AIIB, even assuming the UK would be following a "trend towards constant accommodation of China, which is not the best way to engage a rising power" (Anderlini and Mitchel 2015). However, shortly after that, several other European states, amongst them Germany, France, and Italy, declared their intention to join the AIIB. Deliberately "ignoring direct pleas from the Obama administration" (Higgings and Sanger 2015), the three European states proclaimed their willingness to significantly contribute to the new development bank and actively engage in its establishment as "an institution that follows the best standards and practices in terms of governance, safeguards, debt and procurement policies" (Higgings and Sanger 2015).

With its strongly export-oriented economy, Germany in particular had a profound interest in diversifying its development policies beyond the realm of the large-scale and universal World Bank by participating in the more regionally focused and, at the same time, strongly specialized AIIB. It anticipated the possibility of increased political leverage over infrastructure development projects in Asia and associated export opportunities for German companies. Then German Finance Minister Wolfgang Schäuble declared, for instance, that "we [the German government] want to make a contribution to the positive development of the Asian economy, in which German companies are actively taking part" (Schäuble 2015, qtd. in Mercopress 2015). The government's decision to join the AIIB was also enthusiastically welcomed by the Federation of German Industries (BDI). Stefan Mair, member of the Federation's executive board stated that:

> it makes sense for Germany to participate as a founding member. It is strategically important for Germany to have a say in the AIIB as an export nation. From the point of view of German industry, it is important that the programs of the AIIB and existing institutions such as the World Bank and the Asian Development Bank, in which Germany also holds capital shares, complement each other well. The Asia-Pacific region is one of the world's most important growth regions and will be one of the world's largest too in the coming decades. A sustainably developed infrastructure is central to further investment. (Mair 2015, qtd. in BDI 2015)[6]

For the German government and its highly influential industrial association, the AIIB was thus considered a welcome venue for fostering economic ties with Asia, inasmuch as it increased their political and economic leverage in infrastructure financing. The German government did not feel obliged to foster development projects exclusively via universalist institutions like the WB. Quite the opposite: The absence of network effects incentivized it to diversify its cooperative efforts through parallel, independent, and even competing institutions. As the benefits associated with institutionalized forms of cooperation remain the same with increasing numbers of participating states, regionally focused and more specialized institutions like the AIIB are considered desirable institutional alternatives to the WB.

In sum, the analysis of the process leading to the institutionalization of the AIIB supports the argument that the absence of positive network effects associated with institutionalized cooperation on the issue of development aid created centrifugal effects on the structure of the underlying institution complex. For many states, pursuing development aid not only via large-scale, universalistic institutions like the World Bank but also via more specialized small-scale alternatives like the AIIB appeared highly attractive. Due to greater interest homogeneity, and the associated greater political leverage on infrastructure projects and anticipated economic gains within regional and specialized MDBs, many states decided to join the World Bank's competitor despite US diplomatic efforts to prevent their allies from doing so.

Compared to the policy field of financial stability, where strongly positive network effects inhibited interinstitutional competition to the advantage of the large-scale and universal IMF, institutionalized cooperation among states in the field of development aid was much more competitive. This does not necessarily imply, however, that universalistic cooperation in the field of development aid will become irrelevant or marginal in the future. It suggests rather that large-scale institutions like the World Bank might be forced to sharpen their lending profile vis-à-vis their institutional competitors to remain an attractive venue for states wishing to foster development cooperation. While it thus seems unlikely that the IMF will lose its central position within the institutional complex of financial stability, the World Bank might have to reinforce its reformist efforts. It could do so by, e.g., reducing its funding conditions to maintain its position in the institutional hierarchy within the institutional complex of development aid. Several recent studies point in this direction: The World Bank's lending conditions have become less restrictive over time, and competition among development aid donors for "in play" countries, especially in the Asian region, has increased (Hernandez 2017; Vadlamannati et al. 2019). Table 6.3 sums up

Table 6.3 Network Effects in the Policy Fields of Development Aid and Financial Stability and the Structure of their Underlying Institutional Complexes: Empirical Observations

Structural Characteristics	Policy Field	Financial Stability	Development Aid
Empirical evidence for Network effects (+ "present"/ - "absent") and mechanisms of institutional competition		(+) The regional and small-scale alternatives to the IMF like the BRICS CRA, the LARF, and the ESM lack the financial capability to address financial crises and contagion independently of IMF resources owing to their limited and economically homogenous membership. (+) The IMF, due to its universal and heterogenous membership can attach conditions to its loans, whereas its regional and smaller-scale institutional alternatives fail to provide the necessary political cover for unpalatable policies and consequently have to tie large shares of their loans to IMF conditions *(Invisibility of individual responsibility is desired).*	(-) States' particular development interests cannot be pursued efficiently via large-scale institutions like the World Bank due to the interest heterogeneity stemming from universal membership—regional and specialized development institutions like the AIIB are thus attractive alternative venues for states with specialized development interests. (-) States strive to increase their economic leverage in Asia by joining the more regionally focused and specialized AIIB—for them, participation is considered an opportunity to gain economic and political influence over infrastructure projects in Asia *(Visibility of individual responsibility is desired).*
Long-term effect on institutionalization processes		– States tie regional and small-scale alternative institutions strongly to IMF procedures and regulations; they do not operate independently. – Centripetal effects	– States engage in creating specialized and regional alternatives to large-scale MDBs like the WB. – Centrifugal effects
Topology of the institutional complex		– Centralized	– Decentralized

the findings from the preceding analyses conducted in this chapter: While strongly positive network effects have impeded institutionalization efforts in the policy field of financial stability, the process leading to the establishment of the AIIB suggests the absence of network effects in development aid.

Consequently, while decentralization tendencies due to centrifugal effects are immanent within the institutional complex of development aid, that of financial stability is marked by a clearly defined hierarchy headed by the IMF.

Conclusion

This chapter provides a comparative analysis of the institutional topologies underlying the international regime complexes of financial stability and tax avoidance. The chapter began by laying out the fundamental similarities in states' cooperation issues in both areas. In both policy fields, states set up institutions to regulate, strengthen, and stabilize global economic development. In both, states tackle the consequences of disparate developments in national economies, which are perceived as harmful to global economic growth. Moreover, the financial stability and development aid policy areas exhibit relatively high entry barriers. To establish institutionalized forms of cooperation in the fields of financial stability and development aid, states need to obtain significant fiscal and political power. Moreover, the chapter demonstrated that in both policy fields, states cooperate in providing public goods, which are essentially nonexcludable and are associated with benefits for states, irrespective of their direct contribution to financial stability or development aid institutions.

However, the chapter demonstrated that the two issues differ significantly regarding the network effects associated with institutionalized forms of interstate cooperation. In the case of financial stability, large-scale institutions like the IMF come with significant functional advantages compared to their more limited regional competitors. Due to its large and heterogenous membership, the IMF pools more extensive financial resources enabling it to address liquidity problems affecting its members. It can also more easily accumulate additional funds from the private sector due to its high creditworthiness stemming from risk diversification among its broad membership. Moreover, large-scale institutions in the issue area of balance of payments assistance provide the significant network effect of blame diffusion. Due to its universal membership, the IMF constitutes an attractive lender of last resort that can push through harsh conditionalities while providing other members with political cover. In the policy field of development aid, the opposite is the case. Development projects are attractive sources of soft power for states. They can be used to leverage reputation or even to influence domestic politics in recipient countries directly. States are not interested in political cover and blame diffusion but in the visibility of their contribution. The more states contribute to any project, the less visible individual contributions become, which is why marginal reputation gains decrease with increasing numbers of participating member states.

Moreover, larger-scale institutions make it more difficult for states to push through their individual development interests, whereas more regionally focused and small-scale institutions allow more specialized projects to be pursued by groups of like-minded states with similar development interests and agendas. The resulting dynamics, it has been argued, result in long-term centripetal effects on institutional topologies in the case of financial stability but long-term centrifugal effects in the case of development aid.

The subsequent comparative network analysis of the interinstitutional structures underlying both regime complexes corroborates these theoretical expectations. While the networks underlying the financial stability complex are strongly centralized, with the IMF as the clear-cut institutional center, the networks underlying the development aid complex are significantly more decentralized. Here, the World Bank faces several alternative international institutions with comparably central positions. The qualitative analysis of institutionalization processes within the issue area of development aid demonstrates that this more decentralized structure was strongly influenced by the functional attractiveness of more regionally focused, specialized MDBs due to the absence of network effects. Since many states were not bound to universal forms of cooperation as they were in the issue area of financial stability, they were eager to join new, regionally focused, and specialized MDBs like the AIIB. The case study of institutionalization processes in financial stability demonstrates the opposite of institutional dynamics. Here, strong network effects and the associated functional advantages of large-scale cooperation tied states to the universal IMF, despite their political desire and actions to create independent alternatives. As a result, in the field of financial stability, strong, long-term centripetal dynamics strengthened the IMF as the most central and comparatively uncontested institution of the complex.

Notes

1. For the policy field of development aid, the OCED dataset on official development assistance (ODA) was consulted to identify the 24 most active states in terms of development assistance as percentage of gross national income within the period of 2013–18 (OECD 2019a). For the policy field of financial stability, the IMF dataset on the current account balance of 195 states defined as the "the record of all transactions in the balance of payments covering the exports and imports of goods and services, payments of income, and

current transfers between residents of a country and nonresidents" (IMF 2019) was used to identify the 24 most relevant states in terms of balance of payments.
2. A detailed description of the case selection logic and the operationalization can be found in Appendix A.
3. Membership status was gathered from the official institutional websites of each organization, or, if available, in up-to-date documents containing membership status information.
4. Note that if a state terminated its membership of a particular institution within the period of observation (2013–18), the IO–state relationship in terms of membership was coded "0." This ensures that the membership networks reflect the most recent patterns of institutionalized state cooperation, i.e., membership status in the analyzed institution up to the end of the year 2018.
5. For a comprehensive discussion of the conceptualization of interinstitutional network structures and the applicability and interpretability of network centrality measures, see also Chapter 4 of this book.
6. The original quote in German was translated by the author.

7

Diminishing Barriers to Entry and the Gradual Decentralization of Institutional Topologies in the Energy Regime Complex

The previous two empirical chapters provided static and paired comparisons of the institutional complexes underlying the policy areas of tax avoidance and intellectual property rights, as well as financial stability and development aid. This structural comparison allowed the effect of market characteristics on institutional topologies within these issue areas of global governance to be assessed. More precisely, I compared policy areas that are similar in respect to some market characteristics, but differ strongly regarding one specific market characteristic of interest. Following the logic of most-similar-system designs allowed me to isolate the influence of network effects and the type of good characteristics on interinstitutional topologies by keeping other important policy area characteristics constant. In the empirical chapter that now follows, I will analyze the effect of the third important market characteristic of policy fields, i.e., barriers to entry, by following a different research logic.

In contrast to the previous empirical chapters, this one will not engage in a static and paired comparison of the institutional topologies underlying two policy areas but in a longitudinal analysis of one complex and its underlying market characteristics and topology. This empirical chapter is, therefore, not interested in variation regarding institutional topologies across policy fields but in variation within one specific policy field over time. By assessing the gradual development of the energy governance complex from both a quantitative network and a qualitative process-tracing perspective, I seek to assess whether gradual but profound changes regarding barriers to entry, and hence the propensity for institutional competition, covary with the policy field's underlying institutional topologies.

There are particular reasons why it appears appropriate to analyze variation over time to assess the effect of changing barriers to entry into an institutional

The Institutional Topology of International Regime Complexes. Benjamin Daßler, Oxford University Press.
© Benjamin Daßler (2023). DOI: 10.1093/oso/9780198881926.003.0007

complex. Compared to market characteristics, network effects, and the type of good provided by institutionalized forms of cooperation, which refer to costs and benefits for states resulting from cooperation, barriers to entry refer to *ex ante* costs associated with the establishment of institutionalized forms of cooperation. The former concepts are more directly linked to the fundamental cooperation problem underlying a respective policy issue and are thus less prone to profound change over time. The latter, however, also capture structural conditions present in a particular policy field, like the exclusivity of cooperation due to the issue-specific distribution of capacities among states or the accessibility of technologies necessary to engage in cooperation (Lipscy 2017: 28–30). This chapter demonstrates how such hindrances to fostering cooperation via international institutions can be subject to profound change over time. Diminishing barriers to entry gradually allow more states to pursue cooperative benefits from institutionalized cooperation, increasing the overall propensity for interinstitutional competition within the complex. To assess these dynamics within the institutional complex of energy governance, I therefore analyze both changes in the institutional topology underlying the complex over time and the gradual changes regarding barriers to entry to institutionalized forms of cooperation on the policy issue. The underlying cooperation problem and, thus, costs and benefits stemming from institutionalized cooperation have not changed significantly over time. Barriers to entering the policy field, on the other, have changed significantly through recent decades. This chapter will demonstrate how both political and material (economic) hurdles to cooperation on the issue of energy governance diminished significantly and how this development translated into centrifugal effects on the regime complex's underlying institutional topology.

To this end, I first define and characterize the policy field of global energy governance. Subsequently, I lay out the market characteristics of network effects and good provision associated with institutionalized forms of cooperation in the issue area. I then provide a longitudinal network analysis of the institutional complex for 1993–2018 to assess the development of institutional topologies within the complex over the last 25 years. Finally, I trace the processes leading to the creation of the Energy Charter Treaty (ECT) in 1991, and the International Renewable Energy Agency (IRENA) in 2009. I will argue that, over time, significant changes regarding political, and material hindrances to alternative forms of cooperation that occurred within the issue area of energy governance increased the number of states interested in and, most importantly, capable of engaging in institutionalized forms of energy governance. For these states, pursuing alternative forms of institutionalized cooperation parallel to established institutions like the Organization of Petroleum Exporting Countries (OPEC) and the International Energy Agency (IEA) became increasingly attractive. The members of these established institutions had created and designed them in a way that for a long time had exploited the prohibitively high barriers to entry in order to engage in cartel-like cooperation. These institutions allowed their members to maximize their fossil-resource price-oriented (producer or consumer) interests. Diminishing barriers to entry incentivized states that had thus far not been capable of "entering the market" to create alternative institutions. Over time, the strengthening and creation of additional venues of cooperation on global energy created centrifugal effects on the institutional topology underlying the regime complex.

Market Characteristics and Institutional Competition in Global Energy Governance

Broadly speaking, states pursue institutionalized forms of cooperation in the policy field of energy governance to regulate and stabilize international markets on which the supply of and the demand for energy meet (van de Graaf 2013b; Van de Graaf and Colgan 2016; Goldthau and Witte 2010; Florini and Sovacool 2009). Most importantly, the rules and cooperative mechanisms underlying institutions in the policy field of energy governance "are designed to correct market failures" (Goldthau and Witte 2010: 7). So, institutions are set up to avoid price shocks during periods of energy crisis by, e.g., urging their members to make provisions that allow them to overcome potential breakdowns of supply.

Moreover, institutionalized forms of cooperation in the policy field of energy governance aim at lowering transaction costs for states, for instance, through sharing and pooling energy-market-relevant information (Goldthau and Witte 2010: 8). The frequent exchange of individual supply and demand expectations can help states to overcome uncertainty regarding the development of prices and production volumes of others. A third important reason for states to institutionalize their cooperation in the field of energy governance is that these institutions provide them with rules and standards for market exchange which can constrain or enable the behavior of states participating in the international energy markets (Goldthau and Witte 2010: 8–9). I thus conceive of institutions as part of the energy regime complex if they enable the exchange of energy-related information or provide their member states with rules and standards for the international supply and exchange of energy.

In the policy field of energy governance, institutionalized cooperation among states is associated with relatively modest network effects. On the one side, as far as energy-consuming states are concerned, an institution's having more members is associated with more significant leverage vis-à-vis energy-producing states. Institutions representing large parts of the "demand side" of the energy market can better push through their interests in negotiations with energy-exporting states, e.g., concerning prices or delivery volumes. This is because larger institutions are better able to build up higher oil and gas reserves and offer a larger market for oil suppliers, which, in turn, allows them to negotiate better prices for their members (Bamberger 2004: 154–5). At the same time, having more member states in an institution comes with potentially more significant interest heterogeneity. Growing numbers of potentially conflicting interests regarding the size of such reserves due to, for example, varying energy-import needs make finding a common position more difficult. The same holds for states interested in institutionalized cooperation with regard to coordinating the supply of energy resources. While their ability to increase energy prices in a monopolistic fashion increases as growing numbers of energy-producing states join an institution, it becomes increasingly difficult to coordinate potentially disparate interests. So, for energy-producing states with higher numbers of participants in existing institutions too, the "marginal utility of joining an activity" (Lipscy 2017: 28) does not necessarily increase. On the contrary, the more members access an institution that coordinates the supply and hence the prices of energy resources, the greater the potential for conflicting interests. For instance, with more large-scale energy-producing states joining in, the institution's supply quotas may decrease to stabilize or increase its overall energy output prices.

Especially for economically weaker, energy-producing countries, binding themselves to stricter supply quotas comes with potentially high economic costs. For instance, in late 2019 Ecuador declared that it would be terminating its membership of OPEC in 2020 because it perceived the quotas proposed by the other member states as obstructing its efforts to ensure its fiscal stability (Valencia 2019). Pursuing energy cooperation outside of the broader OPEC context allows Ecuador to increase its oil output in the market as "the countries would not be subject to OPEC's production limit anymore" (Jeremiah 2019). Thus, especially for states with national economies heavily dependent on energy exports, larger numbers of institutional members do not necessarily increase, and can even decrease the marginal utility derived from their membership of the institutions in question. These states actually benefit from relatively small-scale forms of institutionalized cooperation with limited membership.

Over time, the relatively modest network effects associated with institutionalized forms of cooperation have mostly stayed the same. Despite the development of new energy sources and technologies and the associated new possibilities for states to diversify their production portfolios (Francés et al. 2013), the utility of joining institutions aimed at governing the demand and supply of energy does not significantly increase with growing numbers of cooperators. Quite the opposite. Especially for states with particular interests in cooperation on renewable energy sources and technologies, pursuing cooperation with like-minded states outside of more broadly focused institutions with universal membership appears to be more beneficial. Cooperating on renewable energy technologies on a relatively small scale allows for the maximization of intra-group benefits without having to share patents or technology-related know-how with potential competitors.

Moreover, over time, there has been no substantial change concerning the (non) excludability of benefits associated with institutional cooperation in the policy field. Institutional cooperation in global energy governance and especially the associated energy infrastructures have also been aimed at regulating the use of common-pool resources (Goldthau 2014). As most energy resources, like oil or gas, and including some renewable resources, like hydropower, are not infinite, they are essentially objects of rivalry as far as their consumption by states is concerned. Still, without institutional mechanisms aimed at the regulation of their use, states and private actors can hardly be excluded from their consumption effectively.[1]

States therefore have incentives to engage in institutionalized cooperation to regulate access to these resources, thereby turning common-pool resources into club goods from whose consumption others can be excluded. For instance, the initial reason that the oil-producing Arab states engaged in the cooperation that ultimately led to the creation of OPEC in the 1960s, was to use it "as a vehicle to reduce dependence on the international oil companies by discussing royalties and taxes" (Colgan et al. 2012: 124). Such incentives to restrain access to energy resources are even visible in the realm of renewable energy. Access to certain renewable energy technologies is restricted to institutional members so that "with the depletion of nonrenewable resources such as oil and coal, substitutes become available [exclusively] for the members of the group" (Platje 2011: 15). For instance, such institutional "technology pools," including public–private partnerships, allow states to use and share patents and pool research and development information among the club members involved (Rossi 2014). Thus, the type of good provided by institutions in the policy field and, hence, the excludability of benefits derived from institutionalized forms of cooperation on the issue of energy governance have not changed significantly over time.

To sum up, network effects associated with institutionalized cooperation on the issue of energy governance and the excludability of benefits stemming from institutionalized forms of cooperation have not been subject to fundamental changes in recent decades. However, barriers to entering the regime complex have changed dramatically during that time. Due to these eroding barriers to entry, the number of states capable of initiating institutionalized forms of cooperation to regulate the supply and demand of energy sources has increased. While prohibitively high barriers to entry suppressed interinstitutional competition throughout what I will refer to as the "Fossil Age," the successive transformation of the global political economy of energy, marked by the gradual development and expansion of renewable and alternative energy sources, allowed more states to enter the institutional arena of energy governance. During the Fossil Age, these states were confronted with high barriers to entry to institutionalized forms of cooperation due to the high concentration of the international production profile of oil and gas (Lipscy 2017: 29). Many countries lacked access to natural oil or gas resources and were thus unable to engage in institutionalized cooperation on energy-related issues. On the contrary, these states were highly dependent on cooperative outcomes by states that controlled high oil and gas reserves (see, e.g., Rose 2004).

Besides these material barriers, there were also political hurdles to engaging in institutionalized forms of cooperation throughout the Cold War. Many states were restricted with regard to institutionalized cooperation on the supply of energy simply because they belonged to either the "East" or the "West" (see, e.g., Perović 2017). Especially during periods of dramatic tension between the two political blocs, the dominant superpowers, the US and the Soviet Union, engaged in policies that aimed at obstructing efforts to consolidate inter-bloc energy exchange or institutionalized forms of energy cooperation (Painter 2017). From the beginning of the 1990s at the latest, this changed. Not only did the collapse of the Soviet Union open new markets for oil-exporting countries, it also offered new potential oil and gas suppliers for significant energy consumers. Until then, these major consumers were heavily dependent on oil and gas imports from the Middle Eastern states and other oil suppliers, almost all OPEC members (Axelrod 1996; Andrews-Speed 1999). This political change came with rapid technological innovations, which increasingly allowed the replacement of crude oil as the most crucial energy resource by alternatives. These structural and political changes successively removed preexisting high barriers to engaging in institutionalized forms of institutional cooperation on energy. Cooperation outside of established institutions became feasible and increasingly attractive for states, especially those that had so far found themselves heavily dependent on cooperative outcomes of institutions like OPEC, which they had not been able to access. Thus, over time, diminishing barriers to entry within the policy field of energy governance significantly encouraged interinstitutional competition. Figure 7.1 illustrates some of these structural changes regarding the supply of and demand for energy from 1993 to 2017.

During the Fossil Age, when oil and gas were hardly substitutable, the governance of the pricing and trade of these central resources was highly exclusive. The number of states obtaining the lion's share of high-yield oil and gas reserves was limited and, to a great extent, organized within OPEC. For states outside of existing institutional arrangements like OPEC, it was prohibitively costly to set up alternative institutions throughout the Fossil Age. Not only did they lack the capacities and resources to compete against OPEC's regulatory power, but they also lacked the political capacities to set up energy trade arrangements with consuming states on a competitive basis (Jones 1990; Rose 2004). As far as major oil-importing countries were concerned, exclusivity regarding the governance of energy imports was also high, as the IEA, with its highly industrialized member states, unified the lion's share of oil demands and therefore had the capacity to supply high amounts of oil reserves to its members (Florini 2011: 41). For non-OECD states, it was comparatively tricky and costly to set up comparable reserves and to compete with the sheer market size offered by IEA member states to oil exporting countries.

With the end of the Soviet Union and the gradual opening of the energy markets in Eastern Europe, Russia, and Central Asia, competition between the two sides, major energy producers and major energy consumers, increased as new consumers and producers of energy resources entered the field of global energy governance (Konoplyanik and Walde 2006: 524). This development decreased barriers to entry, as cooperation outside the existing institutions became much more feasible and less costly as the new market players offered new resources to govern energy supply effectively. Moreover, during the late 1990s, and more rapidly from the beginning of the 2000s, technological progress and innovation spurred the development of renewable and alternative energy sources, as well as the exploitation of new oil and gas fields, and strongly diversified energy supply in terms of energy-exporting countries (Cohen et al. 2011: 27). This trend towards diversification of energy suppliers significantly reduced exclusivity as well as setup costs for alternative institutions. Institutional arrangements governing alternative energy sources

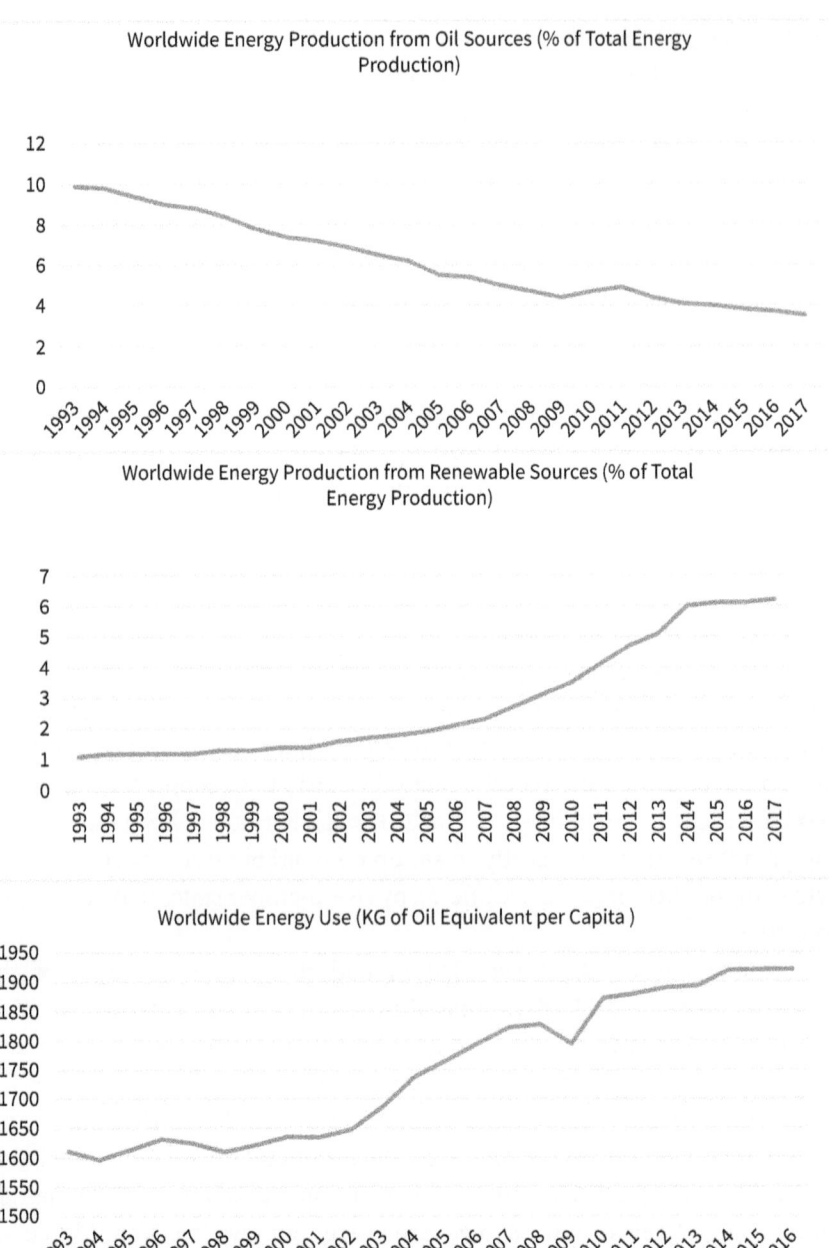

Figure 7.1 Structural Changes in the Policy Field of Global Energy Governance
1993–2017

Note: Own illustration based on data from the International Energy Agency (2018) and World Bank (2018b).

to oil and gas became much more feasible. Organizations with no explicit specialization in either governing the production and export of energy (like OPEC) or its consumption and supply (like the IEA) could be established to provide fora for consumer–producer dialogue and cooperation. Thus, these structural changes within the field of global energy governance successively eroded the preexisting high barriers to entry. It became more attractive and feasible to engage in cooperation outside the preexisting supply and demand fora and, over time, the propensity for competition increased steadily.

In the next section of this empirical chapter, I analyze whether and how these eroding barriers to entry institutionalized forms of cooperation in the field of energy governance affected topologies among institutions set up by states in the field. More specifically, I will map changes regarding the network structures underlying the institutional complex of energy governance over a period of 25 years. After that, the remainder of this chapter will provide a qualitative assessment of the proposed causal mechanisms of my theoretical argument by tracing the processes leading to the institutionalization of the ECT, the International Energy Forum (IEF), and the IRENA. In all three cases, eroding barriers to entry led to efforts to establish new institutional arrangements: Initiator states anticipated the lower political and material costs of engaging in institutionalized forms of cooperation and associated benefits vis-à-vis the institutional status quo. The more competitive institutional environment finally led to the participation of member states who had dominated and defended the institutional status quo. Thus, diminishing barriers over time increased the policy field's propensity for interinstitutional competition, producing long-term centrifugal effects on the institutional complex.

A Longitudinal Network Analysis of the Institutional Complex of Global Energy Governance

As in the previous empirical chapters of this book, I collected official documents from the most relevant international institutions in the field of global energy governance in order to map institutional topologies. For selecting relevant institutions, I again relied on prominent studies examining this governance area and its underlying institutions.[2] I included the G7/G8 and the G20 despite their relatively informal organizational character, not only because of their explicit focus on fostering sustainable cooperation among member states on global energy security but also because the G20 in particular increasingly served as an institutional opportunity for states to foster energy cooperation within a high-level forum and is therefore considered an essential institutional actor in the field (van de Graaf and Westphal 2011; Lesage et al. 2009). Table 7.1 lists the selected institutions and the date of their creation.

To measure the network structure among these institutions over time, just as in the previous empirical chapters of this book, I analyzed instances of references and coordination among all relevant institutions within the complex. To this end, I collected official documents from each institution for the survey period (1993–2017). These documents included official institutional disclosures published regularly, like annual reports, bulletins, or policy recommendations. Such publications comprise, e.g., narratives on institutional projects, analyses of and recommendations for cooperation and trade flows within the global energy network, and references to, or reports about, concrete energy-related projects within and conducted by states and private actors. The network graphs resulting from these references thus represent the intensity and direction of reciprocal references among the institutions involved during the period of investigation. To minimalize the effects of random events on the frequency of reciprocal references, I subdivided the period of observation (1993–2017) into intervals of five years. For every five years, I weighted the number of references within a specific set of institutional documents by their relative size, i.e., the relative number of document pages collected for a particular institution. Based on the results of this quantitative document analysis, I subsequently created sociomatrices in which each cell contained the weighted value of a referential tie between each pair of institutions.

As in the previous empirical chapters of this study, I further mapped the networks resulting from membership in the institutions in question by the

Table 7.1 International Institutions in the Policy Field of Energy Governance

	Institution	Year of Creation
Global Energy Governance	Organization of the Petroleum Exporting Countries (OPEC)	1960
	G7/G8	1975
	G20	1999
	International Energy Agency (IEA)	1974
	Energy Charter Treaty (ECT)	1994
	International Energy Forum (IEF)	2000
	International Renewable Energy Agency (IRENA)	2009

most relevant states in terms of their cooperative engagement in the policy field. To map variation within these membership networks for the policy field of energy governance over time, I created a sample of the most active states in terms of intergovernmental policy coordination on the issue.

The selection was based on quantitative criteria indicating the degree to which a state had a substantial interest in policy coordination on the issue in question.[3] To assess variation over time, I created two separate samples, one containing the most relevant states at the beginning of the longitudinal analysis, i.e., in 1993 and at the end of the period of observation, i.e., in 2017. The resulting membership networks for both points in time are undirected as they are solely based on the membership status of states in the IOs within a particular institutional complex. The ties among states and institutions were thus coded in a binary way: "1" indicated membership and "0" indicated nonmembership of a particular institution. Based on this coding, sociomatrices were constructed indicating the membership of the previously selected states engaged in international energy governance just before the starting point for the longitudinal analysis in 1992 and after the end of the period of observation, i.e., in 2018.

The following network graphs map gradual changes in topologies among institutions in the global energy governance complex. In the reference network graphs, the relative size of each node is based on its in-degree centrality. The color shade of a node, on the other hand, uniquely indicates its betweenness centrality, i.e., the relative number of shortest paths between all pairs of institutions that pass through the institution in question. The "thickness" of ties among institutions further indicates the intensity of a particular IO relation: The more a specific pair of institutions refer to one another, the more pronounced their respective ties are in the network graph. In the membership network graphs, which are undirected, the size of each node solely indicates its degree centrality, i.e., the overall number of connections a node has with all other nodes of the network. Thus, the size of each institution's node indicates the number of relevant states obtaining formal membership. The following Figures 7.2 and 7.3 compare the reference networks over time (1993–2017) and the membership networks reflecting state membership in 1992 as compared to 2018 in the policy field of global energy governance.

The reference and the membership network graphs indicate that the institutional topology underlying the energy governance complex became more decentralized over the observation period. During the early 1990s, the reference, as well as the membership networks of the institutional complex, exhibited two clear-cut institutional centers, OPEC, representing the institutional forum of energy-producing countries, and the IEA, representing the

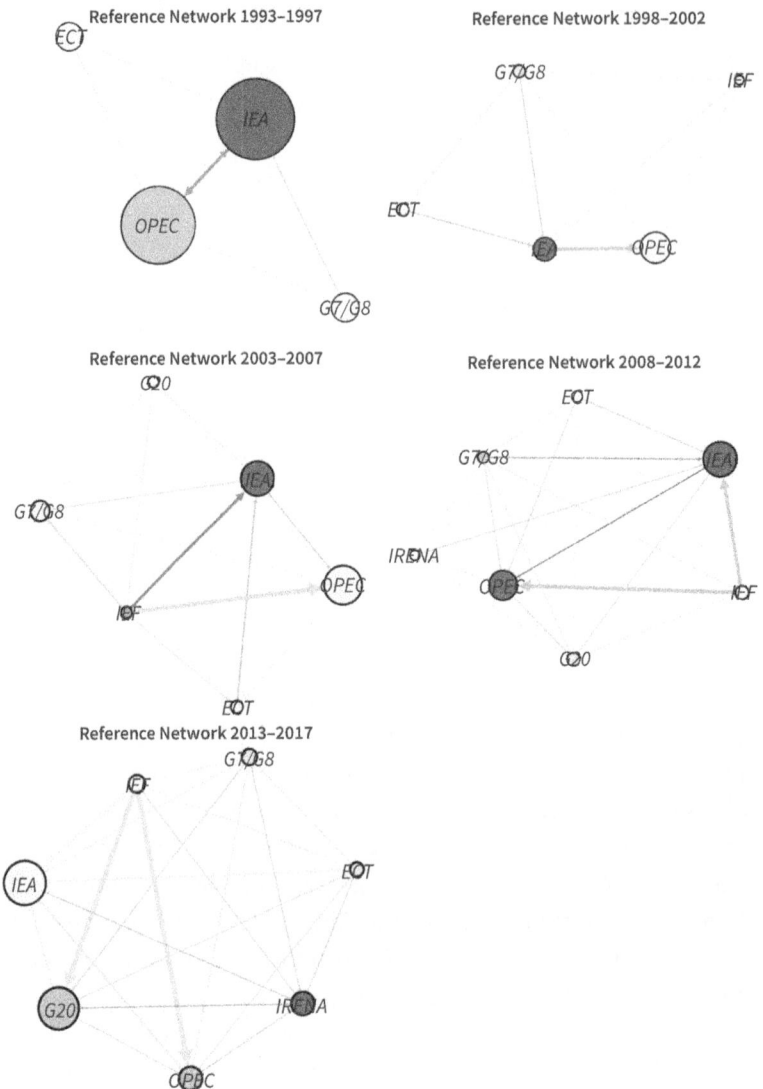

Figure 7.2 Reference Networks of the Institutional Complexes of Energy Governance (1993–2017).

Note: Graphs created with the network visualization tool Gephi (v. 0.9.2). The size of the nodes indicates an institution's weighted in-degree centrality, i.e. the number of weighted references by all other institutions. The color shade of the node indicates its betweenness centrality

venue for cooperation on the demand side. Over time several alternative institutional fora were created, like the IEF, the G20, and IRENA, which have successively occupied more central positions within the reference network underlying the energy governance complex.

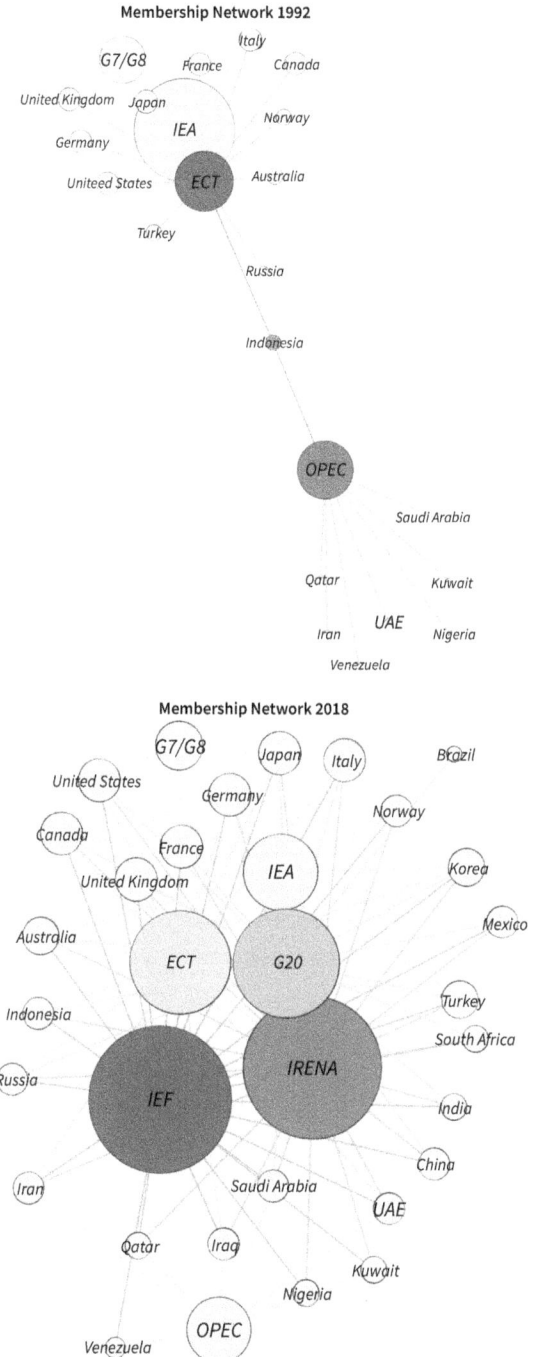

Figure 7.3 Membership Networks of the Institutional Complex of Energy Governance (1992 and 2018)

The network graphs indicate that, since its formal creation in 2009, IRENA has improved its position within both the reference and membership network of the complex. The same holds for the G20, which since, its initial gathering in 1999, has continuously strengthened its network centrality in the interinstitutional complex of global energy governance. As of the last period of observation (2013–17), in terms of weighted in-degree centrality, it holds a similarly central position in the reference network of international energy institutions like the IEA and OPEC. Albeit less significantly than the G20, the IEF too, since its formal establishment in 1991, has consolidated its position within the reference network of the energy governance complex. Especially in terms of membership by relevant states engaging the policy field, the IEF has gathered a focal position vis-à-vis other institutions like the ECT or OPEC. Most importantly, like IRENA, it has managed to include both major energy-consuming and producing states among its members.

Compared to the starting point of the longitudinal analysis, i.e., the beginning of the 1990s, when the IEA and OPEC were the most central institutions in the regime complex of energy governance, its topology today appears to be much more decentralized. Not only have states set up several alternatives to OPEC and IEA, these institutions have gradually moved into more central positions within the reference networks over time. Today, authority among institutions thus appears to be much more fragmented, not only in terms of membership by important states but also in terms of interinstitutional references by other institutions of the field. To systematically capture these differences over time, Figure 7.4 compares the weighted in-degrees of institutions in the energy governance complex, which capture the weighted number of incoming referential ties to each institution by all other institutions in the reference network.

While the IEA and OPEC today can still be considered focal institutions in terms of interinstitutional references, the analysis indicates that the institutional topology underlying the energy governance complex has become more decentralized as other institutions have caught up with both institutions regarding network centrality. Within the most recent observation period (2013–17), the G20 has almost caught up with the IEA and OPEC as the institutions with the highest number of weighted incoming references in the network. Although other institutions like IRENA and the IEF are still less central in terms of their weighted in-degree centrality, over time, they have gained more central positions in the energy governance reference network.

This trend towards a decentralized topology of the complex is also reflected in the distribution of betweenness centralities among institutions within

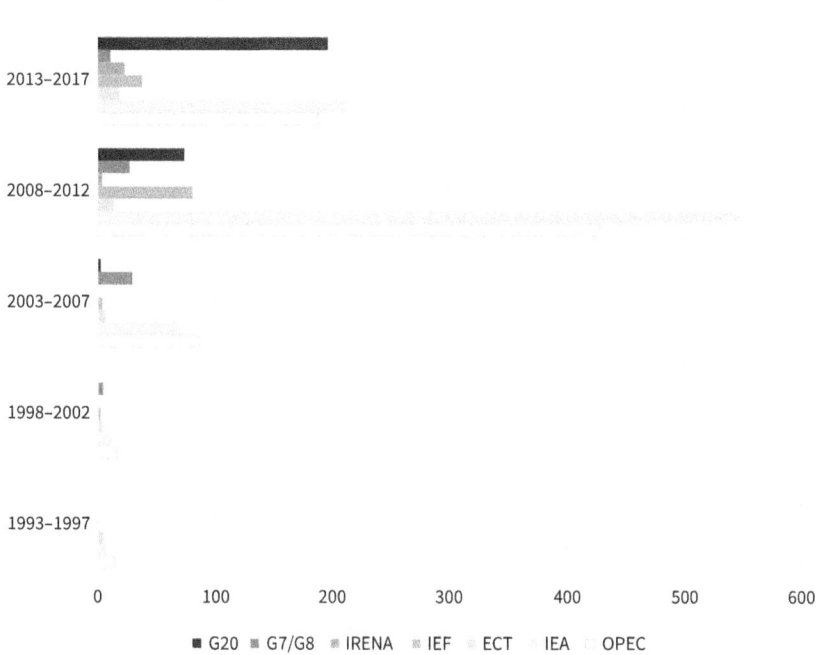

Figure 7.4 Weighted In-Degrees by Institution and Period of Observation: Energy Governance Complex

their reference networks over time. Recalling that betweenness centrality is based on shortest paths, i.e., the minimum number of edges lying between a particular pair of institutions, the concept allows one to assess whether all other institutions of the network are indirectly connected via the institution in question. It thus indicates the centrality of an institution in terms of information transmission or interinstitutional coordination. Institutions that hold high betweenness centralities can be conceived of as having brokerage positions among other institutions in their network. They connect otherwise rather isolated parts of the overall network. Therefore, they can use their network positions to influence the flow and transmission of information and initiate interactions among unconnected nodes. Institutions with high betweenness centralities can obtain high degrees of communicative control and structural autonomy within their respective interinstitutional networks. Figure 7.5 compares the normalized betweenness centralities of institutions within their respective reference networks over time.

Over time, the betweenness centralities of institutions within the reference network of global energy governance have converged and, in the most recent period of observation, IRENA has become the most central institution in terms of betweenness followed by the G20 and OPEC. The IEA's betweenness centrality score, by contrast, has steadily decreased throughout the five periods of observation. This indicates that especially IRENA's but also the G20's increase in betweenness centrality was mainly at the expense of the IEA. While the former two institutions have gained structural autonomy and communicative control within the reference network of international energy institutions, the latter organization seems to have lost, at least partially, this kind of influence over time.

In sum, the longitudinal analysis of the reference and membership networks underlying the energy governance complex suggests that its topology has changed over time. OPEC and the IEA dominated the reference and membership networks underlying the complex of during the first observation periods. Although it has not vanished completely, this dominance in

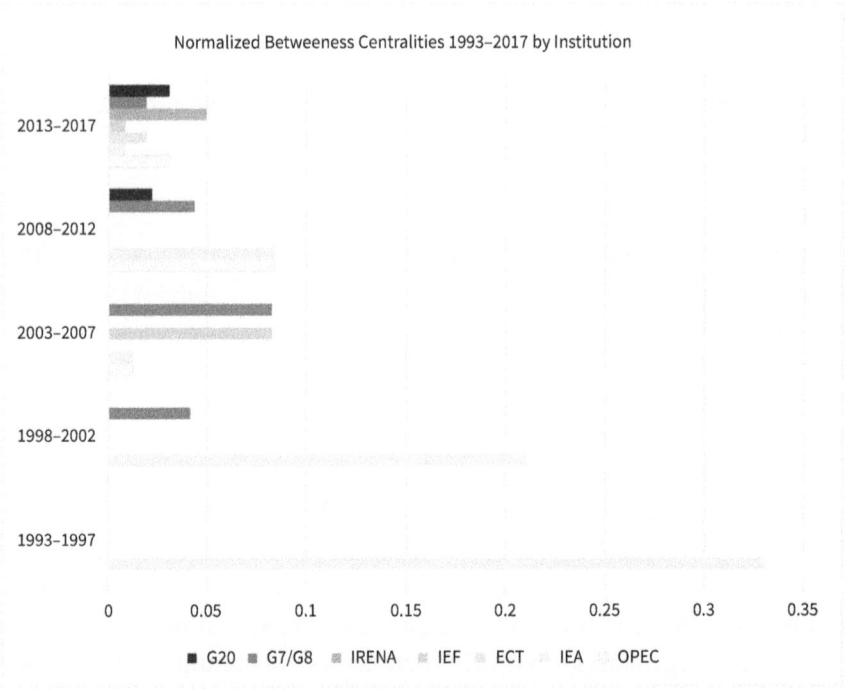

Figure 7.5 Normalized Betweenness Centralities by Institution and Period of Observation: Energy Governance Complex

terms of network centrality has partially eroded over recent decades. IRENA and the G20 in particular have increased their reference and membership network positions vis-à-vis OPEC, the IEA, and the G7/8. The analysis conducted in this section thus indicates that institutional authority within the complex of energy governance has become increasingly contested over the last 25 years. How can this variation over time be explained? In the following, I will qualitatively trace the associated institutionalization processes in the energy governance complex over these nearly thirty years. The subsequent case studies pinpoint the causal effect of the change in barriers to entry to the complex as far as states were concerned. While high barriers to entry at the beginning of the 1990s prohibited many of them from engaging in institutionalized cooperation on the issue, over time these barriers eroded significantly and the number of states entering the arena of global energy governance increased enormously, as did their ability to engage in alternative regime creation. Thanks to significant structural changes diminishing barriers to entry, and thereby prompting interinstitutional competition in the policy field, it became increasingly attractive for these states to foster cooperation via alternative or even competitive institutions.

The previous section demonstrated that both the network effects associated with cooperation on the issue of energy and the type of good provided by the policy field's institutions have not changed over the last decades. What, however, has changed dramatically over the last decades are barriers to entry. Due to fundamental political and technological changes, the number of actors capable of engaging in institutionalized forms of cooperation on the issue of energy governance has increased enormously. Lower barriers to entry into the "institutional arena" of energy governance has encouraged interinstitutional competition in the policy field and created incentives for states to engage in alternative and even competitive institution building.

In the subsequent sections of this empirical chapter, I will trace the processes leading to the initiation of the Energy Charter Process, culminating in the establishment of the ECT in the early 1990s and the IRENA in 2009. Both cases empirically illustrate how political and technological changes created opportunities for states to engage in institutionalized forms of cooperation that they had not been able to engage in before. As these states were dissatisfied with existing institutional arrangements, lower barriers to entry incentivized them to foster the creation of alternative and new institutions, thereby producing centrifugal effects on institutional topologies underlying the institutional complex of energy governance.

The Fall of the Iron Curtain and the Institutionalization of the Energy Charter Process

The fall of the Iron Curtain and the collapse of the Soviet Union at the beginning of the 1990s dramatically changed the general geopolitical momentum and notably altered the incentives and constraints affecting states' desire to engage in institutionalized forms of cooperation. During the period of the Cold War, the hardened political and, especially, economic fronts between the political blocs of West and East represented prohibitively high barriers to states interested in fostering cooperation on energy across the boundaries of the two political units (see, e.g., Perović 2017; Painter 2017). With the end of the Soviet Union and the emergence of new and politically independent Central and Eastern European states, these hurdles diminished. While the growing economies in Western Europe controlled only minimal fossil energy sources and were therefore strongly dependent on imports mainly from the Arab Region, "former Soviet Republics were rich in energy but needed fresh investments to rebuild their economies and overcome political-economic divisions" (Iacob and Cirlig 2016: 72). Especially during the Oil Crisis in the early 1970s, Western European states recognized their vulnerability regarding disruptions of the supply of oil, especially by OPEC (Kohl 1976). Although the IEA had been founded in response to the crisis in 1974 with the primary goal of being better able to respond to physical disruption of oil supplies, most of its members were net importers of energy. Even the powerful and resource-rich United States could not act as a supplier for Western Europe and Japan due to its rapidly growing demand (Kohl 1976: 82).

Thus, for a long time, there was an intense desire among Western European governments to engage in institutionalized forms of cooperation on the issue of energy with the resource-rich countries of Eastern Europe and Central Asia. Nevertheless, the strong political and economic divisions during the period of the Cold War represented significant political hurdles to institutionalizing cooperation beyond the borders of either bloc. The efforts of Italy and especially its oil company "Ente Nazionale Idrocarburi" (ENI) to deepen and expand institutionalized cooperation on oil supply with the Soviet Union may serve as a good example. To relax their national oil dependency, the Italian government, together with ENI, initiated several deals with the Soviet Union to institutionalize the exchange of energy resources for Italian petrochemical and industrial products during the 1960s (Bini 2017). Due to security and geopolitical considerations, the US strongly opposed and even interfered with these Italian policies, claiming that these deals represented "a threat to the North Atlantic Treaty Organization's (NATO's) stability and security, … a challenge to the control oil majors had over international oil resources, and, in particular, … an expression of a growing divergence between the United States (US) and Italy" (Bini 2017: 202). The US administration consequently undertook solid diplomatic efforts to interfere in Italy´s cooperative engagement with the Soviet Union and to avoid a deepening of this institutionalization of inter-bloc cooperation by the Italians (Bini 2017: 206).

With the end of the Soviet Union, these substantial political barriers to entering institutionalized forms of cooperation with Eastern and Central European States diminished. Not surprisingly, in June 1990 Dutch Prime Minister Rudd Lubbers presented his idea of a European Energy Charter at a European Council meeting to enhance industrial cooperation in the field of energy governance, which was intended also to catalyze the economic revival of the former Soviet Republics (Axelrod 1996: 497). At the same time, the proposed institution should "improve the security of supply prospects for those Contracting Parties, mainly western, central and eastern European countries, which are energy consumers and dependent on imports" (Papaioannou 1995: 35). Thus, the prospect of decreasing dependency on Arab oil imports while at the same time enhancing industrial export opportunities created strong incentives to engage in the creation of a new international energy institution. In contrast to the existing IEA, this new institution would explicitly consist of both large net consumers of energy and large net producers of energy. With the end of the Cold War, this constellation of institutional members was finally possible. Due to its institutional design as an explicit subsidiary organization of the OECD, the IEA can be considered relatively rigid with regard to the admission of new member states. Therefore, incentives to engage in institutionalized forms of cooperation outside existing fora were high.

Even for former Soviet states lacking significant oil or gas resources, the diminishing political barriers in the context of the fall of the Iron Curtain created strong incentives to engage in institutionalized cooperation under a new Energy Charter. Many of these states, such as Armenia and Georgia, can be considered as vital transit countries because they are geographically surrounded by major energy supply and demand states. Especially with respect to the transfer of gas from Eastern to Western Europe, institutionalized cooperation would help such states to raise transit fees, which represented a potentially good source of income (Andrews-Speed 1999: 125). Thus, with the fall of the Iron Curtain, the number of states interested in and capable of initiating alternative forms of institutionalized cooperation on the issue of energy governance grew dramatically due to significantly diminished barriers to entry.

In December 1991, just one and a half years after the Dutch prime minister had first proposed it, the European Energy Charter was signed, following a conference in The Hague, by 49 states and the European Union, amongst them several non-European states such as Australia, Canada, and the United States. In its initial form, the European Energy Charter resembled a nonbinding memorandum of understanding. However, it already included important foundational principles which paved the way for the intensification and deepening of the so-called Energy Charter Process that followed. In the founding document, the member states directly referred to the structural changes in the policy field of energy governance and the associated need to expand institutionalized forms of cooperation beyond existing ones by declaring that they were:

> aware that account must be taken of the problems of reconstruction and restructuring in the countries of Central and Eastern Europe and in the USSR and that it is desirable for the signatories to participate in joint efforts aimed at facilitating and promoting market-oriented reforms and modernization of energy sectors in these countries. (Energy Charter Secretariat 2016: 27)

In the years that followed, the Energy Charter Process was intensified, culminating in the signing of the Energy Charter Treaty and the Energy Charter Protocol on Energy Efficiency and Related Environmental Aspects (PEEREA) in Lisbon in 1994. Membership of this now legally binding multilateral treaty was further expanded with the joining of other important member states such as Japan, Russia, and Turkey (Konoplyanik and Walde 2006: 525). Compared to preexisting multilateral arrangements in the field of global energy governance like the IEA, the G7/8 or OPEC, the ECT, for the first time, established concrete legally binding mechanisms for the solution of energy-related disputes among participating states, reflecting the diversity of its membership in terms of energy supply and demand interests. Many observers even considered the ECT to be "the multilateral investment treaty with the widest scope; it is distinct from all other bilateral treaties by the fact that it is only applicable to energy—defined in a wide way" (Konoplyanik and Walde 2006: 528) as it allows even private entities to make use of a separate "Investor–state dispute settlement" (ISDS) mechanism to sue states in an international forum (Tienhaara and Downie 2018).

Without the fundamental political and structural changes that took place with the end of the Soviet Union and the economic liberalization processes in large parts of Eastern Europe and Central Asia, the success of the Energy Charter Process is difficult to imagine. With the entrance of several resource-rich states into the then open global oil and gas market, incentives to institutionalize the exchange of energy between them and the major energy-demanding states of the West grew dramatically. Thus, while interinstitutional competition was severely restricted throughout the period of the Cold War due to the high political costs of institutionalized forms of cooperation on energy involving the East and the West, this changed with the fall of the Iron Curtain. Within a brief period, incentives for creating alternative institutions capable of promoting cooperation among major energy-demanding states and states able and willing to supply energy resources increased strongly.

The Proliferation and Expansion of Renewable Energies and the Creation of IRENA

The previous section traced the process leading to the institutionalization of the Energy Charter Process in the early 1990s. Diminishing political and economic barriers to establishing new institutional forms of cooperation on the issue of energy governance significantly spurred that process. This section demonstrates how the shrinking of another major hurdle to engagement in institutionalized forms of cooperation on the supply and demand of energy provided further incentives for states to create alternative institutions: The increasing availability of renewable energy sources and the associated relaxation of one-sided supply–demand dependencies among states. As the previous case study demonstrated, at the beginning of the 1990s, the propensity for competition in the policy area of global energy governance altered due to fundamental political changes associated with the fall of the Iron Curtain and the liberalization of parts of the Eastern European energy markets. These changes had an effect on the incentives and obstacles to states engaging in institutionalized forms of cooperation, culminating in the intensification and institutionalization of the Energy Charter Process. The policy field was further affected by structural changes in energy production portfolios over time, which also fundamentally affected the policy field's underlying propensity for interinstitutional competition. The significant expansion of renewable energy technologies increased the number of states with fundamental interests in coordinating and institutionalizing the exchange and transfer of such technologies while at the same time reducing costs associated with the establishment of alternative institutions due to relaxed dependencies on major energy-producing states.

Especially developed economies with vital technology-based industries in Western and northern Europe—Germany, Denmark, and Spain, for example—regarded the institutionalization of cooperation on the issue of renewable energies as a promising tool to emancipate themselves more thoroughly from existing institutions like the IEA, which, in their eyes, had been "captured by specific interests ... without fully reflecting the potential of renewable energies" (Urpelainen and Van de Graaf 2015: 813). Germany had been a strong proponent of enhanced international cooperation on the issue of renewable energies since the early 1990s, and even more forcefully in the context of its *"Energiewende"* [energy turn] when it proposed to institutionalize cooperation outside of existing fossil- and nuclear-energy-focused existing institutions (Hake et al. 2015; Eurosolar 2009).

The high degree of exclusivity in institutionalized cooperation on the issue of energy governance before technological innovations allowed industrialized states to diversify their energy supply beyond fossil and nuclear sources had strongly tied many states to existing forms of institutional cooperation. Most importantly, fostering institutionalized cooperation outside existing arrangements dominated by fossil energy-rich states was associated with high material and political costs. These states used to obstruct any efforts to coordinate international cooperation on the issue of renewable energies because of it having the potential to endanger their market dominance. Herrmann Scheer, a social democratic German politician and one of the leading political proponents of the creation of a new institution with a focus on renewable energy sources and especially solar power, claimed in 1993 that:

> time is overdue for the majority of states not to let themselves be prevented from recognizing and acting on their interests by a minority of oil-producing and industrial countries. It is absurd to make the establishment of an International Solar Energy Agency dependent on the agreement of those governments who do not want it in the first place, and whose involvement would only do damage because they would obstruct the agency's efforts. (Scheer 1993: 21)

Nonetheless, at that time, the governments of those states capable of promoting and setting up such an institution, like Japan, Germany, and other industrialized "green economies," in light of their being still strongly dependent on fossil energy sources, considered upsetting significant fossil energy-producing states by such a move as too risky and associated with potentially high costs. For instance, the US and Japanese governments eventually shot down a proposal to create a UN agency to support solar energy. During the preparatory conference in the runup to the UN Earth Summit in Rio in 1992, they insisted that "it would make little sense to create yet another international agency; existing ones could or should handle this additional task" (Scheer 1993: 21).

Reluctance to engage in institutional conflict with major oil and gas suppliers, especially on the part of Germany at the beginning of the 1990s, perfectly reflects its strong economic dependence on oil and gas imports at that time (Hake et al. 2015: 237–8). This dependency represented a major barrier to pursuing alternative institutionalized cooperation outside existing international fora. The major renewable energy sources at that time, hydro, wind, and solar, comprised only a fraction of the overall German energy consumption in 1990.

In the years that followed, however, particularly solar but also wind energy capacities witnessed "an unimaginable market expansion from about 20 MW [megawatts] in 1989 to close on 490 MW in 1995" (Jacobsson and Lauber 2006: 264). This increasingly diverse energy market in Germany and other industrialized European states also resulted in a "growth in the 'political' strength of the industry association organizing suppliers and owners of wind turbines who were now able to add economic arguments to environmental ones in favour of wind energy" (Jacobsson and Lauber 2006: 265). Compared to 1990, the share of electricity production from renewable energy sources climbed from only 4 percent to 33.3 percent in 2015 (Bundesverband Erneuerbare Energien 2015). On the one hand, the rapid expansion of renewable energy sources in industrialized economies significantly decreased Germany´s dependence on energy imports. At the same time, however, it enormously increased incentives to engage in institutionalized cooperation on the issue to pursue cooperative benefits, e.g., by initiating the exchange of technology or spurring investments in research and development on renewable energy sources.

This strong interest is, for instance, reflected in the official initiative for the foundation of an international institution with a focus on renewable energies brought to the German Bundestag by the then German government coalition of Social Democrats and Greens in 2003, which claimed that:

[t]he promotion of renewable energies is no longer just a question of commercial energy supply but in many cases one of autonomous energy use and the introduction of appropriate technologies. Since renewable energies allow decentralized energy use to exploit their potential, it is essential to broaden the knowledge base in many different professional fields. (German Bundestag 2004: 2, translated by the author)

With the significant expansion of renewable energies within Germany's energy portfolio, barriers to engaging in institutionalized forms of cooperation on renewable energies decreased. Compared to the status quo ante, Germany was less dependent on the energy interests of major fossil-energy-exporting countries. As one of the leading countries in the development of renewable energy technologies, pursuing institutionalized cooperation on energy issues outside of existing institutions like the IEA—which was perceived to be controlled by fossil industrial interests—became much more feasible and attractive. Thus, with the expansion of renewable energies within major industrialized countries, institutional competition in the policy field of energy governance increased strongly.

In the years following the official German initiative for the foundation of IRENA, Spain and Denmark joined German lobbying efforts for a new institution. Both countries also had strong corporate interests in the expansion and technological diffusion of renewables. Of the global top ten wind turbine manufacturers, four were based in Germany, two in Spain, and the largest one in Denmark (Van de Graaf 2013a: 27). Together, these three countries started several initiatives at international level to push for an agreement on the establishment of the agency (Van de Graaf 2013a: 26–7; Roehrkasten and Westphal 2013: 7–8).

Renewable energy's expansion and technological development also brought another big player onto the scene. The United Arab Emirates (UAE), over time, has developed a significant strategic interest in the diffusion of renewable energy technologies. At the same time, in light of its investments and expertise in the sector, it faced comparatively few barriers to getting involved in creating a new institution. Due to its vast oil and gas reserves, the UAE possessed the material capability to invest in a new agency that perfectly matched its political ambitions to reduce its economic dependency on oil (Madichie 2011: 41–2). Thus, the UAE joined the "coalition of the willing" led by Germany and declared its support for the foundation of a new institution. Moreover, the UAE promised to provide substantial financial contributions worth US$160 million over the first six years to the new organization, which far outweighed Germany's proposed contribution of US$11 million (Van de Graaf 2013a: 24). In exchange for these massive contributions, the coalition of the willing agreed to locate the headquarters of the new agency in Abu Dhabi, the UAE's capital, while Germany reached an agreement to set up an "IRENA Innovation and Technology Center" in Bonn, Germany (Roehrkasten and Westphal 2013: 10).

Over time, the expansion of renewable energy production portfolios and the rapidly increasing commercial interests in many developed countries outweighed the costs of engaging in institutional conflict with major fossil energy producers. Barriers to entry to institutionalized forms of cooperation on renewable energy issues decreased. Hence, the attractiveness of alternatives to existing institutions like the IEA, with its strong focus on the interests of the fossil energy industry, increased drastically. For industrialized and technologically advanced states like Germany, Spain, and Denmark, creating an independent institution outside of the institutional environment of the IEA was considered an attractive opportunity to give the development of renewables "an 'additional push' because it lagged behind fossil and nuclear energy in terms of market structures, technology development, and established industries" (Van de Graaf 2013a: 26).

To sum up, the issue area of energy governance has witnessed profound structural changes over the last three decades, which have strongly affected the difficulties and costs for states of engaging in institutionalized forms of cooperation on the issue. These changes fundamentally altered the market structure underlying the policy field of energy governance, thereby enormously increasing its underlying propensity for interinstitutional competition. At the beginning of the 1990s, political transformations like the opening of the former Soviet Republics' energy markets and associated decrease in one-sided dependency among energy-consuming and energy-producing states significantly lowered the hurdles to engaging in institutionalized cooperation for many states, especially industrialized states from Western Europe, which had so far been strongly dependent on energy imports, especially from fossil-rich states organized under the umbrella of OPEC, faced new and desirable opportunities to cooperate on the issue of sustainable energy supply.

These political transformations were accompanied by profound technological changes in the field of renewable energy sources, which further altered the competitive structure under which states negotiated their institutionalized cooperation on energy supply. Many states, like Germany, Spain, and Denmark, which had long been heavily dependent on energy imports, saw the rapid growth of their renewable energy industry as a chance to decrease this dependence. They hoped to expand their energy production portfolios further by fostering institutionalized forms of cooperation on renewables. Compared to the status quo ante, the attractiveness of creating alternative institutions to existing fora like the IEA was significantly higher for them. This, in turn, altered the competitive structure in the policy field as it increased the number of actors interested and capable of engaging in the creation of new and alternative international energy institutions. The IEA had been the uncontested center of coordination and cooperation on Western states' energy supply. However, in the course of an accelerated global energy transition, its centrality in the complex decreased significantly. With diminishing political and material hurdles, many states began to engage in alternative institution building. Over time, this reinforced institutional competition and created centrifugal effects on the topologies underlying the energy governance complex, while interinstitutional topologies within the complex became more fragmented and contested.

Conclusion

This chapter conducted a longitudinal analysis of the evolution of the institutional topology underlying the international regime complexes of energy governance during recent decades. The chapter began by introducing the different research logic it used to examine the effect of market entry barriers on institutional topologies. Unlike the previous two chapters, this chapter did not make a static comparison of two specific policy fields, instead analyzing institutional structures and the propensity for institutional competition in the energy policy field over time. It then demonstrated that the network effects associated with institutionalized cooperation on the issue of energy governance and the excludability of benefits stemming from institutionalized forms of cooperation were not subject to fundamental change during the last few decades. However, barriers to entering the regime complex changed dramatically. Due to the erosion of these barriers to entry, the number of states capable of initiating institutionalized forms of cooperation to regulate the supply of and demand for energy resources increased over the period. While prohibitively high barriers to entry had suppressed interinstitutional competition throughout what I referred to as the "Fossil Age," the successive transformation of the global political energy economy, marked by the gradual development and expansion of renewable and alternative energy sources, allowed more states to enter the institutional arena of energy governance.

Two qualitative case studies of institutionalization processes in the issue area demonstrated that, due to technological progress and geopolitical developments, entry barriers to institutionalized forms of cooperation diminished significantly over the last few decades, prompting the formation of new institutional arrangements like the Energy Charter Treaty or the International Renewable Energy Agency. The chapter finds that, while institutionalized forms of cooperation on energy governance were an exclusive option for a small group of powerful states before and throughout the 1990s, declining political, material, and technological barriers significantly increased the propensity for institutional competition over time. The liberalization of the energy market after the end of the Cold War, the potential to exploit new energy resources in many regions, and the exponential increase in the availability of renewable energy technologies spurred the creation of the Energy Charter Treaty that regulates Pan-European investment in energy, and the International Renewable Energy Agency, created to reinforce intergovernmental cooperation on the issue of renewable energy transition. The longitudinal analysis of the interinstitutional networks underlying the regime complex presented in this chapter shows how the complex's underlying topology became more decentralized and contested over time. This gradual fragmentation came particularly at the expense of the IEA, which had been a central authority in global energy policy for many decades but has since found itself increasingly contested and partially replaced by new institutions like the IRENA or the more informal Group of 20 (G20).

Notes

1. Although the production of hydropower energy is infinite in the sense that the amount of available resources is reduced the more it is consumed (like in the case of oil and gas), the availability of accessible hydropower is still limited as the natural habitats necessary to install hydropower plants are finite and give rise to distributional conflicts (see, e.g., Hommes and Boelens 2018; Butcher et al 1986; Frey and Linke 2002).
2. A detailed description of the case selection logic and the operationalization can be found in Appendix A.
3. For the field of energy governance, I consulted the World Bank's "World Development Indicators" dataset (2019) including net energy imports by country over time to identify countries with the highest (hence positive) and lowest (hence negative) net energy imports.

PART IV

REFLECTIONS AND CONCLUSIONS

8

The Moderating Effect of Market Characteristics on Institutionalization Processes in Regime Complexes

In Chapter 3, I put forward the argument that the lack of comparative perspectives in the literature on regime complexity has not only made the comparison of interinstitutional structures across policy fields difficult, it has also led to the nature of their underlying cooperation problem having hardly played a role in theorizing the evolution of these structures. By drawing on, but also complementing, Lipscy's (2015; 2017) theory of policy area competition and intra-institutional change and making it fruitful for analyzing institutional topologies, I have introduced the market characteristics of issue areas as highly relevant scope conditions shaping how states can negotiate or renegotiate institutionalized forms of cooperation. Considering these significant differences in the underlying cooperation problems in policy areas, I argue, helps close the comparative gap in the regime complexity literature.

However, it is essential to emphasize that, given its research design, the book did not have the ambition to rigorously rule out alternative explanations for the evolution of issue-area-specific institutional landscapes. The theory developed in Chapter 3 of this book is not deterministic. Rather, the theoretical argument contributes to a better understanding of the long-term effect that the specific market characteristics of individual regime complexes' underlying cooperation problems exert on the evolution of different institutional topologies. The argument stresses that the individual regime complexes' configurations of the three market characteristics—excludability/nonexcludability of institutional benefits, network effects, and barriers to entry—shape the competitive structure and hence, the centrifugal or centripetal trajectories of institutionalization processes in regime complexes. Within the competitive or anticompetitive markets underlying the policy arenas of global governance, the power, interests, and geopolitical ambitions of states are of the utmost importance for the substantial qualitative outcome of these institutionalization processes. The qualitative empirical

The Institutional Topology of International Regime Complexes. Benjamin Daßler, Oxford University Press.
© Benjamin Daßler (2023). DOI: 10.1093/oso/9780198881926.003.0008

case studies in part three of this book underscore in particular the relevance of these factors in the negotiations of institutionalized forms of cooperation among states.

However, as I will argue in this chapter, these factors interact with policy fields' specific configurations of market characteristics. Specifically, I will show how the effect of state power and institutional design features on the institutional topologies underlying regime complexes are moderated by the market characteristics of issue areas. Based on the empirical evidence presented in this book's case studies, this chapter argues that varying market characteristics in different issue areas can reinforce or attenuate the effect of state power and interest, as well as the functional benefit of specific institutional design characteristics, on the long-term centripetal or centrifugal trajectory of regime complexes. Thus, whether and how particular power configurations among states or the heterogeneity of interests among them translate into their desired institutional outcomes depends on the propensity to competition underlying the issue area in which they operate. Whether and how states can draw on and utilize their power to pursue their interests in institutionalization processes depends on the configuration of market characteristics of issue areas.

Despite these interaction effects, it is important to stress that my comparative research design and the application of a most-similar-system design allow for inferences about the relevance of market characteristics to the evolution of institutional topologies beyond the policy fields examined here. In the following section, I will reflect upon the relationship between my structural explanation and alternative explanations for institutional topologies in greater detail. More specifically, I will lay out how my theory on market characteristics and institutional topology does not contradict but rather complements two prominent perspectives that were put forward by the literature on regime complexity, namely neorealist, power-based accounts and functionalist explanations emphasizing the role of institutional design. I also show that, while these perspectives provide important insights into institutionalization processes within particular complexes, they fall short of accounting for variation across issues because they have not considered the interplay of their main explanatory factors and the market characteristics of political issues.

State Power, Interests, and the Configuration of Market Characteristics

Many scholars interested in the causal foundations of regime complexity have analyzed their underlying structures by drawing on power-based explanations (Benvenisti and Downs 2007; Drezner 2009; Sell 2010b; Ikenberry and Lim 2017). These neorealist accounts claim, often more by implication, that the interinstitutional structures of regime complexes are epiphenomenal to state power (Mearsheimer 1994; Gruber 2001). Thereby, they implicitly put forward the argument that whether we observe centralized or decentralized institutional topologies depends on the power distribution among states engaging in institutionalized forms of cooperation. Institutional complexes will exhibit centralized topologies if centralized forms of institutionalized cooperation are in the interests of, and therefore supported by, powerful states. Even if states that might be considered weaker in terms of their power capabilities were interested in creating alternative institutions and thereby contesting these centralized structures, from a neorealist perspective, powerful states would always be able to prevent them from doing so by using their material strength to coerce the weaker ones into centralized forms of institutionalized cooperation. Conversely, if power tends to shift, resulting in a relatively more equal distribution of material capabilities among states, neorealist accounts expect institutional authority to become more contested, and institutional complexes to be marked by more decentralized topologies. From a purely neorealist perspective, therefore, institutional topologies should mirror prevailing power relations between states and their respective preferred institutional arrangements.

There is no doubt that, in many instances, institutional trajectories are crucially shaped by the relative distribution of power among states. Powerful states have the means to incentivize—in many cases even to force—less powerful states into forms of institutionalized cooperation that reflect their (the powerful states') interests most adequately. In tracing institutionalization processes throughout the empirical chapters of this book, I have shown that powerful states like the United States or China have used their material strength to push for forms of institutionalized cooperation that best fit their interests. For instance, China used its market power to incentivize states to join its newly founded Asian Infrastructure Investment Bank (AIIB) by offering participation in economically promising infrastructure development projects in Asia. The United States, despite initial resistance by some EU members, made use of its financial statecraft and influence to push for a strong IMF involvement in the EU's institutional response to the financial and debt crisis. Depending on their policy-specific interests, the use of material capabilities by powerful states thus either strengthened existing interinstitutional structures or severely weakened them.

Even so, a perspective that focuses exclusively on power distributions among states has significant shortcomings when it comes to explaining the institutional topologies *between policy fields* revealed in this book. Most importantly, the use of power capabilities is significantly restrained by the market characteristics underlying particular policy fields, resulting in diverging institutional structures across different issue areas even when those areas can be considered very similar in terms of the distribution of power among states. I argue therefore that the propensity for competition, determined by a policy field's underlying market characteristics, operates as a *moderating variable*. Depending on its degree, the propensity for competition either significantly restricts states from using their power capabilities to shape the institutional topologies underlying institutional complexes in accordance with their interests or significantly enhances their ability to do so.

For instance, although the US always has the economic capabilities to shape institutionalization processes in the policy areas of development aid and financial stability, the strong propensity for competition in the former significantly restrained the US's use of its hard power to shape the structure of the institutional complex in accordance with its interests. Although the US threatened to use economic sanctions to prevent countries' accession to the World Bank's (WB's) most recent institutional competitor, the AIIB, they could not prevent allies like Germany, France, and the UK from joining the competitor institution. As I pointed out in my empirical analysis, when considering and ultimately negotiating the terms of their participation, the representatives of these states proved themselves to be perfectly aware of the benefits associated with small-scale, more regionally focused development cooperation of the kind initiated by China via the AIIB. They therefore felt it was imperative to emphasize that participation in the new regional development bank for the Asian region would allow them to get a slice of the big pie of future infrastructure projects in this emerging region. For these states, the absence of network effects in the field of development aid rendered cooperation via the WB less attractive as their development policy interests in regional infrastructure projects were much more difficult to pursue in an inclusive and universal institutional environment marked by highly heterogenous interest constellations. Thus, especially for those states with profound economic interests in infrastructure development projects throughout Asia, US threats to sanction participation in the AIIB appeared less credible and fearsome in a setting of heightened institutional competition.

Pursuing institutional outside options via more regionally focused and specialized institutions like the AIIB appeared highly attractive by contrast, and I argue that these centrifugal effects in the policy field of development aid strongly constrained the US in the use of its hard power capabilities to prevent counter-institutionalization: Their threats to sanction accession to the WB's newly created competitor by, e.g., giving states that wished to accede less consideration in the allocation of WB projects, were not credible as all of those states were perfectly aware of their ability to pursue the very same projects equally effective outside of the WB. For them, the costs of sanctions within existing institutions were lower than the benefits associated with parallel participation in the more specialized and regionally focused AIIB.

The contrary is the case in the policy field of financial stability. Despite economic power distributions comparable to those in the field of development aid, the propensity for competition in the field is low. [1] This, I argue, led to the development of entirely different institutional topologies. As revealed by the case studies in Chapter 6 of this book, even though many states attempted to create alternative, independent, and more regional institutional arrangements to rival or replace the IMF, these attempts were largely unsuccessful in as much as all the alternatives remained heavily dependent on, and institutionally tied to, the IMF. In Chapter 6, I demonstrated how this failure came about because institutionalized cooperation on the issue of financial stability, unlike that of development aid, was associated with strong network effects. These effects render cooperation via large-scale and universal institutions such as the IMF highly attractive while aggravating and hindering the creation of credible outside options.

These strong network effects also allowed the US to use its hard power capabilities much more effectively to sustain the central and dominant role of the IMF within the institutional complex, since all credible alternative regional institutions remained heavily dependent on the IMF. As my empirical analysis throughout Chapter 6 shows, states that endeavored to institutionalize alternatives to the IMF were perfectly aware of the benefits associated with the more inclusive and larger-scale form of cooperation via the IMF. Furthermore, they knew perfectly well that these benefits could not be adequately replicated within alternative, more regionally focused, smaller-scale institutions. As a result, the US could effectively insist on involving the IMF in the alternative institutional arrangements to solve the balance of payments issues the newer institutions were meant to address. As the most prominent and influential leader of the IMF, the US was therefore still capable of significantly influencing important policy decisions in the context of financial crises as well as influencing, at least indirectly, decisions in regional alternative institutions like the ESM or the CMI.

Power capabilities are an important explanatory factor that helps us to understand which states can create alternative institutions, thereby contesting the preexisting institutional topologies underlying regime complexes. Power is, therefore, necessary for states to effectively initiate institutionalization processes aimed at (re)shaping interinstitutional structures underlying institutional complexes in accordance with their interests. However, states are constrained in their use of these capabilities by the market characteristics underlying the issue areas of global governance. Within issue areas marked by a strong propensity for competition, the use of hard power to constrain and limit centrifugal tendencies affecting the topology of the institutional complex is much less effective, as states interested in counter-institutionalization are much less dependent on existing institutional structures if desirable outside options are available. Threats to sanction counter-institutionalization strategies within existing institutions are therefore much less credible, since the benefits of participating in the newly created arrangements outweigh the costs of the potential sanctions.

By contrast, policy fields exhibiting low propensities for competition enable powerful states to exert their strength much more effectively, since states interested in counter-institutionalization face much less attractive and costlier outside options and are thus much more dependent on existing institutional structures, which renders threats by powerful states to sanction counter-institutionalization attempts much more credible. The costs of contesting the authority of existing institutions are quite high. Being excluded from IMF programs is associated with high costs in relation to the benefits associated with participation in more regionally focused and smaller-scale alternative financial stability institutions. This clearly privileges powerful states, which are able use their capabilities effectively to strengthen existing institutional topologies reflecting their policy-specific interests. In sum, I claim that considering the constraining or enabling effects of policy area competition on the use of power capabilities by states complements and modifies neorealist accounts. This allows for a more convincing explanation of varying institutional topologies across different issue areas as compared to perspectives focusing on the distribution of material power capabilities alone.

The Rational-Design Approach and the Market Structure of Policy Fields

The second prominent alternative explanation draws on functionalist arguments that focus explicitly on institutional design to explore the causal foundations of institutional structures underlying regime complexes (Abbott and Snidal 1998; Koremenos et al. 2001; Abbott and Snidal 2009; Keohane and Victor 2011; Jupille et al. 2013; Koremenos 2016). In essence, this perspective argues that states design international institutions in a way that maximizes the utility they derive from institutionalized cooperation. As Rosendorff and Milner (2001), for instance, show, states design trade institutions with escape clauses that are neither so cheap that states can use them at will, nor so expensive that they cannot deviate from their obligations without abandoning the institution. Hence, those institutions with the most "fitting" design in terms of utility maximization for participating states should occupy the most central position within the institutional network of an institutional complex. Accordingly, decentralized institutional structures should be especially prevalent within complexes consisting of poorly designed preexisting institutions which, in turn, incentivizes states to create more adequately designed institutional competitors, thereby exerting centrifugal effects on the issue areas' institutional topologies. By contrast, in complexes where well-designed institutions enabling efficient interstate cooperation for their members exist, interinstitutional structures should be centralized around these institutions.

I hold that the rational-design perspective provides important explanatory factors that help us to understand when and how states face incentives to use existing institutions rather than create alternatives or vice versa. Nevertheless, I argue that these perspectives oftentimes underestimate the restricting or enabling effects of policy area competition on a state's ability to consider strategies like selection or creation (Jupille et al. 2013). More precisely, just as purely neorealist accounts neglect the interaction of market characteristics with power capabilities, the rational-design approach underestimates the moderating role of a policy field's underlying propensity for competition on states' ability to design institutions in a way that maximizes their utility. Policy areas marked by strong propensities for competition make institutions with rigid distributive rules much more difficult to establish, even if they would maximize the benefits for states interested in cooperation. In policy areas where outside options are feasible and attractive, inflexible and rigid designs may incentivize states to shift their cooperative efforts to competing institutions with a more efficient and flexible design. This, in turn, creates centrifugal effects on the institutional complex's underlying topology.

By contrast, uncompetitive policy areas incentivize states to refrain entirely from multilateral cooperation, especially if the provision of nonexcludable goods is a characteristic of the policy field. In these policy areas, states have strong incentives to free ride on the provision of institutional benefits by other states. States interested in cooperation need to design their institutions carefully in a way that accommodates those with little interest in cooperation on the policy issue in question. As laid out in the theory chapter of this book, one way to accommodate nonmembers is to design institutional arrangements that allow for selective participation and to emphasize the nonbinding character of the institutions' underlying rules, though, while this may increase the institution's attractiveness for nonparticipants, it decreases the utility of cooperation for members. Consequently, institutions in uncompetitive environments tend to prevail, even if poorly designed, because they do not necessarily have to maximize their members' utility.

Therefore, in uncompetitive policy areas, even if states are very interested in creating institutional alternatives due to the inefficient design of existing institutions, they are strongly restrained from doing so by the realities of the policy area. All in all, while uncompetitive policy fields provide structural conditions under which even poorly designed, rigid, and inflexible institutions can occupy central positions within their complex, issue areas marked by a high propensity for competition privilege institutions with a "most fitting design" that will allow member states to maximize the utility derived from cooperation in addressing the area's underlying policy issue.

In Chapter 5 of this book, I analyzed the OECD's resilience as the uncontested institutional center of the tax avoidance regime complex. Due to the nonexcludability of benefits derived from cooperation on the issue, I claimed that the propensity for competition in that policy field was low: Nonmembers could free ride on the competitive advantages associated with OECD members' formal commitments. The OECD therefore had to accommodate the interests of nonmembers to ensure their participation. By trading institutional strength and effectiveness for support, it would be able to convince reluctant nonmembers to join its soft institutional arrangements like the Global Forum or its Base Erosion and Profit Shifting Arrangement (BEPS). Albeit many members indicated that they would have preferred much more rigid and thus more effective institutional instruments, they were held back from designing their initiatives in that way owing to the uncompetitive character of the issue area and the strong incentives for free riding. While these initiatives clearly cannot be considered utility-maximizing as far as OECD members were concerned, the nonbinding and voluntary design of its institutional arrangements consolidated the OECD's central position within the institutional complex of tax avoidance. Despite several initiatives aimed at creating more inclusive and more rigidly designed institutions outside of the OECD environment, e.g., under the umbrella of the UN Tax Committee, the OECD has been able to reinforce its central position within the complex.

Institutionalization processes within the policy field of intellectual property (IP), on the other hand, which I analyzed in Chapter 5 of this book, proceeded in a much more competitive policy environment owing to the excludability of institutional benefits. As I pointed out in of the chapter, the process leading to the establishment of the TRIPS agreement, the excludability of (economic) benefits derived from institutionalized forms of cooperation on the issue of IP forced developing countries in particular to join a comparatively rigid and inflexible institution. Confronted with the strongly negative consequences of strict and inflexible IP rules for their economies, however, these states were strongly incentivized to engage in counter-institutionalization. Accordingly, they shifted their cooperative activities to alternative institutions like the CBD or the WHO that operated under more flexible IP rules. Consequently, the central position of TRIPS in the underlying interinstitutional structure of the IP complex became increasingly contested.

As compared to the issue area of tax avoidance, therefore, in which the nonexcludability of institutional benefits and the associated low propensity for competition exerted centripetal effects on the structure of the complex, clearly strengthening the authoritative position of rather poorly designed institutional arrangements under the OECD umbrella, the excludability of institutional benefits in the policy field of IP and the associated strong propensity for competition exercised centrifugal effects on the structure of the complex favoring less rigidly designed alternative institutions to TRIPS. I hold, therefore, that institutional design features alone cannot explain the variance in institutional topologies across different issue areas. While institutional design features matter when explaining the dissatisfaction of states and associated incentives to contest institutional authority, this effect is moderated by a policy field's underlying propensity for competition: Institutional design features matter differently, depending on the policy field's competitive structure.

To sum up, in this section, I have presented two alternative theoretical perspectives on the question of why institutional complexes differ regarding their underlying topologies. While both accounts provide important explanatory factors that improve our understanding of institutionalization processes within policy fields and, in particular, of which states can shape institutionalization process in accordance with their own interests, they nevertheless fall short of accounting for the full variation of topologies between the various regime complexes of global governance. I claim that purely neorealist accounts overlook the constraining or enabling effects respectively of policy area competition on states' ability to use their power to pursue their interests when it comes to institutionalization processes. Moreover, I argue that the rational-design approach underestimates the moderating role of policy area competition on the persistence and perceived utility for states of different institutional design features and, hence, on incentives to either strengthen or weaken their position in regime complexes. My theory emphasizing the importance of policy area characteristics is compatible with both alternative explanations, yet complements both as well. Most importantly, in contrast to explanations focusing on power or institutional design features alone, my framework helps us to better understand issue-specific variation in institutional topologies. The market characteristics of issue areas do not contradict; rather, they moderate the effects of power and institutional design characteristics on the evolution of different interinstitutional structures.

Note

1. Some scholars have argued that, to some extent, the US is even less powerful in the issue area of financial stability than in that of development aid. They argue that Asian states such as Japan, China, and Korea are among the top holders of foreign exchange reserves in the world, with reserves far exceeding those of Western states, which is why one should expect them to be capable of "going it alone" by creating institutional alternatives independent from the IMF and its associated US influence (Lipscy 2017: 87).

9
Conclusion
Summary, Reflections, and Outlook

This book has pursued two main research objectives in order to close gaps within the existing literature on international regime complexes.

Its first contribution has been to provide a coherent conceptualization of institutional topologies that allows for cross-issue area comparisons. By introducing the network approach, I have proposed a concept of these structures that is both theoretically grounded and feasible in terms of its empirical operationalization.

The book's second contribution has been the development of a structural theory that improves our understanding of the long-term effects of the market characteristics of issue areas on the evolution of the different interinstitutional structures underlying regime complexes in global governance. More precisely, in this book, I have developed a structural theory that stresses the relevance of the market characteristics of policy fields and their resultant underlying propensity for competition: Acknowledging the centrifugal and centripetal effects respectively that competitive and uncompetitive environments tend to have on institutionalization processes allows for a deeper understanding of why institutional topologies have evolved differently across the issue areas of global governance. The following section will first summarize and reflect on this book's main conceptual and theoretical contributions before doing the same for its main empirical findings. In conclusion, I will reflect upon implications of these findings and delineate avenues for further research.

Networks, Interinstitutional Topologies, and Policy Area Competition

Even though the existing literature on regime complexity has for a long time, at least implicitly, recognized that the international institutions set up to govern the very same policy issues tend to develop "rival authority claims"

The Institutional Topology of International Regime Complexes. Benjamin Daßler, Oxford University Press.
© Benjamin Daßler (2023). DOI: 10.1093/oso/9780198881926.003.0009

(Alter and Raustiala 2018: 332) and thus implicit interinstitutional structures, it has so far fallen short of conceptually grasping and empirically measuring the degree of their centralization/decentralization. Moreover, as a result of the "within-case perspective" adopted predominantly within the literature, there has so far been no coherent understanding of what the interinstitutional structures underlying regime complexes are and, most importantly, how they can be measured.

This book proposed to synthesize insights from the network approach with literature on institutional authority to overcome this gap. Suppose we conceive institutional authority to be an institution's recognized claim to govern within a particular policy field. In that case, the network approach provides us with the conceptual and methodological toolkits to assess and compare the degree of institutional (de)centralization, i.e., the institutional topologies, across various institutional complexes. As a coherently structural approach, network theory allows for the fine-grained conceptualization of interinstitutional relations. It not only allows the positions of individual institutions to be compared vis-à-vis their institutional competitors, it also provides measures to assess the structural characteristics of institutional complexes, thus allowing comparisons to be made across different complexes. As research on regime complexes has so far produced many theoretical claims about the nature of interinstitutional structures but has fallen short in respect of providing feasible and consistent conceptualizations of them, in proposing a concept that helps to overcome this gap, this book contributes to "strengthen[ing] the foundation for comparative analysis of regime complexes" (Henning and Pratt 2020).

Moreover, the book has put forward a theoretical framework that helps to understand better why institutional topologies vary across issue areas. Drawing on, but also refining, Lipscy's theory of policy area competition and intrainstitutional change, it has highlighted the importance of three "market characteristics" of policy fields that impact the evolution of the institutional topologies underlying regime complexes: network effects associated with institutionalized forms of cooperation, the (non-) excludability of institutional benefits, and barriers to entry to institutionalized forms of cooperation within a particular issue area. It has argued that these three market characteristics influence a policy field's underlying propensity for competition, which, in turn, crucially shapes the conditions under which states negotiate institutionalized forms of cooperation within institutional complexes. As I have shown, the scope for action by states as regards institutionalized forms of cooperation varies wildly, depending on the propensity of a particular policy area for competition. Policy fields exhibiting strong propensities for competition can strongly incentivize states to engage in counter-institutionalization strategies like regime shifting, forum shopping, or regime creation, thereby exercising a centrifugal effect on institutional topologies. Such strategies are, however, much more difficult to pursue in policy fields marked by low-level propensities for competition in which outside options are much less attractive. Institutionalization processes in noncompetitive policy fields are subject to strong centripetal effects: states are bound to rather universalistic, large-scale forms of institutionalized cooperation and face fewer incentives to contest existing institutional structures.

In sum, the main argument made by my theoretical framework is that institutional topologies underlying institutional complexes are crucially shaped by their policy area's underlying propensity for competition. As such, I claim that a comprehensive understanding of these structures can only be achieved if the constraining or enabling effects of market characteristics on institutionalization efforts undertaken by states are considered.

Empirical Findings: Centripetal and Centrifugal Tendencies in Five Issue Areas of Global Governance

Drawing on a most-similar-system research design, throughout the three empirical chapters of this book I have provided real-world evidence for the plausibility of my theory: Comparing issue areas that are most similar to one another regarding two of the three market characteristics and other important properties but still differ regarding that other one has allowed me to isolate the effect of this particular characteristic on the institutional complex's underlying topology. Following the logic of covariation analysis, in a first section of each empirical chapter, I checked whether the differences in market characteristics covaried with the institutional complex's underlying topology, which I mapped using comparative network analyses. To go beyond mere covariation analysis, I complemented these findings with qualitative case studies of institutionalization processes within the two policy fields compared in each of my three empirical chapters. I thereby provided evidence not only for the covariance among my independent (i.e., the policy fields' market characteristics) and dependent variable (i.e., the underlying topologies of institutional complexes) but also for the causal mechanism underlying my theoretical argument: While competitive policy environments give rise to centrifugal effects on the respective institutional complex's topology since they incentivize states to engage in counter-institutionalization strategies, uncompetitive policy environments tend to produce centripetal effects on these structures as they strongly bind states to existing institutional arrangements, rendering outside options much more costly and hence unattractive to pursue.

Chapter 5 provided a detailed and structured comparison of the institutional topologies underlying the complexes of tax avoidance and intellectual property. The chapter laid out the main similarities between the two issue areas before elaborating on the most crucial difference: the excludability/nonexcludability of benefits associated with institutionalized forms of cooperation. I pointed out that, while in the issue area of tax avoidance, nonparticipating states cannot be excluded from the benefits associated with the cooperative efforts by others, in the issue area of intellectual property protection institutional benefits are essentially limited to cooperators. The propensity for competition in the tax avoidance complex is comparatively low, as nonparticipating states face the attractive option of free riding on the benefits of existing institutions and the associated competitive self-restraint of their members without bearing any costs themselves. The exclusive character of cooperation on Intellectual Property Rights (IPRs) through its strong links to trade privileges, on the other hand, forces states to actively engage in institutionalized forms of cooperation if they want to enjoy these benefits, albeit developing countries in particular may be forced to join existing institutional arrangements that are essentially against their economic interest. This, in turn, provides strong incentives for those states to engage in counter-institutionalization strategies like forum shopping or regime shifting, creating strong centrifugal effects on the institutional complex's underlying topology.

As the comparative network analysis revealed, these differences in the two policy fields' underlying propensities for competition do in fact covary with the topologies underlying their institutional complexes: While the institutional complex underlying the issue area of tax avoidance is strongly centralized around the OECD, interinstitutional structures underlying the issue area of intellectual property are much more decentralized. By tracing the process leading to the establishment of the OECD's "Global Forum on Transparency and Exchange of Information for Tax Purposes" as well as its more recent efforts to establish a legal framework addressing the issue of tax avoidance, which led to the successful creation of the "Inclusive Framework on BEPS," I have shown that the OECD's central position in the authority network underlying the tax avoidance complex can to a large extent be attributed to that policy field's low propensity for competition. Due to the nonexcludability of institutional benefits, the OECD was forced to trade institutional weakness for support by nonmembers. Nonmembers like China were perfectly aware of their ability to free ride on the tax-related competitive self-restraint of OECD members, which is why they initially shied away from joining the OECD's proposed arrangements. Only by catering to the interests of China and other nonmembers, particularly by offering soft and predominantly nonbinding forms of institutionalized cooperation, was the OECD able to "buy nonmembers in," thereby increasing the utility derived from cooperation for its members. At the same time, the soft and flexible arrangements further decreased incentives for nonmembers to engage in counter-institutionalization—for instance, under the umbrella of the United Nations Tax Committee—as they allowed them to sporadically cooperate on the issue in perfect accordance with their interests. Thus, the nonexcludability of benefits derived from cooperation on the issue of tax avoidance strongly constrained interinstitutional competition in the field, which, in turn, had a strongly centripetal effect of the OECD on the institutional complex's underlying structure in favor. According to the results of my network analysis, the OECD has fortified its central position in the complex over the past decades, albeit at the price of weakly institutionalized rules and the rather voluntary, nonbinding character of its tax avoidance initiatives.

By contrast, within the institutional complex of intellectual property rights, I showed that the excludability of institutional benefits provided a strong incentive for interinstitutional competition leading to centrifugal tendencies within the institutional complex of the issue area. Because participation in critical trade networks was institutionally coupled with formal participation in TRIPS, many emerging and developing countries joined the institution despite their reluctance and inability to comply with its legal provisions. Still, they considered exclusion from the institution and the associated negative economic consequences to be the greater evil and ultimately made up their minds to join TRIPS. At the same time, excludability strongly incentivized these states to engage in counter-institutionalization processes to combat the adverse effects associated with their participation in TRIPS: They shifted their institutionalization efforts away from the WTO environment towards other, competing IP institutions like the CBD and WHO, which promoted less strict IP standards more in line with developing economies' interests. On the other hand, developed countries engaged in counter-institutionalization by forcefully pushing for even stricter and more exclusive forms of institutionalized IP cooperation via bi- and minilateral trade agreements for which they formulated even stricter IP rules than those enshrined in TRIPS. This, in turn, created centrifugal effects on the topology underlying the institutional complex, as it gradually undermined the position of WIPO and TRIPS, which had been its focal institutions up to then. At the same time, it increased the centrality of alternative institutional arrangements like the CBD, WHO, or FAO, promoters of less stringent IP rules. It also encouraged IP proponents to draw bi- and minilateral treaties promoting rules even stricter than the WTO's. Overall, the high exclusivity of institutionalized forms of cooperation in the field of IP spurred interinstitutional competition, resulting in much more contested and fragmented topologies underlying the IP complex.

Chapter 6 provided a detailed comparison of the policy fields of financial stability and development aid in order to assess the influence on institutional topologies of varying network effects associated with institutionalized forms of cooperation. I pointed out that while the two policy fields are remarkably similar when it comes to their fundamental cooperation problems, resource allocations among states and, most importantly, the other two market characteristics, barriers to entry and the nonexcludability of institutional benefits, they nevertheless differ significantly with regard to the network effects associated with institutionalized forms of cooperation. While in the policy field of financial stability, cooperating states benefit greatly from more significant numbers of participating states, in the policy field of development aid large-scale, universalistic cooperation is not associated with such benefits. In particular, within the policy field of financial stability, large-scale, universalistic institutions provide political cover for painful and unpopular austerity measures associated with bailout programs for financially struggling member states. Moreover, institutions with a universal membership are much better at preventing financial contagion during financial crises due to their global reach: Compared to regionally limited institutions, global institutions can take quick measures by reallocating resources from nonaffected to affected countries, thereby containing the spread of liquidity crises among members. As my case studies of attempts to build independent, more regionally focused financial stability institutions outside of the IMF's influence, like the Latin American Reserve Fund (LARF), The European Stability Mechanism (ESM), or the Chiang Mai Initiative (CMI) revealed, the strong network effects associated with cooperation on the issue of financial stability produced strong centripetal effects since they bound states to existing, large-scale institutions while rendering regionally more limited alternatives unattractive and ineffective. In all of these cases, states carefully designed their alternative institutional arrangements to be closely related, both functionally and legally, to the IMF. Therefore, and in line with my network analysis of institutional topologies within the complex, the IMF, despite having been harshly criticized and contested throughout recent decades, appears to have strengthened its central and dominant position within the complex vis-à-vis alternative institutions.

However, within the policy field of development aid, large-scale forms of institutionalized cooperation are not associated with network effects. On the contrary, as this book's case study on the process leading to the establishment of the Asian Infrastructure Investment Bank (AIIB) revealed, states are aware of the benefits associated with more regionally focused, specialized, and relatively small-scale forms of cooperation. As large-scale cooperation comes with a much more pronounced heterogeneity of interest among institutional members, pursuing specialized and more regionally focused development interests is much more difficult in large-scale institutions like the World Bank (WB). Still, strengthening the individual economic profile and enhancing the visibility of individual development measures in order to increase political leverage are critical drivers of state development policies. Thus, compared to financial stability, there are no benefits to be derived from having more significant numbers of participating states in development aid institutions. So states are less bound to existing large-scale institutions, while alternative, more specialized, and regional arrangements like the AIIB are perceived as much more attractive. In line with the results of my network analysis, then, which revealed much more decentralized network structures underlying the development aid, despite the fierce resistance of the US, many of whose allies decided to join the newly founded WB competitor, the AIIB, thereby significantly weakening the WB's authority.

In the last of the three empirical chapters, I analyzed the effect of the third important market characteristic highlighted by my theoretical framework: barriers to entry. Instead of comparing two issue areas, as in the previous two empirical chapters, in Chapter 7 I engaged in a longitudinal analysis of the policy field of energy governance and its underlying institutional complex. I showed first that over the last three decades, though many policy area characteristics remained similar, the policy field changed significantly as regards barriers to entry to institutionalized forms of cooperation on the issue of energy governance. Not only has the number of states interested in, and capable of, sustaining institutionalized forms of cooperation grown significantly, but the issue area itself has witnessed profound structural changes that have significantly lowered the hurdles and costs for states wishing to engage in institutionalized forms of cooperation on the issue. These changes, I argued, have strongly increased the policy field's underlying propensity for interinstitutional competition, resulting in increasingly centrifugal effects on the topology underlying the institutional complex.

By mapping the institutional networks underlying the policy field of energy governance for the period from 1993 to 2017 in the following section, I demonstrated that institutional topologies underlying the complex have indeed become more fragmented. In the early 1990s, the IEA and OPEC appeared to be the uncontested institutional centers of their networks, throughout the years that followed, however, their central position became increasingly contested by alternative institutions like the International Energy Forum (IEF) and the International Renewable Energy Agency (IRENA). This was also reflected in the 'overall properties of the complex's underlying reference network, which have exhibited a continuous trend toward more dispersed and less centralized patterns of interinstitutional recognition over time.

In the section that followed, I provided a qualitative analysis of the processes leading to the establishment of the Energy Charter Treaty (ECT) in the early 1990s and IRENA in 2009, underscoring the plausibility of my theory's causal claim: While at the beginning of the 1990s both political and material obstacles to the creation of alternative institutions to OPEC and the IEA were high, many of these barriers to entry were successively reduced through the following decades. The founding members of the ECT anticipated a decrease in the political costs associated with institutionalizing the economic ties between Western and Eastern Europe after the fall of the Iron Curtain and associated opportunities to diversify their energy supply by institutionalizing the trade in fossil energy sources with former Soviet states; the founding members of IRENA, on the other hand, anticipated fewer material obstacles to the expansion and proliferation of alternative and renewable energy sources, thereby decreasing their dependence on fossil imports while presenting them with new market opportunities. The policy field of energy governance thus witnessed both profound changes in political structures in favor of more diverse energy trading opportunities, as well as far-reaching technological developments enhancing the ability of many actors to increase their autonomy regarding energy supplies. Both developments significantly lowered the barriers to entry to institutionalized forms of cooperation on energy governance, thereby increasing the policy field's underlying propensity for competition. While at the beginning of the 1990s institutionalized cooperation on the issue of energy supply and demand was highly exclusive due to a monopolistic distribution of resources and the high political hurdles hampering the institutionalization of the supply chain across political blocs, over the decades that followed, these barriers successively diminished. This, in turn, strongly incentivized states to create and strengthen alternative arrangements to existing energy institutions.

Finally, Chapter 8 reflects on the relationship between my theoretical argument, my empirical findings, and two prominent alternative explanations of institutional authority: neorealist accounts emphasizing the importance of

material power capabilities of states and rational-design approaches stressing the relevance of individual, institutional design properties to explaining
interinstitutional topologies. In essence, I put forward the argument that my
explanation, by highlighting the constraining and enabling effects of market
characteristics of policy fields, is compatible with and complementary to both
alternative accounts. More precisely, I laid out how the market characteristics of policy fields and their resulting propensity for competition moderate
the effect of the main explanatory factors of both alternative accounts of the
development of institutional topologies underlying institutional complexes.

Whereas within policy fields marked by a strong propensity for competition, states are much more constrained in the use of their power, within issue
areas where, owing to their underlying market characteristics, the propensity
for competition is low, powerful states can make full use of their capabilities to enforce institutionalized forms of cooperation that fit their interest
best. Owing to the lack of attractive outside options, less powerful states are
much more tied to, and dependent on, existing institutional arrangements
sustained by more powerful states. By contrast, in issue areas marked by a
high propensity for competition institutional outside options are attractive
and feasible, even for less powerful states. They are much less vulnerable there
to institutional action by powerful states to preserve the status quo in the
complex as they are less dependent on existing institutional structures. For
powerful states it is, therefore, more challenging to use their power to shape
the topology of institutional complexes in accordance with their interest if a
policy field's underlying propensity for competition is high.

The same goes for the effect of institutional design properties on institutional topologies. Within competitive policy environments it is very important for states to design institutions carefully so as to allow efficient and
effective coordination of the issue in question. But policy fields marked by
a low propensity for competition may even favor the dominance and per-
manence of poorly designed institutions. It is necessary, in fact, to design
rather weak and informal institutions in uncompetitive policy environments
in order to sustain a minimum degree of cooperation. Owing to the unattrac-
tiveness of outside options, states interested in cooperation need to design
their institutions carefully in a way that accommodates those states in particular that have little interest in cooperation on the policy issue in question. But,
while this may increase the institution's attractiveness for nonparticipants,
it decreases the utility of cooperation for members. Given a constellation
of strongly anticompetitive market characteristics, multilateral institutions
tend to survive even if they are poorly designed. Even if states are very interested in creating institutional alternatives because of the inefficient design of

existing institutions, they are firmly restrained from doing so by the realities of the policy area in question. In a nutshell, I claim that while the rational-design approach provides important explanatory factors that help to understand the sources of states' dissatisfaction with preexisting institutions and their institutional contestation strategies, it falls short of accounting for the variance in these structures across issue areas: In uncompetitive policy environments, even poorly designed and weak institutions may occupy central positions within their respective institutional complexes. However, in competitive ones, efficient and attractive institutional design is a prerequisite for acquiring a central and thus authoritative position within a particular institutional complex.

The substantial variation in institutional topologies mapped in this book has important implications beyond questions about regime complexity and global governance. Today's international relations scholarship is understandably concerned with the tectonic geopolitical shifts that are taking place in the context of an increasingly conflictual international system marked by power shifts among states and fundamental ideological cleavages within their societies. Many scholars regard the Liberal International Order (LIO) and its underlying institutions as threatened by a domestic nationalist and populist backlash and the associated shrinking of support in liberal democracies or by the rising influence of autocratic states like China in global governance (Stephen 2014; Stephen and Zürn 2019; De Vries et al. 2021; Söderbaum et al. 2021; Kruck et al. 2022).

As the Russian invasion of Ukraine, which ruthlessly breached international law and its fundamental humanitarian principles, demonstrated so terribly, concerns about the fragility of LIO and its underlying international institutions are legitimate. These changes in the conflictual nature of the international system are generally undermining institutionalization efforts across many issue areas. The damage done by Russia's war against Ukraine to institutionalized forms of cooperation in the issue area of nuclear arms control is devastating. In many other sensitive issue areas of global governance, such as trade, the repercussions of Russian aggression go far beyond the sanctions taken by the West and their effects on the global trading network. Already existing mistrust between "the West and the Rest" has been worsened, deepening preexisting skepticism about the future of LIO.

Nonetheless, this book's central argument and empirical findings suggest that issue-area-specific institutional opportunity structures may shape the speed and degree of disruption caused by this geopolitical transformation and the disruptive effect they have on multilateral cooperation through liberal international institutions: In some issue areas, the long-term centripetal dynamics of anticompetitive configurations of market characteristics are likely strengthening the resilience of pre-existing liberal institutions. As a result of the uncompetitive nature of their underlying market characteristics, in these issue areas states tend to be bound to existing institutions, shying away from the enormous costs of competitive regime creation. In policy fields where states cooperate on the provision of nonexcludable goods, free-riding incentives may further curb escalatory tendencies by revisionist states toward existing liberal institutions. In these issue areas, therefore, liberal institutions should be more resilient to revisionist and illiberal attacks, both from within and without. However, in issue areas already marked by high degrees of interinstitutional competition, the effects of the increasingly con-flictive and disruptive nature of international politics will be and already are much more visible. The absence of long-term centripetal dynamics in issue areas marked by pro-competitive configurations of market characteristics provides strong incentives for revisionist states to expand and reinforce their counter-institutionalization efforts in these areas. The creation of alterna-tive institutions with strongly diverging normative foundations by emerging powers like China and its BRICS allies will likely accelerate in issue areas marked by high degrees of competition. In the development aid field, China has reinforced its counter-institutionalization efforts under its Belt and Road Initiative, whether more or less unintentionally (Jones 2020), or through the gradual, subversive externalization of its nonliberal model of political economy (Stephen and Skidmore 2019). In any event, in this competitive policy area, long-term centrifugal dynamics appear to reinforce and acceler-ate processes of normative change triggered by geopolitical transformations. Therefore, it is crucial to understand the endogenous effects that policy area characteristics exert on the evolution of different institutional topologies, and how these long-term effects constrain or enable states in pursuing their issue-specific normative or functional interests.

Outlook and Avenues for Further Research

I would like to highlight three more general (in both theoretical and empirical terms) implications of the book's findings and associated opportunities for further research on international regime complexes.

First, as the marked variation revealed in institutional topologies across issue areas shows, it is necessary to expand and complement comparative research on international regime complexes. While the dominance of more qualitative "within-policy-field" perspectives in the existing literature has produced important insights into the trajectories of institutionalization processes and the causal mechanisms underlying these developments, the lack of more structural, comparative perspectives has led to an underestimation of how these processes are actually affected by varying policy area realities. By pointing to the particular relevance of market characteristics, which tend to differ greatly across issue areas of global governance, I have shown that states do indeed face different constraints or incentives to institutionalize their cooperative activities across different issue areas.

As set out in Chapter 8 of this book, my arguments are not at odds with, but complement, existing neorealist and rational-design approaches on interinstitutional configurations in global governance. While power capabilities of states and individual institutional design features are important variables shaping institutionalization processes within institutional complexes, I claim that their effect on the overall topologies of regime complexes is moderated by the market characteristics of a particular policy field. To understand the observed variance in institutional topologies across different issue areas of global governance, it is, in my view, crucial to consider the interaction of policy area characteristics with explanatory factors put forward by alternative explanations. As the aim of this book was not to provide a rigorous empirical test of the argument presented with a high risk of falsification, but rather to demonstrate its plausibility and applicability, further research applying more robust conceptualization and measurement of these alternative explanatory factors is necessary to deepen our understanding of this assumed interaction. For instance, going beyond case comparisons following the logic of most-similar-system designs, future research should consider comparing larger numbers of issue areas and their underlying institutional topologies. Depending on the number of cases, applying the method of qualitative comparative analysis (QCA) (see, e.g., Marx et al. 2014) might allow the causal effects of market characteristics vis-à-vis alternative explanatory factors to be assessed. More specifically, such a methodology might enable an investigation into how the combination of these factors is associated with different institutional topologies.

Second, my book shows that it is indeed possible to compare institutional topologies across issue areas by applying coherent concepts and methods. Conceptualizing these structures from a network perspective allows for a fine-grained measurement and thus comparison of institutional authority. Furthermore, conceiving of institutional authority as an institution's recognized claim to govern has proven to be a feasible way to combine insights from the literature on institutional authority with network theory. This synthesis, I claim, allows the interinstitutional topologies underlying different issue areas of global governance to be conceptualized and measured. My conceptualization, furthermore, allowed me to gather comparable and original institutional data at the individual level and to use it to map interinstitutional authority at a structural one. The operationalization of institutional topologies as recognition networks among international institutions governing the same policy field thus also provides us with the opportunity to engage in the analysis of more specific interinstitutional constellations.

For instance, going beyond the description of the overall structure of institutional networks by engaging in an assessment of more detailed properties of these networks might contribute to enhancing our understanding of even more specific social foundations underlying regime complexes. My research indicates that institutional networks underlying different issue areas differ not only in their overall topology, but also with regard to specific clusters of states and institutions. Investigating how these clusters or "cliques" of states and institutions evolve and, more specifically, how these "institutional cliques" differ from and relate to each other, would further contribute to our understanding of the specific patterns of cooperation underlying international regime complexes. Authority within institutional complexes could be investigated not only on the level of institutions, but also on that of clusters of states and institutions. Recent studies indicate that, on the level of states, these clusters in intergovernmental organization networks have become less fragmented over time (Greenhill and Lupu 2017). Even so, these studies only focus on clusters of states based on their overlapping membership of certain institutions, they do not investigate policy-area-specific variance. The data gathered in the context of this book could be used to further expand the analysis of such clusters by exploring issue-area-specific differences. In this way, the network data gathered throughout this book could be used to create new knowledge of the apparently changing nature of interstate cooperation in global governance.

In this book, I have used an original dataset consisting of more than 73,000 pages of official institutional documents to map institutional topologies in a purely quantitative sense. My data could also be used qualitatively to assess the social ties underlying each network: Following a more constructivist approach to institutional authority (see, e.g., Deitelhoff and Zimmermann 2020; Dingwerth et al. 2019; Struett et al. 2013), the references I found in my data could also be evaluated regarding their specific quality and sentiment. Analyzing and categorizing the qualitative content of these acts of recognition would allow the discursive structure underlying institutional complexes to be mapped. It would also enable differences in these discourses across issue areas to be identified and whether institutional complexes are marked by more confrontational forms of institutional interaction or a collaborative division of labor. In view of the theoretical argument proposed in this book as well as the empirical evidence presented, one might expect that especially those issue areas marked by a highly competitive market structure would tend to exhibit more confrontational and conflictual discursive structures. Policy fields marked by uncompetitive market characteristics, on the contrary, should produce more cooperative forms of interinstitutional interaction tailored to the authoritative center of the complex. Research following more qualitatively oriented designs might come up with interesting regularities of this kind regarding the competitive environment of issue areas and interinstitutional discourses.

Third and finally, my research shows that there appears to be no uniform empirical trend regarding the development of institutional topologies underlying regime complexes. In contrast to what some regime complexity theories might lead us to expect, it appears that there is neither a stringent development towards an ever-growing density and fragmentation nor signs of a general trend towards the (re)centralization of institutional complexes or even the marginalization or complete disappearance of multilateral institutions. Beyond this, it appears that it is not necessarily the complexity *within institutional complexes* but rather, and primarily, the complexity stemming from varying institutional structures *across different issue areas* of global governance that will present state decision makers with challenges in the future. Navigating between highly diverse institutional structures makes it more difficult to engage in negotiation strategies like issue linking, or to transfer cooperative efforts from one policy field to another.

This implication also offers one of the most relevant and theoretically interesting avenues for further research. What are the politics of regime complexity? We know very little about the actual intentions and strategies of newly created IOs and their principals once they enter preexisting regime complexes. The findings of this book suggest that their prospects of gaining a foothold in their complex differs across issue areas. What does this imply for their strategy vis-à-vis established institutional contenders? Are interinstitutional relations more conflictive in areas marked by high propensities for competition? When and how do newly emerged institutional actors decide to cooperate with legacy institutions? What strategies do newly created competitor institutions adopt to gain a foothold in their regime complex? These are all highly relevant questions that should be addressed in future research to enable us to fully understand whether global governance finds itself on a path toward an increasingly conflictual and disruptive order, or whether there is indeed hope that the LIO and its normative foundation of peaceful cooperation is indeed resilient despite current geopolitical transformations.

During times when the distribution of power among states undoubtedly shifts and uncertainty in the international system appears to increase, the prospects for successful institutionalized forms of cooperation may be determined even more by the policy environment and its underlying propensity for institutional competition. In uncompetitive policy fields, where monopolistic institutions lock in the privileges of established powers, topologies among institutions can be expected to be more enduring. Still, as the established powers that once upon a time created these monopolistic institutions to serve their own ends decline, their interest in preserving the institutional status quo may be waning as well. As the aggressive rhetorical and institutional actions of the Trump administration vis-à-vis many multilateral institutions indicate, the waning influence of the US in relation to China and other emerging powers might indeed result in a gradual retreat from its institutional commitments. In the light of this book's theory, this is particularly bad news for institutionalized forms of cooperation within uncompetitive policy environments where incentives for emerging powers to engage in the creation of institutional alternatives are low. By contrast, within policy fields marked by highly competitive market characteristics, it appears much more likely that institutional topologies will adapt to the new realities, as emerging powers face strong incentives to create and sustain institutional alternatives. Consequently, even in the light of increasing uncertainty and a more complex, multipolar world, it is not unlikely that the expansion and proliferation of international institutions that has taken place over recent decades will continue. Still, the extent to which this will affect the underlying topology of institutional complex and the overall prospects for successful intergovernmental cooperation may be subject to strong, issue-area-specific variance.

Appendices

Case Selection Logic, Operationalization, and Robustness

The 48 institutions representing the five individual regime complexes were all selected following the same consistent deductive and inductive logics. First, all institutions mentioned in relevant studies on the corresponding regime complexes were identified (listed for all issue areas below). This was followed by obtaining the official documents from this deductively selected sample of institutions. Based on these documents (listed in Appendix B below), a further inductive search was conducted to identify additional IOs, including regional ones, that were mentioned to a significant extant by the deductively elicited institutions. To identify the membership status of the selected sample of states for each regime complex, up-to-date information from the institutions' official websites was consulted.

- **Intellectual Property:**

For the deductive case selection step for the issue area of Intellectual Property, I consulted Helfer (2004) and Helfer (2009), Raustiala and Victor (2004), Yu (2007), Sell (2010a; 2010b), Erstling and Boutillon (2005), and Pratt (2018) to identify the multilateral institutions in the field highlighted as the most relevant by these studies. For the complementary inductive case selection step, I further consulted an official outlet by the African Regional Intellectual Property Organization (ARIPO). The document contains a list of, amongst other things, international institutions which have been set up by states to cooperate on the issue of Intellectual Property protection (ARIPO 2019). It is important to note that this case selection logic resulted in a different sample of institutions as compared to Pratt (2018). My inductive search identified additional IOs not covered in Pratt's (2018) sample, including regional and highly specialized ones, that were mentioned to a significant extant by the deductively elicited institutions like, e.g., the International Union for the Protection of New Varieties of Plants (UPOV), an institution that is of particular importance when it comes to the patenting and commercial use of biological resources, an issue of major concern for developing countries (see, e.g. Robinson 2008; Dutfield 2008). Moreover, Pratt's (2018) sample includes the United Nations as a separate institution. For my analysis, I decided to exclude the UN due the fact that the World Intellectual Property Organization (WIPO), which is part of my sample, has become an institutional part of the UN system by officially gaining the status of a specialized agency of the United Nations in 1974. This raises doubt on whether references between the UN umbrella organization and its specialized agency as well as state membership of both institutions are independent from each other or whether including both institutions could not rather compromise the results. However, Pratt's (2018) findings on the Intellectual Property complex serve as a perfect cross-validity check here, as he shows that if the UN is included, the patterns of interinstitutional deference remain strongly decentralized, which is perfectly in line with this book's findings on the Intellectual Property complex (Pratt 2018: 757).

- **Tax Avoidance**

For the deductive case selection step for the issue area of Intellectual Property, I consulted Rixen (2008a; 2008b; 2011), Lesage and Van De Graaf (2013: 84–7), Brauner (2002), Christians (2010), and Rosenbloom et al. (2014: 61–76) to identify the multilateral tax institutions highlighted as the most relevant by these studies. For the complementary inductive case selection step, I further consulted the OECD's report on the "platform for collaboration on tax." The document explicitly lists other multilateral tax organizations with whom it seeks to "establish an effective institutional setting [...] and to produce concrete outputs" (OECD 2016: 6) on the policy issue of Tax Avoidance. Both documents were consulted to complement further the list of the most relevant multilateral institutions engaging in the policy field.

- **Financial Stability**

For the deductive case selection step for the issue area of Financial Stability, I consulted Lipscy (2015; 2017), Schüller and Wogart (2017), Biziwick et al. (2015), Sussangkarn (2011), Ciorciari (2011), Lütz and Kranke (2014), Eichengreen (2007), and Desai and Vreeland (2011) to identify the most important multilateral Financial Stability institutions set up by states to provide balance of payments assistance to member countries. For the complementary inductive case selection step, I additionally consulted an IMF report about its engagement with other multilateral financial institution where it lists institutions that were established to avert financing instability or due to dissatisfaction with Fund conditionality and concerns about Fund governance (see IMF 2013; Lipscy 2017: 75).

- **Development Aid**

For the deductive case selection step for the issue area of Development Aid, I consulted Lipscy 2015 and 2017, Tierney et. al 2011, Hook and Rumsey 2016, Nielson et. al 2017, Findley et al. 2017, Wang 2017, Faure et al. 2015, and Park and Strand 2015 to identify the most important Multilateral Development Banks actively engaging in the provision of financial aid to developing countries. The institutions identified within these studies were further cross- checked by consulting the OECD's list of multilateral donors (OECD 2019b). For the complementary inductive case selection step, I consulted an official list provided by the World Bank containing multilateral institutions that share the task of providing financial support to developing countries, including MBDs and other multilateral financial institutions (World Bank 2018a).

- **Energy Governance**

For the deductive case selection step for the issue area of Energy Governance, I consulted Lesage and Van de Graaf (2013, 2016), Van de Graaf and Colgan (2016), Van de Graaf (2017), Goldthau and Witte (2010), and Wilson (2015). The regional Organization of Arab Petroleum Exporting Countries (OAPEC) had to be excluded from the main longitudinal analysis. Unfortunately, the organization has not published official documents like annual reports or regular bulletins before 2014. To increase confidence in the identified general pattern of an increasingly decentralized topology underlying the regime complex of energy governance, I used available data on OAPEC to replicate the network structures including this additional energy institutions. As a robustness check, I used the available membership information and all available reports and bulletins published by OAPEC since the beginning of 2014 to map both membership networks (1990 and 2018) and the reference network for the period with available documents (2013–17) below. Both analyses corroborate the findings of the main analysis. Figure A1.1 comparing the membership networks of the Energy Governance complex 1992 with 2018 is in line with the finding of the main analysis that the network has become more decentralized. Furthermore, Figure A1.2 corroborates the findings of the main analysis that the 2013–17 reference network exhibits high degrees of decentralization. Including OAPEC in the network reinforces the impression of an increasingly fragmented regime complex, with this particularly specialized regional energy producer institution occupying a similarly peripheral position within the reference network like the ECT or the International Energy Forum. While obtaining particularly close ties with OPEC, certainly due to the many shared interests of their (partially overlapping) membership, it is also connected to other specialized institutions like the IEF, IRENA, or the G7 and G20. The robustness of this general decentralization trend is further supported by the slight increase of the reference network's modularity from 0.105 to 0.193 when including OAPEC to the network indicating an even more separated and decentralized topology.

Membership Network 1990 including OAPEC

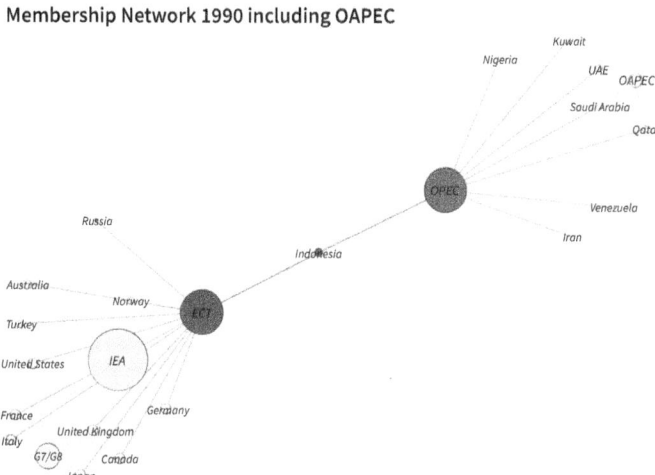

Membership Network 2018 including OAPEC

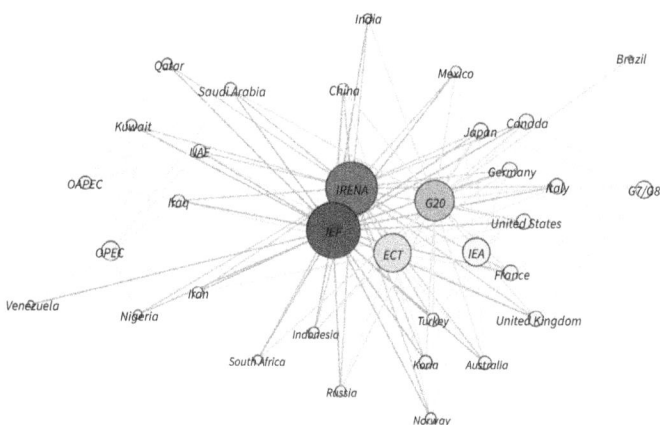

Figure A1.1 Energy Governance Membership Networks (1992 vs. 2018) Including OAPEC

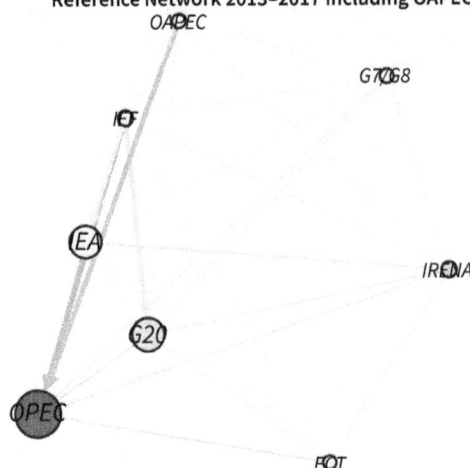

Figure A1.2 Energy Governance Reference
Network 2013–2014 Including OAPEC

List of Documents

- **Tax Avoidance**

IO	Documents
Organization for Economic Cooperation and Development (OECD)	OECD Taxation Working Papers No. 36 (2018) Domestic Revenue Mobilisation: A new database on tax levels and structures in 80 countries; OECD SECRETARY-GENERAL REPORT TO THE G20 FINANCE MINISTERS AND CENTRAL BANK GOVERNORS WASHINGTON D.C. APRIL 2015; OECD SECRETARY-GENERAL REPORT TO G20 FINANCE MINISTERS Istanbul, Turkey, February 2015; OECD Council 2015 DRAFT RESOLUTION OF THE COUNCIL RENEWING AND REVISING THE MANDATE OF THE GLOBAL FORUM ON TRANSPARENCY AND EXCHANGE OF INFORMATION FOR TAX PURPOSES Doc. Number C(2015)127; OECD Centre for Tax Policy and Administration Brochure: OECD Work on Taxation 2018–19; OECD Global Forum on Transparency and Exchange of Information for Tax Purposes: Progress Report to the G20 Finance Ministers and Central Bank Governors: Update on Effectiveness and On-going Monitoring, September 2014; OECD SECRETARY-GENERAL REPORT TO G20 FINANCE MINISTERS Shanghai People's Republic of China 26–27 February 2016; OECD SECRETARY-GENERAL REPORT TO G20 LEADERS Brisbane, Australia November 2014; OECD SECRETARY-GENERAL REPORT TO G20 FINANCE MINISTERS Ankara, Turkey September 2015; OECD SECRETARY-GENERAL REPORT TO G20 FINANCE MINISTERS Washington D.C. United States April 2016; OECD SECRETARY-GENERAL REPORT TO G20 FINANCE MINISTERS AND CENTRAL BANK GOVERNORS Buenos Aires, Argentina March 2018; OECD SECRETARY-GENERAL REPORT TO G20 FINANCE MINISTERS Baden-Baden, Germany March 2017; OECD SECRETARY-GENERAL REPORT TO G20 FINANCE MINISTERS Washington D.C. October 2016; OECD SECRETARY-GENERAL REPORT TO G20 LEADERS Buenos Aires, Argentina December 2018; OECD SECRETARY-GENERAL REPORT TO G20 LEADERS Hamburg, Germany July 2017; OECD SECRETARY-GENERAL REPORT TO G20 LEADERS Antalya, Turkey November 2015;

Continued

IO	Documents
	OECD SECRETARY-GENERAL REPORT TO G20 LEADERS Hangzhou, China September 2016; OECD Taxation Working Papers No. 18 Tax Policy and Tax Reform in the People's Republic of China; OECD Taxation Working Papers No. 17 (2013) The Tax Policy Landscape Five Years after the Crisis; OECD Taxation Working Papers No. 16 (2013) Effective Personal Tax Rates on Marginal Skills Investments in OECD Countries; OECD Taxation Working Papers No. 15 (2013) Average Personal Income Tax Rate and Tax Wedge Progression in OECD Countries; OECD Taxation Working Papers No. 21 (2014) The Diesel Differential DIFFERENCES IN THE TAX TREATMENT OF GASOLINE AND DIESEL FOR ROAD USE; OECD Taxation Working Papers No. 20 (2014) Personal Tax Treatment of Company Cars and Commuting Expenses ESTIMATING THE FISCAL AND ENVIRONMENTAL COSTS; OECD Taxation Working Papers No. 19 (2013) Taxation of Dividend, Interest, and Capital Gain Income; OECD Taxation Working Papers No. 29 (2016) The Impact of Tax and Benefit Systems on the Workforce Participation Incentives of Women; OECD Taxation Working Papers No. 28 (2016) Distinguishing between "normal" and "excess" returns for tax policy; OECD Taxation Working Papers No. 27 (2016) Fiscal incentives for R&D and innovation in a diverse world; OECD Taxation Working Papers No. 26 (2016) Tax Design for Inclusive Economic Growth; OECD Taxation Working Papers No. 40 (2018) Tax policies for inclusive growth in a changing world; OECD Taxation Working Papers No. 39 (2018) Simplified registration and collection mechanisms for taxpayers that are not located in the jurisdiction of taxation; OECD Taxation Working Papers No. 38 (2018) Corporate Effective Tax Rates MODEL DESCRIPTION AND RESULTS FROM 36 OECD AND NON-OECD COUNTRIES; OECD Taxation Working Papers No. 37 (2018) Unintended technology-bias in corporate income taxation THE CASE OF ELECTRICITY GENERATION IN THE LOW-CARBON TRANSITION; OECD Taxation Working Papers No. 34 (2018) Statutory tax rates on dividends, interest and capital gains THE DEBT EQUITY BIAS AT THE PERSONAL LEVEL; OECD Taxation Working Papers No. 32 (2018) Legal tax liability, legal remittance responsibility and tax incidence THREE DIMENSIONS OF BUSINESS TAXATION; OECD Global Forum on Transparency and Exchange of Information for Tax Purposes Progress Report to the G20Leaders: Global Forum Update on Effectiveness and On-going Monitoring September 2013
African Tax Administration Forum (ATAF)	ATAF The African Tax Outlook 2016 (1st Edition); ATAF The African Tax Outlook 2017 (2nd Edition); ATAF The African Tax Outlook 2018 (3rd Edition); African Tax Administration Forum Annual Report 2013; African Tax Administration Forum Annual Report 2014; African Tax Administration Forum Annual Report 2015; African Tax Administration Forum Annual Report 2016; African Tax Administration Forum Annual Report 2017; ATAF High-Level Tax Policy Dialogue: Forging the Nexus between Tax Policy and Tax Administration in Africa Outcome Statement, 17

IO	Documents
	August 2017; ATAF eNewsletter December 2017; ATAF eNewsletter June2017; ATAF HIGH-LEVEL TAX POLICY DIALOGUE: REINFORCING AFRICA'S POSITION TO BENEFIT FROM THE GLOBAL TAX AGENDA SUMMARY OF THE MEETING 31 July 2018
The Commonwealth Association of Tax Administrators (CATA)	37TH CATA ANNUAL TECHNICAL CONFERENCE FINAL COMMUNIQUE- CATA 7th to 11th November 2016; The Commonwealth Association of Tax Administrators NEWSLETTER December 2013 Issue 4; The Commonwealth Association of Tax Administrators NEWSLETTER June 2013 Issue 2; The Commonwealth Association of Tax Administrators NEWSLETTER September 2013 Issue 3; The Commonwealth Association of Tax Administrators NEWSLETTER March 2014 Issue 1; 36th Annual Technical Conference of CATA COMMUNIQUE 16th to 20th November 2015; 38TH CATA ANNUAL TECHNICAL CONFERENCE FINAL COMMUNIQUE—CATA 6th to 10th November 2017; 39th CATA Technical Conference Communique Sheraton Fiji Resort, Nadi, Fiji 12–16 November 2018; Commonwealth Association of Tax Administrations (CATA) 2017 Technical Conference Background paper: Using Technology Effectively to Ensure Reporting Compliance at the Canada Revenue Agency; CATA NEWSLETTER DECEMBER 2015; The Commonwealth Association of Tax Administrators NEWSLETTER December 2018; 37TH CATA ANNUAL TECHNICAL CONFERENCE FINAL COMMUNIQUE- CATA 7th to 11th November 2016; Discussion Note Commonwealth Senior Finance Officials Meeting 2016 Domestic Revenue Mobilisation, Tax Reform and the Role of Finance Ministries Prepared by the Economic Policy Division, the Commonwealth Secretariat; CATA NEWSLETTER June 2017; CATA NEWSLETTER June 2018; CATA NEWSLETTER June 2014 Issue 2; KENYA COUNTRY PAPER 2017 CATA CONFERENCE, ACCRA GHANA, 6TH–10TH NOVEMBER, 2017 THEME: LEVERAGING TECHNOLOGY TO ENHANCE REVENUE COLLECTION TITLE: FACILITATING, MONITORING AND ENABLING COMPLIANCE THROUGH TECHNOLOGY; Malaysia Background CATA Conference 2017 Paper Theme: Leveraging technology to enhance revenue administration Topic 1: Facilitating, monitoring and enabling compliance through technology; CATA NEWSLETTER March 2017; CATA Newsletter March 2018; CATA NEWSLETTER March 2013 Issue 1; Mauritius Background Paper CATA Conference 2017 Topic 1: Facilitating, monitoring and enabling compliance through technology; Media Release November 16th, 2015 Media Release Malaysia LHDN CATA 36TH ANNUAL TECHNICAL CONFERENCE'S MAIN FOCUS ON GOVERNANCE AND INTEGRITY IN TAX ADMINISTRATION; Media Release November 17th, 2015: CATA MEMBER COUNTRIES SERIOUS IN OVERCOMING TRANSFER PRICING AND BASE EROSION AND PROFIT SHIFTING ISSUES (BEPS); Media Release November

Continued

IO	Documents
	18th, 2015: DELEGATES OF CATA ARE IMPRESSED BY MELAKA'S UNIQUENESS; Media Release November 19th, 2015: TOGETHERNESS IN RESOLVING BEPS; SAMOA 2017: BACKGROUND PAPER THEME: Leveraging technology to enhance revenue administration Topic 1: Facilitating, monitoring and enabling compliance through technology Topic 2: Equipping staff with skills to deliver in an increasingly digital environment; CATA NEWSLETTER September 2016; CATA NEWSLETTER September 2018
Inter-American Centre of Tax Administrations (CIAT)	CIAT Technical Conference Nairobi, Kenya September 9–12, 2013 Prevention and control of tax evasion; Inter-American Center of Tax Administrations—CIAT State Agency of Tax Administration—KRA CIAT TECHNICAL CONFERENCE: "THE OPTIMIZATION OF RESOURCES AND PROCESSES OF THE TAX ADMINISTRATIONS" Santiago de Compostela, Spain October 6 to 9, 2014. CIAT Technical Conference 2015 ROME: "The Tax Administration's Examination Function" Rome, Italy, September 28th–October 1st, 2015; CIAT 2016 TECHNOLOGY MEETING October, 10–12, 2016 Hilton Hotel Downtown, Miami, Florida, USA: "TECHNOLOGY IN TAX ADMINISTRATION" PROGRAM; CIAT Technical Conference 2017 DAILY SCHEDULE OF ACTIVITIES "Advances of the tax administrations in relation to the problem of tax base erosion and profit shifting"; CIAT and IOTA Tax Summit Lisbon 2018: TAX ADMINISTRATIONS AND THE CHALLENGES OF THE DIGITAL WORLD; Overview of Tax Expenditures in Latin American statistics of the CIAT Database CIAT Working Paper 2018
Le Centre des Recontres et d'Etudes des Dirigeants des Administration Fiscales (CREDAF)	CREDAF 2014 GUIDE D'AIDE A LA MISE EN OEUVRE DES CONVENTIONS FISCALES INTERNATIONALES; CREDAF 2015 GUIDE GUIDE MÉTHODOLOGIQUE EVALUATION DES DÉPENSES FISCALES; CREDAF GUIDE 2017 GUIDE DE LA FISCALITE DES INDUSTRIES EXTRACTIVES; CREDAF 2018 Rapport
Commission of the European Union (EU COM)	European Commission 2016 Directorate General Taxation and Customs Union's (TAXUD) Annual Activity Report DG TAXATION AND CUSTOMS UNION; European Commission 2013 Directorate General Taxation and Customs Union's (TAXUD) Annual Activity Report DG TAXATION AND CUSTOMS UNION; European Commission 2014 Directorate General Taxation and Customs Union's (TAXUD) Annual Activity Report DG TAXATION AND CUSTOMS UNION; European Commission 2015 Directorate General Taxation and Customs Union's (TAXUD) Annual Activity Report DG TAXATION AND CUSTOMS UNION; European Commission 2017 Directorate General Taxation and Customs Union's (TAXUD) Annual Activity Report DG TAXATION AND CUSTOMS UNION; COMMISSION STAFF WORKING DOCUMENT Fiscalis 2020 Programme—Progress Report 2016; COMMISSION STAFF WORKING DOCUMENT Commission Staff Working Papers on Fiscalis 2020 programme Progress Report for 2014; COMMISSION STAFF WORKING DOCUMENT Fiscalis

IO	Documents
	2020 programme Progress Report for 2015; COMMISSION STAFF WORKING DOCUMENT Fiscalis 2020 programme Progress Report for 2017; REPORT FROM THE COMMISSION TO THE EUROPEAN PARLIAMENT AND THE COUNCIL on overview and assessment of the statistics and information on the automatic exchanges in the field of direct taxation; European Commission TAXATION PAPERS Taxation and Customs Union WORKING PAPER N. 64—2016 The Impact of Tax Planning on Forward-Looking Effective Tax Rates; European Commission TAXATION PAPERS Taxation and Customs Union WORKING PAPER No 73—2018 FISCALIS Tax Gap Project Group THE CONCEPT OF TAX GAPS Corporate Income Tax Gap Estimation Methodologies; European Commission Report "VAT refunds and reimbursements: A quantitative and qualitative study Final Report TAXUD/2017/DE/328 FWC No. TAXUD/2015/CC/131
Group of 20 (G20)	Group of 20 Communiqué Meeting of Finance Ministers and Central Bank Governors Moscow, 19–20 July 2013; G20 Labour and Employment Ministers' Declaration Moscow, 18–19 July 2013; Communiqué Meeting of Finance Ministers and Central Bank Governors Washington, 10–11 October 2013; Communiqué Meeting of Finance Ministers and Central Bank Governors Sydney, 22–23 February 2014; Communiqué Meeting of G20 Finance Ministers and Central Bank Governors Washington D.C., 10–11 April 2014; Meeting of G20 in Hamburg 2017 Official Brochure "Shaping an interconnected world"; G20 Meeting in Hamburg 2017: PRIORITIES OF THE 2017 G20 SUMMIT Document; G20 Meeting in Hamburg 2017 Annex to G20 Leaders Declaration G20 High Level Principles on Organizing Against Corruption; G20 Meeting in Hamburg Annex to G20 Leaders Declaration G20 High Level Principles on Countering Corruption in Customs; G20 Meeting in Hamburg Action Plan July 2017; G20 Meeting in Hamburg HAMBURG ANNUAL PROGRESS REPORT ON G20 DEVELOPMENT COMMITMENTS; G20 Meeting Hamburg 2017 Official Leaders' Declaration "Shaping an interconnected world"; OECD G20 Joint Policy Paper on Economic Resilience and Structural Policies November 2016; Report to G20 Deputy Finance Ministers and Deputy Central Bank Governors on MDB Internal Incentives for Crowding-in Private Investment in Infrastructure 1 December 2016; IMF to the G20 Report A Macroeconomic Perspective on Resilience November 2016; IMF to the G20 Report Increasing Resilience to Large and Volatile Capital Flows: The Role of Macroprudential Policies November 2016; IMF to the G20 Report Toward A More Resilient Global Financial Architecture November 2016; G20 Meeting Buenos Aires 2018 Communiqué Annex Finance Ministers & Central Bank Governors 19–20 March 2018, Buenos Aires, Argentina; Communiqué Finance Ministers & Central Bank Governors 19–20 March 2018, Buenos Aires, Argentina; Meeting of G20 in Buenos Aires 2018 Official Brochure; OVERVIEW OF ARGENTINA'S G20 PRESIDENCY 2018 BUILDING CONSENSUS FOR FAIR AND SUSTAINABLE

Continued

IO	Documents
	DEVELOPMENT; Communiqué G20 Finance Ministers and Central Bank Governors Meeting 9–10 February 2015, Istanbul; Communiqué G20 Finance Ministers and Central Bank Governors Meeting 16–17 April 2015, Washington D.C., USA; Joint Meeting of G20 Finance and Labor Ministers September 4, 2015 CHAIR'S STATEMENT; Communiqué G20 Finance Ministers and Central Bank Governors Meeting 4-5 September 2015, Ankara, Turkey; Communiqué G20 Finance Ministers and Central Bank Governors Meeting Baden-Baden, Germany, 17–18 March 2017; Statement—G20 Finance Ministers Meeting Brisbane, November 15, 2014 Check against delivery; G20 Meeting in Buenos Aires 2018 BUENOS AIRES ACTION PLAN; G20 Leaders' declaration Buenos Aires 2018 Building consensus for fair and sustainable development; BUENOS AIRES UPDATE Moving forward the G20 Action Plan on the 2030 Agenda for Sustainable Development; Communiqué G20 Finance Ministers and Central Bank Governors Meeting Chengdu, China, July 24, 2016; Communiqué Meeting of G20 Finance Ministers and Central Bank Governors Cairns, 20–21 September 2014; Communiqué of Meeting of G20 Finance Ministers and Central Bank Governors Moscow, February 16, 2013; The G20 Labour and Employment and Finance Ministers' Communiqué Moscow, July 19, 2013; Communiqué G20 Finance Ministers and Central Bank Governors Meeting Shanghai, February 27, 2016; Communiqué G20 Finance Ministers and Central Bank Governors' Meeting Washington, April 15, 2016; Communiqué G20 Meeting of Finance Ministers and Central Bank Governors Washington DC, April 19, 2013
Intra-European Organisation of Tax Administrations (IOTA)	IOTA The Tax Tribune magazine 38th Edition January 2019; IOTA Publication DISRUPTIVE BUSINESS MODELS based on technical session of the 21st IOTA General Assembly, Kyiv, 28–30 June 2017; IOTA The Tax Tribune magazine 37th Edition June 2018; IOTA NEWSLETTER 2018/3. SEPTEMBER–DECEMBER; IOTA NEWSLETTER 2018/2. MAY–AUGUST; IOTA NEWSLETTER 2018/1. JANUARY–APRIL; IOTA NEWSLETTER 2017/3. SEPTEMBER–DECEMBER; IOTA NEWSLETTER October–December 2016; IOTA NEWSLETTER May–September 2016; IOTA NEWSLETTER January–April 2016; IOTA NEWSLETTER 12 April–30 June; IOTA NEWSLETTER 2 January–7 April 2017; IOTA The Tax Tribune magazine 30th Edition January 2013; IOTA The Tax Tribune magazine 31th Edition January 2014; IOTA The Tax Tribune magazine 33th Edition January 2015; ; IOTA The Tax Tribune magazine Issue 35 2016; IOTA The Tax Tribune magazine 36th Edition 2018; IOTA The Tax Tribune magazine Issue 34 Special Edition Celebrating IOTA´s 20th anniversary; IOTA The Tax Tribune magazine 32th Edition 2015;
United Nations Tax Committee (UNTC)	UN ECOSOC Newsletter of FfDO/DESA Number 2013/1, April 2013; Newsletter of FfDO/DESA Number 2013/2, May 2013; Newsletter of FfDO/DESA Number 2013/3, May 2013; Newsletter of FfDO/DESA Number 2013/4, May 2013; Newsletter of FfDO/DESA Number 2013/5, June 2013; Newsletter of FfDO/DESA Number

IO	Documents
	2013/6, June 2013; Newsletter Number 2013/7 3 October 2013; Newsletter of FfDO/DESA Number 2014/1, April 2014; Newsletter of FfDO/DESA Number 2014/2, June 2014; Newsletter of FfDO/DESA Number 2014/3, June 2014; Newsletter of FfDO/DESA Number 2014/4, June 2014; Newsletter of FfDO/DESA Number 2014/5, June 2014; Newsletter of FfDO/DESA Number 2015/1, April 2015; Newsletter of FfDO/DESA Number 2015/2, April 2015; UNTC 2017 United Nations Handbook on Selected Issues for Taxation of the Extractive Industries by Developing Countries; UNTC 2017 United Nations Practical Manual on Transfer Pricing for Developing Countries; United Nations 2017 Model Double Taxation Convention between Developed and Developing Countries; Committee of Experts on International Cooperation in Tax Matters Report on the ninth session (21–25 October 2013); Committee of Experts on International Cooperation in Tax Matters Report on the tenth session (27-31 October 2014); Committee of Experts on International Cooperation in Tax Matters Report on the eleventh session (19–23 October 2015); Committee of Experts on International Cooperation in Tax Matters Report on the twelfth and thirteenth sessions (11–14 October 2016 and 5-8 December 2016); Committee of Experts on International Cooperation in Tax Matters Report on the fifteenth session (17–20 October 2017); Committee of Experts on International Cooperation in Tax Matters Report on the fourteenth session (3–6 April 2017); Committee of Experts on International Cooperation in Tax Matters Report on the seventeenth session (16–19 October 2018); Committee of Experts on International Cooperation in Tax Matters Report on the sixteenth session (14–17 May 2018)

- **Intellectual Property**

IO	Title of Documents
African Regional Intellectual Property Organization (ARIPO)	African Regional Intellectual Property Organization (ARIPO) Annual Report 2014; African Regional Intellectual Property Organization (ARIPO) Annual Report 2015; African Regional Intellectual Property Organization (ARIPO) Annual Report 2016; African Regional Intellectual Property Organization (ARIPO) Annual Report 2017; ARIPO Magazine Vol. 4, No.4, October–December 2014; ARIPO Magazine Vol. 6, No. 3, July–September 2016; ARIPO Magazine Vol. 6, No. 4, October–December 2016; ARIPO Magazine Vol. 7, No. 1 January–March 2017; ARIPO Magazine Vol. 7, No. 2 April–June 2017; ARIPO Magazine Vol. 7, No. 3 July–September 2017; ARIPO Magazine Vol. 7, No. 4

Continued

IO	Title of Documents
	October–December 2017; ARIPO Magazine Issue 1, January–March 2018; ARIPO Magazine Issue 2, April–June 2018; ARIPO Magazine Issue 3, July–September 2018; ARIPO Magazine Vol. 5, No. 1, January–March 2015; ARIPO Magazine Vol. 5, No. 2, April–June 2015; ARIPO Magazine Vol. 5, No. 3, July–September 2015; ARIPO Magazine Vol. 5, No. 4, October–December 2015; ARIPO Magazine Vol. 6, No. 1, January–March 2016; ARIPO Magazine Vol. 6, No. 2, April–June 2016;
Eurasian Patent Organization (EAPO)	Eurasian Patent Organization Annual Report 2012; Eurasian Patent Organization Annual Report 2013; Eurasian Patent Organization Annual Report 2014; Eurasian Patent Organization Annual Report 2015; Eurasian Patent Organization Annual Report 2016;
European Patent Organization (EPO)	EPO Environmental Report 2016; EPO Environmental Report 2017; Environmental statement 2009 in accordance with Regulation EG 761/2001; EPO Facts and Figures 2015; EPO Facts and Figures 2016; EPO Facts and Figures 2017; European Patent Office Financial Statements Accounting Period 2016; European Patent Office Social Report for the year 2013; Social Report for the year 2014; European Patent Office Financial Statements Accounting Period 2013; European Patent Office Financial Statements Accounting Period 2014; European Patent Office Financial Statements Accounting Period 2015; European Patent Office Financial Statements Accounting Period 2017; Modernizing the EPO for excellence and sustainability Achievements 2010 to 2018; EPO Quality Report 2017; EPO Social Report for the year 2015; EPO Social Report for the year 2016;
Convention on Biological Diversity (CBD)	Convention on Biological Diversity Secretariat 2018 REPORT OF THE ONLINE FORUM IN PREPARATION FOR THE CAPACITY DEVELOPMENT PROGRAMME ON NATIONAL ARRANGEMENTS ON TRADITIONAL KNOWLEDGE FOR ACHIEVING TARGET 18 AND CONTRIBUTING TO TARGET 16 OF THE STRATEGIC PLAN FOR BIODIVERSITY 2011–2020; CBD Secretariat 2015: REPORT OF THE INTERNATIONAL TRAINING WORKSHOP ON COMMUNITY-BASED MONITORING, INDICATORS ON TRADITIONAL KNOWLEDGE AND CUSTOMARY SUSTAINABLE USE AND COMMUNITY PROTOCOLS, WITHIN THE STRATEGIC PLAN FOR BIODIVERSITY 2011–2020; CBD Secretariat 2018 UPDATE ON EXISTING CAPACITY-BUILDING AND DEVELOPMENT INITIATIVES AND RESOURCES SUPPORTING THE IMPLEMENTATION OF THE NAGOYA PROTOCOL ON ACCESS AND BENEFIT-SHARING AND LESSONS LEARNED; CBD Secretariat 2018 REVIEW OF THE OUTCOMES OF THE SECOND MEETING OF THE CONFERENCE OF THE PARTIES SERVING AS THE MEETING OF THE PARTIES TO THE NAGOYA PROTOCOL REGARDING ITEMS RELEVANT TO COMPLIANCE; CBD Technical Note Series No. 84 2016

IO	Title of Documents
	UPDATE ON CLIMATE GEOENGINEERING IN RELATION TO THE CONVENTION ON BIOLOGICAL DIVERSITY: POTENTIAL IMPACTS AND REGULATORY FRAMEWORK; CBD Technical Note Series No. 86 Synthesis report on experiences with ecosystem-based approaches to climate change adaptation and disaster risk reduction; CBD Technical Note Series No. 88 Restoring Life on Earth: Private-sector Experiences in Land Reclamation and Ecosystem Recovery; CBD Technical Note Series No. 89 THE LIMA DECLARATION ON BIODIVERSITY AND CLIMATE CHANGE: Contributions from Science to Policy for Sustainable Development; Hyderabad, India, 8–19 October 2012 REPORT OF THE ELEVENTH MEETING OF THE CONFERENCE OF THE PARTIES TO THE CONVENTION ON BIOLOGICAL DIVERSITY; Montreal Canada 2015 Ad-Hoc Inter-Sessional Working Group "REPORT OF THE AD HOC OPEN-ENDED INTER-SESSIONAL WORKING GROUP ON ARTICLE 8(j) AND RELATED PROVISIONS OF THE CONVENTION ON BIOLOGICAL DIVERSITY ON ITS NINTH MEETING"; Pyeongchang, Republic of Korea, 6–17 October 2014 REPORT OF THE EIGHTH MEETING OF THE AD HOC OPEN-ENDED INTER-SESSIONAL WORKING GROUP ON ARTICLE 8(j) AND RELATED PROVISIONS OF THE CONVENTION ON BIOLOGICAL DIVERSITY; Report of the International Training Workshop on Community-Based Monitoring, Indicators on Traditional Knowledge and Customary Sustainable Use and Community Protocols, Within the Strategic Plan for Biodiversity 2011–2020; CBD Secretariat 2014 Global Biodiversity Outlook A mid-term assessment of progress towards the implementation of the Strategic Plan for Biodiversity 2011–2020; CBD Secretariat 2018 CONFERENCE OF THE PARTIES TO THE CONVENTION ON BIOLOGICAL DIVERSITY SERVING AS THE MEETING OF THE PARTIES TO THE NAGOYA PROTOCOL ON ACCESS TO GENETIC RESOURCES AND THE FAIR AND EQUITABLE SHARING OF BENEFITS ARISING FROM THEIR UTILIZATION Third meeting Sharm El-Sheikh, Egypt, 17–29 November 2018 Agenda item 5 COMPLIANCE WITH THE PROTOCOL; CBD Secretariat 2018 CONFERENCE OF THE PARTIES TO THE CONVENTION ON BIOLOGICAL DIVERSITY SERVING AS THE MEETING OF THE PARTIES TO THE NAGOYA PROTOCOL ON ACCESS TO GENETIC RESOURCES AND THE FAIR AND EQUITABLE SHARING OF BENEFITS ARISING FROM THEIR UTILIZATION ASSESSMENT AND REVIEW OF THE EFFECTIVENESS OF THE PROTOCOL (ARTICLE 31); CBD Secretariat 2018 CONFERENCE OF THE PARTIES TO THE CONVENTION ON BIOLOGICAL DIVERSITY SERVING AS THE MEETING OF THE PARTIES TO THE NAGOYA PROTOCOL ON ACCESS TO GENETIC RESOURCES AND THE FAIR AND EQUITABLE SHARING OF BENEFITS ARISING FROM THEIR UTILIZATION

Continued

IO	Title of Documents
	"SPECIALIZED INTERNATIONAL ACCESS AND BENEFIT SHARING INSTRUMENTS IN THE CONTEXT OF ARTICLE 4, PARAGRAPH 4, OF THE NAGOYA PROTOCOL"; CBD Secretariat 2018 CONFERENCE OF THE PARTIES TO THE CONVENTION ON BIOLOGICAL DIVERSITY SERVING AS THE MEETING OF THE PARTIES TO THE NAGOYA PROTOCOL ON ACCESS TO GENETIC RESOURCES AND THE FAIR AND EQUITABLE SHARING OF BENEFITS ARISING FROM THEIR UTILIZATION "MEASURES TO RAISE AWARENESS OF THE IMPORTANCE OF GENETIC RESOURCES AND ASSOCIATED TRADITIONAL KNOWLEDGE (ARTICLE 21)"; CBD Secretariat 2018 CONFERENCE OF THE PARTIES TO THE CONVENTION ON BIOLOGICAL DIVERSITY SERVING AS THE MEETING OF THE PARTIES TO THE NAGOYA PROTOCOL ON ACCESS TO GENETIC RESOURCES AND THE FAIR AND EQUITABLE SHARING OF BENEFITS ARISING FROM THEIR UTILIZATION "MONITORING AND REPORTING (ARTICLE 29)"; CBD Secretariat 2018 CONFERENCE OF THE PARTIES TO THE CONVENTION ON BIOLOGICAL DIVERSITY SERVING AS THE MEETING OF THE PARTIES TO THE NAGOYA PROTOCOL ON ACCESS TO GENETIC RESOURCES AND THE FAIR AND EQUITABLE SHARING OF BENEFITS ARISING FROM THEIR UTILIZATION "FINANCIAL MECHANISM"; CBD Secretariat BIANNUAL REPORT ON THE ADMINISTRATION OF THE CONVENTION ON BIOLOGICAL DIVERSITY (January–June 2013); CBD Secretariat BIANNUAL REPORT ON THE ADMINISTRATION OF THE CONVENTION ON BIOLOGICAL DIVERSITY (July–December 2013); CBD Secretariat BIANNUAL REPORT ON THE ADMINISTRATION OF THE CONVENTION ON BIOLOGICAL DIVERSITY (January–June 2014); CBD Secretariat BIANNUAL REPORT ON THE ADMINISTRATION OF THE CONVENTION ON BIOLOGICAL DIVERSITY (July–December 2014); CBD Secretariat BIANNUAL REPORT ON THE ADMINISTRATION OF THE CONVENTION ON BIOLOGICAL DIVERSITY (January–June 2015); CBD Secretariat BIANNUAL REPORT ON THE ADMINISTRATION OF THE CONVENTION ON BIOLOGICAL DIVERSITY (July—December 2015); CBD Secretariat BIANNUAL REPORT ON THE ADMINISTRATION OF THE CONVENTION ON BIOLOGICAL DIVERSITY (January–June 2016); CBD Secretariat BIANNUAL REPORT ON THE ADMINISTRATION OF THE CONVENTION ON BIOLOGICAL DIVERSITY (July–December 2016); CBD Secretariat BIANNUAL REPORT ON THE ADMINISTRATION OF THE CONVENTION ON BIOLOGICAL DIVERSITY (July–December 2017); CBD Secretariat 2015 REPORT OF THE DIALOGUE WORKSHOP ON ASSESSMENT OF COLLECTIVE ACTION OF INDIGENOUS PEOPLES AND LOCAL COMMUNITIES IN BIODIVERSITY CONSERVATION AND

IO	Title of Documents
	RESOURCE MOBILIZATION; CBD Brochure "THE CONVENTION ON BIOLOGICAL DIVERSITY: SOCIAL, ECONOMIC AND LEGAL CHALLENGES; Square Brackets CBD Newsletter October 2013 Issue 8; Square Brackets CBD Newsletter July 2014 Issue 9; Square Brackets CBD Newsletter May 2016 Issue 10; CBD Brochure "THE CONVENTION ON BIOLOGICAL DIVERSITY: THE ROLE OF SCIENCE, TECHNOLOGY, AND TECHNICAL EXPERTISE"; CBD Secretariat 2017 AD HOC OPEN-ENDED INTER-SESSIONAL WORKING GROUP ON ARTICLE 8(j) AND RELATED PROVISIONS OF THE CONVENTION ON BIOLOGICAL DIVERSITY Tenth meeting Montreal, Canada, 13–16 December 2017 Agenda item 4 "RECOMMENDATION ADOPTED BY THE WORKING GROUP"; CBD Secretariat 2017 AD HOC OPEN-ENDED INTER-SESSIONAL WORKING GROUP ON ARTICLE 8(j) AND RELATED PROVISIONS OF THE CONVENTION ON BIOLOGICAL DIVERSITY Tenth meeting Montreal, Canada, 13–16 December 2017 Agenda item 4 "RECOMMENDATION ADOPTED BY THE WORKING GROUP (2)"; CBD Secretariat 2017 AD HOC OPEN-ENDED INTER-SESSIONAL WORKING GROUP ON ARTICLE 8(j) AND RELATED PROVISIONS OF THE CONVENTION ON BIOLOGICAL DIVERSITY Tenth meeting Montreal, Canada, 13 16 December 2017 Agenda item 4 "RECOMMENDATION ADOPTED BY THE WORKING GROUP (3)"; AD HOC OPEN-ENDED INTER SESSIONAL WORKING GROUP ON ARTICLE 8(j) AND RELATED PROVISIONS OF THE CONVENTION ON BIOLOGICAL DIVERSITY Tenth meeting Montreal, Canada, 13–16 December 2017 Agenda item 8 "RECOMMENDATION ADOPTED BY THE WORKING GROUP 10/6 Recommendations from the United Nations Permanent Forum on Indigenous Issues to the Convention on Biological Diversity"
Food and Agriculture Organization (FAO)	FAO Secretariat 2018 INTERNATIONAL TREATY ON PLANT GENETIC RESOURCES FOR FOOD AND AGRICULTURE EIGHTH MEETING OF THE AD HOC OPEN-ENDED WORKING GROUP TO ENHANCE THE FUNCTIONING OF THE MULTILATERAL SYSTEM Rome, Italy, 10–12 October 2018 SUBMISSIONS FROM CONTRACTING PARTIES AND STAKEHOLDERS ON MATTERS TO BE DISCUSSED AT THE EIGHTH MEETING OF THE WORKING GROUP; FAO OFFICE OF EVALUATION Thematic evaluation series April 2016 Evaluation of FAO's work in Genetic Resources; FAO Secretariat 2018 An overview of legal and institutional frameworks and opportunities, challenges and recommendations for geographical indication products in Armenia, Georgia, Kyrgyzstan, the Republic of Moldova and the Russian Federation Synthesis Report; FAO Annual Report 2013 THE STATE OF FOOD AND AGRICULTURE; FAO Annual Report 2014 THE STATE OF FOOD AND AGRICULTURE; FAO

Continued

IO	Title of Documents
	Special Annual Report 2014 of FAO Expert Working Group Research Approaches and Methods for Evaluating the Protein Quality of Human Food; FAO Annual Report 2015 THE STATE OF FOOD AND AGRICULTURE: Social protection and agriculture: breaking the cycle of rural poverty; FAO Annual Report 2016 THE STATE OF FOOD AND AGRICULTURE: CLIMATE CHANGE, AGRICULTURE AND FOOD SECURITY; FAO Special Annual Report 2016 "POTENTIALS OF NON-WOOD FOREST PRODUCTS (NWFP) FOR VALUE CHAIN DEVELOPMENT, VALUE ADDITION AND DEVELOPMENT OF NWFP-BASED RURAL MICROENTERPRISES IN SUDAN CONSULTANCY REPORT; FAO Special Report 2016 "National gender profile of agriculture and rural livelihoods"
African Intellectual Property Organization (OAPI)	OAPI Magazine Le trimestriel d'informations de l'Organisation Africaine de la Proprieté Intellectuelle No. 31 June 2017; OAPI Magazine Le trimestriel d'informations de l'Organisation Africaine de la Proprieté Intellectuelle No. 32 Decembre 2017; OAPI Magazine Le trimestriel d'informations de l'Organisation Africaine de la Proprieté Intellectuelle No. 19 Mars 2013; OAPI Magazine Le trimestriel d'informations de l'Organisation Africaine de la Proprieté Intellectuelle No. 20 Juillet 2013; OAPI Magazine Le trimestriel d'informations de l'Organisation Africaine de la Proprieté Intellectuelle No. 21 Decembre 2013; OAPI Magazine Le trimestriel d'informations de l'Organisation Africaine de la Proprieté Intellectuelle No. 22 Mars 2014; OAPI Magazine Le trimestriel d'informations de l'Organisation Africaine de la Proprieté Intellectuelle No. 33 Aout 2014; OAPI Magazine Le trimestriel d'informations de l'Organisation Africaine de la Proprieté Intellectuelle No. 24 Decembre 2014; OAPI Magazine Le trimestriel d'informations de l'Organisation Africaine de la Proprieté Intellectuelle No. 25 Mars 2015; OAPI Magazine Le trimestriel d'informations de l'Organisation Africaine de la Proprieté Intellectuelle No. 26 Juillet 2015; OAPI Magazine Le trimestriel d'informations de l'Organisation Africaine de la Proprieté Intellectuelle No. 27 Decembre 2015; OAPI Magazine Le trimestriel d'informations de l'Organisation Africaine de la Proprieté Intellectuelle No. 28 June 2016; OAPI Magazine Le trimestriel d'informations de l'Organisation Africaine de la Proprieté Intellectuelle No. 29 Septembre 2016
World Trade Organization/ Trade-Related Aspects of Intellectual Property (WTO/TRIPS)	World Trade Organization (WTO) ANNUAL REPORT (2013) OF THE COUNCIL FOR TRIPS; World Trade Organization (WTO) ANNUAL REPORT (2014) OF THE COUNCIL FOR TRIPS; World Trade Organization (WTO) ANNUAL REPORT (2015) OF THE COUNCIL FOR TRIPS; World Trade Organization (WTO) ANNUAL REPORT (2015) OF THE COUNCIL FOR TRIPS Addendum; World Trade Organization (WTO) ANNUAL REPORT (2015) OF THE COUNCIL FOR TRIPS Addendum (2); World Trade Organization (WTO) ANNUAL REPORT (2016) OF THE COUNCIL FOR TRIPS; World Trade Organization (WTO)

IO	Title of Documents
	ANNUAL REPORT (2017) OF THE COUNCIL FOR TRIPS; World Trade Organization (WTO) ANNUAL REPORT (2018) OF THE COUNCIL FOR TRIPS; WTO Council for Trade-Related Aspects of Intellectual Property Rights Special Session MULTILATERAL SYSTEM OF NOTIFICATION AND REGISTRATION OF GEOGRAPHICAL INDICATIONS FOR WINES AND SPIRITS Report by the Chairman, Ambassador Darlington Mwape (Zambia) to the Trade Negotiations Committee for the purpose of the TNC stocktaking exercise; TRIPS Council 2014 Council for Trade-Related Aspects of Intellectual Property Rights Special Session MULTILATERAL SYSTEM OF NOTIFICATION AND REGISTRATION OF GEOGRAPHICAL INDICATIONS FOR WINES AND SPIRITS REPORT BY THE CHAIRMAN, AMBASSADOR ALFREDO SUESCUM (PANAMA); TRIPS Council 2015 Council for Trade-Related Aspects of Intellectual Property Rights Special Session MULTILATERAL SYSTEM OF NOTIFICATION AND REGISTRATION OF GEOGRAPHICAL INDICATIONS FOR WINES AND SPIRITS REPORT BY THE CHAIRMAN, AMBASSADOR DACIO CASTILLO (HONDURAS); TRIPS Council 2016 Council for Trade-Related Aspects of Intellectual Property Rights Special Session MULTILATERAL SYSTEM OF NOTIFICATION AND REGISTRATION OF GEOGRAPHICAL INDICATIONS FOR WINES AND SPIRITS REPORT BY THE CHAIRMAN, AMBASSADOR DACIO CASTILLO (HONDURAS); TRIPS Council 2017 Council for Trade-Related Aspects of Intellectual Property Rights Special Session MULTILATERAL SYSTEM OF NOTIFICATION AND REGISTRATION OF GEOGRAPHICAL INDICATIONS FOR WINES AND SPIRITS REPORT BY THE CHAIRMAN, AMBASSADOR DACIO CASTILLO (HONDURAS); TRIPS Council 2017 Ministerial Conference Eleventh Session Buenos Aires, 10–13 December 2017 TRIPS NON-VIOLATION AND SITUATION COMPLAINTS MINISTERIAL DECISION OF 13 DECEMBER 2017; TRIPS Council 2013 Council for Trade-Related Aspects of Intellectual Property Rights MINUTES OF MEETING HELD IN THE CENTRE WILLIAM RAPPARD ON 5–6 MARCH 2013 Chairperson: Ambassador Dacio Castillo (Honduras); TRIPS Council 2013 Council for Trade-Related Aspects of Intellectual Property Rights MINUTES OF MEETING HELD IN THE CENTRE WILLIAM RAPPARD ON 11–12 JUNE 2013 Chairperson: Ambassador Alfredo Suescum (Panama) Addendum; TRIPS Council 2013 Council for Trade-Related Aspects of Intellectual Property Rights MINUTES OF MEETING HELD IN THE CENTRE WILLIAM RAPPARD ON 10–11 OCTOBER 2013 CHAIRPERSON: AMBASSADOR ALFREDO SUESCUM (PANAMA) Addendum; TRIPS Council 2013 Council for Trade-Related Aspects of Intellectual Property Rights MINUTES OF MEETING HELD IN THE CENTRE WILLIAM

Continued

IO	Title of Documents
	RAPPARD ON 10–11 OCTOBER 2013 CHAIRPERSON: AMBASSADOR ALFREDO SUESCUM (PANAMA) Corrigendum; Council for Trade-Related Aspects of Intellectual Property Rights MINUTES OF MEETING HELD IN THE CENTRE WILLIAM RAPPARD ON 25–26 FEBRUARY 2014 Interim Chairperson: Ambassador Dacio Castillo (Honduras); Council for Trade-Related Aspects of Intellectual Property Rights MINUTES OF MEETING HELD IN THE CENTRE WILLIAM RAPPARD ON 11 JUNE 2014 Chairperson: Ambassador Mothusi Palai (Botswana); Council for Trade-Related Aspects of Intellectual Property Rights MINUTES OF MEETING HELD IN THE CENTRE WILLIAM RAPPARD ON 28–29 OCTOBER 2014 Chairperson: Ambassador Mothusi Palai (Botswana); Council for Trade-Related Aspects of Intellectual Property Rights MINUTES OF MEETING HELD IN THE CENTRE WILLIAM RAPPARD ON 24–25 FEBRUARY 2015 Chairperson: Ambassador Mothusi Palai (Botswana); Council for Trade-Related Aspects of Intellectual Property Rights MINUTES OF MEETING HELD IN THE CENTRE WILLIAM RAPPARD ON 15–16 OCTOBER, 6 NOVEMBER AND 23 NOVEMBER 2015 Chairpersons: Ambassador Al-Otaibi (Kingdom of Saudi-Arabia) and Ambassador Alfredo Suescum (Panama); Council for Trade-Related Aspects of Intellectual Property Rights MINUTES OF MEETING HELD IN THE CENTRE WILLIAM RAPPARD ON 1 MARCH 2016 Chairperson: Ambassador Al-Otaibi (Kingdom of Saudi-Arabia); Council for Trade-Related Aspects of Intellectual Property rights MINUTES OF MEETING HELD IN THE CENTRE WILLIAM RAPPARD ON 7–8 JUNE 2016 Chairperson: Ambassador Mero (United Republic of Tanzania); Council for Trade-Related Aspects of Intellectual Property rights MINUTES OF MEETING HELD IN THE CENTRE WILLIAM RAPPARD ON 7–8 JUNE 2016 Chairperson: Ambassador Mero (United Republic of Tanzania) Addendum; Council for Trade-Related Aspects of Intellectual Property Rights MINUTES OF MEETING HELD IN THE CENTRE WILLIAM RAPPARD ON 8–9 NOVEMBER 2016 Chairperson: Ambassador Mero (United Republic of Tanzania); MINUTES OF MEETING Council for Trade-Related Aspects of Intellectual Property Rights MINUTES OF MEETING HELD IN THE CENTRE WILLIAM RAPPARD ON 30 JANUARY 2017 Chairperson: Ambassador Mero (United Republic of Tanzania); Council for Trade-Related Aspects of Intellectual Property Rights MINUTES OF MEETING HELD IN THE CENTRE WILLIAM RAPPARD ON 13 JUNE 2017 Chairperson: Ms Irene Young (Hong Kong, China); Council for Trade-Related Aspects of Intellectual Property Rights MINUTES OF MEETING HELD IN THE CENTRE WILLIAM RAPPARD ON 19–20 OCTOBER 2017 Chairperson: Ms Irene Young (Hong Kong, China); Council for Trade-Related Aspects of Intellectual Property Rights MINUTES OF MEETING HELD IN THE CENTRE WILLIAM RAPPARD ON 19–20 OCTOBER 2017 Chairperson: Ms Irene Young (Hong Kong, China) Corrigendum;

IO	Title of Documents
	Council for Trade-Related Aspects of Intellectual Property Rights MINUTES OF MEETING HELD IN THE CENTRE WILLIAM RAPPARD ON 27 FEBRUARY 2018 Chairperson: Ms Irene Young (Hong Kong, China); Council for Trade-Related Aspects of Intellectual Property Rights MINUTES OF MEETING HELD IN THE CENTRE WILLIAM RAPPARD ON 27 FEBRUARY 2018 Chairperson: Ms Irene Young (Hong Kong, China) Addendum; Council for Trade-Related Aspects of Intellectual Property Rights MINUTES OF MEETING HELD IN THE CENTRE WILLIAM RAPPARD ON 5–6 JUNE 2018 Chairperson: H.E. Ambassador Dr Walter Werner (Germany) Addendum; World Health Organization, World Intellectual Property Organization and World Trade Organization 2013 "Promoting Access to Medical Technologies and Innovation Intersections between public health, intellectual property and trade"; WTO 2013 Council for Trade-Related Aspects of Intellectual Property Rights WTO SECRETARIAT TECHNICAL COOPERATION IN THE TRIPS AREA NOTE BY THE SECRETARIAT; WTO 2015 Council for Trade-Related Aspects of Intellectual Property Rights WTO SECRETARIAT TECHNICAL COOPERATION IN THE TRIPS AREA NOTE BY THE SECRETARIAT; WTO 2017 Council for Trade-Related Aspects of Intellectual Property Rights WTO SECRETARIAT TECHNICAL COOPERATION IN THE TRIPS AREA NOTE BY THE SECRETARIAT; WTO 2018 Council for Trade-Related Aspects of Intellectual Property Rights WTO SECRETARIAT TECHNICAL COOPERATION IN THE TRIPS AREA NOTE BY THE SECRETARIAT
International Union for the Protection of New Varieties of Plants (UPOV)	INTERNATIONAL UNION FOR THE PROTECTION OF NEW VARIETIES OF PLANTS COUNCIL Forty-Seventh Ordinary Session Geneva, October 2013 ANNUAL REPORT OF THE SECRETARY-GENERAL FOR 2012; INTERNATIONAL UNION FOR THE PROTECTION OF NEW VARIETIES OF PLANTS COUNCIL Forty-Seventh Ordinary Session Geneva, October,2014 ANNUAL REPORT OF THE SECRETARY-GENERAL FOR 2013; INTERNATIONAL UNION FOR THE PROTECTION OF NEW VARIETIES OF PLANTS COUNCIL Forty-Seventh Ordinary Session Geneva, October 2016 ANNUAL REPORT OF THE SECRETARY-GENERAL FOR 2015; INTERNATIONAL UNION FOR THE PROTECTION OF NEW VARIETIES OF PLANTS COUNCIL Forty-Seventh Ordinary Session Geneva, October 2017 ANNUAL REPORT OF THE SECRETARY-GENERAL FOR 2016; INTERNATIONAL UNION FOR THE PROTECTION OF NEW VARIETIES OF PLANTS COUNCIL Forty-Seventh Ordinary Session Geneva, October 2018 ANNUAL REPORT OF THE SECRETARY-GENERAL FOR 2017; UPOV PLANT VARIETY PROTECTION GAZETTE AND NEWSLETTER No. 106—December 2013; UPOV PLANT VARIETY PROTECTION

Continued

IO	Title of Documents
World Health Organization (WHO)	GAZETTE AND NEWSLETTER No. 107—February 2015; UPOV PLANT VARIETY PROTECTION GAZETTE AND NEWSLETTER No. 108—December 2015 WHO Annual Technical Report July 2014 ACCESS TO ANTIRETROVIRAL DRUGS IN LOW- AND MIDDLE-INCOME COUNTRIES; WHO 2014 Report Increasing access to HIV treatment in middle-income countries Key data on prices, regulatory status, tariffs and the intellectual property situation; WHO Annual Technical Report 2016 The role of intellectual property in local production in developing countries Opportunities and challenges; WHO Technical Report 2015 Trade and Health: Towards building a National Strategy; WHO Technical Report 2016 PATENT SITUATION OF KEY PRODUCTS FOR TREATMENT OF HEPATITIS C WORKING PAPER Update and revised version June 2016
World Intellectual Property Organization (WIPO)	WIPO Magazine Special Issue November 2015; WIPO Magazine No 1 February 2014; WIPO Magazine No 2 April 2014; WIPO Magazine No 3 June 2014; WIPO Magazine No 4 August 2014; WIPO Magazine No 5 October 2014; WIPO Magazine No 6 December 2014; WIPO Magazine No 7 February 2015; WIPO Magazine No 8 April 2015; WIPO Magazine No 9 June 2015; WIPO Magazine No 10 August 2015; WIPO Magazine No 11 October 2015; WIPO Magazine No 12 December 2015; WIPO Magazine No 1 February 2016; WIPO Magazine No 2 April 2016; WIPO Magazine No 3 June 2016; WIPO Magazine No 4 August 2016; WIPO Magazine No 5 October 2016; WIPO Magazine Special Supplement November 2016; WIPO Magazine No 6 December 2016; WIPO Magazine No 1 February 2017; WIPO Magazine No 2 April 2017; WIPO Magazine No 3 June 2017; WIPO Magazine No 4 August 2017; WIPO Magazine No 5 October 2017; WIPO Magazine No 6 December 2017; WIPO; WIPO Magazine No 2 April 2018; WIPO Magazine No 3 June 2018; WIPO Magazine No 4 August 2018; WIPO Magazine No 5 October 2018; WIPO Magazine Special Issue October 2018; World Intellectual Property Organization (WIPO) World Intellectual Property Indicators Annual Report 2014; World Intellectual Property Organization (WIPO) World Intellectual Property Indicators Annual Report 2015; World Intellectual Property Organization (WIPO) World Intellectual Property Indicators Annual Report 2016; World Intellectual Property Organization (WIPO) World Intellectual Property Indicators Annual Report 2017

- **Development Aid**

Institution	Title of Documents
World Bank (WB)	*World Bank Annual Report 2013: End Extreme Poverty—Promote shared Prosperity; World Bank Annual*

Institution	Title of Documents
	Report 2014; World Bank Annual Report 2015; World Bank Annual Report 2016; World Bank Annual Report 2017: End Extreme Poverty—Boost Shared Prosperity; World Bank Annual Report 2018: Investing in Opportunity—Ending Poverty
Asian Development Bank (ADB)	*Asian Development Bank Donor Report 2013; Asian Development Bank: Financial Report 2013; Asian Development Bank Annual Report 2013; Asian Development Bank Annual Report 2014; Summary of Proceedings, 47th Annual Meeting of the Board of Governors 2014; Asian Development Bank Financial Report 2014; Asian Development Bank Donor Report 2014; Asian Development Bank Annual Report 2015; Summary of Proceedings, 48th Annual Meeting of the Board of Governors 2015; Asian Development Bank Financial Report 2015; Asian Development Bank Donor Report 2015; Asian Development Bank Annual Report 2016; Asian Development Bank Donor Report 2016; Asian Development Bank Financial Report 2016; Summary of Proceedings, 49th Annual Meeting of the Board of Governors 2016; Asian Development Bank Annual Report 2017; Asian Development Bank Financial Report 2017; Asian Development Bank Donor Report 2017; Summary of Proceedings, 50th Annual Meeting of the Board of Governors 2017; Summary of Proceedings, 51st Annual Meeting of the Board of Governors 2018*
African Development Bank (AFDB)	*African Development Group 2015–2017 Rolling Plan and Budget Document: Towards an efficient, effective and adaptable organization; African Development Report 2014: Regional Integration for Inclusive Growth; African Development Report 2015: Growth, Poverty and Inequality Nexus: Overcoming Barriers to Sustainable Development; African Development Bank Annual Report 2013; African Development Bank Annual Report 2014; African Development Bank Annual Report 2015; African Development Bank Annual Report 2016; African Development Bank Annual Report 2017; The Africa Competitiveness Report 2015; The Africa Competitiveness Report 2013; The Africa Competitiveness Report 2017; African Development Report 2012; African Development Bank 2016–2018 Work Programme and Budget Document: Accelerating Africa´s Growth and Transformation; African Development Bank The 2013–2015 Three Year Rolling Plan and Budget Proposal; African Development Group 2014–2016 Rolling Plan and Budget Document: Supporting Africa´s Transformation; African Development Bank 2017–2019 Work Programme and Budget Document; African Development Bank 2018–2020 Work Programme and Budget Document*
Development Bank of Latin America (CAF)	*Development Bank of Latin America Annual Report 2013; Development Bank of Latin America Annual Report 2014; Development Bank of Latin America Annual Report 2015; Development Bank of Latin America Annual Report 2016; Development Bank of Latin America Annual Report 2017; CAF Joint Progress Report (2014–2015) of the MDB Working Group on Sustainable Transport; Sustainability Report CAF 2015–2016*

Continued

Institution	Title of Documents
European Bank for Reconstruction and Development (EBRD)	*European Bank for Reconstruction and Development Annual Report 2013; European Bank for Reconstruction and Development Annual Report 2014; European Bank for Reconstruction and Development Annual Report 2015; European Bank for Reconstruction and Development Annual Report 2016; European Bank for Reconstruction and Development Annual Review 2017*
Inter-American Development Bank (IADB)	*Inter-American Development Bank Annual Report 2013: The Year in Review; Inter-American Development Bank Annual Report 2014: The Year in Review; Inter-American Development Bank Annual Report 2015: The Year in Review; Inter-American Development Bank Annual Report 2016: The Year in Review; Inter-American Development Bank Annual Report 2017: The Year in Review; Inter-American Development Bank 2015 Partnership Report; Inter-American Development Bank 2016 Partnership Report; Inter-American Development Bank 2017 Partnership Report; Inter-American Development Bank Development Effectiveness Overview 2014; Inter-American Development Bank Development Effectiveness Overview 2015; Inter-American Development Bank Development Effectiveness Overview 2016; Inter-American Development Bank Development Effectiveness Overview 2018; Inter-American Development Bank Cultural Center Annual Report 2013*
Islamic Development Bank (IsDB)	*Islamic Development Bank Annual Report 2013; Islamic Development Bank Annual Report 2014; Islamic Development Bank Annual Report 2016; Islamic Development Bank Annual Report 2017; "IsDB Group and World Bank Launch Second Edition of Global Report on Islamic Finance" Media Release April, 2nd 2018; Islamic Development Bank Development Effectiveness Report 2017; Islamic Development Bank IDGB Operations at a Glance Q2 2018 Update; Islamic Development Bank Media Release: "IDB Doubles its Annual financing rate to 30% annually over coming 3 years" June 10th, 2009; Islamic Development Bank Group ANNUAL EVALUATION REPORT FOR THE YEAR 1436 H; Islamic Development Bank Group Operations Evaluation Department In Brief; Islamic Development Bank Annual Work Program of the Operations Evaluations Department for the Year 2018 G; Islamic Development Bank Annual Work Program of the Operations Evaluations Department for the Year 2017 G; Islamic Development Bank Annual Evaluation Report of the Operations Evaluations Department for the Year 2016 G*
New Development Bank	*New Development Bank Annual Report 2016; New Development Bank Annual Report 2017; Agreement on the New Development Bank—Fortaleza, July 15 2014; New Development Bank: MINUTES OF THE FOURTH AUDIT, RISK, BUDGET AND COMPLIANCE MEETING OF THE NEW DEVELOPMENT BANK HELD AT SHANGHAI, CHINA ON 18 JUNE 2017; New Development Bank: MINUTES OF THE FIRST ANNUAL MEETING OF THE BOARD OF GOVERNORS OF THE NEW DEVELOPMENT BANK HELD*

Institution	Title of Documents
	IN SHANGHAI, CHINA ON 20 JULY 2016; New Development Bank: MINUTES OF THE SECOND ANNUAL MEETING OF THE BOARD OF GOVERNORS OF THE NEW DEVELOPMENT BANK HELD IN NEW DELHI, INDIA ON 1 APRIL 2017; New Development Bank: Independent Auditor's Report and Financial Statements for the period from 3rd July 2015 until 31st December 2016; NDB: MINUTES OF THE 1st MEETING OF THE BUDGET, HUMAN RESOURCES AND COMPENSATION COMMITTEE OF THE NEW DEVELOPMENT BANK HELD AT SHANGHAI, CHINA ON MARCH 1, 2018; NDB: MINUTES OF THE SECOND MEETING OF THE BUDGET, HUMAN RESOURCES AND COMPENSATION COMMITTEE OF THE NEW DEVELOPMENT BANK HELD AT SHANGHAI, CHINA ON MAY 28, 2018; NDB: MINUTES OF THE THIRD AUDIT, RISK AND BUDGET COMPLIANCE MEETING OF THE NEW DEVELOPMENT BANK HELD AT NEW DELHI, INDIA ON 31 MARCH 2017; NDB: MINUTES OF THE THIRD MEETING OF THE BUDGET, HUMAN RESOURCES AND COMPENSATION COMMITTEE OF THE NEW DEVELOPMENT BANK HELD AT SHANGHAI, CHINA ON SEPTEMBER 17, 2018; NDB: MINUTES OF THE SIXTH AUDIT, RISK AND COMPLIANCE MEETING OF THE NEW DEVELOPMENT BANK HELD AT SHANGHAI, CHINA ON MARCH 1, 2018; NDB: MINUTES OF THE SEVENTH AUDIT, RISK AND COMPLIANCE COMMITTEE MEETING OF THE NEW DEVELOPMENT BANK HELD AT SHANGHAI, CHINA ON MAY 28, 2018; NDB: MINUTES OF THE 7TH MEETING OF THE BOARD OF DIRECTORS OF THE NEW DEVELOPMENT BANK HELD AT THE NEW DEVELOPMENT BANK, SHANGHAI, CHINA ON 22 NOVEMBER 2016; NDB: MINUTES OF THE EIGHTH AUDIT, RISK AND COMPLIANCE COMMITTEE MEETING OF THE NEW DEVELOPMENT BANK HELD AT SHANGHAI, CHINA ON SEPTEMBER 17, 2018; NDB: MINUTES OF THE 8TH MEETING OF THE BOARD OF DIRECTORS OF THE NEW DEVELOPMENT BANK HELD AT THE NEW DEVELOPMENT BANK, SHANGHAI, CHINA ON 22 FEBRUARY 2017; NDB: MINUTES OF THE 9TH MEETING OF THE BOARD OF DIRECTORS OF THE NEW DEVELOPMENT BANK HELD AT NEW DELHI, INDIA ON 31 MARCH 2017; NDB: MINUTES OF THE 10TH MEETING OF THE BOARD OF DIRECTORS OF THE NEW DEVELOPMENT BANK HELD AT SHANGHAI, CHINA ON 18 JUNE 2017; NDB: MINUTES OF THE 11TH MEETING OF THE BOARD OF DIRECTORS OF THE NEW DEVELOPMENT BANK (TELECONFERENCE) HELD ON 30 AUGUST 2017; NDB: MINUTES OF THE 14TH MEETING OF THE BOARD OF DIRECTORS OF THE NEW DEVELOPMENT BANK HELD AT SHANGHAI, CHINA ON MAY 28, 2018; NDB: MINUTES OF THE 15TH MEETING OF THE BOARD OF DIRECTORS OF THE NEW DEVELOPMENT BANK HELD IN BUENOS AIRES ON JULY 20, 2018; NDB: MINUTES OF THE

Continued

Institution	Title of Documents
	16th MEETING OF THE BOARD OF DIRECTORS OF THE NEW DEVELOPMENT BANK HELD IN SHANGHAI ON SEPTEMBER 18, 2018; NDB: THE NEW DEVELOPMENT BANK SUMMARY OF THE BUDGET FOR 2017
European Investment Bank (EIB)	*European Investment Bank: Report on results of EIB operations outside the EU 2013; European Investment Bank Sustainability Report 2013; European Investment Bank Sustainability Report 2014; European Investment Bank Sustainability Report 2015; European Investment Bank Sustainability Report 2016; European Investment Bank FEMIP Annual Report 2013; EIB Audit Committee Annual Reports for the year 2014; EIB Audit Committee Annual Reports for the year 2016; EIB Audit Committee Annual Reports for the year 2017; Annual Report on EIB operations inside the EU 2015 With the three pillar assessment methodology; EIB Statistical Report 2017*
United Nations Development Group (UNDG)	*UNDG: Local Insight, Global Ambitions: UNLOCKING SDG FINANCING: GOOD PRACTICES FROM EARLY ADOPTERS; UNDG STANDARD OPERATING PROCEDURES FOR "DELIVERING AS ONE" 2015 PROGRESS REPORT; UNDG SWITCHING GEARS FOR 2030 RESULTS OF DEVELOPMENT COORDINATION IN 2017; UNDG TOGETHER POSSIBLE GEARING UP FOR THE 2030 AGENDA 2015 RESULTS OF UNDG COORDINATION; UNDG Lift off—Agenda 2013: Shared Results of the UNDG 2016; UNDG TOGETHER POSSIBLE: GEARING UP FOR THE 2030 AGENDA EXECUTIVE SUMMARY OF 2015 RESULTS OF UNDG COORDINATION; The impact of UN coordination: Stories from the field—UN Synthesis of 2011/12 Resident Coordinator Annual Reports; UNDG 2015 Report A Million Voices The World We Want A Sustainable Future with Dignity for all; UNDG 2016 The Sustainable Development Goals are Coming to Life: Stories of Country Implementation and UN Support; UNDG Transition Report 2016: Looking Back, Leaping Forward Moving from MDGs to SDGs in Europe and Central Asia; UNDG 2015 THE GLOBAL CONVERSATION BEGINS: Emerging Views for a New Development Agenda; UNDG 2014 Delivering the Post-2015 Development Agenda: Opportunities at the national and local level*
Council of Europe Bank (CEB)	*Council of Europe Development Bank Report of the Governor 2013; Council of Europe Development Bank Report of the Governor 2014; Council of Europe Development Bank Report of the Governor 2015; Council of Europe Development Bank Report of the Governor 2016; Council of Europe Development Bank Report of the Governor 2017; Council of Europe Development Bank Financial Report 2016; Council of Europe Development Bank Financial Report 2017; Council of Europe Development Bank Financial Statements 2015; Council of Europe Development Bank Financial Statements 2014; Council of Europe Development Bank Financial Statements 2013*
Arab Bank for Economic Development in Africa (BADEA)	*ARAB BANK FOR ECONOMIC DEVELOPMENT IN AFRICA Annual Report 2013; ARAB BANK FOR ECONOMIC DEVELOPMENT IN AFRICA Annual Report 2014; ARAB BANK*

Institution	Title of Documents
	FOR ECONOMIC DEVELOPMENT IN AFRICA Annual Report 2015; ARAB BANK FOR ECONOMIC DEVELOPMENT IN AFRICA Annual Report 2016; ARAB BANK FOR ECONOMIC DEVELOPMENT IN AFRICA Annual Report 2017
OPEC Fund for International Development (OPECFID)	*The OPEC Fund for International Development Annual Report 2013; The OPEC Fund for International Development Annual Report 2014; The OPEC Fund for International Development Annual Report 2015; The OPEC Fund for International Development Annual Report 2016; The OPEC Fund for International Development Annual Report 2017; OPECFID Quarterly January 2019: BRIDGE BUILDERS Industry, infrastructure and innovation for future generations; OPECFID Quarterly July 2017: Today's children: In safe hands? OPECFID Quarterly April 2018; OPECFID Quarterly April 2017; OPECFID Quarterly January 2018 OPECFID Quarterly January 2017; OPECFID Quarterly July 2018; OPECFID Quarterly October 2018; OPECFID Quarterly October 2017*
Eurasian Development Bank (EDB)	*Eurasian Development Bank Annual Report 2013; Eurasian Development Bank Annual Report 2014; Eurasian Development Bank Annual Report 2015; Eurasian Development Bank Annual Report 2017*
Asian Infrastructure Investment Bank (AIIB)	*Asian Infrastructure Investment Bank Annual Report and Financials 2016; Asian Infrastructure Investment Bank Annual Report and Financials 2017; Asian Infrastructure Investment Bank Annual Report and Financials 2018; ASIAN INFRASTRUCTURE FINANCE 2019 Bridging Borders: Infrastructure to Connect Asia and Beyond*
Caribbean Development Bank (CDB)	*CARIBBEAN DEVELOPMENT BANK ANNUAL REPORT 2013 VOLUME ONE; CARIBBEAN DEVELOPMENT BANK ANNUAL REPORT 2013 VOLUME TWO; CBD Office of INTEGRITY, COMPLIANCE AND ACCOUNTABILITY Annual Report 2018; CARIBBEAN DEVELOPMENT BANK ANNUAL REPORT 2016; CARIBBEAN DEVELOPMENT BANK ANNUAL REPORT 2017; CARIBBEAN DEVELOPMENT BANK ANNUAL REPORT 2015; CARIBBEAN DEVELOPMENT BANK ANNUAL REPORT 2014 Volume ONE; CARIBBEAN DEVELOPMENT BANK ANNUAL REPORT 2014 Volume TWO*

- **Financial Stability**

IO	Title of Documents
International Monetary Fund (IMF)	INTERNATIONAL MONETARY FUND ANNUAL REPORT 2013 Promoting a more secure and stable global economy; INTERNATIONAL MONETARY FUND ANNUAL REPORT 2014: From Stabilization to Sustainable Growth; INTERNATIONAL MONETARY FUND ANNUAL REPORT

Continued

IO	Title of Documents
	2015: Tackling Challenges together; INTERNATIONAL MONETARY FUND ANNUAL REPORT 2016: Finding Solutions Together; INTERNATIONAL MONETARY FUND ANNUAL REPORT 2017: Promoting Inclusive Growth
BRICS Contingency Reserve Arrangement (CRA)	BRICS Leaders' Informal Meeting on the margins of the G20 Summit Joint Communique Hangzhou, China, 4 September 2016; BRICS Fortaleza Declaration, 15 July 2014; 10TH BRICS SUMMIT JOHANNESBURG DECLARATION BRICS in Africa: Collaboration for Inclusive Growth and Shared Prosperity in the 4th Industrial Revolution; BRICS Joint Statistical Publication 2013; BRICS Joint Statistical Publication 2014; BRICS Joint Statistical Publication 2015; BRICS Joint Statistical Publication 2016; BRICS Joint Statistical Publication 2017; Media note at the conclusion of the BRICS Leaders' meeting held on the margins of the G20 Leaders' Summit, St Petersburg, Russia, 5 September 2013; BRICS Xiamen Declaration, Xiamen, China, 4 September 2017
Chiang Mai Initiative (CMI)	ASEAN+3 The Joint Statement of the 15th ASEAN+3 Finance Ministers and Central Bank Governors' Meeting 3 May 2012, Manila, the Philippines; AMRO Research Office 2nd High-Level RFA Dialogue: New Development, Cooperation and Capacity Building Joint Statement Washington D.C., 11 October 2017; AMRO Annual Report 2017; AMRO Annual Report 2016; ASEAN+3 The Joint Statement of the 18th ASEAN+3 Finance Ministers and Central Bank Governors' Meeting (3 May 2015 /Baku, Azerbaijan); ASEAN+3 The Joint Statement of the 16th ASEAN+3 Finance Ministers and Central Bank Governors' Meeting 3 May 2013, Delhi, India; Joint Statement of the 21stASEAN+3 Finance Ministers' and Central Bank Governors' Meeting (Manila, Philippines, 4 May 2018); The Joint Statement of the 19th ASEAN+3 Finance Ministers' and Central Bank Governors' Meeting (May 3, 2016 Frankfurt, Germany); The Joint Statement of the 20th ASEAN+3 Finance Ministers' and Central Bank Governors' Meeting (Yokohama, Japan, May 5th 2017)
EU Balance of Payment Assistance (BoP/ESM)	EU Commission Press release 27th March 2017: European Union EUR 600 million tap on 0.750% benchmark due April 4th, 2031; EU Commission 2014 Annual Activity Report Economic and Financial Affairs; EU Commission 2015 Annual Activity Report Economic and Financial Affairs; EU Commission 2016 Annual Activity Report Economic and Financial Affairs; EU Commission 2017 Annual Activity Report Directorate General for Economic and Financial Affairs; EU Commission 2013 EU BALANCE-OF-PAYMENTS ASSISTANCE TO HUNGARY: THIRD REVIEW UNDER POST-PROGRAMME SURVEILLANCE; EU Commission 201 EU BALANCE-OF-PAYMENTS ASSISTANCE TO HUNGARY: FOURTH REVIEW UNDER POST-PROGRAMME SURVEILLANCE; EU Commission 2015 EU BALANCE-OF-PAYMENTS ASSISTANCE TO HUNGARY: FIFTH REVIEW UNDER POST-PROGRAMME SURVEILLANCE; EU Commission 2015 EU BALANCE-OF-PAYMENTS ASSISTANCE

IO	Title of Documents
	TO HUNGARY: SIXTH REVIEW UNDER POST-PROGRAMME SURVEILLANCE; EU Commission 2013 EU BOP ASSISTANCE TO LATVIA—THIRD REVIEW UNDER POST-PROGRAMME SURVEILLANCE; EU Commission 2014 EU BOP ASSISTANCE TO LATVIA—FOURTH REVIEW UNDER POST-PROGRAMME SURVEILLANCE; EU Commission 2014 EU BOP ASSISTANCE TO LATVIA—FIFTH REVIEW UNDER POST-PROGRAMME SURVEILLANCE; EU Commission 2014 EU BOP ASSISTANCE TO LATVIA—SIXTH REVIEW UNDER POST-PROGRAMME SURVEILLANCE; EU Commission Balance of Payments Assistance Programme Romania, 2013–2015 INSTITUTIONAL PAPER 012, NOVEMBER 2015; Post-Programme Surveillance Report Romania, Spring 2016 INSTITUTIONAL PAPER 029, JULY 2016; Post-Programme Surveillance Report Romania, Spring 2017 INSTITUTIONAL PAPER 054, MAY 2017; Post-Programme Surveillance Report Romania, Autumn 2017 INSTITUTIONAL PAPER 068, DECEMBER 2017
Arab Monetary Fund (AMF)	Arab Monetary Fund Annual Report 2013; Arab Monetary Fund Annual Report 2014; Arab Monetary Fund Annual Report 2015; Arab Monetary Fund Annual Report 2016; Arab Monetary Fund Annual Report 2017
Latin American Reserve Fund (LARF)	Fondo Latinoamericano de Reservas Memoria Anual 2013; Fondo Latinoamericano de Reservas Memoria Anual 2014; Fondo Latinoamericano de Reservas Memoria Anual 2016; Fondo Latinoamericano de Reservas Memoria Anual 2017

- **Energy Governance**

IO	Period	Title of Documents
Organization of the Petroleum Exporting Countries (OPEC)	1993–1997	OPEC Bulletin, Vol 24 No.1, January 1993; OPEC Bulletin, Vol 24 No.2, February 1993; OPEC Bulletin, Vol 24 No.3, March 1993; OPEC Bulletin, Vol 24 No.4, April 1993; OPEC Bulletin, Vol 24 No.5, May 1993; OPEC Bulletin, Vol 24 No.6, June 1993; OPEC Bulletin, Vol 24 No.7 July/August 1993; OPEC Bulletin, Vol 24 No.8, September 1993; OPEC Bulletin, Vol 24 No.9, October 1993; OPEC Bulletin, Vol 24 No.10, November/December 1993; OPEC Review 1993, 17(4), 451–468; OPEC Bulletin, Vol 25 No.1, January 1994; OPEC Bulletin, Vol 25 No.2, February 1994; OPEC Bulletin, Vol 25 No.3, March 1994; OPEC Bulletin, Vol 25 No.4, April 1994; OPEC Bulletin, Vol 25 No.5, May 1994; OPEC Bulletin, Vol 25 No.6, June 1994; OPEC

Continued

IO	Period	Title of Documents
		Bulletin, Vol 25 No.7, July/August 1994; OPEC Bulletin, Vol 25 No.8, September 1994; OPEC Bulletin, Vol 25 No.9, October 1994; OPEC Bulletin, Vol 25 No.10, November/December 1994; OPEC Bulletin, Vol 26 No.1, January 1995; OPEC Bulletin, Vol 26 No.2, January 1995; OPEC Bulletin, Vol 26 No.3, March 1995; OPEC Bulletin, Vol 26 No.4, April 1995; OPEC Bulletin, Vol 26 No.5, May 1995; OPEC Bulletin, Vol 26 No.6, June 1995; OPEC Bulletin, Vol 26 No.7, July/August 1995; OPEC Bulletin, Vol 26 No.8, September 1995; OPEC Bulletin, Vol 26 No.9, October 1995; OPEC Bulletin, Vol 26 No.10, November/December 1995; OPEC Bulletin, Vol 27 No.1, January 1996; OPEC Bulletin Vol 27 No.2, February 1996; OPEC Bulletin Vol 27 No.3, March 1996; OPEC Bulletin Vol 27 No.4, April 1996; OPEC Bulletin Vol 27 No.5, May 1996; OPEC Bulletin Vol 27 No.6, June 1996; OPEC Bulletin Vol 27 No.7, July/August 1996; OPEC Bulletin Vol 27 No.8, September 1996; OPEC Bulletin Vol 27 No.9, October 1996; OPEC Bulletin Vol 27 No.10, November/December 1996; OPEC Bulletin Vol 28 No.1, January 1997; OPEC Bulletin Vol 28 No.2, February 1997; OPEC Bulletin Vol 28 No.3, March 1997; OPEC Bulletin Vol 28 No.4, April 1997; OPEC Bulletin Vol 28 No.5, May 1997; OPEC Bulletin Vol 28 No.6, June 1997; OPEC Bulletin Vol 28 No.7, July/August 1997; OPEC OPEC Bulletin Vol 28 No.8, September 1997; Bulletin Vol 28 No.9, October 1997; OPEC Bulletin Vol 28 No.10, November/December 1997
	1998–2002	OPEC Annual Report 1998; OPEC Annual Statistical Bulletin 1999; OPEC Annual Statistical Bulletin 2000; OPEC Annual Report 2001; OPEC Annual Report 2002; OPEC Bulletin, Vol 31 No.1, January 2000; OPEC Bulletin, Vol 31 No.5, May 2000; OPEC Bulletin, Vol 31 No.8, August 2000; OPEC Bulletin, Vol 31 No.9, September 2000; OPEC Bulletin, Vol 31 No.10, October 2000; OPEC Bulletin, Vol 31 No.12, December 2000; OPEC Bulletin OPEC Bulletin, Vol 32 No.1, January 2001; OPEC Bulletin, Vol 33 No.1, January 2002; OPEC Bulletin, Vol 32 No.2, February 2001; Vol 33 No.2, February 2002; OPEC Bulletin, Vol 32 No.3, March 2001; OPEC Bulletin, Vol 33 No.3, March 2002; OPEC Bulletin, Vol 32 No.4, April 2001; OPEC Bulletin, Vol 33 No.4, April 2002; OPEC Bulletin, Vol 33 No.5, May 2002; OPEC Bulletin, Vol 32 No.5, May 2001; OPEC Bulletin, Vol 32 No.6, June 2001; OPEC Bulletin, Vol 33 No.6, June 2002; OPEC Bulletin, Vol 33 No.7, July 2002; OPEC Bulletin, Vol 32 No.67 July 2001; OPEC Bulletin, Vol 32 No.8, August 2001; OPEC Bulletin, Vol 32 No.9, September 2001; OPEC Bulletin, Vol 33 No.9, September 2002; OPEC Bulletin, Vol 32 No.10, October 2001; OPEC Bulletin, Vol 32 No.11, November 2001;

IO	Period	Title of Documents
		OPEC Bulletin, Vol 33 No.11, November 2002; OPEC Bulletin, Vol 33 No.12, December 2002; OPEC Bulletin, Vol 32 No.12, December 2001
	2003–7	OPEC Annual Report 2003; OPEC Annual Report 2004; OPEC Annual Report 2005; OPEC Annual Report 2006; OPEC Annual Report 2007; OPEC Bulletin Vol.37, No.1, January–February 2006; OPEC Bulletin Vol.37, No.2, March–April 2006; OPEC Bulletin Vol.37, No.3, May–June 2006; OPEC Bulletin Vol.38, No.3, May–June 2007; OPEC Bulletin Vol.37, No.4, July–August 2006; OPEC Bulletin Vol.36, No.4, July–August 2005; OPEC Bulletin Vol.38, No.4, July–August 2007; OPEC Bulletin Vol.37, No.5, September–October 2006; OPEC Bulletin Vol.38, No.5, September–October 2007; OPEC Bulletin Vol.36, No.6, November–December 2005; OPEC Bulletin Vol.37, No.6, November–December 2006; OPEC Bulletin Vol.35, No.1, January–February 2004; OPEC Bulletin Vol.36, No.1, January–February 2005; OPEC Bulletin Vol.38, No.1,
		January 2007; OPEC Bulletin Vol.34, No.1, January–February 2003; OPEC Bulletin Vol.36, No.2, February 2005; OPEC Bulletin Vol.38, No.2, February 2007; OPEC Bulletin Vol.35, No.2, March 2004; OPEC Bulletin Vol.38, No.3, March 2007; OPEC Bulletin Vol.34, No.3, March-April 2003; OPEC Bulletin Vol.35, No.3, April 2004; OPEC Bulletin Vol.38, No.4, April 2007; OPEC Bulletin Vol.35, No.4, May 2004; OPEC Bulletin Vol.34, No.3, May-June 2003; OPEC Bulletin Vol.35, No.5, June 2004; OPEC Bulletin Vol.36, No.6, June 2005; OPEC Bulletin Vol.34, No.4, July–August 2003; OPEC Bulletin Vol.35, No.6, July–August 2004; OPEC Bulletin Vol.35, No.7, September 2004; OPEC Bulletin Vol.36, No.8, September 2005; OPEC Bulletin Vol.34, No.5, September–October 2003; OPEC Bulletin Vol.35, No.8, October 2004; OPEC Bulletin Vol.36, No.9, October 2005; OPEC Bulletin Vol.38, No.8, November 2007; OPEC Bulletin Vol.34, No.6, November–December 2003; OPEC Bulletin Vol.35, No.9, November–December 2004; OPEC Bulletin Vol.38, No.9, December 2007
	2008–2012	OPEC Annual Report 2008; OPEC Annual Report 2009; OPEC Annual Report 2010; OPEC Annual Report 2011; OPEC Annual Report 2012; OPEC Bulletin Vol. 41, No.1, January–February 2010; OPEC Bulletin Vol. 41, No.2, March 2010; OPEC Bulletin Vol. 41, No.3, April 2010; OPEC Bulletin Vol. 41, No.4, May 2010; OPEC Bulletin Vol. 41, No.5, June 2010; OPEC Bulletin Vol. 41, No.6, July–August 2010; OPEC Bulletin Vol. 41, No.7, January–February 2010; OPEC Bulletin Vol. 41, No.8, September 2010; OPEC Bulletin Vol. 41, No.9, October

Continued

IO	Period	Title of Documents
		2010; OPEC Bulletin Vol. 41, No.10, November–December 2010; OPEC Bulletin Vol. 42, No.1, January–February 2011; OPEC Bulletin Vol. 42, No.2, March 2011; OPEC Bulletin Vol. 42, No.3, April 2011; OPEC Bulletin Vol. 42, No.4, May 2011; OPEC Bulletin Vol. 42, No.5, June 2011; OPEC Bulletin Vol. 42, No.6, July–August 2011; OPEC Bulletin Vol. 42, No.7, September 2011; OPEC Bulletin Vol. 42, No.8, October 2011; OPEC Bulletin Vol. 42, No.9, November–December 2011; OPEC Bulletin Vol. 43, No.1, December 2011–January 2012; OPEC Bulletin Vol. 43, No.2, February 2012; OPEC Bulletin Vol. 43, No.3, March–April 2012; OPEC Bulletin Vol. 43, No.4, May 2012; OPEC Bulletin Vol. 43, No.5, June–July 2012; OPEC Bulletin Vol. 43, No.6, August–September 2012; OPEC Bulletin Vol. 43, No.7, October–December 2012; OPEC Bulletin Vol. 43, No.8, October 2012; OPEC Bulletin Vol. 43, No.9, November–December 2012; OPEC Bulletin Vol. 39, No.1, January 2008; OPEC Bulletin Vol. 39, No.2, February 2008; OPEC Bulletin Vol. 39, No.3, March–April 2008; OPEC Bulletin Vol. 39, No.4, May 2008; OPEC Bulletin Vol. 39, No.5, June 2008; OPEC Bulletin Vol. 39, No.6, June 2008; OPEC Bulletin Vol. 39, No.7, July–August 2008; OPEC Bulletin Vol. 39, No.8, September 2008; OPEC Bulletin Vol. 39, No.9, October 2008; OPEC Bulletin Vol. 39, No.10, November–December 2008; OPEC Bulletin Vol. 40, No.1, January 2009; OPEC Bulletin Vol. 40, No.2, February 2009; OPEC Bulletin Vol. 40, No.3, March–April 2009; OPEC Bulletin Vol. 40, No.4, May 2009; OPEC Bulletin Vol. 40, No.5, June 2009; OPEC Bulletin Vol. 40, No.6, July 2009; OPEC Bulletin Vol. 40, No.7, August–September 2009; OPEC Bulletin Vol. 40, No.8, October–November 2009; OPEC Bulletin Vol. 40, No.9, December 2009
	2013–2017	OPEC Annual Report 2013; OPEC Annual Report 2014; OPEC Annual Report 2015; OPEC Annual Report 2016; OPEC Annual Report 2017; OPEC Bulletin Vol 44, No.1, January 2013; OPEC Bulletin Vol 44, No.2, February–March 2013; OPEC Bulletin Vol 44, No.3, April 2013; OPEC Bulletin Vol 44, No.4, May 2013; OPEC Bulletin Vol 44, No.5, June–July 2013; OPEC Bulletin Vol 44, No.6, August 2013; OPEC Bulletin Vol 44, No.7, September 2013; OPEC Bulletin Vol 44, No.8, October–November 2013; OPEC Bulletin Vol 44, No.9, December 2013; OPEC Bulletin Vol 45, No.1, January 2014; OPEC Bulletin Vol 45, No.2, February–March 2014; OPEC Bulletin Vol 45, No.3, April 2014; OPEC Bulletin Vol 45, No.4, May 2014; OPEC Bulletin Vol 45, No.5, June 2014; OPEC Bulletin Vol 45, No.6, July 2014; OPEC Bulletin Vol 45, No.7, August–September 2014; OPEC Bulletin Vol 45, No.8, October 2014; OPEC Bulletin Vol

IO	Period	Title of Documents
		45, No.9, November–December 2014; OPEC Bulletin Vol 46, No.1, January–February 2015; OPEC Bulletin Vol 46, No.2, March 2015; OPEC Bulletin Vol 46, No.3, April 2015; OPEC Bulletin Vol 46, No.4, May 2015; OPEC Bulletin Vol 46, No.5, June 2015; OPEC Bulletin Vol 46, No.6, July–August 2015; OPEC Bulletin Vol 46, No.7, September 2015; OPEC Bulletin Vol 46, No.8, October 2015; OPEC Bulletin Vol 46, No.9, November 2015; OPEC Bulletin Vol 46, No.10, December 2015; OPEC Bulletin Vol 47, No.1, January–February 2016; OPEC Bulletin Vol 47, No.2, March 2016; OPEC Bulletin Vol 47, No.3, April 2016; OPEC Bulletin Vol 47, No.4, May 2016; OPEC Bulletin Vol 47, No.5, June–July 2016; OPEC Bulletin Vol 47, No.6, August–September 2016; OPEC Bulletin Vol 47, No.7, October 2016; OPEC Bulletin Vol 47, No.8, November–December 2016; OPEC Bulletin Vol 48, No.1, January–February 2017; OPEC Bulletin Vol 48, No.2, March-April 2017; OPEC Bulletin Vol 48, No.3, May-July 2017; OPEC Bulletin Vol 48, No.4, August–September 2017; OPEC Bulletin Vol 48, No.5, October 2017; OPEC Bulletin Vol 48, No.6, November 2017
International Energy Agency (IEA)	1993–1997	International Energy Agency (IEA)—World Energy Outlook 1993; International Energy Agency (IEA)—World Energy Outlook 1994; International Energy Agency (IEA)—World Energy Outlook 1995; International Energy Agency (IEA)—World Energy Outlook 1996; International Energy Agency (IEA)—World Energy Outlook 1997
	1998–2002	International Energy Agency (IEA)—World Energy Outlook 1998 Edition; International Energy Agency (IEA)—World Energy Outlook 1999 Edition; International Energy Agency (IEA)—World Energy Outlook 2000 Edition; International Energy Agency (IEA)—World Energy Outlook 2001 Edition; International Energy Agency (IEA)—World Energy Outlook 2002–Part 1; International Energy Agency (IEA)—World Energy Outlook 2002–Part 2
	2003–7	International Energy Agency (IEA)—World Energy Outlook 2003; International Energy Agency (IEA)—World Energy Outlook 2004; International Energy Agency (IEA)—World Energy Outlook 2005; International Energy Agency (IEA)—World Energy Outlook 2006; International Energy Agency (IEA)—World Energy Outlook 2007;
	2008–12	International Energy Agency (IEA)—World Energy Outlook 2008; International Energy Agency (IEA)—World Energy Outlook 2009; International Energy Agency (IEA)—World Energy Outlook 2010; International Energy Agency (IEA)—World Energy Outlook 2011; International Energy Agency (IEA)—World Energy Outlook 2012

Continued

IO	Period	Title of Documents
	2013–17	International Energy Agency (IEA)—World Energy Outlook 2013; International Energy Agency (IEA)—World Energy Outlook 2014; International Energy Agency (IEA)—World Energy Outlook 2015; International Energy Agency (IEA)—World Energy Outlook 2016; International Energy Agency (IEA)—World Energy Outlook 2017; International Energy Agency (IEA)—World Energy Outlook Special Report Energy and Climate Change 2015; International Energy Agency (IEA)—World Energy Outlook Special Report Energy and Air Pollution 2016
Energy Charter Treaty (ECT)	1998–2002	Energy Charter "ENERGY TRANSIT—The Multilateral Challenge" Prepared for G8 Energy Ministerial Meeting Moscow, 1 April 1998; The Energy Charter Treaty Secretariat 2002 "IMPACTS OF MARKET LIBERALISATION ON ENERGY EFFICIENCY POLICIES AND PROGRAMMES"; The Energy Charter Secretariat 2001 "TRADE IN ENERGY WTO Rules Applying under the Energy Charter Treaty"
	2003–7	The Energy Charter Secretariat 2003 "Best Practices Guidelines on Restructuring (including Privatization) in the Energy Sector"; The Energy Charter Secretariat 2003 "THE ROAD TOWARDS AN ENERGY-EFFICIENT FUTURE Report to the Ministerial Conference 'Environment for Europe'"; Kiev, Ukraine, May 21–23 2003; The Energy Charter Secretariat 2004 "Investing in Energy Efficiency Removing the Barriers"; The Energy Charter Secretariat 2005 "Integration of Energy Efficiency and Renewable Energy Policies"; The Energy Charter Secretariat 2007 "DRIVING WITHOUT PETROLEUM? A Comparative Guide to Biofuels, Gas-to-Liquids and Coal-to-Liquids as Fuels for Transportation"; The Energy Charter Secretariat 2006 "Cogeneration and District Heating Best Practices for Municipalities Energy Charter Protocol on Energy Efficiency and Related Environmental Aspects (PEEREA)" The Energy Charter Secretariat 2007 "Policy Developments and Challenges in Delivering Energy Efficiency Energy Charter Secretariat"; The Energy Charter Secretariat 2006 "Energy Efficiency and Emissions Trading A PEEREA perspective after the entry into force of the Kyoto Protocol and of the EU ETS"; The Energy Charter Secretariat 2006 "GAS TRANSIT TARIFFS in selected Energy Charter Treaty Countries"; The Energy Charter Secretariat 2006 "The Impact of CO2 Reduction Measures on Energy Trade"; The Energy Charter Secretariat 2007 "Putting a Price on Energy International Pricing Mechanisms for Oil and Gas Energy"; The Energy Charter Secretariat 2007 "FROM WELLHEAD TOMARKET OIL PIPELINE TARIFFS AND TARIFF METHODOLOGIES IN SELECTED ENERGY CHARTER MEMBER COUNTRIES"

IO	Period	Title of Documents
	2008–12	The Energy Charter Secretariat Annual Report 2011; The Energy Charter Secretariat Annual Report 2012; The Energy Charter Secretariat 2009 "Investment and Market Development in Carbon Capture and Storage Role of the Energy Charter Treaty"; Energy Charter Secretariat 2010 "PUTTING A PRICE ON ENERGY: INTERNATIONAL COAL PRICING"; Energy Charter Secretariat 2012 "Analysis on Issues Related to Competition under the Energy Charter Treaty"; The ECT Secretariat 2012 "EXPROPRIATION REGIME under the ENERGY CHARTER TREATY" The ECT Secretariat 2012 "Bringing Gas to the Market—Gas Transit and Transmission Tariffs in Energy Charter Treaty Countries: Regulatory Aspects and Tariff Methodologies"; The ECT Secretariat 2009 "Developments in LNG Trade and Pricing"; The ECT Secretariat 2012 "Transport Tariffs and Underlying Methodologies for Cross—Border Crude Oil and Products Pipelines"; The ECT Secretariat 2011 "Oil Pricing Update"; The ECT Secretariat 2008 "Energy Efficiency in the Public Sector Policies and Programmes in ECT Member Countries"; ECT Secretariat 2008 "Taxation along the oil and gas supply chain"; The ECT Secretariat 2010 "Market Trading Mechanisms for Delivering Energy Efficiency"
	2013–17	The Energy Charter Secretariat Annual Report 2013; The Energy Charter Secretariat Annual Report 2014; The Energy Charter Secretariat Annual Report 2015; The Energy Charter Secretariat Annual Report 2017; The Energy Charter Secretariat Annual Report 2016; The ECT Secretariat 2013 "Exchanges of Business Assets within Investment Activities in the Energy Sector: Key Concepts"; The ECT Secretariat 2014 "Analysis of mutual exchanges of business assets within investment activities in the energy sector"; The ECT Secretariat 2014 "Securing Energy Flows from Central Asia to China: Relevance of the Energy Charter Treaty"; The ECT Secretariat 2013 "Potential Impact of the Energy Charter Treaty on FDI Promotion and Protection in view of Global Trends, Energy Governance and Possible Actions towards ECT Non-Members"; The ECT Secretariat 2013 "Testing the Water for Global Energy Governance Reform: Can the Energy Charter Provide a New Benchmark?"; The ECT Secretariat 2013 "Price of Electricity Transit in Transition Countries"; The Energy Charter Secretariat 2014 "Knitting the Fabric of Regional Governance: the Unique Model of the Gulf Cooperation Council"; The ECT Secretariat 2014 "Price of Electricity Transit in Transition Countries"; The ECT Secretariat 2014 "Energy Cooperation in Central Europe: Interconnecting the Visegrad Region"

Continued

IO	Period	Title of Documents
International Energy Forum (IEF)	2003–7	International Energy Forum Secretariat (IEFS) IEF Newsletter December 2004, Issue 1; International Energy Forum Secretariat (IEFS) IEF Newsletter July 2005, issue 3; International Energy Forum Secretariat (IEFS) IEF Newsletter October 2005, issue 4; International Energy Forum Secretariat (IEFS) IEF Newsletter Issue 2, April 2005; International Energy Forum Secretariat (IEFS) IEF Newsletter International July 2007, issue 10; Energy Forum Secretariat (IEFS) JODI NEWSLETTER No. 1, March, 2005; Energy Forum Secretariat (IEFS) JODI NEWSLETTER No. 2, April 2005; JODI NEWSLETTER No. 1, March, 2005; Energy Forum Secretariat (IEFS) JODI NEWSLETTER No. 3, May 2005; Energy Forum Secretariat (IEFS) JODI NEWSLETTER No. 4, June 2005; Energy Forum Secretariat (IEFS) JODI NEWSLETTER No. 5, May 2005; Energy Forum Secretariat (IEFS) JODI NEWSLETTER No. 6, January 2006; Energy Forum Secretariat (IEFS) JODI NEWSLETTER Issue 6, May 2006; Energy Forum Secretariat (IEFS) JODI NEWSLETTER No. 7, April, 2006; Energy Forum Secretariat (IEFS) JODI NEWSLETTER January 2007, issue 8; Energy Forum Secretariat (IEFS) JODI NEWSLETTER No. 10, March, 2007; Energy Forum Secretariat (IEFS) JODI NEWSLETTER No. 11, December, 2007
	2008–12	The IEF Secretariat PRESS RELEASE "The 7 JODI organizations call on Ministers to reaffirm their commitment to JODI Rome, 21 April 2008"; International Energy Forum Secretariat (IEFS) IEF Newsletter May 2009 Issue 13; International Energy Forum Secretariat (IEFS) IEF Newsletter Issue 14; International Energy Forum Secretariat (IEFS) IEF Newsletter Issue 15; International Energy Forum Secretariat (IEFS) IEF Newsletter Issue 16; International Energy Forum Secretariat (IEFS) IEF Newsletter Issue 17; Energy Forum Secretariat (IEFS) JODI NEWSLETTER Issue 12; Energy Forum Secretariat (IEFS) JODI NEWSLETTER Issue 13; Energy Forum Secretariat (IEFS) JODI NEWSLETTER Issue 14; Energy Forum Secretariat (IEFS) JODI NEWSLETTER Issue 15; Energy Forum Secretariat (IEFS) JODI NEWSLETTER Issue 16; International Energy Forum Secretariat (IEFS) JODI NEWSLETTER Issue 17; International Energy Forum Secretariat (IEFS) JODI NEWSLETTER Issue 11; International Energy Forum Secretariat (IEFS) PRESS RELASE "OPEC OIL OUTLOOK STRESSES UNPRECEDENTED CHALLENGES FOR OIL INVESTMENT"; International Energy Forum Secretariat (IEFS) 2012 "IEF THOUGHT-LEADERS ROUNDTABLE ON GAS"; Joint IEA-IEF-OPEC Report on the 2nd Symposium Energy Outlooks 23–24 January 2012, Riyadh; IEA-IEF-OPEC Symposium on Energy Outlooks

IO	Period	Title of Documents
		23rd–24th January 2012 Riyadh Introductory paper; IEF Secretariat "Energy Sustainability—13TH INTERNATIONAL ENERGY FORUM"; International Energy Forum Event Reports (as published on their website) 2008–2012
	2013–17	International Energy Forum Event Reports and News (as published on their website) 2013–2017; International Energy Forum September 2014 "Executive View—Aldo Flores-Quiroga: Power Steering"; IEF Secretariat 2013 Third IEA-IEF-OPEC Symposium on Energy Outlooks Riyadh, 22 January 2013 "Opening remarks by Aldo Flores-Quiroga Secretary General of the IEF"; IEF Secretariat 2013 "Practical Recommendations for Increasing Transparency in International Gas and Coal Markets Report by IEA, IEF and OPEC to G20 Finance Ministers", May 2013; IEF Secretariat 2013 "Opening Speech by Aldo Flores-Quiroga Secretary General International Energy Forum 3rd IEF NOC-IOC Forum New Delhi June 11–12, 2013; IEF Publication 2013 'INSIGHTS INTO PRICE FORMATION IN OIL MARKETS'; IEF Publication 2013 'INSIGHTS INTO UNCONVENTIONALS IN THE US AND BEYOND'; IEF Document LISTS OF HEADS OF DELEGATIONS 5TH ASIAN MINISTERIAL ENERGY ROUNDTABLE MEETING 2013"
G7/G8	1993–7	Heads of States Communique Denver 1997; Communique Denver 1997 Foreign Minister's Progress Report; "Confronting Global Economic and Financial Challenges: Denver Summit Statement by Seven"; Final Report to the G7 Heads of State and Government on Promoting Financial Stability; Halifax Summit Communique Halifax, June 16, 1995; The Halifax Summit Review of the International Financial Institutions: Background Document; Economic Communique: Making a Success of Globalization for the Benefit of All Lyon, France, June 28, 1996; Finance Ministers Report to the Heads of State and Government on International Monetary Stability Lyon, France, June 28, 1996; Transcript of the Press Conference Given by the President of the French Republic Jacques Chirac, President, France Lyon, France, 28 June 1996; Summit Communique July 9, 1994, Naples; Towards the Meeting of Boris Yeltsin, President of the Russian Federation, with the Leaders of the G7 July 1994, Naples; Economic Declaration: A Strengthened Commitment to Jobs and Growth July 6–9, 1993, Tokyo; Tokyo Summit Political Declaration: Striving for a More Secure and Humane World July 8, 1993, Tokyo; Strengthening G7 Cooperation to Promote Employment and

Continued

IO	Period	Title of Documents
		Noninflationary Growth G7 Finance Minister' Report to the Tokyo Summit July 8, 1993
	1998–2002	G8 Heads of State Communique Birmingham, 17 May 1998; Political Statement on Regional issues Birmingham, 15 May 1998; TRANSCRIPT "A" OF THE PRESS CONFERENCE GIVEN BY THE PRIME MINISTER, MR TONY BLAIR IN BIRMINGHAM 17 May 1998; G7 Chairman's Statement Birmingham, 15 May 1998; G-8 Energy Ministers Meeting: Co-Chairs' Statement May 2–3, 2002, Detroit; The G8 Energy Ministerial Meeting On The World Energy Future Communique Moscow, Russia Federation, April, 1998; G8 Heads of State Communique Genova, July 22 2001; G8 Heads of State STATEMENT Genova, July 20, 2001; Communique G8 Environment Ministers' Meeting in Trieste, 2–4 March 2001; The Kananaskis Summit Chair's Summary Kananaskis, June 27,2002; Statement by G7 Leaders Delivering on the Promise of the Enhanced HIPC Initiative Kananaskis, June 27, 2002; Cooperative G8 Action on Transport Security Kananaskis, June 26, 2002; G8 Heads of State Communique Cologne 1999 Final Germany, June 20, 1999; GS Statement on Regional Issues Köln, Germany, June 20, 1999; Köln Charter: Aims and Ambitions for Lifelong Learning Cologne, June 18, 1999; G7 Statement Köln, Germany, June 18, 1999; Conclusions of the Meeting of the G8 Foreign Ministers Cologne, June 10, 1999; G8 Communique Okinawa 2000 Okinawa, Japan, July 23, 2000; G7 Statement Okinawa, July 21, 2000; Summit Meeting in Tokyo Among President Olusegun Obasanjo of the Federal Republic of Nigeria, President Thabo Mbeki of the Republic of South Africa, President Abdelaziz Boutemca of the Democratic People's Republic of Algeria, Prime Minister Chuan Leekpai of the Kingdom of Thailand and G8 Leaders Tokyo, July 20, 2000; Actions Against Abuse of the Global Financial System Report from G7 Finance Ministers to the Heads of State and Government Okinawa, July 21, 2000; Poverty Reduction and Economic Development Report from G7 Finance Ministers to the Heads of State and Government Okinawa, July 21, 2000
	2003–7	G8 Energy Ministers Meetings Chairman's Conclusions London, November 1, 2005; Factsheet: New Developments in UK Activities in Support of Gleneagles Plan of Action London, November 1, 2005; Summary Documents Evian 2003: Chair's Summary Evian, July 3 2003; Co-operative G8 Action on Trade Evian, June 2, 2003; G8 Finance Ministers Meetings Finance Ministers' Statement Deauville, May 17, 2003G8 Environmental Minister´s Meeting, Paris April 2003 Communiqué; Trade Union Statement to the Evian G8 economic Summit and OECD

IO	Period	Title of Documents
		ministerial council April-June 2003; Energizing Global Sustainable Development: Promising Prospects for the Gleneagles G8 Professor John Kirton Director, G8 Research Group, University of Toronto; Statement on the Final Day of the Summit Gleneagles, July 8, 2005 (midday); UK PRESIDENCY G8 2005 FACTSHEET: CLEANER FOSSIL FUELS; Summary of Proceedings: Energy and Environment Ministerial Roundtable London, March 16, 2005; Chairs Summary Prime Minister Tony Blair Gleneagles, July 8, 2005 (final press conference); Summit 2005 Factsheet: CLIMATE CHANGE, CLEAN ENERGY AND SUSTAINABLE DEVELOPMENT; GLENEAGLES PLANOFACTION CLIMATE CHANGE, CLEAN ENERGY AND SUSTAINABLE DEVELOPMENT; The 2005 G8 Summit Gleneagles Communique; GLENEAGLES PLAN OF ACTION CLIMATE CHANGE, CLEAN ENERGY AND SUSTAINABLE DEVELOPMENT; G8 Gleneagles 2005 Plan for Africa; Gleneagles Summit 2005 "GLOBAL ECONOMY AND Oil"; G8 Summit Heiligendamm 2007 GROWTH AND RESPONSIBILITY IN THE WORLD ECONOMY Summit Declaration (7 June 2007); G8 Summit 2007 RESPONSIBILITY FOR RAW MATERIALS: TRANSPARENCY AND SUSTAINABLE GROWTH; Joint Statement by the German G8 Presidency and the Heads of State and/or Government of Brazil, China, India Mexico and South Africa on the occasion of the G8 Summit in Heiligendamm, Germany, I June 2007; Chair´s Summary Sea Island Summit June 2004; Science and Technology for Sustainable Development: "3rd" Action Plan and Programme on Implementation Sea Island June 2004; Global Energy Security G8 Summit St. Petersburg, July 16, 2006; Chair's Summary St. Petersburg, July 17, 2006; Report on the G8 Global Partnership St. Petersburg, July 17, 2006
	2008–12	G8 Hokkaido Toyako Summit Leaders' Declaration July 8, 2008; National Reports on Global Energy Security Principles and St. Petersburg Plan of Action July 2008; St. Petersburg Plan of Action Global Energy Security; Report to the G8 Summit The IEA, supporting the Gleneagles Action Plan; G8 Summit Hokkaido INTERNATIONAL INITIATVE ON 3S-BASED NUCLEAR ENERGY INFRASTRUCTURE; Declaration of Leaders Meeting of Major Economies on Energy Security and Climate Change Hokkaldo Toyako July 9, 2008; Chair's Summary Hokkaido Toyako Summit July 9, 2008; Joint Statement of Energy Ministers of The People's Republic of China, India, Japan, the Republic of Korea and the United States Aomori, Japan on 7 June 2008; G8 Leaders DECLARATION

Continued

IO	Period	Title of Documents
		INTERNATIONAL PARTNERSIDP FOR ENERGY EFFICIENCY COOPERATION [IPEEC]; G8 Summit L´Aquila 2009 RESPONSIBLE LEADERSHIP FOR A SUSTAINABLE FUTURE; G8 Preliminary Accountability Report L' Aquila G8 Summit (8–10 July 2009); L' Aquila G8 Summit 'Political Issues'; G8 L´Aquila Summit Declaration 2009 'PROMOTING THE GLOBAL AGENDA'; The Agenda of the HEILIGENDAMM—L' AQUILA PROCESS (HAP) 2009; Chair's Summary L" Aquila, 10 July 2009; JOINT STATEMENT BY THE G8 ENERGY MINISTERS AND THE EUROPEAN ENERGY COMMISSIONER; Report on the G8 Global Partnership 2010 Muskoka, June 26, 2010; Muskoka Declaration: Recovery and New Beginnings Muskoka, Canada, June 26, 2010; Muskoka Accountability Report—Assessing Action and Results against development- related commitments; G8 Conference of Senior Officials on Capacity Building: Chair's Report to G8 Sherpas; G8 Declaration: Renewed Commitment for Freedom and Democracy Deauville, May 26–7, 2011; G8/Africa Joint Declaration: Shared Values, Shared Responsibilities Deauville, May 27, 2011; G8 Global Partnership: Assessment and Options for Future Programming Deauville, May 26–27, 2011; G8 Meeting of Foreign Ministers: Chair's Summary March 15, 2011, Paris; Camp David Declaration Camp David, Maryland, United States, May 19, 2012; Statement by the G8 on Global Oil Markets Camp David, Maryland, United States, May 19, 2012; Camp David 2012 Accountability Report—Actions, approach and results; Fact Sheet: G8 Action on Energy and Climate Change U.S. State Department, May 19, 2012
	2013–17	Lough Erne G8 Summit 2013 "Communique on Global Economic Working Session"; Lough Erne G8 Summit 2013 "Leaders Communique"; Lough Erne G8 2013 Summit Accountability Report Keeping our promises"; G7 Brussels Summit Declaration 2014; G7 Leaders Communique on Foreign Policy Brussels 2014; G7 Leaders Declaration Elmau 2015; Annex to the Leaders Declaration Elmau 2015; G7 Elmau 2015 Progress Report- Biodiversity—A vital foundation for sustainable development; Code of Conduct of the G7 CONNEX Initiative—Elmau 2015; G7 Summit Elmau 2015 "Compact on Economic Governance of the Deauville Partnership; Elmau 2015 Background Report on Long- Term Climate Finance prepared by CICERO for G7 Summit Elmau; G7 Hamburg Initiative for Sustainable Energy Security; The Progress Reporton G7 Energy Sector Support for Ukraine—G7 Energy Ministerial Meeting Kitakyushu 2016; G7 Rome Energy Ministerial Meeting 2017—Energy Security: From Rome 2014 to Rome 2017: Chair's Summary

IO	Period	Title of Documents
G20	2003–7	FIFTH G-20 FINANCE MINISTERS' AND CENTRAL BANK GOVERNORS, MEETING Morelia, Mexico October 26–27, 2003 MORELIA COMMUNIQUE; Mexico 2003: G20 Work Program; COMMUNIQUÉ Meeting of Finance Ministers and Central Bank Governors Berlin, 20–21 November 2004; Berlin 2004 "G-20 ACCORD FOR SUSTAINED GROWTH—Stability, Competition and Empowerment: Mobilising Economic Forces for Satisfactory Long-Term Growth"; Berlin 2004 G20 REFORM AGENDA Agreed actions to implement the G-20 Accord for Sustained Growth; G20 STATEMENT ON TRANSPARENCY AND EXCHANGE OF INFORMATION FOR TAX PURPOSES; Communique de presse conjoint Jacques Chirac, president de la Republique francaise, et Hu Jintao, president de la Republique Populaire de Chine Beijing, 10 octobre 2004; "Shaping globalisation together 20. January 2004"—Joint Statement by the Federal Ministry of Finance and the Deutsche Bundesbank to mark Germany's taking on the chairmanship of the Group of Twenty (G-20) in 2004; Pess Release Nr. 144e/2004 German Federal Government from 21 November 2004 "G-20 Finance Ministers meeting successfully concluded"; Shaping Globalisation Together: Work Programme of the German G-20 Presidency 2004–January 2004; Meeting of G-20 Finance and Central Bank Deputies Chongqing, P.R. China, 14–15 March, 2005 Administrative Circular; G20 COMMUNIQUÉ Meeting of Finance Ministers and Central Bank Governors Xianghe, Hebei, China, October 15–16, 2005; G20 Meeting 2005 "The G-20 Statement on Reforming the Bretton Woods Institutions"; G20 Meeting 2005 Bejing "The G-20 Statement on Global Development Issues"; G-20 Reform Agenda 2005 Agreed actions to implement the G-20 Accord for Sustained Growth; G20 Statement on Global Development Issues Meeting of Finance Ministers and Central Bank Governors Xianghe, Hebei, China, October 16, 2005; G20 Meeting of Ministers and Governors in Melbourne, 18–19 November 2006 "Communique"; G-20 Work Programme for 2006 — Building and Sustaining Prosperity; Meeting of Ministers and Governors in Melbourne, 18–19 November 2006; Meeting of Ministers and Governors in Kleinmond, South Africa, 17–18 November 2007 Communique; G–20 WORK PROGRAMME FOR 2007 SHARING—INFLUENCE, RESPONSIBILITY, KNOWLEDGE; Meeting of Ministers and Governors in Kleinmond, South Africa, 17–18 November 2007 G–20 REFORM AGENDA 2007 Agreed Actions to Implement the G–20 Accord for Sustained Growth

Continued

IO	Period	Title of Documents
	2008–12	Communiqué Meeting of Ministers and Governors São Paulo—Brazil 8–9 November 2008; MINISTRY OF FINANCE G-20 Leaders' Meeting on Financial Markets and Global Economy Washington—November 15th, 2008 Global financial governance Brazilian proposal; Annex to Communiqué—G20 Finance Ministers and Central Bank Governors—14 March 2008 Restoring lending: a framework for financial repair and recovery; Communiqué Meeting of G20 Finance Ministers and Central Bank Governors, United Kingdom, 7 November 2009; DECLARATION ON DELIVERING RESOURCES THROUGH THE INTERNATIONAL FINANCIAL INSTITUTIONS LONDON SUMMIT, 2 APRIL 2009; DECLARATION ON STRENGTHENING THE FINANCIAL SYSTEM—LONDON SUMMIT, 2 APRIL 2009; PROGRESS REPORT ON THE ECONOMIC AND FINANCIAL ACTIONS OF THE LONDON, WASHINGTON AND PITTSBURGH G20 SUMMITS PREPARED BY THE UK CHAIR OF THE G20 ST ANDREWS, 7 NOVEMBER 2009; Progress Report on the Immediate Actions of the Washington Action Plan prepared by the UK Chair of the G20 Summit 2009; Cannes Summit Final Declaration 2011; Cannes Summit 2011 G20 Leaders Communique; Cannes 2001 Summit Action Plan for Growth and Jobs; The G20 Toronto Summit Declaration 2010; Draft G20 Summit Declaration Toronto 2010; Toronto Summit 2010 "Joint Letter from G20 Leaders"; Statement by the Prime Minister of Canada at the World Economic Forum January 2010; The G20 Toronto Summit Commitments; THE G20 SEOUL SUMMIT LEADERS' DECLARATION NOVEMBER 11–12, 2010; THE SEOUL SUMMIT DOCUMENT: Framework for Strong, Sustainable and Balanced Growth; G20 Summit Seoul 2010 "Seoul Development Consensus for Shared Growth"; Seoul Summit 2010 "MULTI-YEAR ACTION PLAN ON DEVELOPMENT"; G20 Anti-Corruption Action Plan G20 Agenda for Action on Combating Corruption, Promoting Market Integrity, and Supporting a Clean Business Environment—Seoul 2010; Seoul Summit 2010 Table: Policy Commitments by G20 Members; Davos Forum Special Address Seoul G20 Summit: Priorities and Challenges Lee Myung-bak President, Republic of Korea 28th January, 10:35–10:55 Congress Centre; G20 Labour and Employment Ministers' Conclusions Paris, 26–27 September 2011; Global Financial Partnership for Financial Institutions Report to the Leaders G20 Leaders' Summit, Cannes, November 5th, 2011; The Cannes Summit 2011: What Outcomes—Statement by the French Presidency; B20 and L20 Joint Statement Cannes 2011; Governance for growth Building consensus for the future A 2011 report by David

IO	Period	Title of Documents
		Cameron, Prime Minister of the United Kingdom; G20 Action Plan to Support the Development of Local Currency Bond Markets as endorsed by G20 Finance Ministers and Central Bank Governors October 15, 2011; G20 Coherent Conclusions for the Management of Capital Flows Drawing on Country Experiences as endorsed by G20 Finance Ministers and Central Bank Governors October 15, 2011; G20 Principles for Cooperation between the IMF and Regional Financing Arrangements as endorsed by G20 Finance Ministers and Central Bank Governors October 15, 2011; G20 Leaders Declaration Los Cabos Mexico 2012; G20 Summit 2012 Mexico THE LOS CABOS GROWTH AND JOBS ACTION PLAN; POLICY COMMITMENTS BY G20 MEMBERS LOS CABOS SUMMIT, JUNE 18–19, 2012; G20 2012 PROGRESS REPORT OF THE DEVELOPMENT WORKING GROUP; G20 Labour and Employment Ministers' Conclusions Guadalajara, Mexico, 17–18 May 2012; G20 Mexico 2012 Agriculture Vice Ministers/Deputies Meeting REPORT Mexico City, May 18th 2012; L20 Statement to the G20 Summit in Cabos 2012; DISCUSSION PAPER MEXICO'S PRESIDENCY OF THE G-20 January 2012; "The Current Challenges for Global Growth," Los Catbos Summit 2012; Communique of the International Monetary and Financial Committee of the Board of Governors of the International Monetary Fund Washington DC, October 11, 2008; Meeting of Finance Ministers and Central Bank Governors June 2005 Communique; Meeting of Finance Ministers and Central Bank Governors Communique, September 5, 2009, London; Communique of the G20 Finance Ministers and Central Bank Governors Paris, October 15, 2011; Declaration of the G20 Summit on Financial Markets and the World Economy Washington DC, November 1 5, 2008; The G20 Pittsburgh Summit Commitments contained in the G20 Leaders Statement Issued in Pittsburgh September 25, 2009; G20 Declaration on Further Steps to Strengthen the Financial System September 5, 2009, London; London Summit—Leaders' Statement 2 April 2009; On the Way to a Global Economic Order; Report of the press conference with German chancellor Angela Merkel and German finance minister Steinbrück after the G20 leaders summit in Washington DC, November 1 5, 2008; G20 Leaders Statement: The Pittsburgh Summit September 24–25, 2009, Pittsburgh; Press Briefing by U.S. Treasury Secretary Tim Geithner on the G20 Meetings September 24, 2009, Pittsburgh; DECLARATION ON STRENGTHENING THE FINANCIAL SYSTEM LONDON SUMMIT, 2 APRIL 2009; Statement of the Finance Ministers of Brazil, China, Russia and India, March 14, 2009

Continued

IO	Period	Title of Documents
	2013–17	G20 Leaders Declaration Summit St Petersburg September 6, 2013; G20 Ministerial Moscow 2013 Finance Minister´s Communique; G20 Meeting in Washington 2013 Finance Minister´s Communique; G20 Summit in St Petersburg 2013 "Advancing Transparency in Regional Trade Agreements"; G20 Summit St Petersburg 2013 "Action Plan"; "Annex" G20 Summit St Petersburg "St. Petersburg Fiscal Templates—G-20 Advanced Economies"; Annex 2: St. Petersburg Fiscal Templates—G-20 Emerging Market Economies; G20 Workplan on Financing for Investment Study Group's Findings and Ways Forward July 2013; G20/OECD HIGH-LEVEL PRINCIPLES OF LONG-TERM INVESTMENT FINANCING BY INSTITUTIONAL INVESTORS September 2013; G20 Roadmap towards Strengthened Oversight and Regulation of Shadow Banking; Saint Petersburg Accountability Report on G20 Development Commitments Saint Petersburg, Russia 2013; G20 ANTI-CORRUPTION WORKING GROUP PROGRESS REPORT 2013 September, 2013; G20 5th Anniversary Statement St Petersburg 2013; Tax Annex to the St Petersburg G20 Leaders' Declaration; Saint Petersburg G20 2013 Summit Development Outlook; G20 Joint Statement on Syria St Petersburg Summit 2013; Vladimir Putin's News Conference Following the G20 Summit in St Petersburg 2013; A Narrative Progress Report on Financial Reform Report of the Financial Stability Board to G20 Leaders; THE RUSSIAN PRESIDENCY OF THE G20 2013: OUTLINE December, 2012; Brisbane G20 Leaders' Communique 2014; G20 Brisbane Summit Leaders' Statement on Ebola 2014; Brisbane Action Plan November 2014; Brisbane 2014 The G20 Global Infrastructure Initiative; 2014 Financial Inclusion Action Plan 2 September 2014; G20 PLAN TO FACILITATE REMITTANCE FLOWS Brisbane 2014 Summit; G20 FOOD SECURITY AND NUTRITION FRAMEWORK Brisbane 2014; G20 DEVELOPMENT WORKING GROUP ACCOUNTABILITY FRAMEWORK 5 SEPTEMBER 2014 Brisbane Summit 2014; G20 2014—Brisbane Anti-Corruption Update; G20 High-Level Principles on Beneficial Ownership Transparency Brisbane 14; G20 Principles on Energy Cooperation—November 2014; G20 ENERGY EFFICIENCY ACTION PLAN VOLUNTARY COLLABORATION ON ENERGY EFFICIENCY 16 NOVEMBER 2014; G20 Accountability Assessment Framework Going Forward November 2014; November 14, 2014 The Brisbane Accountability Assessment; G20 Labour and Employment Minister Declaration G20 Summit Moscow 2013; G20 FINANCE MINISTERS AND CENTRAL BANK GOVERNORS MEETING THURSDAY

IO	Period	Title of Documents
		10—FRIDAY 11 APRIL 2014 WASHINGTON D.C., USA-FINAL AGENDA; GLOBAL PROSPECTS AND POLICY CHALLENGES Meetings of G-20 Finance Ministers and Central Bank Governors February 2014 Sydney, Australia; MACROECONOMIC AND REFORM PRIORITIES Prepared by IMF Staff with inputs from the OECD and the World Bank for the Meetings of G-20 Finance Ministers and Central Bank Governors February 22–23, 2014 Sydney, Australia; OVERCOMING CONSTRAINTS TO THE FINANCING OF INFRASTRUCTURE Success Stories and Lessons Learned: Country, Sector and Project Examples of Overcoming Constraints to the Financing of Infrastructure—February 2014 for the G20; PRACTICAL SOLUTIONS AND MODELS FOR ADDRESSING OBSTACLES TO INSTITUTIONAL INVESTMENT IN INFRASTRUCTURE IN DEVELOPING COUNTRIES—Prepared by the Staff of the World Bank Group for the G20 Investment and Infrastructure Working Group, January 2014; OECD SECRETARY-GENERAL REPORT TO THE G20 FINANCE MINISTERS AND CENTRAL BANK GOVERNORS SYDNEY FEBRUARY 2014; 17 February 2014 To G20 Finance Ministers and Central Bank Governors Financial Reforms—Progress and Challenges; Australian G20 Presidency—Korean Government Summary of G20 Seoul Conference; Communique G20 Finance Ministers and Central Bank Governors Ankara 2015; Chair's Statement G20 Finance Ministers and Central Bank Governors Ankara 2015; Communique G20 Finance Ministers and Central Bank Governors Washington 2015; Communique G20 Finance Ministers and Central Bank Governors Istanbul February 2015; Communique G20 Finance Ministers and Central Bank Governors Shanghai February 2016; Communique G20 Finance Ministers and Central Bank Governors Washington 2016; Communique G20 Finance Ministers and Central Bank Governors Shengdu, China 2016; Communique G20 Finance Ministers and Central Bank Governors Baden-Baden 2017; IMF for G20 Ministerial—Increasing Resilience to Large and Volatile Capital Flows: The Role of Macroprudential Policies November 2016; IMF for G20 Ministerial 2016—Macroeconomic Perspective on Resilience November 2016; November 14, 2016 OECD G20 Policy Paper on Economic Resilience and Structural Policies; Economic resilience: a financial perspective Note submitted to the G20 on 7 November 2016; Report to G20 Deputy Finance Ministers and Deputy Central Bank Governors on MDB Internal Incentives for Crowding-in Private Investment in Infrastructure 1 December 2016

Continued

IO	Period	Title of Documents
International Renewable Energy Agency (IRENA)	2008–12	First meeting of the Council of IRENA 10–11 July 2011, Abu Dhabi, United Arab Emirates—REPORT OF THE FIRST MEETING OF THE COUNCIL OF THE INTERNATIONAL RENEWABLE ENERGY AGENCY; IRENA Secretariat 2012—Renewable Energy Jobs & Access; CONFERENCE ON THE ESTABLISHMENT OF THE INTERNATIONAL RENEWABLE ENERGY AGENCY Resolution on Establishing a Preparatory Commission for the International Renewable Energy Agency Monday, 26 January 2009, Bonn, World Conference Center IRENA/FC/res.1; First session of the Assembly Distribution: General 4–5 April 2011, Abu Dhabi, United Arab Emirates 16 August 2011 REPORT OF THE FIRST SESSION OF THE ASSEMBLY OF THE INTERNATIONAL RENEWABLE ENERGY AGENCY; CONFERENCE ON THE ESTABLISHMENT OF THE INTERNATIONAL RENEWABLE ENERGY AGENCY Conference Report Monday, 26 January 2009, Bonn, World Conference Center IRENA/FC/CR; Capacity Building Strategic Framework for IRENA (2012–2015) November 2012; INTERNATIONAL RENEWABLE ENERGY AGENCY Third meeting of the Council Abu Dhabi, 05—06 June 2012 The Working Capital Fund of IRENA Report of the Director-General; INTERNATIONAL RENEWABLE ENERGY AGENCY Third meeting of the Council Abu Dhabi, 05—–06 June 2012 Proposed Medium-term Strategy of IRENA Report of the Director-General; INTERNATIONAL RENEWABLE ENERGY AGENCY Second session of the Assembly Abu Dhabi, 14–15 January 2012—Report of the Director-General on the Implementation of the Work Programme and Budget for 2011; INTERNATIONAL RENEWABLE ENERGY AGENCY First Session of the Assembly Abu Dhabi, 4–5 April 2011 Report on the activities of the Preparatory Commission; Update on the Implementation of the 2011 Work Programme and Budget—July 2011; INTERNATIONAL RENEWABLE ENERGY AGENCY First meeting of the Council Abu Dhabi, 10 and 11 July 2011 List of International Organisations with envisaged or on-going cooperation; INTERNATIONAL RENEWABLE ENERGY AGENCY Second meeting of the Council Abu Dhabi, 13–14 November 2011 Secondment of staff to the International Renewable Energy Agency Report of the Director-General; INTERNATIONAL RENEWABLE ENERGY AGENCY Second meeting of the Council Abu Dhabi, 13–14 November 2011 IRENA Programmatic and Budgetary Cycle Note of the Director-General; INTERNATIONAL RENEWABLE ENERGY AGENCY Second meeting of the Council Abu Dhabi, 13 and 14 November 2011 Report of the Director-General on the Implementation of

IO	Period	Title of Documents
		the Work Programme and Budget for 2011; INTERNATIONAL RENEWABLE ENERGY AGENCY Second meeting of the Council Abu Dhabi, 13–14 November 2011 Agenda of the second meeting of the Council of the International Renewable Energy Agency; IRENA Event Reports (from the official website) 2011–2012; IRENA Newsletters 2011 (Issues 1&2); IRENA Newsletters 2012 (Issue 3&4); Second session of the Assembly Abu Dhabi, 14–15 January 2012 30 January 2012 Decision on the establishment of the Working Capital Fund of IRENA; Second session of the Assembly Abu Dhabi, 14–15 January 2012 30 January 2012 Decision on Rules of Procedure for subsidiary organs to be included in the Provisional Rules of Procedure of the Assembly and of the Council
	2013–17	IRENA Event Reports 2013–2017 (from the official website); IRENA Quarterly 2017/Q1; IRENA Quarterly 2017/2; IRENA Quarterly 2017/Q4; IRENA Quarterly 2015/ Q1; IRENA Quarterly 2015/Q2; IRENA Quarterly 2015/Q3; IRENA Quarterly 2015/Q4; IRENA Quarterly 2014/Q4; IRENA Quarterly 2014/Q3; IRENA Quarterly 2014/Q2; IRENA Quarterly 2016/Q1; IRENA Quarterly 2016/Q4; IRENA Quarterly 2016/Q2; IRENA Quarterly 2016/Q3; Seventh session of the Assembly of IRENA Abu Dhabi, 14–15 January 2017 REPORT OF THE SEVENTH SESSION OF THE ASSEMBLY OF THE INTERNATIONAL RENEWABLE ENERGY AGENCY; INTERNATIONAL RENEWABLE ENERGY AGENCY Seventh meeting of the Assembly Abu Dhabi, 14–15 January 2017 Annual Report of the Director-General on the Implementation of the Work Programme and Budget for 2016–2017; INTERNATIONAL RENEWABLE ENERGY AGENCY Sixth session of the Assembly Abu Dhabi, 16–17 January 2016 Annual report of the Director-General on the Implementation of the Work Programme and Budget for 2014–2015; INTERNATIONAL RENEWABLE ENERGY AGENCY Fifth session of the Assembly Abu Dhabi, 17–18 January 2015 Annual report of the Director-General on the Implementation of the Work Programme and Budget for 2014–2015; INTERNATIONAL RENEWABLE ENERGY AGENCY Fourth session of the Assembly Abu Dhabi, 18–19 January 2014 Report of the Director-General on the Implementation of the Work Programme and Budget for 2013; INTERNATIONAL RENEWABLE ENERGY AGENCY Fourth session of the Assembly Abu Dhabi, 18–19 January 2014 Work Programme and Budget for 2014–2015 Report of the Director-General; INTERNATIONAL RENEWABLE ENERGY AGENCY

Continued

IO	Period	Title of Documents
		Third session of the Assembly Abu Dhabi, 13–14 January 2013 Work Programme and Budget for 2013 Report of the Director-General
Organization of Arab Petroleum Exporting Countries (OAPEC)	2013–17	ORGANIZATION OF ARAB PETROLEUM EXPORTING COUNTRIES (OAPEC) The Secretary General's 41st Annual Report 2014; ORGANIZATION OF ARAB PETROLEUM EXPORTING COUNTRIES (OAPEC) The Secretary General's 42nd Annual Report 2015; OAPEC Special Issue on THE 24TH FORUM ON THE FUNDAMENTALS OF OIL AND GAS INDUSTRY April 2017; OAPEC Arab Electricity Cooperation—Promising Future for Integration and Development April 2016; OPAEC Bulletin August & September 2016 Increased Investment Needed to Underwrite Market Stability; OAPEC Bulletin August & September 2017; OAPEC Bulletin December 2015; OAPEC Bulletin December 2016; OAPEC Bulletin February 2017; OAPEC Bulletin February 2016; OAPEC Bulletin January 2017; OAPEC Bulletin July 2017; OAPEC Bulletin July 2016; OAPEC Bulletin June 2016; OAPEC Bulletin June 2017; OAPEC Bulletin March 2017; OAPEC Bulletin March 2016; OAPEC Bulletin May 2016; OAPEC Bulletin November–December 2017; OAPEC Bulletin November 2016; OAPEC Bulletin October 2017; OAPEC Bulletin October 2016

References

Abbott, K. W. (2012). "The transnational regime complex for climate change." *Environment and Planning C: Government and Policy*, 30(4), 571–590.

Abbott, K. W., Genschel, P., Snidal, D., & Zangl, B. (Eds.). (2015). *International Organizations as Orchestrators*. Cambridge University Press.

Abbott, K. W., & Snidal, D. (1998). "Why states act through formal international organizations." *Journal of Conflict Resolution*, 42(1), 3–32.

Abbott, K. W., & Snidal, D. (2000). "Hard and soft law in international governance." *International Organization*, 54(3), 421–456.

Abbott, K. W., & Snidal, D. (2009). "Strengthening international regulation through transnational new governance: Overcoming the orchestration deficit." *Vandderbilt Journal of Transnational Law*, 42, 501.

Adede, O. (2003). "Origins and History of the TRIPS Negotiations." In: *Trading in Knowledge: Development Perspectives on TRIPS, Trade and Sustainability*, edited by C. Bellman, G. Dutfield, & R. Meléndez-Ortiz, Earthscan, 23–35.

African Regional Intellectual Property Organization (ARIPO) (2019). Cooperation Agreements. Available at: https://www.aripo.org/cooperation-agreements/. Accessed August 21, 2019.

Agosin, M. R. (2001). "Strengthening regional financial cooperation." *Cepal Review*, No. 73, 31–50.

Alston, P., & Mégret, F. (Eds.). (2020). *The United Nations and Human Rights: A Critical Appraisal*. Oxford University Press.

Alter, K. J., & Meunier, S. (2009). "The politics of international regime complexity." *Perspectives on Politics*, 7(1), 13–24.

Alter, K. J., & Raustiala, K. (2018). "The rise of international regime complexity." *Annual Review of Law and Social Science*, 14, 329–349.

Anckar, C. (2008). "On the applicability of the most similar systems design and the most different systems design in comparative research." *International Journal of Social Research Methodology*, 11(5), 389–401.

Andean Group (1976). "Treaty for the creation of the Andean Reserve Fund." *International Legal Materials*, 18(5), 1191–1202.

Anderlini, J., & Mitchell, T. (2015). "UK move to join AIIB meets mixed response in China." *Financial Times*, March 13, 2015. Available at: https://www.ft.com/content/c3189416-c965-11e4-a2d9-00144feab7de. Accessed June 21, 2019.

Andrade, J. C. S., & de Oliveira, J. A. P. (2015). "The role of the private sector in global climate and energy governance." *Journal of Business Ethics*, 130(2), 375–387.

Andrews-Speed, P. (1999). "The politics of petroleum and the Energy Charter Treaty as an effective investment regime." *Journal of Energy Finance & Development*, 4(1), 117–135.

Artana, D. (2010). Why Banco del Sur is a bad idea. *Americas Quarterly*, February 24. Available at: https://www.americasquarterly.org/artana-banco-del-sur. Accessed June 21, 2019.

Asian Development Bank Institute. (2009). *Infrastructure for a seamless Asia*. Asian Development Bank. Available at: https://www.adb.org/publications/infrastructure-seamless-asia. Accessed July 19, 2019.

Asian Infrastructure Investment Bank (2019). *Articles of Agreement*. Available at: https://www.aiib.org/en/about-aiib/basic-documents/articles-of-agreement/index.html. Accessed July 19, 2019.

Auster, R. D. (1977). "Private markets in public goods (or qualities)." *The Quarterly Journal of Economics*, 91(3), 419–430.

Avant, D. D., Finnemore, M., & Sell, S. K. (Eds.). (2010). *Who Governs the Globe?* Cambridge University Press.

Avi-Yonah, R., & Xu, H. (2018). "China and BEPS." *Laws*, 7(1), 1–26.

Axelrod, R. S. (1996). "The European energy charter treaty: reality or illusion?" *Energy Policy*, 24(6), 497–505.

Baccini, L., Poast, P., & Urpelainen, J. (2011) "The return of hegemonic theory: Dominant states and the origins of international cooperation." Available at: https://vdocuments.site/the-return-of-hegemonic-theory-dominant-states-and-the-origins-of-international.html?page=1. Accessed February 22, 2023.

Bäckstrand, K. (2006). "Democratizing global environmental governance? Stakeholder democracy after the World Summit on Sustainable Development." *European Journal of International Relations* 12(4), 467–498.

Baig, T., & Goldfajn, I. (1999). "Financial market contagion in the Asian crisis." *IMF Staff Papers*, 46(2), 167–195.

Baistrocchi, E. A. (2013). "The international tax regime and the BRIC world: Elements for a theory." *Oxford Journal of Legal Studies*, 33(4), 733–766.

Bamberger, C. (2004). *IEA, the First Thirty Years: The History of the International Energy Agency, 1974–2004.* OECD.

Baran, K. S., Fietkiewicz, K. J., & Stock, W. G. (2015). "Monopolies on Social Network Services (SNS) Markets and Competition Law." In: *Reinventing Information Science in the Networked Society: Proceedings of the 14th International Symposium on Information Science*, edited by F. Pehar, C. Schlögl, & C. Wolff, Verlag Werner Hülsbusch, 424–436.

Barnett, G. A., Park, H. W., Jiang, K., Tang, C., & Aguillo, I. F. (2014). "A multi-level network analysis of web-citations among the world's universities." *Scientometrics*, 99(1), 5–26.

Barnett, M., & Finnemore, M. (2004). *Rules for the World: International Organizations in Global Politics.* Cornell University Press.

Barrett, S. (2007). *Why Cooperate?: The Incentive to Supply Global Public Goods.* Oxford University Press.

BDI (Bund Deutscher Industrie) (2015). "Der asiatisch-pazifische Raum ist eine der bedeutendsten Wachstumsregionen weltweit." Statement by Stefan Mair, member of the BDI executive board. Available at: https://bdi.eu/artikel/news/der-asiatisch-pazifische-raum-ist-eine-der-bedeutendsten-wachstumsregionen-weltweit/. Accessed July 12, 2019.

Benvenisti, E., & Downs, G. W. (2007). "The empire's new clothes: political economy and the fragmentation of international law." *Stanford Law Review*, 60, 595–631.

Bernauer, T. (1995a). "Theorie der Klub-Güter und Osterweiterung der NATO." *Zeitschrift für Internationale Beziehungen*, 2(1), 79–105.

Bernauer, T. (1995b). "The effect of international environmental institutions: How we might learn more." *International Organization*, 49(2), 351–377.

Betts, A. (2013). "Regime complexity and international organizations: UNHCR as a challenged institution." *Global Governance: A Review of Multilateralism and International Organizations*, 19(1), 69–81.

Biermann, F., & Kim, R. E. (Eds.). (2020) *Architectures of Earth System Governance: Institutional Complexity and Structural Transformation.* Cambridge University Press.

Biermann, F., Pattberg, P., Van Asselt, H., & Zelli, F. (2009). "The fragmentation of global governance architectures: A framework for analysis." *Global Environmental Politics*, 9(4), 14–40.

Biermann, F., Pattberg, P., & Zelli, F. (Eds.). (2010). *Global Climate Governance beyond 2012: Architecture, Agency and Adaptation.* Cambridge University Press.

Biermann, R. (2008) "Towards a theory of inter-organizational networking: The Euro-Atlantic security institutions interacting." *Review of International Organizations*, 3(2), 151–177.

Bini, E. (2017). "A Challenge to Cold War Energy Politics? The US and Italy's Relations with the Soviet Union, 1958–1969." In: *Cold War Energy: A Transnational History of Soviet Oil and Gas*, edited by J. Perović, Palgrave Macmillan, 201–230.

Biziwick, M., Cattaneo, N., & Fryer, D. (2015). "The rationale for and potential role of the BRICS Contingent Reserve Arrangement." *South African Journal of International Affairs*, 22(3), 307–324.

Bjorvatn, K., & Schjelderup, G. (2002). "Tax competition and international public goods." *International Tax and Public Finance*, 9(2), 111–120.

Blustein, P. (2015). *Laid Low: The IMF, the Euro Zone and the First Rescue of Greece*. CIGI (Centre for International Governance Innovation). Available at: https://www.cigionline.org/sites/default/files/cigi_paper_no.61web.pdf. Accessed July 24, 2019.

Bogdandy, A., Wolfrum, R., Bernstorff, J., Dann, P., & Goldmann, M. (Eds.). (2010). *The Exercise of Public Authority by International Institutions: Advancing International Institutional Law*. Springer Science & Business Media.

Bond, P. (2016). "BRICS banking and the debate over sub-imperialism." *Third World Quarterly*, 37(4), 611–629.

Brandes, U. (2001). "A faster algorithm for betweenness centrality." *Journal of Mathematical Sociology*, 25(2), 163–177.

Brauner, Y. (2002). *An International Tax Regime in Crystallization—Realities, Experiences, Opportunities*. NYU Public Law Research Paper.

Braunstein, Y. M., & White, L. J. (1985). "Setting technical compatibility standards: An economic analysis." *The Antitrust Bulletin*, 30(2), 337–355.

BRICS (2014). "Treaty for the Establishment of a BRICS Contingent Reserve Arrangement. Fortaleza, July 15, 2014." Available at: http://www.brics.utoronto.ca/docs/140715-treaty.html. Accessed July 27, 2019.

Brosig, M (2011). "Overlap and interplay between international organisations: Theories and approaches." *South African Journal of International Affairs*, 18(2), 147–167.

Brosig, M. (2015). *Cooperative Peacekeeping in Africa: Exploring Regime Complexity*. Routledge.

Brosig, M. (2017). "Regime Complexity and Resource Dependence Theory in International Peacekeeping. In: *Palgrave Handbook of Inter-Organizational Relations in World Politics*, edited by J. A. Koops & R. Biermann, Palgrave Macmillan, 447–470.

Brown, W. (2000). "Restructuring north–south relations: ACP–EU development co-operation in a liberal international order." *Review of African Political Economy*, 27(85), 367–383.

Brummer, C. (2007). "Regional integration and incomplete club goods: A trade perspective." *Chicago Journal of International Law*, 8(2), 535–551.

Bry, S. H. (2017). "Brazil's soft-power strategy: The political aspirations of south–south development cooperation." *Foreign Policy Analysis*, 13(2), 297–316.

Bryson, J. R., & Rusten, G. (2010). *Design Economies and the Changing World Economy: Innovation, Production and Competitiveness*. Routledge.

Buchanan, J. M. (1965). "An economic theory of clubs." *Economica*, 32(125), 1–14.

Buck, M., & Hamilton, C. (2011). "The Nagoya Protocol on access to genetic resources and the fair and equitable sharing of benefits arising from their utilization to the Convention on Biological Diversity." *Review of European Community & International Environmental Law*, 20(1), 47–61.

Bundesverband Erneuerbare Energien (2015). Factsheet Renewables from Germany. Available at: https://docslib.org/doc/9178188/factsheet-renewables-from-germany. Last accessed June 12, 2019.

Burke-White, W. (2003). "International legal pluralism." *Michigan Journal of International Law*, 25, 963–979.

Busch, M. L. (2007). "Overlapping institutions, forum shopping, and dispute settlement in international trade." *International Organization*, 61(04), 735–761.

Butcher, W. R., Wandschneider, P. R., & Whittlesey, N. K. (1986). "Competition between Irrigation and Hydropower in the Pacific Northwest." In: *Scarce Water and Institutional Change*, edited by K. D. Frederick, Routledge, 25–66.

Cabral, L. M., Salant, D. J., & Woroch, G. A. (1999). "Monopoly pricing with network externalities." *International Journal of Industrial Organization*, 17(2), 199–214.

Callaghan, M., & Hubbard, P. (2016). "The Asian infrastructure investment bank: Multilateralism on the silk road." *China Economic Journal*, 9(2), 116–139.

Carpenter, C., Duygulu, S., Montgomery, A. H., & Rapp, A. (2014). "Explaining the advocacy agenda: Insights from the human security network." *International Organization*, 68(2), 449–470.

Carraro, C., & Siniscalco, D. (1998). "International institutions and environmental policy: International environmental agreements—incentives and political economy." *European Economic Review*, 42(3-5), 561–572.

Caves, R. E., & Porter, M. E. (1977). "From entry barriers to mobility barriers: Conjectural decisions and contrived deterrence to new competition." *The Quarterly Journal of Economics*, 91(2), 241–261.

Cetorelli, N., & Strahan, P. E. (2006). "Finance as a barrier to entry: Bank competition and industry structure in local US markets." *The Journal of Finance*, 61(1), 437–461.

Chabchitrchaidol, A., Nakagawa, S., & Nemoto, Y. (2018). "Quest for financial stability in East Asia: Establishment of an independent surveillance unit "AMRO" and its future challenges." *Public Policy Review*, 14(5), 1001–1024.

China Daily (2015). "BRICS Contingency Fund expected to be operational in 30 days." *China Daily Online*, July 1 2015. Available at: http://www.chinadaily.com.cn/world/2015xiatbricssco/2015-07/01/content_21154058.htm. Accessed June 21, 2019.

Chong, A., & Gradstein, M. (2008). "What determines foreign aid? The donors' perspective." *Journal of Development Economics*, 87(1), 1–13.

Chow, D. C. (2016). "Why China established the Asia infrastructure investment bank." *Vanderbilt Journal of Transnational Law*, 49, 1255.

Christians, A. (2010). "Taxation in a time of crisis: Policy leadership from the OECD to the G20." *Northwestern Journal of Law and Social Policy*, 5, 19–40.

Christians, A. (2016). "BEPS and the new international tax order." *Brigham Young University Law Review*, (6), 1603–1647.

Ciorciari, J. D. (2011). "Chiang Mai initiative multilateralization: International politics and institution-building in Asia." *Asian Survey*, 51(5), 926–952.

Claessens, S., & Forbes, K. (2004). "International financial contagion: The theory, evidence and policy implications." Paper presented at the conference "The IMF's Role in Emerging Market Economies: Reassessing the Adequacy of its Resources," Amsterdam.

Clark, P. B., & Huang, H. (2001). *International Financial Contagion and the IMF: A Theoretical Framework*. IMF Working Paper, No. 01/137. International Monetary Fund.

Clark, R. (2021). "Pool or duel? Cooperation and competition among international organizations." *International Organization*, 75(4), 1133–1153.

Clark, R. (2022). "Bargain down or shop around? Outside options and IMF conditionality." *The Journal of Politics*, 84(3), 1791–1805.

Clark, R., & Dolan, L. R. (2021). "Pleasing the principal: US influence in World Bank policymaking." *American Journal of Political Science*, 65(1), 36–51.

Clarke, E. H. (1971). "Multipart pricing of public goods." *Public Choice*, 11(1), 17–33.

Clifton, J., & Díaz-Fuentes, D. (2014). "The OECD and 'The Rest': Analyzing the limits of policy transfer." *Journal of Comparative Policy Analysis: Research and Practice*, 16(3), 249–265.

Climie, C. (2018). "The European Stability Mechanism and the IMF: From the enhanced cooperation to embedded supervisor." *Canadian Journal of European and Russian Studies*, 12(1), 1–15.

Cockfield, A. J. (2005). "The rise of the OECD as informal world tax organization through national responses to E-commerce tax challenges." *Yale Journal of Law & Technology*, 8, 136–187.

Coglianese, C. (2000). "Globalization and the Design of International Institutions." In: *Governance in a Globalizing World*, edited by J. S. Nye Jr. & J. D. Donohue, Brookings, 297–318.

Cohen, G., Joutz, F., & Loungani, P. (2011). "Measuring energy security: Trends in the diversification of oil and natural gas supplies." *Energy Policy*, 39(9), 4860–4869.

Colgan, J. D., Keohane, R. O., & Van de Graaf, T. (2012). "Punctuated equilibrium in the energy regime complex." *The Review of International Organizations*, 7(2), 117–143.

Conner, K. R. (1991). "A historical comparison of resource-based theory and five schools of thought within industrial organization economics: Do we have a new theory of the firm?" *Journal of Management*, 17(1), 121–154.

Constancio, V. (2012). "Contagion and the European debt crisis." *Financial Stability Review*, 16, 109–121.

Convention on Biological Diversity (CBD) (2002). "Access and benefit-sharing as related to genetic resources." COP 6, Decision VI/24. Sixth Ordinary Meeting of the Conference of the Parties to the Convention on Biological Diversity, April 7–19, 2002, The Hague, Netherlands. Available at: https://www.cbd.int/decision/cop/?id=7198. Accessed September 12, 2019.

Cooper, A. F. (2016). *The BRICS: A Very Short Introduction*. Oxford University Press.

Coriat, B. (Ed.). (2008). *The Political Economy of HIV/AIDS in Developing Countries: TRIPS, Public Health Systems and Free Access*. Edward Elgar Publishing.

Cornes, R., & Sandler, T. (1996). *The Theory of Externalities, Public Goods, and Club Goods*. Cambridge University Press.

Correa, C. M. (2000). *Intellectual Property Rights, the WTO and Developing Countries: The TRIPS Agreement and Policy Options*. Zed books.

Crockett, A. (1997). "Why is financial stability a goal of public policy?" *Economic Review—Federal Reserve Bank of Kansas City*, 82, 5–22.

Dagan, T. (2004). "The Costs of International Tax Cooperation." In: *The Welfare State, Globalization, and International Law*, edited by E. Benvenesti & G. Nolte, Springer, 49–77.

Danner, L. K. (2019). "European involvement in China's Asian Infrastructure Investment Bank: Geopolitical Pragmatism or Normative Engagement?" In: *EU Development Policies*, edited by S. L. Beringer, S, Maier, & M. Thiel, Palgrave Macmillan, 79–93.

Daßler, B. (2022). "Good (s) for everyone? Policy area competition and institutional topologies in the regime complexes of tax avoidance and intellectual property." *Journal of International Relations and Development*, 25, 993–1019.

Daßler, B., Kruck, A., & Zangl, B. (2019). "Interactions between hard and soft power: The institutional adaptation of international intellectual property protection to global power shifts." *European Journal of International Relations*, 25(2), 588–612.

Dauvergne, P., & Farias, D. (2012). "The rise of Brazil as a global development power." *Third World Quarterly*, 33(5), 903–917.

Davis, C. L. (2009). "Overlapping institutions in trade policy." *Perspectives on Politics*, 7(1), 25–31.

Dehejia, V. H., & Genschel, P. (1999). "Tax competition in the European Union." *Politics & Society*, 27(3), 403–430.

Deere, C. (2009). *The Implementation Game: The TRIPS Agreement and the Global Politics of Intellectual Property Reform in Developing Countries*. Oxford University Press.

Deitelhoff, N., & Zimmermann, L. (2020). "Things we lost in the fire: How different types of contestation affect the robustness of international norms." *International Studies Review*, 22(1), 51–76.

Desai, R. M., & Vreeland, J. R. (2011). "Global governance in a multipolar world: The case for regional monetary funds." *International Studies Review*, 13(1), 109–121.

De Vries, C. E., Hobolt, S. B., & Walter, S. (2021). "Politicizing international cooperation: The mass public, political entrepreneurs, and political opportunity structures." *International Organization*, 75(2), 306–332.

Dietrich, S. (2016). "Donor political economies and the pursuit of aid effectiveness." *International Organization*, 70(1), 65–102.

Dingwerth, K., Witt, A., Lehmann, I., Reichel, E., & Weise, T. (2019). *International Organizations under Pressure: Legitimating Global Governance in Challenging Times*. Oxford University Press.

Doleac, C. (2015). *Development Bank in Latin America: Towards a So-Called Radical Emancipatory Project?* Council of Hemispheric Affairs. Available at: https://www.coha.org/development-bank-in-latin-america-towards-a-so-called-radical-emancipatory-project/. Accessed February 23, 2023.

Dorussen, H., & Ward, H. (2008). "Intergovernmental organizations and the Kantian peace: A network perspective." *Journal of Conflict Resolution*, 52(2), 189–212.

Dosi, G., & Stiglitz, J. E. (2014). "The Role of Intellectual Property Rights in the Development Process, with Some Lessons from Developed Countries: An Introduction." In: *Intellectual Property Rights: Legal and Economic Challenges for Development*, edited by M. Cimoli, Oxford University Press, 1–53.

Drahos, P. (2002). "Developing countries and international intellectual property standard-setting." *The Journal of World Intellectual Property*, 5(5), 765–789.

Dreher, A. (2009). "IMF conditionality: Theory and evidence." *Public Choice*, 141(1–2), 233–267.

Dreher, A., Sturm, J. E., & Vreeland, J. R. (2009). "Development aid and international politics: Does membership on the UN Security Council influence World Bank decisions?" *Journal of Development Economics*, 88(1), 1–18.

Dreher, A., & Vaubel, R. (2004). "Do IMF and IBRD cause moral hazard and political business cycles? Evidence from panel data." *Open Economies Review*, 15(1), 5–22.

Drezner, D. W. (2009). "The power and peril of international regime complexity." *Perspectives on Politics*, 7(01), 65–70.

Duffield, J. (2007). "What are international institutions?" *International Studies Review*, 9(1), 1–22.

Dutfield, G. (2010). *Intellectual Property, Biogenetic Resources and Traditional Knowledge*. Routledge.

Dutfield, G. (2008). "Turning Plant Varieties into Intellectual Property: The UPOV Convention." In: *The Future Control of Food: A Guide to International Negotiations and Rules on Intellectual Property, Biodiversity and Food Security (1st ed.)*, edited by G. Tansey, Routledge, 27–47.

Dutt, N. K. (1997). "The United States and the Asian Development Bank." *Journal of Contemporary Asia*, 27(1), 71–84.

Eberhartinger, E., & Petutschnig, M. (2015). *Practicing Experts' Views on BEPS: A Critical Analysis*. WU International Taxation Research Paper Series (2015–27).

Eden, L., & Kudrle, R. T. (2005). "Tax havens: Renegade states in the international tax regime?" *Law & Policy*, 27(1), 100–127.

Efrat, A., & Newman, A. L. (2016). "Deciding to defer: The importance of fairness in resolving transnational jurisdictional conflicts." *International Organization*, 409–441.

Eichengreen, B. (2007). "Insurance underwriter or financial development fund: What role for reserve pooling in Latin America?" *Open Economies Review*, 18(1), 27–52.

Emmert, F. (1990). "Intellectual property in the Uruguay Round negotiating strategies of the western industrialized countries." *Michigan Journal of International Law*, 11 (4), 1317–1399.

Energy Charter Secretariat (2016). *The International Energy Charter Consolidated Energy Charter Treaty with Related Documents*. Available at: https://www.energychartertreaty.org/treaty/other-documents/european-energy-charter-1991/. Accessed May 23, 2019.

Erstling, J., & Boutillon, I. (2005). "The Patent Cooperation Treaty: At the center of the international patent system." *William Mitchell Law Review*, 32, 1583–1601.

EU Council (2002). "Council Regulation (EC) No 332/2002 of 18 February 2002 establishing a facility providing medium-term financial assistance for Member States' balances of payments." *Official Journal of the European Communities*, 45, 1–3, February 23, 2002.

EU Council (2010). "Statement by the Heads of State and Government of the Euro Area. Council Decision of March 24th 2010." Available at: https://www.consilium.europa.eu/uedocs/cms_data/docs/pressdata/en/ec/113563.pdf. Accessed July 24, 2019.

EU Council (2012). "Treaty Establishing the European Stability Mechanism." Available at: https://www.esm.europa.eu/sites/default/files/20150203_-_esm_treaty_-_en.pdf. Accessed July 24, 2019.

Eurosolar and World Council for Renewable Energy (2009). *The Long Road to IRENA: From the Idea to the Foundation of the International Renewable Energy Agency. Documentation 1990–2009.* Ponte Press, Bochum.

Faure, R., Prizzon, A., & Rogerson, A. (2015). *Multilateral development banks.* Overseas Development Institute.

Feldenkirchen, M., Reiermann, C., Sauga, M., & Schlamp, H. J. (2010). "Merkel takes on the EU and her own finance minister." *Spiegel Online*, March 22, 2010. Available at: https://www.spiegel.de/international/germany/berlin-divided-on-greece-merkel-takes-on-the-eu-and-her-own-finance-minister-a-684968.html. Accessed June 21, 2019.

Findley, M. G., Milner, H. V., & Nielson, D. L. (2017). "The choice among aid donors: The effects of multilateral vs. bilateral aid on recipient behavioral support." *The Review of International Organizations*, 12(2), 307–334.

Finger, J. M., & Nogues, J. J. (2002). "The unbalanced Uruguay Round outcome: The new areas in future WTO negotiations. *The World Economy*, 25(3), 321–340.

Finger, J. M., & Schuler, P. (Eds.). (2004). *Poor People's Knowledge: Promoting Intellectual Property in Developing Countries.* The World Bank and Oxford University Press.

Fischbacher, U., & Gachter, S. (2010). "Social preferences, beliefs, and the dynamics of free riding in public goods experiments." *American Economic Review*, 100(1), 541–556.

Fisher, R., Ury, W. L., & Patton, B. (2011). *Getting to Yes: Negotiating Agreement without Giving In.* Penguin.

Florini, A. (2011). "The International Energy Agency in global energy governance." *Global Policy*, 2(1), 40–50.

Florini, A., & Sovacool, B. K. (2009). "Who governs energy? The challenges facing global energy governance." *Energy Policy*, 37(12), 5239–5248.

Fondo Latinoamericano de Reservas (FLAR) (2000). *Ampliación de las funciones del Fondo Latinoamericano de Reservas (FLAR) a las de un Fondo Monetario Regional.* [Extension of the Functions of the Latin American Reserve Fund (FLAR) Toward a Regional Mutual Fund]. Working Paper, FLAR, Bogotá.

Francés, G. E., Marín-Quemada, J. M., & González, E. S. M. (2013). "RES and risk: Renewable energy's contribution to energy security. A portfolio-based approach." *Renewable and Sustainable Energy Reviews*, 26, 549–559.

Francis, D. C. (2010). "Merkel praised in Germany for hard line on Greece debt crisis." *The Christian Science Monitor*, March 26, 2010. Available at: https://www.csmonitor.com/World/Europe/2010/0326/Merkel-praised-in-Germany-for-hard-line-on-Greece-debt-crisis. Accessed February 23, 2023.

Freeman, L. C. (1977). "A set of measures of centrality based on betweenness." *Sociometry*, 40(1), 35–41.

Frey, B. S. (1984). "The public choice view of international political economy." *International Organization*, 38(1), 199–223.

Frey, G. W., & Linke, D. M. (2002). "Hydropower as a renewable and sustainable energy resource meeting global energy challenges in a reasonable way." *Energy Policy*, 30(14), 1261–1265.

Gandal, N. (2002). "Compatibility, standardization, and network effects: Some policy implications." *Oxford Review of Economic Policy*, 18(1), 80–91.

Garcia, G. (2016). "The rise of the Global South, the IMF and the future of law and development. *Third World Quarterly*, 37(2), 191–208.

Gehring, T., & Faude, B. (2013). "The dynamics of regime complexes: Microfoundations and systemic effects." *Global governance*, 19(1), 119–130.

Gehring, T., & Faude, B. (2014). "A theory of emerging order within institutional complexes: How competition among regulatory international institutions leads to institutional adaptation and division of labor." *The Review of International Organizations*, 9(4), 471–498.

Genschel, P., & Plümper, T. (1997). "Regulatory competition and international co-operation." *Journal of European Public Policy*, 4(4), 626–642.

Genschel, P., & Seelkopf, L. (2016). "Did they learn to tax? Taxation trends outside the OECD." *Review of International Political Economy*, 23(2), 316–344.

George, K., Joll, C., & Lynk, E. L. (2005). *Industrial Organization: Competition, Growth and Structural Change*. Routledge.

German Bundestag (2004). "Initiative zur Gründung einer Internationalen Agentur zur Förderung der Erneuerbaren Energien (International Renewable Energy Agency—IRENA)." Drucksache 15/811, 15. Wahlperiode, 08.04.2003.

Gholiagha, S., Holzscheiter, A., and Liese, A. (2020) "Activating norm collisions: Interface conflicts in international drug control." *Global Constitutionalism*, 9(2), 290–317.

Gilpin, R. (2016). *The Political Economy of International Relations*. Princeton University Press.

Goertz, G. (2006). *Social Science Concepts: A User's Guide*. Princeton University Press.

Goldthau, A. (2014). "Rethinking the governance of energy infrastructure: Scale, decentralization and polycentrism." *Energy Research & Social Science*, 1, 134–140.

Goldthau, A., & Witte, J. M. (Eds.). (2010). *Global Energy Governance: The New Rules of the Game*. Brookings Institution Press.

Gomel, G. (2017). "Crisis prevention and the role of IMF conditionality." In *Governing Global Finance: New Challenges, G7 and IMF Contributions*, edited by M. Fratianni, P. Savola, & J. J. Kirton, Routledge, 167–175.

Gould, D. M., & Gruben, W. C. (1996). "The role of intellectual property rights in economic growth." *Journal of Development Economics*, 48(2), 323–350.

Gowa, J. (1989). "Rational hegemons, excludable goods, and small groups: An epitaph for hegemonic stability theory?" *World Politics*, 41(3), 307–324.

Grabel, I. (2019). "Continuity, discontinuity and incoherence in the Bretton Woods order: A Hirschmanian reading." *Development and Change*, 50(1), 46–71.

Grace, C. (2004). *The Effect of Changing Intellectual Property on Pharmaceutical Industry Prospects in India and China*. Report of the Department for International Development Health Systems Resource Centre. Available at: https://www.eldis.org/document/A16619. Accessed February 25, 2023,

Graham, E. R. (2014). "International organizations as collective agents: Fragmentation and the limits of principal control at the World Health Organization." *European Journal of International Relations*, 20(2), 366–390.

Gravelle, J. G. (2015). *Tax Havens: International Tax Avoidance and Evasion*. Congressional Research Service, Library of Congress. Available at: https://fas.org/sgp/crs/misc/R40623.pdf. Accessed July 24, 2019.

Green, J. F. (2014). *Rethinking Private Authority: Agents and Entrepreneurs in Global Environmental Governance*. Princeton University Press.

Green, J. F. (2022). "Hierarchy in regime complexes: Understanding authority in Antarctic governance." *International Studies Quarterly*, 66(1), sqab084.

Greenhill, B. (2008). "Recognition and collective identity formation in international politics." *European Journal of International Relations*, 14(2), 343–368.

Greenhill, B., & Lupu, Y. (2017). "Clubs of clubs: Fragmentation in the network of intergovernmental organizations." *International Studies Quarterly*, 61(1), 181–195.

Grinberg, I. (2016). "Does FATCA Teach Broader Lessons about International Tax Multilateralism?" In: Global Tax Governance: What Is Wrong and How to Fix It, edited by T. Rixen & P. Dietsch, ECPR Press, 157–174.

Group of 20 Heads of State (2009). "Declaration on Strengthening the Financial System—London Summit, 2 April 2009." Available at: http://www.g20.utoronto.ca/2009/2009ifi.pdf. Accessed August 23, 2019.

Group of 20 Heads of State (G20) (2013). "G20 Leaders' Declaration Saint Petersburg Summit, September 2013." Available at: http://www.g20.utoronto.ca/2013/Saint_Petersburg_Declaration_ENG.pdf. Accessed September 12, 2019.

Groves, L., & Hinton, R. (Eds.). (2013). *Inclusive Aid: Changing Power and Relationships in International Development*. Routledge.

Gruber, L. (2001). "Power politics and the free trade bandwagon." *Comparative Political Studies*, 34(7), 703–741.

Güven, A. B. (2017). "Defending supremacy: how the IMF and the World Bank navigate the challenge of rising powers." *International Affairs*, 93(5), 1149–1166.

Guzman, A. T. (2002). "International antitrust and the WTO: The lesson from intellectual property." *Vanderbilt Journal of International Law*, 43, 933–957.

Hafner-Burton, E. M., Kahler, M., & Montgomery, A. H. (2009). "Network analysis for international relations." *International Organization*, 63(3), 559–592.

Haftel, Y. Z., & Hofmann, S. C. (2019). "Rivalry and overlap: Why regional economic organizations encroach on security organizations." *Journal of Conflict Resolution*, 63(9), 2180–2206.

Haftel, Y. Z., & Lenz, T. (2021) "Measuring institutional overlap in global governance." *The Review of International Organizations*, 17, 323–347.

Haihong, G. (2017). "The RMB internationalization and the reform of the international monetary system." *Global Economic Observer*, 5(1), 113.

Hake, J. F., Fischer, W., Venghaus, S., & Weckenbrock, C. (2015). "The German Energiewende—History and status quo." *Energy*, 92, 532–546.

Hakelberg, L. (2015). "The power politics of international tax co-operation: Luxembourg, Austria and the automatic exchange of information." *Journal of European Public Policy*, 22(3), 409–428.

Hakelberg, L. (2016). "Coercion in international tax cooperation: Identifying the prerequisites for sanction threats by a great power." *Review of International Political Economy*, 23(3), 511–541.

Hämmerli, A., Gattiker, R., & Weyermann, R. (2006). "Conflict and cooperation in an actors' network of Chechnya based on event data." *Journal of Conflict Resolution*, 50(2), 159–175.

Hanrieder, T. (2015). *International Organization in Time: Fragmentation and Reform*. Oxford University Press.

Harsch, M. F. (2015). *The power of Dependence: NATO-UN Cooperation in Crisis Management*. Oxford University Press.

Hart-Landsberg, M. (2009). "Learning from ALBA and the Bank of the South: Challenges and possibilities." *Monthly Review*, 61(4), 1–20.

Hathaway, O. A., & Shapiro, S. J. (2017). *The Internationalists: How a Radical Plan to Outlaw War Remade the World*. Simon and Schuster.

Hawkins, D. G., Lake, D. A., Nielson, D. L., & Tierney, M. J. (Eds.). (2006). *Delegation and Agency in International Organizations*. Cambridge University Press.

Hecan, M. (2016). "Dynamics of institutional proliferation in financing for development: The birth of the AIIB." *Development*, 59(1–2), 158–166.

Helfer, L. R. (2004). "Regime shifting: The TRIPs agreement and new dynamics of international intellectual property lawmaking." *Yale Journal of International Law*, 29, 1–83.

Helfer, L. R. (2009). "Regime shifting in the international intellectual property system." *Perspectives on Politics*, 7(1), 39–44.

Helleiner, E., & Wang, H. (2018). "Limits to the BRICS' challenge: Credit rating reform and institutional innovation in global finance." *Review of International Political Economy*, 25(5), 573–595.

Henning, C. R. (2017). "Avoiding fragmentation of global financial governance." *Global Policy*, 8(1), 101–106.

Henning, C. R. (2019). "Regime complexity and the institutions of crisis and development finance." *Development and Change*, 50(1), 24–45.

Henning, C. R., & Pratt, T. (2020). "Hierarchy and differentiation in international regime complexes: A theoretical framework for comparative research." Unpublished manuscript. Available at: https://www.peio.me/wp-content/uploads/2020/01/PEIO13_paper_66.pdf. Accessed May 6, 2020.

Heredia, L. (2007). "Why South America wants a new bank." BBC News, December 10, 2007. Available at: http://news.bbc.co.uk/2/hi/americas/7068124.stm. Accessed June 13, 2019.

Hernandez, D. (2017). "Are 'new' donors challenging World Bank conditionality?" *World Development*, 96, 529–549.

Heubaum, H., & Biermann, F. (2015). "Integrating global energy and climate governance: The changing role of the International Energy Agency." *Energy Policy*, 87, 229–239.

Heupel, M., & Zürn, M. (Eds.). (2017). *Protecting the Individual from International Authority: Human Rights in International Organizations*. Cambridge University Press.

Higgings, A., & Sanger, D. E. (2015). "3 European powers say they will join China-Led bank." *The New York Times*, March 17, 2015. Available at: https://www.nytimes.com/2015/03/18/business/france-germany-and-italy-join-asian-infrastructure-investment-bank.html. Accessed July 12, 2019.

Hofmann, S. C. (2009). "Overlapping institutions in the realm of international security: The case of NATO and ESDP." *Perspectives on Politics*, 7(1), 45–52.

Hofmann, S. C. (2011). "Why institutional overlap matters: CSDP in the European security architecture." *Journal of Common Market Studies*, 49(1), 101–120.

Hommes, L., & Boelens, R. (2018). "From natural flow to 'working river': Hydropower development, modernity and socio-territorial transformations in Lima's Rímac watershed." *Journal of Historical Geography*, 62, 85–95.

Honneth, A. (1995). *The Struggle for Recognition: The Moral Grammar of Social Conflicts*. MIT Press.

Hooghe, L., Lenz, T., & Marks, G. (2019). *A Theory of International Organization*. Oxford University Press.

Hooghe, L., & Marks, G. (2015). "Delegation and pooling in international organizations." *The Review of International Organizations*, 10, 305–328.

Hook, S. W., & Rumsey, J. G. (2016). "The Development Aid regime at fifty: policy challenges inside and out." *International Studies Perspectives*, 17(1), 55–74.

Houben, A. C., Kakes, J., & Schinasi, G. J. (2004). *Toward a Framework for Safeguarding Financial Stability* (Vol. 4). International Monetary Fund.

Howarth, D., & Schild, J. (2021). "Nein to 'Transfer Union': The German brake on the construction of a European Union fiscal capacity." *Journal of European Integration*, 43(2), 209–226.

Humphrey, C. (2014). "The politics of loan pricing in multilateral development banks." *Review of International Political Economy*, 21(3), 611–639.

Humrich, C. (2013). "Fragmented international governance of arctic offshore oil: Governance challenges and institutional improvement." *Global Environmental Politics*, 13(3), 79–99.

Hurd, I. (1999). "Legitimacy and authority in international politics." *International Organization*, 53(2), 379–408.

Iacob, I. G., & Cirlig, R. E. (2016). "The Energy Charter Treaty and settlement of disputes—current challenges." *Juridical Tribune Journal–Tribuna Juridica*, 6(1), 71–83.

Ikenberry, G. J., & Lim, D. J. (2017). *China's Emerging Institutional Statecraft*. The Asian Infrastructure Investment Bank and the Brookings Institute.

International Energy Agency (2018). "Data and Statistics." Available at: https://www.iea.org/data-and-statistics. Accessed September 12, 2018.

International Monetary Fund (IMF) (2013). "Stocktaking the Fund's engagement with regional financing arrangements." Washington, D.C. Available at: https://www.imf.org/external/np/pp/eng/2013/041113b.pdf. Accessed June 30, 2019.

International Monetary Fund (IMF) (2019). "IMF Data Mapper. Current account balance U.S. dollars." Available at: https://www.imf.org/external/datamapper/BCA@WEO/OEMDC/ADVEC/WEOWORLD. Accessed June 30, 2019.

Jacobsson, S., & Lauber, V. (2006). "The politics and policy of energy system transformation—explaining the German diffusion of renewable energy technology." *Energy Policy*, 34(3), 256–276.

Jacoby, C. D., & Weiss, C. (1997). "Recognizing property rights in traditional biocultural contribution." *Stanford Environmental Law Journal*, 16, 74.

Jansen, D. (2006). *Einführung in die Netzwerkanalyse: Grundlagen, Methoden, Forschungsbeispiele*. Springer, Wiesbaden.

Jeremiah, K. (2019). "Stakeholders downplay Ecuador's exit from OPEC." *The Guardian*, October 4, 2019. Available at: https://guardian.ng/business-services/stakeholders-downplay-ecuadors-exit-from-opec/. Accessed October 21, 2019.

Johnson, T., & Urpelainen, J. (2012). "A strategic theory of regime integration and separation." *International Organization*, 66(4), 645–677.

Johnston, A. I. (2001). "Treating international institutions as social environments." *International Studies Quarterly*, 45(4), 487–515.

Jones, C. T. (1990). "OPEC behaviour under falling prices: Implications for cartel stability." *The Energy Journal*, 11(3), 117–129.

Jones, L. (2020). "Does China's belt and road initiative challenge the liberal, rules-based order?" *Fudan Journal of the Humanities and Social Sciences*, 13(1), 113–133.

Jupille, J. H., Mattli, W., & Snidal, D. (2013). *Institutional Choice and Global Commerce*. Cambridge University Press.

Kahn, R. (2014). "BRICS and mortals." Council on Foreign Relations, July 15, 2014. Blog post. Available at: https://www.cfr.org/blog/brics-and-mortals. Accessed February 12, 2019.

Kalantzis-Cope, P. (2016). "Geopolitical structuring in the age of information: Imagining order, understanding change." *Alternatives* 41(4), 179–193.

Kamau, E. C., Fedder, B., & Winter, G. (2010). "The Nagoya Protocol on access to genetic resources and benefit sharing: What is new and what are the implications for provider and user countries and the scientific community." *Law Environment & Development Journal*, 6(3), 246–262.

Kaminski, M. E. (2013). "The capture of international intellectual property law through the US trade regime." *Southern California Law Review*, 87, 977.

Kammas, P., & Philippopoulos, A. (2009). "The role of international public goods in tax cooperation." *CESifo Economic Studies*, 56(2), 278–299.

Kastner, S. L., Pearson, M. M., & Rector, C. (2016). "Invest, hold up, or accept? China in multilateral governance." *Security Studies*, 25(1), 142–179.

Katz, M. L., & Shapiro, C. (1985). "Network externalities, competition, and compatibility." *The American Economic Review*, 75(3), 424–440.

Katz, M. L., & Shapiro, C. (1994). "Systems competition and network effects." *Journal of Economic Perspectives*, 8(2), 93–115.

Kaul, I., Conceicao, P., Le Goulven, K., & Mendoza, R. U. (Eds.). (2003). *Providing Global Public Goods: Managing Globalization*. Oxford University Press.

Kaul, I., Grunberg, I., & Stern, M. A. (Eds.). (1999). *Global Public Goods: International Cooperation in the 21st Century*. Oxford University Press.

Kavalski, E. (2013). "The struggle for recognition of normative powers: Normative power Europe and normative power China in context." *Cooperation and Conflict*, 48(2), 247–267.

Kawai, M. (2017). "Asia's Financial Stability as a Regional and Global Public Good." In: *21st Century Cooperation: Regional Public Goods, Global Governance, and Sustainable Development*, edited by A. Estevadeordal & L. Goodman, Routledge, 312–335.

Keen, M., & Marchand, M. (1997). "Fiscal competition and the pattern of public spending." *Journal of Public Economics*, 66(1), 33–53.

Kelley, J. (2009). "The more the merrier? The effects of having multiple international election monitoring organizations." *Perspectives on Politics*, 7(1), 59–64.

Kellow, A. (2012). "Multi-level and multi-arena governance: The limits of integration and the possibilities of forum shopping." *International Environmental Agreements: Politics, Law and Economics*, 12(4), 327–342.

Keohane, R. O., & Victor, D. G. (2011). "The regime complex for climate change." *Perspectives on Politics*, 9(1), 7–23.

Kerzner, D. S., & Chodikoff, D. W. (2016). *International Tax Evasion in the Global Information Age*. Springer.

Kilby, C. (2006). "Donor influence in multilateral development banks: The case of the Asian Development Bank." *The Review of International Organizations*, 1(2), 173–195.

Kilby, C. (2011). "Informal influence in the Asian development bank." *The Review of International Organizations*, 6(3–4), 223–257.

Kilby, C. (2013). "An empirical assessment of informal influence in the World Bank." *Economic Development and Cultural Change*, 61(2), 431–464.

Kim, R. E. (2020). "Is global governance fragmented, polycentric, or complex? The state of the art of the network approach." *International Studies Review*, 22(4), 903–931.

Kohl, W. L. (1976). "The United States, Western Europe, and the energy problem." *Journal of International Affairs*, 30(1), 81–96.

Kölliker, A. (2001). "Bringing together or driving apart the union? Towards a theory of differentiated integration." *West European Politics*, 24(4), 125–151.

Konoplyanik, A., & Walde, T. (2006). "Energy Charter Treaty and its role in international energy." Journal of Energy and Natural Resources Law, 24 (4), 523–558.

Koremenos, B. (2016). *The Continent of International Law: Explaining Agreement Design*. Cambridge University Press.

Koremenos, B., Lipson, C., & Snidal, D. (2001). "The rational design of international institutions." *International Organization*, 55(4), 761–799.

Kreuder-Sonnen, C., & Zürn, M. (2020) "After fragmentation: Norm collisions, interface conflicts, and conflict management." *Global Constitutionalism*, 9(2), 241–267.

Kruck, A., Heinkelmann-Wild, T., Daßler, B., & Hobbach, R. (2022). "Disentangling institutional contestation by established powers: Types of contestation frames and varying opportunities for the re-legitimation of international institutions." *Global Constitutionalism*, 11(2), 344–368.

Kruck, A., & Zangl, B. (2019). "Trading privileges for support: The strategic co-optation of emerging powers into international institutions." *International Theory*, 11(3), 318–343.

Kruger, M. (2001). "Harmonizing TRIPS and the CBD: A proposal from India." *Minnesota Journal of International Law*, 10, 169–207.

Kudrle, R. T. (2008). "The OECD's harmful tax competition initiative and the tax havens: From bombshell to damp squib." *Global Economy Journal*, 8(1), 1850128.

Kudrle, Robert T. (2014). "The OECD and the International Tax Regime: Persistence Pays Off." *Journal of Comparative Policy Analysis: Research and Practice*, 16(3), 201–215.

Lake, D. A. (2009). "Relational authority and legitimacy in international relations." *American Behavioral Scientist*, 53(3), 331–353.

Lake, D. A. (2011). *Hierarchy in International Relations*. Cornell University Press.

Lee, J. W., & Shin, K. (2008). "IMF bailouts and moral hazard." *Journal of International Money and Finance*, 27(5), 816–830.

Lenz, T. (2021). *Interorganizational Diffusion in International Relations: Regional Institutions and the Role of the European Union*. Oxford University Press.

Lesage, D., & Van de Graaf, T. (Eds.). (2015). *Rising Powers and Multilateral Institutions*. Springer.

Lesage, D. (2010). "The G20 and tax havens: maintaining the momentum?" Paper presented at the conference "Governing the Global Economy: The Role of the G20," Toronto. Available at: http://www.g20.utoronto.ca/biblio/lesage-tax-havens.pdf. Accessed February 21, 2019.

Lesage, D., & Van de Graaf, T. (2013). "Thriving in complexity? The OECD system's role in energy and taxation. *Global Governance: A Review of Multilateralism and International Organizations*, 19(1), 83–92.

Lesage, D., & Van de Graaf, T. (2016). *Global Energy Governance in a Multipolar World*. Routledge.

Lesage, D., Van de Graaf, T., & Westphal, K. (2009). "The G8's role in global energy governance since the 2005 Gleneagles summit." *Global Governance: A Review of Multilateralism and International Organizations*, 15(2), 259–277.

Levy, J. S. (2008). "Case studies: Types, designs, and logics of inference." *Conflict Management and Peace Science*, 25(1), 1–18.

Li, J. (2016). *China and BEPS: From Norm-Taker to Norm-Shaker*. Osgoode Legal Studies Research Paper Series. 126.

Liao, R. (2015). "Out of the Bretton Woods: How the AIIB is different." *Foreign Affairs*, 27(July), 633–649.

Lim, D. Y. M., & Vreeland, J. R. (2013). "Regional organizations and international politics: Japanese influence over the Asian Development Bank and the UN Security Council." *World Politics*, 65(1), 34–72.

Lipscy, P. Y. (2015). "Explaining institutional change: Policy areas, outside options, and the Bretton Woods institutions." *American Journal of Political Science*, 59(2), 341–356.

Lipscy, P. Y. (2017). *Renegotiating the World Order: Institutional Change in International Relations.* Cambridge University Press.

Lipson, M. (2017). "Organization Theory and Cooperation and Conflict among International Organizations." In: *Palgrave Handbook of Inter-Organizational Relations in World Politics*, edited by J. A. Koops & R. Biermann, Palgrave Macmillan, London, 67–96.

Loewen, H. (2014). "Institutional interplay between the Chiang Mai Initiative and the International Monetary Fund." *European Journal of East Asian Studies*, 13(1), 50–67.

Loewen, H. (2018). "Institutional Development and Institutional Interplay within the Global Financial Regime Complex—the IMF and Regional Financial Cooperation in East Asia." In: *Initiatives of Regional Integration in Asia in Comparative Perspective*, edited by H. Loewen & A. Zoreb, Springer, Dordrecht.

Loewen, H., & Hilpert, H. G. (2010). *Auf dem Weg zu einem asiatischen Währungsfonds?* SWP Aktuell, No. 53. Stiftung Wissenschaft und Politik, Berlin.

Lu, Y., Luo, X., Polgar, M., & Cao, Y. (2010). "Social network analysis of a criminal hacker community." *Journal of Computer Information Systems*, 51(2), 31–41.

Luchtenberg, K. F., & Vu, Q. V. (2015). "The 2008 financial crisis: Stock market contagion and its determinants." *Research in International Business and Finance*, 33, 178–203.

Lumsdaine, D. H. (1993). *Moral Vision in International Politics: The Foreign Aid Regime, 1949–1989.* Princeton University Press.

Lundsgaarde, E. (2012). *The Domestic Politics of Foreign Aid.* Routledge, New York.

Lupu, Y., & Voeten, E. (2012). "Precedent in international courts: A network analysis of case citations by the European Court of Human Rights." *British Journal of Political Science*, 42(2), 413–439.

Lütz, S., and Kranke, M. (2014). "The European rescue of the Washington Consensus? EU and IMF lending to Central and Eastern European countries." *Review of International Political Economy*, 21(2), 310–338.

Madichie, N. O. (2011). "IRENA–Masdar City (UAE)–Exemplars of innovation into emerging markets." *Foresight*, 13(6), 34–47.

Mansfield, E. (1995). *Intellectual Property Protection, Direct Investment, and Technology Transfer: Germany, Japan, and the United States.* The World Bank. Available at: https://elibrary.worldbank.org/doi/abs/10.1596/0-8213-3442-5. Accessed June 12, 2019.

Markovich, S. (2008). "Snowball: A dynamic oligopoly model with indirect network effects." *Journal of Economic Dynamics and Control*, 32(3), 909–938.

Martens, B. (2005). "Why do aid agencies exist?" *Development Policy Review*, 23(6), 643–663.

Martin, L. L. (1992). "Institutions and cooperation: Sanctions during the Falkland Islands conflict." *International Security*, 16(4), 143–178.

Marx, A., Rihoux, B., & Ragin, C. (2014). "The origins, development, and application of Qualitative Comparative Analysis: the first 25 years." *European Political Science Review*, 6(1), 115–142.

Maskus, K. (1998). "The international regulation of intellectual property." *Review of World Economics*, 134(2), 186–208.

Massey, J. A. (2006). "The emperor is far away: China's enforcement of intellectual property rights protection, 1986–2006." *Chinese Journal of International Law*, 7, 231–237.

Mattli, W. (1999). *The Logic of Regional Integration: Europe and Beyond.* Cambridge University Press.

McElhinny, V. (2007). "A look into the Bank of the South. Due to launch in December 2007." Bank Information Center Info Brief (Bank Information Center, Washington, D.C.)

Mearsheimer, J. J. (1994). "The false promise of international institutions." *International Security*, 19(3), 5–49.

Mercopress (2015). "EU main economies announce plans to join China-led development bank, despite US warning." Available at: https://en.mercopress.com/2015/03/18/eu-main-economies-announce-plans-to-join-china-led-development-bank-despite-us-warning. Accessed July 12, 2019.

Milner, C. (2006). "Making NAMA work: Supporting adjustment and development." *World Economy*, 29(10), 1409–1422.

Minasyan, A. (2016). "Your development or mine? Effects of donor–recipient cultural differences on the aid-growth nexus." *Journal of Comparative Economics*, 44(2), 309–325.

Morin, J. F., Louafi, S., Orsini, A., & Oubenal, M. (2017). "Boundary organizations in regime complexes: A social network profile of IPBES." *Journal of International Relations and Development*, 20, 543–577.

Morse, J. C., & Keohane, R. O. (2014). "Contested multilateralism." *The Review of International Organizations*. 9(4), 385–412.

Moschella, M. (2010). *Governing Risk: The IMF and Global Financial Crises*. Springer.

Mosley, P. (1985). "The political economy of foreign aid: A model of the market for a public good," *Economic Development and Cultural Change*, 33(2), 373–393.

Murphy, H., & Kellow, A. (2013). "Forum shopping in global governance: Understanding states, business and NGOs in multiple arenas." *Global Policy*, 4(2), 139–149.

Murphy, S. (2009). "Free trade in agriculture: A bad idea whose time is done." *Monthly Review*, 61(3), 78.

Muzaka, V. (2011). "Linkages, contests and overlaps in the global intellectual property rights regime." *European Journal of International Relations*, 17(4), 755–776.

Ndikumana, L. (2015). *International Tax Cooperation and Implications of Globalization*. CDP Background Paper, UN Department of Economics and Social Affairs.

Nelson, R. M., Nanto, D. K., Sanford, J. E., Weiss, Martin A. (2010). "Frequently asked questions about IMF involvement in the Eurozone debt crisis." Congressional Research Service, Library of Congress. Available at: https://fas.org/sgp/crs/row/R41239.pdf. Accessed March 21, 2019.

Netanel, N. (Ed.). (2009). *The Development Agenda: Global Intellectual Property and Developing Countries*. Oxford University Press.

Nielson, D. L., Parks, B., & Tierney, M. J. (2017). "International organizations and development finance." *Review of International Organizations*, 12(2), 157–169.

Nieto, M. M., & Schinasi, M. G. J. (2007). *EU Framework for Safeguarding Financial Stability: Towards an Analytical Benchmark for Assessing Its Effectiveness* (No. 7–260). International Monetary Fund.

Nye, J. S., Jr. (2002). "Limits of American power." *Political Science Quarterly*, 117(4), 545–559.

Oberthur, S., & Stokke, O. S. (Eds.). (2011). *Managing Institutional Complexity: Regime Interplay and Global Environmental Change*. MIT Press.

Ocampo, J. A., & Titelman, D. (2009). "Subregional financial cooperation: The South American experience." *Journal of Post Keynesian Economics*, 32(2), 249–268.

OECD (1998). *Harmful Tax Competition. An Emerging Global Issue*. OECD, Paris.

OECD (2013). "China signing ceremony of the Multilateral Convention on Mutual Administrative Assistance in Tax Matters. Opening remarks of the OECD Secretary-General, Mr. Angel Gurría, 27 August 2013." Available at: https://www.oecd.org/tax/exchange-of-tax-information/chinasigningceremonyofthemultilateralconventiononmutualadministrativeassistanceintaxmatters.htm. Accessed April 4, 2019.

OECD (2015). OECD/G20 *Base Erosion and Profit Shifting Project 2015 Final Reports. Frequently Asked Questions*. Available at: http://www.oecd.org/ctp/beps-frequently-asked-questions.pdf. Accessed July 7, 2019.

OECD (2016). *The Platform for Collaboration on Tax*. Concept note. Jointly published by the Organization for Economic Cooperation and Development, International Monetary Fund, World Bank and United Nations, 19 April 2016. Available at: https://www1.oecd.org/ctp/concept-note-platform-for-collaboration-on-tax.pdf. Accessed July 7, 2019.

OECD (2017). *Active with the People's Republic of China.* OECD Global Relations Secretariat. Available at: http://www.oecd.org/global-relations/active-with-china.pdf. Accessed July 12, 2019.

OECD (2018). *Active with the People's Republic of China.* OECD Brochure. Available at: https://www.oecd.org/china/active-with-china.pdf. Accessed August 25, 2019.

OECD (2019a). "Net ODA (indicator)." Available at: https://data.oecd.org/oda/net-oda.htm. Accessed July 12, 2019.

OECD (2019b). "DAC list of multilateral donors." Available at: http://www.oecd.org/dac/financing-sustainable-development/development-finance-data/dac-glossary.htm#Multi_Agencies. Accessed July 12, 2019.

OECD (2019c). "Statutory corporate income tax rates 2000–2019." Available at: https://stats.oecd.org/Index.aspx?QueryId=78166. Accessed July 21, 2019.

OECD (2019d). "Convention mutual administrative assistance in tax matters." Available at: http://www.oecd.org/ctp/exchange-of-tax-information/convention-on-mutual-administrative-assistance-in-tax-matters.htm. Accessed October 31, 2019.

OECD (2019e). "What is BEPS?" Available at: http://www.oecd.org/tax/beps/about/. Accessed October 31, 2019.

OECD (2019f). "Members of the OECD/G20 Inclusive Framework on BEPS. Updated October 2019." Available at: http://www.oecd.org/tax/beps/inclusive-framework-on-beps-composition.pdf. Accessed October 31, 2019.

Olson, M., & Zeckhauser, R. (1966). "An economic theory of alliances." *The Review of Economics and Statistics*, 48(3), 266–279.

Orsini, A. (2013). "Multi-forum non-state actors: Navigating the regime complexes for forestry and genetic resources." *Global Environmental Politics*, 13(3), 34–55.

Orsini, A., Morin, J.-F., & Young, O. (2013). "Regime complexes: A buzz, a boom or a boost for global governance?" *Global Governance, A Review of Multilateralism and International Organizations*, 19(1), 27–39.

Ortiz, I. (2007). "New Developments in South–South Cooperation: China ODA, Alternative Regionalisms, Banco Del Sur." International Development Economics Associates (IDEAs). Available at: https://www.networkideas.org/news-analysis/2007/08/new-developments-in-south-south-cooperation/. Accesses February 25, 2023.

Osborne, G. (2015). "Statement on the UK's plans to join Asian Infrastructure Investment Bank from 12th March, 2015." Available at: https://www.gov.uk/government/news/uk-announces-plans-to-join-asian-infrastructure-investment-bank. Accessed July 12, 2019.

Ostrom, E. (1990). *Governing the commons: The Evolution of Institutions for Collective Action.* Cambridge University Press.

Oye, K. A. (1985). "Explaining cooperation under anarchy: Hypotheses and strategies." *World Politics*, 38(1), 1–24.

Painter, D. S. (2017). "From Linkage to Economic Warfare: Energy, Soviet–American Relations, and the End of the Cold War." In: *Cold War Energy: A Transnational History of Soviet Oil and Gas* edited by J. Perović. Palgrave Macmillan, Cham, 283–318.

Papaioannou, A. (1995). "Security of energy supply: The approach in the European Union and the contribution of the Energy Charter Treaty." *Maastricht Journal of European and Comparative Law*, 2(1), 34–62.

Park, S. (2014). "Institutional isomorphism and the Asian Development Bank's accountability mechanism: Something old, something new, something borrowed, something blue?" *The Pacific Review*, 27(2), 217–239.

Park, S., & Strand, J. R. (Eds.). (2015). *Global Economic Governance and the Development Practices of the Multilateral Development Banks.* Routledge.

Parks, B. C., Masaki, T., Faust, J., & Leiderer, S. (2016). "Aid management, trust, and development policy influence: New evidence from a survey of public sector officials in low-income and middle-income countries." *AidData Working Paper* No. 30.

Patnaik, J. K. (1992). "India and the TRIPS: Some notes on the Uruguay Round negotiations." *India Quarterly*, 48(4), 31–42.

Perlez, J. (2015). "China creates a world bank of its own, and the U.S. balks." *The New York Times*, December 4, 2015. Available at: https://www.nytimes.com/2015/12/05/business/international/china-creates-an-asian-bank-as-the-us-stands-aloof.html. Accessed July 12, 2019.

Perović, J. (2017). *Cold War Energy: A Transnational History of Soviet Oil and Gas*. Springer.

Pierson, P. (2000). "Increasing returns, path dependence, and the book of politics." *American Political Science Review*, 94(2), 251–267.

Pincus, J. A. (1965). *Economic Aid and International Cost Sharing*. Johns Hopkins Press.

Platje, J. (2011). "Institutional change for creating capacity and capability for sustainable development: A club good perspective." *Ordnungspolitische Diskurse*, 5(6), 1–19.

Ponsot, J. F. (2009). "New financial architecture and regional monetary integration in Latin America." Paper presented at Colloque international "Économie politique internationale et nouvelles régulations de la mondialisation," Centre de Recherche sur l'Intégration Économique et Financière, Université de Poitiers.

Pratt, T. (2018). "Deference and hierarchy in international regime complexes." *International Organization*, 72(3), 561–590.

Pratt, T. (2021). "Angling for influence: Institutional proliferation in development banking." *International Studies Quarterly*, 65(1), 95–108.

Quintana, S. O. (2008). "The Bank of the South." *Law & Business Review of the Americas*, 14, 737–758.

Raustiala, K. (2006). "Density and conflict in international intellectual property law." *University of California at Davis Law Review*, 40, 1021.

Raustiala, K., & Victor, D. G. (2004). "The regime complex for plant genetic resources." *International Organization*, 58(2), 277–309.

Riles, A. (2014). "Managing regulatory arbitrage: A conflict of laws approach." *Cornell International Law Journal*, 47(1), 63–119.

Rixen, T. (2008a). "Politicization and institutional (non-)change in international taxation." *WZB Discussion Paper* (No. SP IV 2008–306).

Rixen, T. (2008b). *The Political Economy of International Tax Governance*. Springer.

Rixen, T. (2011). "From double tax avoidance to tax competition: Explaining the institutional trajectory of international tax governance." *Review of International Political Economy*, 18(2), 197–227.

Rixen, T., Viola, L. A., & Zürn, M. (Eds.). (2016). *Historical Institutionalism and International Relations: Explaining Institutional Development in World Politics*. Oxford University Press.

Robinson, D. (2008). "Sui Generis plant variety protection systems: Liability rules and non-UPOV systems of protection." *Journal of Intellectual Property Law & Practice*, 3(10), 659–665.

Roehrkasten, S., & Westphal, K. (2013). "IRENA and Germany's foreign renewable energy policy aiming at multilevel governance and an internationalization of the Energiewende." Working Paper FG 8, 2013/01. Available at: https://www.swp-berlin.org/en/publication/irena-and-germanys-foreign-renewable-energy-policy. Accessed February 25, 2023.

Rosales, A. (2013). "The Banco del Sur and the return to development." *Latin American Perspectives*, 40(5), 27–43.

Rose, E. A. (2004). "OPEC's dominance of the global oil market: The rise of the world's dependency on oil." *The Middle East Journal*, 58(3), 424–443.

Rosenbloom, H. D., Noked, N., & Helal, M. (2014). "The unruly world of tax: A proposal for an International Tax Cooperation Forum." *Florida Tax Review*, 57(15). Ohio State Public Law Working Paper No. 433. Available at: https://papers.ssrn.com/sol3/papers.cfm?abstract_id=3085449. Accessed July 12, 2019.

Rosendorff, B. P., & Milner, H. V. (2001). "The optimal design of international trade institutions: Uncertainty and escape." *International Organization*, 55(4), 829–857.

Rossi, C. (2014). "Introducing Public–Private Technology Pools to Address Climate Change." In: *The Way Forward in International Climate Policy*, edited by H. de Cononck, R. Lorch &, A. D. Sagar, Climate Strategies, London, 37–43.

Ruiz Nunez, F., & Wei, Z. (2015). "Infrastructure investment demands in emerging markets and developing economies." Policy Research working paper; no. WPS 7414. Washington, D.C.: World Bank Group.

Runge, C. F. (1984). "Institutions and the free rider: The assurance problem in collective action." *The Journal of Politics*, 46(1), 154–181.

Rusinowska, A., Berghammer, R., De Swart, H., & Grabisch, M. (2011). "Social Networks: Prestige, Centrality, and Influence." In: *Relational and Algebraic Methods in Computer Science, RAMICS 2011*, edited by H. de Swart, Springer, Berlin, Heidelberg, 22–39.

Salines, M., Glöckler, G., & Truchlewski, Z. (2012). "Existential crisis, incremental response: The eurozone's dual institutional evolution 2007–2011." *Journal of European Public Policy*, 19(5), 665–681.

Samarakoon, L. P. (2011). "Stock market interdependence, contagion, and the US financial crisis: The case of emerging and frontier markets." *Journal of International Financial Markets, Institutions and Money*, 21(5), 724–742.

Sandler, T. (2004). *Global Collective Action*. Cambridge University Press.

Sandler, T., & Tschirhart, J. (1997). "Club theory: Thirty years later." *Public Choice*, 93(3-4), 335–355.

Sartori, M., & Schiavo, S. (2015). "Connected we stand: A network perspective on trade and global food security." *Food Policy*, 57, 114–127.

Schaller, S. (2007). "Banco del Sur—Ein neuer Hoffnungsträger?" *Quetzal Politik und Kultur in Lateinamerika Onlinemagazin*. Available at: https://quetzal-leipzig.de/lateinamerika/argentinien/banco-del-sur-ein-neuer-hoffnungstraeger-bank-des-suedens. Accessed February 24, 2019.

Schäuble, W. (2010). "Why Europe's monetary union faces its biggest crisis." *Financial Times*, March 11, 2010. Available at: https://www.ft.com/content/2a205b88-2d41-11df-9c5b-00144feabdc0. Accessed April 23, 2019.

Scheer, H. (1993). "The International Solar Energy Agency—Excerpt from the Book by Hermann Scheer *A Solar Manifesto*." In: Eurosolar and World Council for Renewable Energy (2009). *The Long Road to IRENA: From the Idea to the Foundation of the International Renewable Energy Agency*. Documentation 1990–2009. Ponte Press, Bochum, 20–23.

Schüller, M., & Wogart, J. P. (2017). "The emergence of post-crisis regional financial institutions in Asia—with a little help from Europe." *Asia Europe Journal*, 15(4), 483–501.

Schwarzer, D. (2015). "Building the euro area's debt crisis management capacity with the IMF." *Review of International Political Economy*, 22(3), 599–625.

Scott, J. (2017). *Social Network Analysis*. Sage Publishing.

Seelkopf, L., Lierse, H., & Schmitt, C. (2016). "Trade liberalization and the global expansion of modern taxes." *Review of International Political Economy*, 22(2), 208–231.

Seitz, F., & Jost, T. (2012). "The role of the IMF in the European debt crisis." HAW im Dialog—Weidener Diskussionspapiere No 32. Available at: https://www.econstor.eu/bitstream/10419/56452/1/689266685.pdf. Accessed June 7, 2019.

Sell, S. K. (2003). *Private Power, Public Law: The Globalization of Intellectual Property Rights*. Cambridge University Press.

Sell, S. K. (2010a). "The rise and rule of a trade-based strategy: Historical institutionalism and the international regulation of intellectual property." *Review of International Political Economy*, 17(4), 762–790.

Sell, S. K. (2010b). "TRIPS was never enough: Vertical forum shifting, FTAs, ACTA, and TPP." *Journal of Intellectual Property Law*, 18, 447–478.

Sell, S. K. (2017). "The Politics of International Intellectual Property Law." In: *Research Handbook on the Politics of International Law*, edited by W. Sandholtz and C, A. Whytock, Edward Elgar Publishing, Cheltenham, 307–335.

Sell, S. K., & Prakash, A. (2004). "Using ideas strategically: The contest between business and NGO networks in intellectual property rights." *International Studies Quarterly*, 48(1), 143–175.

Sending, O. J. (2017). "Recognition and liquid authority." *International Theory*, 9(2), 311–328.

Serdült, U. (2002). "Soziale Netzwerkanalyse: Eine Methode zur Untersuchung von Beziehungen zwischen sozialen Akteuren." *Österreichische Zeitschrift für Politikwissenschaft*, 31(2), 127–141.

Shaviro, D. (2001). "Some Observations Concerning Multijurisdictional Tax Competition." In: *Regulatory Competition and Economic Integration: Comparative Perspectives*, edited by D. C. Esty & D. Geradin, Oxford University Press, NY, 49–67.

Sherwood, R. M. (1990). *Intellectual Property and Economic Development*. Routledge.

Singh, J. P. (2006). "The Evolution of National Interests: New Issues and North-South Negotiations during the Uruguay Round." In: *Negotiating Trade: Developing Countries in the WTO and NAFTA*, edited by J. Odell, Cambridge University Press, 41–84.

Slapin, J. B. (2009). "Exit, voice, and cooperation: Bargaining power in international organizations and federal systems." *Journal of Theoretical Politics*, 21(2), 187–211.

Slemrod, J., & Wilson, J. D. (2009). "Tax competition with parasitic tax havens." *Journal of Public Economics*, 93(11–12), 1261–1270.

Snidal, D. (1979). "Public goods, property rights, and political organizations." *International Studies Quarterly*, 23(4), 532–566.

Söderbaum, F., Spandler, K., & Pacciardi, A. (2021). *Contestations of the Liberal International Order: A Populist Script of Regional Cooperation*. Cambridge University Press.

Steil, B., & Walker, D. (2014). "Is the BRICS contingent reserve arrangement a substitute for the IMF?" Council on Foreign Relations, August 6, 2014, Blog post. Available at: https://www.cfr.org/blog/brics-contingent-reserve-arrangement-substitute-imf. Accessed June 21, 2019.

Steins, N. A., & Edwards, V. M. (1999). "Platforms for collective action in multiple-use common-pool resources." *Agriculture and Human Values*, 16(3), 241–255.

Stephen, M. D. (2014). "Rising powers, global capitalism and liberal global governance: A historical materialist account of the BRICs challenge." *European Journal of International Relations*, 20(4), 912–938.

Stephen, M. D., & Skidmore, D. (2019). The AIIB in the liberal international order. *The Chinese Journal of International Politics*, 12(1), 61–91.

Stephen, M. D., & Zürn, M. (Eds.). (2019). *Contested World Orders: Rising Powers, Non-Governmental Organizations, and the Politics of Authority beyond The Nation-State*. Oxford University Press.

Strand, J. R., Flores, E. M., & Trevathan, M. W. (2016). "China's leadership in global economic governance and the creation of the Asian Infrastructure Investment Bank." *Rising Powers Quarterly*, 1(1), 55–63.

Strand, J. R., & Retzl, K. J. (2016). "Did recent voice reforms improve good governance within the World Bank?" *Development and Change*, 47(3), 415–445.

Struett, M. J., Nance, M. T., & Armstrong, D. (2013). "Navigating the maritime piracy regime complex." *Global Governance*, 19(1), 93–104.

Sussangkarn, C. (2011). "Chiang Mai initiative multilateralization: Origin, development, and outlook." *Asian Economic Policy Review*, 6(2), 203–220.

Talley, I. (2015). U.S. looks to work with China-led infrastructure fund. *The Wall Street Journal*, March 22, 2015. Available at: https://www.wsj.com/articles/u-s-to-seek-collaboration-with-china-led-asian-infrastructure-investment-bank-1427057486. Accessed July 22, 2019.

Teune, H., & Przeworski, A. (1970). *The Logic of Comparative Social Inquiry*. Wiley-Interscience.

The Economist (2007). "Hugo Chávez moves into banking: Venezuela and Brazil battle quietly over the shape of a planned regional development bank." May 10, 2007. Available at: https://www.economist.com/the-americas/2007/05/10/hugo-chavez-moves-into-banking. Accessed June 21, 2019.

Tienhaara, K., & Downie, C. (2018). "Risky business? The Energy Charter Treaty, renewable energy, and investor-state disputes." *Global Governance: A Review of Multilateralism and International Organizations*, 24(3), 451–471.

Tierney, M. J., Nielson, D. L., Hawkins, D. G., Roberts, J. T., Findley, M. G., Powers, R. M., & Hicks, R. L. (2011). "More dollars than sense: Refining our knowledge of development finance using AidData." *World Development*, 39(11), 1891–1906.

Trachtman, J. P. (2010). "The international law of financial crisis: Spillovers, subsidiarity, fragmentation and cooperation." *Journal of International Economic Law*, 13(3), 719–742.

Treier, S., & Jackman, S. (2008). "Democracy as a latent variable." *American Journal of Political Science*, 52(1), 201–217.

Troiano, U. (2017). *Intergovernmental Cooperation and Tax Enforcement* (No. 24153). National Bureau of Economic Research, Inc.

Tuman, J. P., & Strand, J. R. (2006). "The role of mercantilism, humanitarianism, and gaiatsu in Japan's ODA programme in Asia." *International Relations of the Asia-Pacific*, 6(1), 61–80.

Urpelainen, J. (2012). "How uncertainty about outside options impedes international cooperation." *International Theory*, 4, 133–163.

Urpelainen, J., & Van de Graaf, T. (2015). "Your place or mine? Institutional capture and the creation of overlapping international institutions." *British Journal of Political Science*, 45(4), 799–827.

Vadlamannati, K. C., Li, Y., Brazys, S. R., & Dukalskis, A. (2019). *Building Bridges or Breaking Bonds? The Belt and Road Initiative and Foreign Aid Competition*. UCD Geary Institute for Public Policy Discussion Paper Series. Available at: http://www.ucd.ie/geary/static/publications/workingpapers/gearywp201906.pdf. Accessed July 19, 2019.

Valencia, A. (2019). "Ecuador to quit OPEC in 2020 in search of bigger export revenue." Available at: https://uk.reuters.com/article/uk-ecuador-opec/ecuador-to-quit-opec-in-2020-in-search-of-bigger-export-revenue-idUKKBN1WG4KD. Accessed October 9, 2019.

van Asselt, H., & Zelli, F. (2014). "Connect the dots: Managing the fragmentation of global climate governance." *Environmental Economic Policy Studies*, 16, 137–155.

Van de Graaf, T. (2013a). "Fragmentation in global energy governance: Explaining the creation of IRENA." *Global Environmental Politics*, 13(3), 14–33.

Van de Graaf, T. (2013b). *The Politics and Institutions of Global Energy Governance*. Palgrave Macmillan.

Van de Graaf, T. (2017). "Organizational Interactions in Global Energy Governance." In: *Palgrave Handbook of Inter-Organizational Relations in World Politics*, edited by J. A. Koops & R. Biermann, Palgrave Macmillan, London, 591–609.

Van de Graaf, T., & Colgan, J. (2016). "Global energy governance: A review and research agenda." *Palgrave Communications* 2, 1–12.

Van de Graaf, T., & Westphal, K. (2011). "The G8 and G20 as global steering committees for energy: Opportunities and constraints." *Global Policy*, 2, 19–30.

Vaubel, R. (1983). "The moral hazard of IMF lending." *World Economy*, 6(3), 291–304.

Vestergaard, J., & Wade, R. H. (2015). "Still in the woods: Gridlock in the IMF and the World Bank puts multilateralism at risk." *Global Policy*, 6(1), 1–12.

Viana, J. M. N. (2002). "Intellectual property rights, the World Trade Organization and public health: The Brazilian perspective." *Connecticut Journal of International Law*, 17(2), 311–318.

Voeten, E. (2001). "Outside options and the logic of Security Council action." *American Political Science Review*, 95(4), 845–858.

Vreeland, J. R. (2006). *The International Monetary Fund (IMF): Politics of Conditional Lending*. Routledge.

Wallbott, L., Wolff, F., & Pozarowska, J. (2014). "The Negotiations of the Nagoya Protocol: Issues, Coalitions and Process." In: Global Governance of Genetic Resources: Access and Benefit Sharing after the Nagoya Protocol, edited by S. Oberthür and G. K. Rosendal, Routledge, Milton Park, Oxon, 33–59.

Wang, H. (2017). "New multilateral development banks: Opportunities and challenges for global governance." *Global Policy*, 8(1), 113–118.

Ward, M. D., Stovel, K., & Sacks, A. (2011). "Network analysis and political science." *Annual Review of Political Science*, 14, 245–264.

Watt, N., Lewis, P., & Branigan, T. (2015). "US anger at Britain joining Chinese-led investment bank AIIB." *The Guardian*, March 13, 2015. Available at: https://www.theguardian.com/us-news/2015/mar/13/white-house-pointedly-asks-uk-to-use-its-voice-as-part-of-chinese-led-bank.

Weiner, J. M., & Ault, H. J. (1998). "The OECD's report on harmful tax competition." *National Tax Journal*, 51(3), 601–608.

Weisbrot, M. (2014). "BRICS' new financial institutions could undermine US–EU global dominance." *Al-Jazeera America*, July 18, 2014. Available at: http://america.aljazeera.com/opinions/2014/7/brics-developmentbankimffinance.html. Accessed March 4, 2019.

Weiss, M. A. (2009). *The Global Financial Crisis: The Role of the International Monetary Fund (IMF)*. Washington, D.C.: Congressional Research Service, Vol. 22976.

Weiss, M. A. (2017). *Asian Infrastructure Investment Bank (AIIB)*. Washington, D.C.: Congressional Research Service, Vol. 44754.

Weissman, R. (1996). "Long, strange trips: The pharmaceutical industry drive to harmonize global intellectual property rules, and the remaining WTO legal alternatives available to third world countries." *University of Pennsylvania Journal of International Economic Law* 17, 1069–1125.

Wendt, A. (2003). "Why a world state is inevitable." *European Journal of International Relations*, 9(4), 491–542.

Widmaier, W. W. (2003). "Constructing monetary crises: New Keynesian understandings and monetary cooperation in the 1990s." *Review of International Studies*, 29(1), 61–77.

Wildasin, D. E. (2002). "Tax coordination: The importance of institutions." *Swedish Economic Policy Review*, 9(1), 171–200.

Wilson, J. D. (2015). "Multilateral organisations and the limits to international energy cooperation." *New Political Economy*, 20(1), 85–106.

World Bank (WB) (2016). "Sector Taxonomy and definitions." Revised July 1, 2016. Available at: http://pubdocs.worldbank.org/en/538321490128452070/Sector-Taxonomy-and-definitions.pdf. Accessed July 19, 2019.

World Bank (WB) (2018a). "List of affiliated institutions." Available at: http://www.worldbank.org/en/about/partners. Accessed July 19, 2019.

World Bank (WB) (2018b). "World development indicators." Available at: https://databank.worldbank.org/reports.aspx?source=world-development-indicators. Accessed June 21, 2018.

World Bank (WB) (2019a). "Projects and Operations." Available at: http://projects.worldbank.org/. Accessed July 19, 2019.

World Bank (WB) (2019b). "International Bank for Reconstruction and Development Subscription and Voting Power of Member Countries." Available at: http://pubdocs.worldbank.org/en/795101541106471736/IBRDCountryVotingTable.pdf. Accessed July 19, 2019.

World Health Organization (WHO) (2001). "Revised drug strategy—Report by the Secretariat." Fifty-Fourth World Health Assembly, Doc. N. A54/17, Provisional agenda item 13.8. 10 April 2001. Available at: http://apps.who.int/medicinedocs/documents/s16337e/s16337e.pdf. Accessed September 22, 2019.

World Health Organization (WHO) (2003). "Intellectual property rights, innovation and public health." Fifty-Sixth World Health Assembly, Doc. N. WHA56.27, Agenda item 14.9. 28 May 2003. Available at: http://apps.who.int/gb/archive/pdf_files/WHA56/ea56r27.pdf. Accessed September 22, 2019.

World Intellectual Property Organization (WIPO) (2018) "World intellectual property indicators." Available at: https://www.wipo.int/edocs/pubdocs/en/wipo_pub_941_2018.pdf. Accessed August 7, 2019.

World Intellectual Property Organization (WIPO) (2019a). "Directory of intellectual property offices." Available at: https://www.wipo.int/directory/en/urls.jsp. Accessed August 7, 2019.

World Intellectual Property Organization (WIPO) (2019b). "WIPO IP statistic data center 1980–2017." Available at: https://www3.wipo.int/ipstats/index.htm?tab=patent. Accessed July 27, 2019.

Würdemann, A. I. (2018). "The BRICS contingent reserve arrangement: A subversive power against the IMF's conditionality?" *The Journal of World Investment & Trade*, 19(3), 570–593.

Yang, D. (2003). "The development of intellectual property in China." *World Patent Information*, 25(2), 131–142.

Yildirim, A. B. (2018). "Domestic political implications of global value chains: Explaining EU responses to litigation at the World Trade Organization." *Comparative European Politics*, 16(4), 549–580.

Yu, P. K. (2007). "Intellectual Property, Economic Development, and the China Puzzle." In: *Intellectual Property, Trade and Development: Strategies to Optimize Economic Development in a TRIPs Plus Era*, edited by D. J. Gervais, Oxford University Press, Oxford, 173–220.

Zangl, B., Heußner, F., Kruck, A., & Lanzendörfer, X. (2016). "Imperfect adaptation: How the WTO and the IMF adjust to shifting power distributions among their members." *The Review of International Organizations*, 11(2), 171–196.

Zelli, F. (2011). "The fragmentation of the global climate governance architecture." *Wiley Interdisciplinary Reviews: Climate Change*, 2(2), 255–270.

Zelli, F., & Van Asselt, H. (2013). "Introduction: The institutional fragmentation of global environmental governance: Causes, consequences, and responses." *Global Environmental Politics*, 13(3), 1–13.

Zhang, N. (1997). "Intellectual property law enforcement in China: Trade issues, policies and practices." *Fordham Intellectual Property, Media & Entertainment Law Journal*, 8, 63.

Zhu, J. (2016). "G20 institutional transition and global tax governance." *The Pacific Review*, 29(3), 465–471.

Zodrow, G. R., & Mieszkowski, P. (1986). "Pigou, Tiebout, property taxation, and the underprovision of local public goods." *Journal of Urban Economics*, 19(3), 356–370.

Zürn, M., Binder, M., & Ecker-Ehrhardt, M. (2012). "International authority and its politicization." *International Theory*, 4(1), 69–106.

Zürn, M., & Faude, B. (2013). "Commentary: On fragmentation, differentiation, and coordination." *Global Environmental Politics*, 13(3), 119–130.

Index

Transformations in Governance

Transformations in Governance is a major academic book series from Oxford University Press. It is designed to accommodate the impressive growth of research in comparative politics, international relations, public policy, federalism, and environmental and urban studies concerned with the dispersion of authority from central states to supranational institutions, subnational governments, and public–private networks. It brings together work that advances our understanding of the organization, causes, and consequences of multilevel and complex governance.

The series is selective, containing annually a small number of books of exceptionally high quality by leading and emerging scholars.

The series is edited by Liesbet Hooghe and Gary Marks of the University of North Carolina, Chapel Hill, and Walter Mattli of the University of Oxford.